Israel's Holocaust and the Politics of Nationhood

The ghost of the Holocaust is ever present in Israel, in the lives and nightmares of the survivors and in the absence of the victims. In this compelling and disturbing analysis, Idith Zertal, a leading member of the new generation of revisionist historians in Israel, considers the ways Israel has used the memory of the Holocaust in order to define and legitimize its existence and politics. Drawing on a wide range of sources, the author exposes the pivotal role of the Holocaust in Israels public sphere, in its project of nation building, in its politics of power, and in its perception of the conflict with the Palestinians. She argues that the centrality of the Holocaust has led to a culture of death and victimhood that permeates Israelis society, and self-image. For the updated paperback edition of the book, Tony Judt, the world-renowned historian and political commentator, has contributed a foreword in which he writes of Zertals courage, the originality of her work, and the unforgiving honesty with which she looks at the moral condition of her own country.

IDITH IERTAL is an Israeli historian and essayist, the author of many books and articles on Jewish, Zionist, and Israeli history. She is currently teaching at the Institute of Jewish Studies at the University of Basel, Switzerland. Her works include *From Catastrophe to Power: Holocaust Survivors and the Emergence of Israel* (1998) and *Lords of the Land: The War over Israel's Settlements in the Occupied Territories, 1967–2007* (co-authored with Akiva Eldar, 2007). *Israel's Holocaust and the Politics of Nationhood* has been published in eight languages.

T0384716

Cambridge Middle East Studies 21

Editorial Board
Charles Tripp (general editor),
Julia Clancy-Smith,
F. Gregory Gause,
Yezid Sayigh,
Avi Shlaim and
Judith E. Tucker

Cambridge Middle East Studies has been established to publish books on the nineteenth- to twenty-first-century Middle East and North Africa. The aim of the series is to provide new and original interpretations of aspects of Middle Eastern societies and their histories. To achieve disciplinary diversity, books will be solicited from authors writing in a wide range of fields including history, sociology, anthropology, political science, and political economy. The emphasis will be on producing books offering an original approach along theoretical and empirical lines. The series is intended for students and academics, but the more accessible and wide-ranging studies will also appeal to the interested general reader.

A list of books in the series can be found after the index

Israel's Holocaust and the Politics of Nationhood

Idith Zertal

Translated by

Chaya Galai

CAMBRIDGE
UNIVERSITY PRESS

CAMBRIDGE UNIVERSITY PRESS
Cambridge, New York, Melbourne, Madrid, Cape Town, Singapore,
São Paulo, Delhi, Dubai, Tokyo, Mexico City

Cambridge University Press
32 Avenue of the Americas, New York, NY 10013–2473, USA

www.cambridge.org
Information on this title: www.cambridge.org/9780521616461

Originally published in Hebrew as "Ha'Umah ve Ha'Mavet, Historia,
Zikaron, Politika," Dvir Publishing House, 2002 and © Idith Zertal 2002.
English translation © Idith Zertal 2005
Foreword © Tony Judt 2011

English edition first published 2005
First paperback edition 2011

A catalog record for this publication is available from the British Library.

ISBN 978-0-521-85096-4 Hardback
ISBN 978-0-521-61646-1 Paperback

Contents

Acknowledgments   *page* ix
Foreword by Tony Judt   xi

Introduction   1

1   The sacrificed and the sanctified   9

2   Memory without rememberers   52

3   From the People's Hall to the Wailing Wall   91

4   Between *Love of the World* and *Love of Israel*   128

5   Yellow territories   164

Biographies   209
Glossary   217
Bibliography   223
Index   231

Acknowledgments

It is a special pleasure for me to thank all those – individuals and institutions – who helped in the process of creating this book.

I am grateful to the International Center of Holocaust Studies at Yad Vashem for the period I spent there. During my fellowship at the Center I began reflecting about the book's main themes.

In 1997–1998, as Senior Fellow at the United States Institute of Peace in Washington DC, I researched and wrote about the effects of the Eichmann trial on Israeli politics and discourse, and especially on the sequence of events that led to the 1967 war. This work found its way into chapter 3 of the present book. I thank the Institute's staff for their generous support.

Parts of my work have been presented over the years at the University of Chicago, New York University, Yad Vashem, the Ecole des Hautes Etudes en Sciences Sociales in Paris, Ben-Gurion University in Beer Sheva, and the Hebrew University of Jerusalem. I thank these institutions for the opportunity to discuss the ideas behind this book.

I thank my students at the Interdisciplinary Center Herzliya and the Hebrew University who took part in my seminars and contributed by their openness and intellectual curiosity to the shaping of this book.

Adi Ophir, Shulamit Aloni, Lior Barshack, Guy Ben Porat, and the late Martin Strauss read the original manuscript or parts of it. Their comments were especially pertinent and precious to me. Shlomo Ben Ami and Avi Shlaim supported my work with rare generosity. I am grateful to each one of them.

I owe special thanks to the late Michael Rogin and *Representations'* editorial board for their enthusiastic reception of my article "From the People's Hall to the Wailing Wall: A Study in Fear, Memory and War," published in the winter of 2000.

I am indebted to research assistants at various institutions: Guy Ben Porat (today a colleague and friend), Chagai Vered, Orit Ziv, and Shlomit Gur. Research for this project was generously supported by the Rich

Foundation and its director, Avner Azulai. My deep gratitude goes to him and to the Foundation.

I would also like to thank my friend Ziv Lewis at my home publishing house, Kinneret-Zmora-Dvir in Israel, for his support and help with the book.

I thank Chaya Galai for an excellent translation of my sometimes untranslatable Hebrew.

Working with Cambridge University Press, especially with its Asia and the Middle East Editor, Marigold Acland, has been an amazing experience: swift, demanding, punctual, and graceful, for which I am very grateful. I also thank Linda Randall for her meticulous copy-editing.

Finally, this book was from its inception closely followed and magnanimously assisted by my friend and mentor Ohad Zmora, whose untimely death is a terrible loss. I dedicate it to his memory, with love.

The preface written for the paperback edition of this book by Professor Tony Judt is immensely precious to me for both its tone and content and the circumstances of its writing, and I am forever grateful for it.

IZ
April 2010

Foreword to the paperback edition

Tony Judt
University Professor and Director of the Remarque Institute, New York University

History should never be mere polemic, but it is frequently and very properly polemical. Written in retrospect, it is often called upon to serve as a witness to and commentator on contemporary political debate. This is not a new experience for historians: even in the early years of the modern state, narratives and chronicles were designed and appropriated to justify or denigrate, support or oppose those in authority. This did not always make historians popular, and as a class of writers and scholars they were frequently exposed to public praise and condemnation or worse.

In the age of the modern nation-state, where founding myths and serviceable back-narratives were crucial to the early legitimacy of newly created territorial polities, the historian came into her own. Every European country, from Belgium to Moldova, can boast a shelf of scholarly tomes identifying the medieval, ancient, or even archaic roots of the country, its language and its people, its sufferings and its claims: these were often the work of talented and widely published historians, themselves prominent actors in the national revivals they helped legitimize. There are statues, monuments, and boulevards named after such historians across every continent. The rise of the modern state, and its enduring legitimacy in the eyes of citizens and foreigners alike, would be inconceivable without them.

But once the new nation-state is established, and always assuming the minimum of political liberty, contestations arise. Just as the prehistory and early years of new countries are marked by official, self-serving, and self-congratulatory national narratives, so the mature state gives rise to historical dissent. New generations of scholars begin to unpick the conveniently tidy skein of national inevitability and progress – questioning the ethnic, geographical, linguistic, and other sources of a presumptively "natural" community of origin and destiny. Above all, the myths and silences that serve to enhance the credibility of the state and the form in which it emerged – or to suppress alternative accounts and un-pursued directions – get exposed to scholarly interrogation.

This is not a comfortable process, and it is frequently accompanied by academic and political conflicts, occasionally violent. Tomas Masaryk, decades before he ascended to the presidency of the country he founded, played a vital but unpopular role in discrediting one of the founding myths – the "invented traditions" – of Czech national identity. Charles de Gaulle, to take a comparably significant case, chose quite deliberately to suppress debate about the extent of support for the Vichy regime in wartime France: not because he was under any illusions on the subject, but because he fervently believed that it would simply not be possible to put the country back together if the unpleasant truth was stated too boldly and too soon. French historians complied – instinctively rather than sycophantically – and it was not until many decades later that the war years became a subject of legitimate historical interrogation.

Israel, the self-described "Jewish state," may be located on the Fertile Crescent of the Middle East, but it is for most historical and emotional purposes the last and most problematic of the European national revivals. Zionism, its founding ideology, emerged in exactly the same time and places as the nationalist movements and myths of German and Slav Europe. The great theorists of a Zionist project came from Odessa and Vienna, from Vilnius and Warsaw. The classic justification for a Jewish state – a landless people unable to live "normally" so long as they were forced to share other peoples' territory – precisely echoes the case made at various stages for the invention of Slovakia and Croatia, Estonia, Moldova – or indeed Belgium.

Jews, of course, are different, but for these purposes merely in the sense that they are like everyone else only more so. Whereas Romanians or Poles had a plausibly continuous history on the territories claimed for their modern national state, it was central to the Jewish national narrative that their history had been interrupted: they used to live in what by the twentieth century was known as Palestine but had been expelled thence millennia ago. The national project for Jews did not just consist of asserting the right to self-government in a country of their own: they had to colonize it first. This was a further controversial step in a narrative bound to intrude on someone else's story – in this case the story of the people already living in Palestine – and here too scholars had a role to play. They still do.

Historians in modern Israel thus occupied and continue to occupy an absolutely crucial space in the making and legitimizing of the state. Indeed, the profession in Israel has taken a unique form – unique at least among historical communities in modern liberal democracies. All the main Israeli universities divide and distinguish among their historians, who form two non-communicating academic subdisciplines: Jewish history – and everything else. It goes without saying that it is those who practice the former who enjoy higher status – not least on account of their more salient political role.

For many decades, essentially from the founding of the state in 1948 until the mid-1980s, Jewish (and Zionist) history was controlled and shaped by an elite community of quasi-official historians. Their self-acknowledged task was to tell the approved story of the Jews – from the earliest biblical times through the present – in a way which confirmed and illustrated its terminus ad quem: the establishment of the state of Israel. Debates within Zionist historiography in particular concentrated on ideological quarrels, strategic and tactical differences, and the complicated and violent history of Zionism's relationship with Arabs, English, and other impediments. But none of the great founding historians of Zionism, nor any of their most prominent students and successors, ever challenged the prevailing national narrative. How could they? They were largely responsible for it and for nurturing its future.

And then came the revisionists. Like their homologues in German or French history, the Israeli revisionist historians made their name by challenging the inherited and official view and targeting the most sensitive moments in the recent past: precisely those that the official historiography and its political apologists were least disposed to debate. Thus the Israeli revisionists focused on the pleasantly reassuring story of Israel's ethically untarnished military, the necessity and essential "cleanliness" of its wars of independence and expansion – and above all, on the question of the Palestinians: the great silence at the heart of the Zionist enterprise.

The best of those early revisionists, scholars like Benny Morris, achieved a very considerable breakthrough. They have given us a completely different and far more troubling narrative of, for example, Israel's war of independence – no longer the heroic struggle of a morally impeccable David faced with the unreasonable and unreasoning might of multiple Arab Goliaths, but a sorry tale of war crimes, dispossession, and political dishonesty. They have opened up disturbing directions for future research: exactly how did Jews acquire land in this new and "empty" territory? Precisely what was done to the indigenous Palestinian population before and after independence? Were the idealistic heroes of Israel's dominant Labour movement so clean of conscience?

Thanks to the revisionists and their own students, we know far, far more than would have been conceivable just a generation back. The myths and the official historiography to which I was exposed as an enthusiastic and naÿve teenager in the Israel of the mid-1960s would be untenable today.

Of all Israel's revisionist historians, Idith Zertal is by far the most courageous and original. A former journalist who has taught at the Hebrew University and other academic institutions, her publications include *From Catastrophe to Power* (1998); *Lords of the Land* (with Akiva Eldar), a 2007 study of the steady Israeli settlement of the Occupied Territories – and above all the present book, originally published in Hebrew in 2002. *From Catastrophe to Power* was Professor Zertal's first discussion of the encounters between the Zionist community in Palestine and Holocaust survivors and of the newfound uses to which Jewish victimhood were put in the service of the state.

A professor of history at the University of Basel in Switzerland, Dr. Zertal is distinctive in her country and her generation. Whereas most of the pathbreaking new scholars in Israeli historiography confined themselves to the classic themes of Zionist history – merely inverting or subverting the interpretation – Idith Zertal has carved out for herself a unique role. She, virtually alone, has opened up the impossibly painful subject of Israel's use and abuse of the Holocaust.

The relationship of the Holocaust to Israel is in one sense perfectly straightforward. If Hitler had not tried to exterminate the Jews of Europe – and come close to succeeding – there would not have been a Jewish state in the Middle East. Zionism was a minority taste even among the secular minority of politicized Jews in prewar Europe and the United States. The Jewish settlement in former Ottoman Palestine was small and unlikely ever to attract the sorts of funding or immigration that would allow it to proceed to independence on the terms it sought.

But the Shoah changed everything. With American (and, briefly but crucially, Soviet) support, the Zionists could argue after 1945 that Jewish survival was a moral obligation history had placed on the rest of the world – and that only in a Jewish state could the surviving Jews count on security and a future. But once Israel existed, the moral benefits of being grounded in a great historical crime became unclear. From the outset, the Jewish state – like the young Zionists who first conceived it – was designed to be everything that Jews in the Diaspora were not: tough, autonomous, independent of spirit, and violently efficient in its response to challenge and persecution. The image of the weak and servile Jews of the shtetl and the ghetto was abhorrent to the Zionist mind: a new sort of Jew was in the making, and he was best defined in apposition to everything that the old sort of Jew stood for. Since in recent memory the Diaspora Jews were best known for having gone – in the clichÕ of the 1950s – "like sheep to the slaughter," the 6 million dead Jews of Europe represented everything that Israel was not and against which it stood.

Thus the uses of the Holocaust in the Israeli national narrative and the tale of the country's foundation were complicated from the outset. On the one hand, Jews were the world's ultimate victim, and Israel had a moral case against everyone else which it never hesitated to press. On the other, the victims were not very attractive in Zionist eyes and were often dismissed with something close to contempt: as Idith Zertal documents, official Israel even went to the trouble of trying Jewish "collaborators" for wartime cooperation with the Nazis – as though to illustrate just how low Jews could sink in the absence of the sort of pride and backbone that only a state can provide.

These complications were resolvable in the 1950s because much of what we take to be a natural attention to the Holocaust had not yet emerged from the relative silence of the postwar years. It was only in the 1960s that trials in Germany and elsewhere highlighted the scale of German criminality and reopened issues of war guilt, genocide, and crimes against humanity. By then, a new generation of Israelis was more open to sympathizing with the victims – just as the older generation of founding fathers like Ben-Gurion were beginning to worry that the arguments for Zionism were no longer as self-evident as they had once seemed (in the eyes of the rest of the world, at least). It seemed to them that the Holocaust might now be put to more active service: as an illustration as well as a justification of the case for a Jewish state. Out of this grew the Eichmann Trial.

The trial, and the agonized debates to which it gave rise, is associated above all with Hannah Arendt's classic account of it, *Eichmann in Jerusalem: A Report on the Banality of Evil*. Arendt's relentlessly honest and intelligent discussion of Nazism, Jewish victimhood, and the problem of evil aroused paroxysms of conformist rage in the Jewish community worldwide and in Israel itself. For many years, her work was not translated into Hebrew, and as Idith Zertal documents in Chapter 4, she became something of a persona non grata in the world of Jewish and Israeli scholarship.

Zertal herself could legitimately claim the honor of being Israel's leading Arendtian today. Indeed, in addition to introducing Arendt and her ideas to Israeli readers – something most academics in Zertal's generation of Israelis were reluctant to do – she is the translator of *The Origins of Totalitarianism*, which has finally and belatedly found an Israeli publisher. Like Arendt, Zertal is unafraid of controversy and has never shown any interest in courting influential favor. Indeed, her Arendtian intellectual style and her unwavering advocacy of Arendt's works ever since the mid-1990s did her no favors: the academic vicissitudes to which she has been exposed can in large measure be attributed to them.

It is thus not by chance that Idith Zertal should have devoted so much of her career to explicating and unraveling the complexities of Israeli history and Holocaust memory: these are consummately Arendtian concerns. Others have narrated the uses to which official Israel puts the Holocaust: memorial days, compulsory school trips to Auschwitz, a lachrymose emphasis on the risks that Jews worldwide run if they let down their guard or take their distance from Israel, and so forth. What is distinctive about Zertal's account is the unforgiving honesty with which she looks at the moral condition of her own country.

In the first place, she brings out more than any other writer I know the complicated subterranean interlacing of national pride and ethnic morbidity that characterizes Israeli identity today. It is a very strange country indeed which is built at once on an assertion of "health and efficiency" in an almost fin-de-siÒcle German way: with an emphasis to the point of obsession on the outdoor life, the landscape, youth, virility, machismo, and physical dominance – and at the same time on an obsession with death. For it is the latter which introduces and locates the Holocaust at the heart of the Israeli psyche (and which has been exported with varying efficiency to Jewish communities across the world). In this way of thinking, the most powerful country in the Middle East – with its own nuclear bomb and by some estimates the fourth-strongest military on the globe – is always about to suffer extermination and collective annihilation.

Whatever its use or value as a moral lever – even if only over Germans and the odd guilty Dutchman and Pole – this conviction that the Jewish state is a perennial candidate for disappearance is a conscious transfer of the narrative of the Holocaust onto the future of its successor state. The pathology of this undertaking is clear in the country's foreign policy: Israel is the only democracy, and one of the few recognized states in the world, that refuses to declare its borders. This insistence on the permanent protean permeability of the territorial identity of the Jews seems to me – on my reading of Zertal – to arise from the obsessive attention paid (first instrumentally, now instinctively) to Jewish loss in the past. The dead Jews of Europe have become live hectares of Jewish land in occupied Palestine: lose one hectare and you risk losing all. We will give up nothing.

More serious still is the harm that Israel's abusive relationship with the Jewish genocide does to the latter's memory. Israeli historians, journalists, commentators, politicians, and teachers are second to none in the attention they pay to the Holocaust. Even in the 1960s I recall having it impressed upon me that this was something that would sooner or later be devalued in non-Jewish memory. They (who, we were always reminded, were the ones who did it) will inevitably relativize and trivialize it, reducing it to just another crime or even the collateral damage of war. It is our duty (as Israelis and Jews, but especially as Israelis) to ensure that its full meaning is always clear and acknowledged.

It is thus multiply tragic that Israel above all is now responsible for the devaluation of the Holocaust and the trivialization of Auschwitz. By forcing the analogy between the challenges facing Israel and the threats to which Diaspora Jews were once exposed, by tendentiously linking Jewish loss and defeat in biblical and post-biblical times to the establishment of the extermination camps, and by forcibly reminding every Israeli schoolchild of the crimes of non-Jews in the past (and implicitly in the future), Israel has linked the fate of the memory of the Holocaust to itself. And in so doing, since Israeli behavior in recent years has incurred a range of international responses reaching from anger to contempt, it risks inviting the charge that the Holocaust is merely an exploitable (and overexploited) historical myth.

I use the term "myth" advisedly, much as Professor Zertal deploys it. There is nothing mythological about what happened in Europe in the

1940s. But the relationship between the situation in which Jews found themselves then and the circumstances that Israel has created for itself today is fictional. It was developed for local political advantage. In this sense, the destruction of the Jews of Europe is a serviceable myth that has been exploited to national ends by a state which did not even exist at the time in question.

This is not, as I observed at the outset, an altogether unique set of circumstances. But it is one thing for Romanian irredentists to exaggerate and idealize the "latinate" origins of their country by telling implausible stories about the history of Transylvania. It is quite another for a democratic state in our own time to put to emotional and political advantage a catastrophic set of events that took place within living memory. The Holocaust is part of a broader history, not just a moral lesson for Jews. If Israel appropriates it in a way that seems to others cynically instrumental, it will itself have been the chief contributor to its devaluation.

No one interested in the history or politics of the contemporary Middle East can ignore this book. As the role of ethnic and religious extremists continues to grow in Israel – facilitated by the illegal Jewish settlements in the Occupied Territories where such extremists flourish and are favored – so Israeli policy will become ever more distorted around themes of victimhood and past suffering. Israel today is self-defined as the nation of the Holocaust: even its founding fathers would have been taken aback at the instrumentalization of Jewish loss for political ends.

This is bad news for Israel – en route to becoming what Idith Zertal wisely describes as an altar and temple of Auschwitz memory – but it is also a grim portent for the rest of us. The Holocaust does not belong to Israel any more than it belongs to Jews. It is, as wise Jewish observers have written, primarily a problem and a challenge for non-Jews. But if Israel continues on its present path, combining insouciant and self-destructive policies with self-pitying attention to its unique claim on Holocaust memory and meaning, we shall soon be dealing with a new generation of Europeans and Americans who – when faced with the obligation to study the history of the Holocaust, or of anti-Semitism – will simply raise their eyebrows and yawn.

There is no law that says that the memory of any given event, much less the meaning we assign to it, is secure and indelibly cast. These things change, and if we wish to maintain some control over their significance for our descendants and ourselves, we should be a little more careful in the use to which we put them. I urge you to read *Israel's Holocaust and the Politics of Nationhood*. It is not a reassuring book, but then this is not a very reassuring subject. It is, however, a major contribution to a debate and a conversation which will only grow more important in years to come.

New York
April 2010

Introduction

"From ... remorselessly accumulating cemeteries," writes Benedict Anderson at the closure of his book *Imagined Communities*, "the nation's biography snatches exemplary suicides, poignant martyrdoms, assassinations, executions, wars and holocausts. But to serve the narrative purpose, these violent deaths must be remembered/forgotten as 'our own'."[1] These words reverberate deep within the present book, which deals with the way the Israeli-Zionist nation's biography in the course of the twentieth century gathered its catastrophes, wars, and victims, embraced them, remembered and forgot them, told their stories in its own way, endowed them with meaning, bequeathed them to its children, shaped its own image through them, viewing itself in them as if it were all these. This is a book about Israeli nation-ness and nationalism, about death in its national public sphere, and the fatal connection between them: about the memory of death and culture of death and the politics of death in the service of the nation. To the same degree, it is a book about collective memory, about memory as an agent of culture, shaping consciousness and identity and shaped by them in a constant reciprocal process;[2] about the way in which Israel's collective memory of death and trauma was created and produced, and how it has been processed, coded, and put to use in Israel's public space, particularly in the half-century which has lapsed since the destruction of European Jewry.

---

[1] Benedict Anderson, *Imagined Communities: Reflections on the Origins and Spread of Nationalism*, London and New York 1983, p. 206.

[2] In the past few decades the question of collective memory has become a central issue in the work and discourse of historians and cultural scholars. A list of books and articles on memory published since Maurice Halbwachs's *La mémoire collective* (*1950–1968*) and particularly since its publication in English (1980), encompasses thousands of items, which cannot be listed here. On the multi-cultural discourse on collective memory, see Kerwin Lee Klein, "On the Emergence of Memory in Historical Discourse," *Representations*, **69**, Winter 2000, pp. 127–150. The article, which analyses the development of research on memory and its relation to history, society, and culture, opens with the words: "Welcome to the memory industry."

To paraphrase Tolstoy, one could say that if prosperous and happy communities are all alike, every unhappy community is unhappy in its own way and each of its offspring is branded with the mark of that unhappiness. Victories and great achievements require neither explication nor sophisticated interpretative structures; self-explanatory, they speak for themselves. By contrast, the more devastating the national debacles and defeats and the more victims they claim, the more they are subject to processes of social taming and domestication, and produce complex edifices of memory and interpretation to enable their reception and comprehension and to overcome them. Thus, they shed one form and take on another form to become tales of empowerment, rituals of initiation, and displays of transcendence.

An essential stage in the formation and shaping of a national community is its perception as trauma-community, a "victim-community," and the creation of a pantheon to its dead martyrs, in whose images the nation's sons and daughters see the reflection of their ideal selves. Through the constitution of a martyrology specific to that community, namely, the community becoming a remembering collective that recollects and recounts itself through the unifying memory of catastrophes, suffering, and victimization, binding its members together by instilling in them a sense of common mission and destiny, a shared sense of nationhood is created and the nation is crystallized. These ordeals can yield an embracing sense of redemption and transcendence, when the shared moments of destruction are recounted and replicated by the victim-community through rituals of testimony and identification until those moments lose their historical substance, are enshrouded in sanctity, and become a model of heroic endeavor, a myth of rebirth.

"Victimization," wrote Martin Jaffee in his article on the victim-community and the Holocaust ritual, "is easily thematized in memory and story as a moment of victory. That is, when transformed by the religious imagination into myth, the experience of victimization can confer a kind of holiness and power upon the victim." In stories constructed around disaster and destruction, "the victim is always both victim and victor, always destroyed but always reborn in a form that overcomes the victimizer." The chief beneficiary of that empowerment, says Jaffee, is the community, which perceives itself as the historical witness to the degradation of the victim and his subsequent transcendence, as the historical body whose very existence preserves and relives the moment of degradation and transfiguration.

By telling and retelling the story of the victim, the community of victimization not only memorializes the victim and stands in solidarity with the victim's fate; it also shares in the victim's triumph and transformation, bringing into its history the power of its myth, and mapping onto its own political and social reality the mythic plot through which it comes to self-understanding as a community of suffering.[3]

Death is never a closed matter. Like history, or as history, the dead do not belong solely to the past; they are a vital and active part of the present.[4] They belong to the present and play a part therein as long as they are recalled and spoken of by the living, who project their own lives on to the dead and draw their own lessons from their death. The living "exhume the dead," summoning them to a second life by giving meaning to their lives and death, a meaning that they themselves did not understand, as the French Revolution's historian, Jules Michelet, wrote.[5] Yet these dead are not the sum total of the dead, nor are they a random selection of them – just as history is not the sum total – or a random selection – of all the events that have occurred since the dawn of time. They are only those who have been chosen at various times by the living and transformed into historic dead or historic events, agents of meaning in the national sphere.

The Holocaust and its millions of dead have been ever-present in Israel from the day of its establishment and the link between the two events remains indissoluble. The Holocaust has always been present in Israel's speech and silences; in the lives and nightmares of hundreds of thousands of survivors who have settled in Israel, and in the crying absence of the victims; in legislation, orations, ceremonies, courtrooms, schools, in the press, poetry, gravestone inscriptions, monuments, memorial books. Through a dialectical process of appropriation and exclusion, remembering and forgetting, Israeli society has defined itself in relation to the Holocaust: it regarded itself as both the heir to the victims and their accuser, atoning for their sins and redeeming their death. The metaphorical bestowal of Israeli citizenship on the 6 million murdered Jews in the early days of statehood,[6] and their symbolic ingathering into the Israeli

---

[3] Martin S. Jaffee, "The Victim-Community in Myth and History: Holocaust Ritual, the Question of Palestine and the Rhetoric of Christian Witness," *Journal of Ecumenical Studies*, 28, Spring 1991, pp. 230–231.

[4] An interesting claim, from a slightly different perspective, can be found in Lior Barshack's analysis of the way in which a constant production of death is crucial to the constitution of any political sphere. See Lior Barshack, "Death and the Political," *Free Associations*, 47, 2001, pp. 435–462.

[5] Jules Michelet, "Histoire du xix siècle," in *Oeuvres complètes*, Paris 1982, vol. XXI, p. 268; Roland Barthes (ed.), *Michelet par lui-même*, Bourges 1954, p. 92; both are cited in Hayden White, *Metahistory: The Historical Imagination in Nineteenth-Century Europe*, Baltimore 1973, pp. 158–159.

[6] As early as 1950 it was proposed to the Prime Minister that symbolic citizenship be bestowed on Holocaust victims within the framework of the law. The proposal was examined by legal experts who recommended that it be accepted. It was extensively discussed but not implemented, yet the idea of granting retroactive citizenship was

body politic, reflected that historical, material, political, psychological, and metaphysical presence in the Israeli collectivity.

According to circumstances of time and place, the Holocaust victims were brought to life again and again and became a central function in Israeli political deliberation, particularly in the context of the Israeli–Arab conflict, and especially at moments of crisis and conflagration, namely, in wartime. There has not been a war in Israel, from 1948 till the present ongoing outburst of violence which began in October 2000, that has not been perceived, defined, and conceptualized in terms of the Holocaust. This move, which initially, more than half a century ago, was goal-restricted and relatively purposeful, aimed at constructing Israeli power and consciousness of power out of the total Jewish powerlessness, became in due course, as the Israeli historical situation was further removed in time and circumstances from the Holocaust, a rather devalued cliché. Auschwitz – as the embodiment of the total, ultimate evil – was, and still is, summoned up for military and security issues and political dilemmas which Israeli society has refused to confront, resolve, and pay the price for, thus transmuting Israel into an ahistorical and apolitical twilight zone, where Auschwitz is not a past event but a threatening present and a constant option.

By means of Auschwitz – which has become over the years Israel's main reference in its relations with a world defined repeatedly as anti-Semitic and forever hostile – Israel rendered itself immune to criticism, and impervious to a rational dialogue with the world around her. Furthermore, while insisting, and rightly so, on the unique nature of the Holocaust in an epoch of genocide and vast-scale human catastrophes,[7] Israel, because of its wholesale and out-of-context use of the Holocaust, became a prime example of devaluation of the meaning and enormity of the Holocaust.

The investigation into the presence of the Holocaust and its dead in Israeli discourse, which constitutes the main part of this book, is flanked – as is the short Zionist century[8] – by two other dead individuals, who, unlike the anonymous mass of the Holocaust victims, are the most celebrated and renowned dead in the annals of Israeli Zionism, particularly because of the special circumstances of their death. The book opens

---

compatible with Ben-Gurion's decision at the time to claim reparations from Germany and his assertion that the State of Israel had the moral right to demand restitution from Germany on behalf of the victims.

[7] "It could be that in our century of genocide and mass criminality ... the extermination of the Jews of Europe is perceived by many as the ultimate standard of evil, against which all degrees of evil may be measured," writes the historian of the Holocaust Saul Friedländer in his book, *Nazi Germany and the Jews*, Vol. I: *The Years of Persecution 1933–1939*, New York 1997, p. 1.

[8] I have borrowed the term from the subtitle of Eric Hobsbawm's book, *Age of Extremes: The Short Twentieth Century, 1914–1991*, London 1994.

with the death in battle of Yosef Trumpeldor on the country's northern border on 1 March 1920, an event which marked the dramatic initiation of the violent conflict over Palestine. It ends with the assassination of Prime Minister Yitzhak Rabin by an Israeli Jew, on 4 November 1995. Both traumatic events – which still reverberate, each in its own way and with its own degree of intensity, in Israel's public space – and their paradigmatic victims, are interpreted in this book not only within the context of the concept of collective memory and its link to nation-building project, but also in their relation – direct (in the case of the Rabin assassination) or oblique (in the case of Trumpeldor) – to the way in which, over the years, the political resource of the Holocaust has been instrumentalized and used in Israel.

The first chapter is a kind of platform for the paradigmatic assumptions examined in the rest of the book. Through three formative historical events in Jewish and Zionist history of the previous century – the battle of Tel-Hai and the death of Trumpeldor (1920), the ghetto uprisings (1943), and the *Exodus* affair (1947) – this chapter examines the discrepancy between the historical dimension of the events and the national memory molded upon them and the way in which historical defeats were transmuted into paragons of triumph and models of identification for a mobilized and combative nation. The mythical and processed story of Tel-Hai and its hero's death served as both a model of identification for the young Jewish ghetto fighters, and – together with Massada's myth – as the diametrical opposite to and reprehension of the death of the Jewish masses during the Holocaust. The two other events examined in the chapter testify to the onset of the process of selective appropriation of the Holocaust and its victims by the Zionist collective in the pre-state period.

The second chapter is devoted to the complex and multi-faceted construct of Holocaust remembering and forgetting in Israel's first decade of statehood. While Israeli society nationalized the memory of the Holocaust – through leaders and spokesmen who had not been "there" – and organized it, within its hegemonic public space, into a ritualized, didactic memory, bearing a national lesson in accord with its vision, it excluded the direct bearers of this memory – some quarter of a million Holocaust survivors who had immigrated to Israel, and altered the country's human landscape. Concurrently, alternative, subversive memories of the disaster[9] were formulated in other sites of the Israeli sphere. Among

---

[9] On individual and communal commemoration of the Holocaust in the first years of statehood, see Judith Baumel, "'In Everlasting Memory': Individual and Communal Holocaust Commemoration in Israel," in Robert Wistrich and David Ohana (eds.), *The Shaping of Israeli Identity: Myth, Memory and Trauma*, London 1995, pp. 146–170.

these sites, on which the chapter dwells, were Israeli courtrooms, where Holocaust survivors were placed on trial in the fifties and early sixties. These Jews, defined as "collaborators" with the Nazis in the extermination of their brethren, were charged under the Nazis and Nazi Collaborators (Punishment) Law 1950. Memories of everyday facts of devastation and the routine of horror were recorded in those courtrooms through the defendants' and witnesses' testimonies, and the inhuman, utterly exceptional dilemmas of behaviour faced by ordinary people were raised. This was a memory, which the "new and pure" Israel[10] did not want and even nowadays rejects.

The third chapter, earlier versions of which were published in the journals *Representations*[11] and *Theory and Criticism*,[12] investigates the ways in which the organized, specific Holocaust discourse formulated at the trial of Adolf Eichmann (1961) affected the civilian and military Israeli elites and leadership and their perception of the crisis of May–June 1967. It also raises the question of the nature of the "Holocaust anxiety" which has swept Israel before the war and has been part of the complex of considerations leading eventually to the decision to launch a "pre-emptive attack" to prevent a new Holocaust. Finally, this chapter deals with the ways the Holocaust discourse shaped the perception of the swift military victory and intensified the sanctifying process of the territories captured by Israel during the war.

Ben-Gurion's last great national project, the trial of Adolf Eichmann, the only Nazi to be charged under the Nazis and Nazi Collaborators (Punishment) Law after a series of Jewish survivors, was one of the most constitutive events in the annals of the state, and contributed to the shaping of the Holocaust memory in western culture. On the other hand, the trial inaugurated an era of critical, secular examination of the numinous event of the Holocaust, and the conduct of human beings, both perpetrators and victims, in the extreme situations it generated. The thinker who, to a large extent, launched this new discussion and formulated its first concepts was Hannah Arendt, the German-Jewish political philosopher, who wrote a series of articles on the trial in the *New Yorker*, later published in book form as *Eichmann in Jerusalem: A Report on the*

---

[10] This term was used by the then Attorney General, Haim Cohen, later to become judge in Israel's Supreme Court, in the context of the Grunewald–Kastner trial, which is discussed in chapters 1 and 2. Quoted by Yehiam Weitz, *Ha'ish She'nirtzah Paamayim: Hayav, Mishpato U'moto shel Dr. Israel Kastner* (*The Man Who Was Murdered Twice: The Life, Trial and Death of Dr. Israel Kastner*), Jerusalem 1995, p. 102.

[11] *Representations*, **69**, Winter 2000, pp. 96–126.

[12] *Theory and Criticism*, **15**, Winter 2000, pp. 19–38 (Hebrew).

Banality of Evil (1963).[13] The articles and the book sparked off immediate intense controversy, and the debate raged throughout the sixties – and
is still ongoing, though the tone has changed – with the author at the
center of the storm. Both Jews and non-Jews took part in that controversy,
particularly in the United States and Europe, and less so in Israel, for
reasons which are debated in chapter 4. One of the most acrid documents
in this polemic was a letter from the renowned Kabbala scholar Gershom
Scholem to Arendt, accusing her of lacking "love of Israel" and of hatred
of Zionism, a charge which clung to her for years. Arendt's penetrating
reply was never published in Hebrew,[14] although Scholem had assured
her that his letter would be published, in whatever forum and language,
together with her reply. The fourth chapter is thus devoted to the stormy
confrontation between these two formidable figures on the event of the
Holocaust, on the trial, and the way in which Israel conducted it. It also
draws an intellectual and personal portrait of Arendt, and proposes
thereby alternative options (other than the Jewish-Israeli) for Jewish
identity in the twentieth century and for the conduct of independently
minded, autonomous dissenters, in "dark times" of national unity/
unanimity, and mass hysteria. To a large degree, the present book is a
homage to Hannah Arendt, whose voice has been silenced in Israel for
many years, and whose writings are indispensable for deciphering the
twentieth century and the understanding of Israel.

The fifth and last chapter examines the evolvement of Holocaust discourse in Israel from an additional angle and in two central contexts: the
building of Israel's military strength and justification of its use, and the
borders of the land. The assimilation of the organized Holocaust memory
into the time-honored Zionist polemic concerning the ideal and longed-
for borders of the Jewish state, and the representation of Israel's international border – particularly since the 1967 war and the widespread
Jewish settlement in the occupied territories – in terms of the Holocaust,
have contributed to the expansion and justification of Israeli occupation
of a land inhabited by another people. They also practically usurped the
course of development of the State of Israel, expropriating it from its
political and historical dimensions; and, at the end of the process which
increasingly appears to mark the end of the Zionist century, have led to
the assassination of an Israeli prime minister who had been trying to
terminate the occupation and withdraw to agreed political borders.

---

[13] The book appeared in Hebrew translation some forty years later, in 2000.
[14] It exists now, in my translation into Hebrew, in the original version of my book, published
in 2002 under the title *Ha'umah Ve'hamavet, Historia Zikaron Politika* (*Death and the
Nation: History Memory Politics*).

The English version of this book is being published in the summer of 2005, almost ten years after the assassination of Prime Minister Rabin, and in the midst of a bloody political storm in Israel, caused by yet another dramatic effort to put an end, at least partially, to Israeli occupation and to disengage from some of the occupied territories. These are dark times for Israel. The ten bad years which have elapsed since Rabin's assassination, with which the book concludes, cast a gloomy light on the (wishful) statement of the assassin's judge that "the murder did not achieve its aim [and] has even created momentary rapprochement."[15] They also offer tragic, almost daily evidence of the impact of the active presence of Holocaust images on the lives and death of Israelis and of their neighbors, and on the perceptions of their lives and their deaths. As in the past, events of the present day would appear to demonstrate how the process of sanctification – which is itself a form of devaluation – of the Holocaust, coupled with the concept of holiness of the land, and the harnessing of the living to this two-fold theology, have converted a haven, a home and a homeland into a temple and an everlasting altar.

---

[15] Edmond Levi, *The State of Israel* v. *Yigal ben Shlomo Amir*, Severe Criminal File (SCF) (Tel Aviv and Jaffa) 498/95, Sentences, p. 5.

1   The sacrificed and the sanctified

Where memory and national identity meet, there is a grave, there lies death. The killing fields of national ethnic conflicts, the graves of the fallen, are the building blocks of which modern nations are made, out of which the fabric of national sentiment grows. The moment of death for one's country, consecrated and rendered a moment of salvation, along with the unending ritual return to that moment and to its living-dead victim, fuse together the community of death, the national victim-community.[1] In this community, the living appropriate the dead, immortalize them, assign meaning to their deaths as they, the living, see fit, and thereby create the "common city," constituted, according to Jules Michelet,[2] out of the dead and the living, in which the dead serve as the highest authority for the deeds of the living. Ancient graves thus generate processes that create fresh graves. Old death is both the motive and the seal of approval for new death in the service of the nation, and death with death shall hold communion. Defeat in battles, those all too effective wholesale manufacturers of death on the altar of the nation, are a vital component in the creation of national identity, and their stories are threaded through national sagas from end to end, becoming in the process tales of triumph and valor, held up for the instruction of the nation's children-soldiers-victims, who learn from these images and imaginings to want to die.[3]

The tales of three constitutive Zionist defeats are the subject of the present chapter. The battle of Tel-Hai, the ghetto uprisings, and the *Exodus* affair – which occurred, respectively, in 1920, 1943, and 1947 – were transformed soon after they had occurred or even while they were still taking place, into mythological tales of heroism and winning

---

[1] Jaffee, "The Victim-Community," pp. 230–231.
[2] Jules Michelet, "Histoire du xix siècle," in *Oeuvres complètes*, Paris 1982, vol. XXI, p. 268; Roland Barthes (ed.), *Michelet par lui-même*, Bourges 1954, p. 92, quoted in White, *Metahistory*.
[3] For an interesting and influential discussion of the component of death in modern nationalism, see Anderson, *Imagined Communities* (especially the two last chapters).

narratives. In these three cases, which differ markedly in scale, substance, and the long-term meanings assigned to them, the defeats were transmuted into tales of victory, although meticulous scrutiny of each event unearths no victory in any of them, definitely not in the immediate, concrete context. The fighters of the northern outpost of Tel-Hai were defeated, six of them were killed, and the site was abandoned; from the very outset, the ghetto uprisings had no chance whatsoever of achieving victory, and the Warsaw ghetto uprising, the most large-scale and dramatic among them, actually ended in an act of collective suicide by the surviving rebels. Moreover, "in terms of saving Jewish souls," as the Zionist poet laureate, Nathan Alterman, later put it,[4] the uprisings contributed nothing, and in fact endangered the lives of the other inhabitants of the ghetto; the passengers on the *Exodus*, most of them Holocaust survivors, who, in accordance with the proclaimed goals of the Zionist project, were to be brought clandestinely to Palestine, not only failed to reach shore, but were forced to return to Germany after a long and miserable journey, and arrived in Israel months, or even years, later. All three cases ended either in tragedy or in great chagrin. How is it then that they were changed into what Liddell Hart called "magnificent defeats"? How were they released from their historical bonds, from the materiality of their factual details, to be elevated to the rank of formative events which shape a new ethos and a new type of man?

Seven days after the Zionist-Jewish defeat at Tel-Hai and the death of its hero, Yosef Trumpeldor, in battle there, the Zionist-Revisionist leader, Zeev Jabotinsky, published a eulogy for the brave of the hour in the daily *Ha'aretz*. In this text he cited Trumpeldor's dying words as quoted by the doctor who treated him. "These were the last words of Yosef Trumpeldor as he witnessed his friends' grief at the enormous sacrifice," Jabotinsky wrote:

"it's nothing! It's good to die for our country" ... "it's nothing." A profound concept, sublime logic and an all-encompassing philosophy are buried in these two words. Events are as nothing when the will prevails. The bitter brings forth sweetness, so long as the will lives on. The will is a living mound (*tel hai*), and as for all the rest – sacrifices, defeats, humiliations – "it's nothing!"

In a quasi-ritual, quasi-biblical requiem for the heroes slain in battle, Jabotinsky alluded to David's lament for Saul and Jonathan, rendering the biblical lament as a blessing, "Ye mountains of Galilee, Tel-Hai and

---

[4] Dan Laor (ed.), *Nathan Alterman Al Shtei Ha'drakhim, Dapim min Ha'pinkas* (*Nathan Alterman's Two Paths, Pages from a Notebook*), Tel Aviv 1989, pp. 13–20.

Kfar Giladi, Chamara and Metula, let there be dew and let there also be
rain upon you. 'It's nothing!' Ours you have been, ours you shall be."[5]

According to his biographer, Jabotinsky's intent, in his farewell to his
revered hero, who was already firing the imaginations of his contempor-
aries, was to portray the whole of Trumpeldor's life and thought through
the recurrent theme, epitomized in the phrase "It's nothing."[6] This was
held to mean that what was to be considered as most important was man's
spirit and will – neither the facts, of and in themselves, nor the events, nor
the "incidents", but the meaning that man's vision and will read into
them, the way in which human beings act upon them, and what they
extract from them. It followed, then, that the decisive factor was not the
specific, contingent death of Trumpeldor, but the way in which his death
was interpreted by those left behind, the memory of the dead as constructed and re-constructed by the living, and, finally, the manner in
which this memory is deployed by the living to their own ends.

In this article, which was one of Jabotinsky's few public references to the
Tel-Hai battle, written when the shock of the tragedy was still fresh in
people's minds, one can already discern Jabotinsky's critical view of the
event itself, if only from the way he devalued the importance of its details.
Elsewhere, in a private letter he wrote over a decade later, he was much
more explicit. "The real murderers" of Trumpeldor and his comrades
killed at Tel-Hai, he wrote, were those "irresponsible" people from the
leadership of the Jewish community ("Yishuv") who, at the time, rejected
his opinion that there was no realistic chance of protecting the isolated
Jewish settlements in northern Upper Galilee, and that consequently all the
settlers should be moved back to the center of the country.[7] In an article
published at the same time that this letter had been written, Jabotinsky
openly denounced the Zionist leadership and the heads of the labor movement for their high-flown rhetoric and their failure to take action, which
had, he had said, combined to cause the tragedy of Tel-Hai.

In the five days between the sixth and the eleventh of the month of Adar it was
incumbent on these people – and they had the necessary time to act – to do one of two
things: either to send in reinforcements or to order Trumpeldor and his comrades to
evacuate the besieged area. If they did neither and instead left a handful of young men
and women alone, on a tiny farm, surrounded by several thousand well-armed
Bedouin, then surely someone is guilty of this terrible folly. Who is guilty?[8]

[5] Zeev Jabotinsky, "Tel Hai," *Ha'aretz*, 8 March 1920.
[6] Shmuel Katz, *Jabo, Biografia shel Zeev Jabotinsky*, vol. I (*Jabo, a Biography of Zeev Jabotinsky*, vol. I), Tel Aviv 1993, p. 369 and chapter 48 in full.
[7] Jabotinsky's letter to Leona Karpi, 24 February 1931, *Ha'Umah*, 11 December 1964, pp. 492–493, Jabotinsky Institute 21/2–1, quoted in Katz, *Jabo*, p. 369.
[8] Ibid., p. 368.

However, Jabotinsky's prolonged silence, prior to that article, about the details and development of the actual events, and his devaluation, in his early eulogy, of the actual historical occurrences, had already paved the way for the great silence which, for years, was to cloak the historical event of Tel-Hai, in direct contrast to the great myth constructed around the battle. "It's nothing," Jabotinsky wrote in the refrain-like conclusion of his eulogy. "It's nothing," he repeated, as if to say that what had transpired was indeed unimportant, unlike the descriptive and interpretative construction that would, in the future, be erected on the vestiges of the event. "Ours you have been, ours you shall be," he declared, addressing the mountains and Jewish settlements of Galilee. But these words also functioned to register full ownership of the story and the memory of the event. Rather than the dead Trumpeldor himself, the theme of Jabotinsky's eulogy was in fact his own early reflections on the remembering subject: on the "prevailing will," which is the motivating force of memory and consciousness, the will that chooses and selects – in keeping with the times, and shifts in the political climate – what is to be preserved and become an ever-living past, extant and active within the present, an eternal living mound, a '*tel hai*'.

Jabotinsky was a European intellectual, the cultural product of the turn of the twentieth century, who had spent three years at the University of Rome studying Roman law, history, and philosophy. In later years he would write on this experience, saying that "If I have a spiritual motherland, it is Italy rather than Russia ... my attitude to the issues of nation, country, and society was formed in those years under Italian influence."[9] As a student in Rome he was apparently aware of the ongoing debate during the first decades of the century among Italian philosophers, most prominently represented by Benedetto Croce, concerning the meaning of history and of historiography. Yet even if he was not directly familiar with Croce's work (which is rather unlikely, since they were both students of the thinker and professor of law, Antonio Labriolla, though several years apart) his comments on Trumpeldor were steeped in the Crocean (and Kantian) conception of "the eternal ghost of the thing in itself," as opposed to the history we know, which is "all the history we need ... at every moment."[10] Indeed, in his words one could detect Jabotinsky's own insight into the way in which people "know" their world, or, in this case,

[9] Katz, *Jabo*, pp. 27–28.
[10] Croce wrote this in a 1912 article, which later appeared, in an amended version, in his book on the theory and history of historiography, published in Italian in 1927. Quoted in Carlo Ginzburg, "Just One Witness," in Saul Friedländer (ed.), *Probing the Limits of Representation: Nazism and the "Final Solution,"* Cambridge, MA, and London 1992, p. 95.

their past; into how they commemorate and appropriate people and events from the past ("ours you shall be"); into the way past events are handed down from generation to generation and how each community organizes its past in keeping with its needs, self-image, and visions: muffling and erasing the troubling chapters on the one hand, while, on the other hand, amplifying and glorifying those aspects of the past which bolster the community's stand and serve its purposes.

The testimonies of those who survived the battle of Tel-Hai are the immediate and, to this day, the principal source for our knowledge of the events of 1 March 1920 (11th Adar, 5680 according to the Hebrew calendar).[11] The first testimonies were recorded immediately and published in issues 29, 30, and 31 of *Kuntress*, the periodical of the labor party of the time, Achdut Ha'avoda, in March and April. In the final analysis, these initial testimonies tell a sad, confused story, the gist of which is a series of misunderstandings and miscalculations, involving a small and isolated group of young Jewish settlers living at the northern frontier of Palestine, without adequate means of defense, embroiled in unnecessary combat with a group of Arab residents of the area. The documentation shows that the battle could have been avoided; that following its outbreak, it could have been better handled, and that by the end of the day, there were six Jewish dead.[12] Among them was Yosef Trumpeldor, regarded as the commander of the place because of his seniority in years and his extensive combat experience, who, even before his death in battle, had been hailed as a hero of the 1905 Russian–Japanese War, where he lost an arm. Three days later, on 4 March, following the hasty burial of the six dead in two common graves – one for the men and one for the two women killed – and following their retreat to the south, the survivors of Tel-Hai reached another Jewish settlement and told their story.

The report spread throughout the country by varied and swift routes, and by the time it had been recorded in writing and published, at the end of the week, and far from the northern frontier, its meaning had already been extracted from its historicity and secularity, and had taken on sacred

[11] The most complete and detailed documentation and analysis of the Tel-Hai affair can be found in the pioneering work by the historian-journalist Nakdimon Rogel, *Tel Hai: Hazit Bli Oref* (*Tel Hai: Front without Hinterland*), Tel Aviv 1979. In 1994 Rogel published an additional book, a collection of documents on the affair, the ultimate source for any discussion of Tel-Hai. See Nakdimon Rogel, *Parashat Tel Hai: Teudot Le'haganat Ha'galil Ha'elyon Be'taraf* (*The Tel Hai Affair: Documents on the Defence of Upper Galilee in 1921*), Jerusalem 1994.
[12] In contrast to many other battles, in which the Jewish-Zionist reports made no reference to the number of enemy dead, in the case of Tel-Hai the first reports already contained estimates of the number of Arab casualties. Harzfeld Report, Labor Archives, 134-IV, File 1a, quoted in Rogel, *Documents*, p. 282.

connotations.[13] The chain of events in northern Galilee leading up to the battle, the pathetic role played by the political leadership of the Jewish community, along with other circumstances, contributed to the immediate sanctification of the abortive battle. Added to that was the rather unique personality of Trumpeldor, different from the other settlers at Tel-Hai and fascinating precisely because of his "exceptionality," who was not supposed to be in Tel-Hai that day, but instead on his way back to Russia to recruit more settlers. The enigmatic figure of Trumpeldor, his coincidental, fatal encounter with the final battle of his life, and his last words, as reported by his doctor, alone sufficed to generate a process of sanctification. The question of whether Trumpeldor did in fact utter these words, a historical fact based on the testimony of two witnesses only, Dr. George Gerry and Abraham Harzfeld, is accordingly irrelevant, though it is of interest.

Trumpeldor did not die immediately, but lingered on till later that night, several hours after his injury, on the way from Tel-Hai to Kfar Giladi, as his comrades were carrying him. When he was asked, in the course of the retreat, how he felt, Trumpeldor said, so both witnesses later reported, "It's nothing, it is good to die for our country."[14] Trumpeldor's supposed last words underwent several minor revisions. Furthermore, the language he was speaking stays to this day unknown. Did he use his broken Hebrew – or, more precisely, could he have even formed a sentence such as that ascribed to him, in a language in which he was far from being fluent? Or did he fall back on his native language, Russian, or recite Horace's lines in Latin? And if he had indeed spoken his stilted Hebrew, how could Dr. Gerry, an American, two weeks in the country and previously unacquainted with Trumpeldor, have understood him? According to other testimonies, in the hours when he lay wounded, Trumpeldor begged in Russian to have his wounds bandaged. One can thus presume that he mumbled at length in his native language while he was still conscious. None of these words were recorded or engraved on

---

[13] In his immediate report, conveyed on the day of the battle and the following day, Harzfeld already used the term *kedoshim* (holy ones). "We grope in the dark – where are our holy ones ... I remained behind to bring down the dead, to collect everything possible for departure and it was decided that we must go up, all of us, but first we must transfer the holy ones and whatever was possible," quoted in Rogel, *Documents*, p. 278.

[14] Dr. Gerry's first testimony was published in *Kuntress*, 29, 12 March 1920. In the first version it was claimed that Trumpeldor said, "It is worth dying for our country." This was later amended to "It is good ... " An anonymous article in *Ha'aretz*, which preceded *Kuntress* by four days, reported that Pinhas Shneourson had also heard Trumpeldor say, a moment before his death, in answer to the question "How are you?" "It is good to die for our country." See Rogel, *Documents*, p. 278. For Harzfeld's evidence see ibid., pp. 434, 440–443.

the memory of coming generations, and they were lost for ever. They were probably superfluous. Yet, the decisive historical "fact" is not the sentence itself, whether uttered or not, but rather the swift absorption of the words ascribed to Trumpeldor, without query as to their "authenticity," at this first, formative stage of the construction of the Hebrew nation in Palestine, and the transformation of these words into the symbol and slogan of a critical period in the history of Zionism.

Frontier and center

The events and moves that preceded the battle of Tel-Hai contributed to the construction of the tragedy and its aura of inevitability, and paved the way for its transformation into a founding myth and a sacred national symbol. Many months before the battle, the four Jewish settlements in the area were exposed to the local inhabitants' hostility. This hostility was part of a larger struggle over the area, whose political status had been in dispute since the end of World War I. The British had evacuated their forces in 1919, under a provisional accord with France, pending final delineation of the northern border of Palestine, while the French fought for control of the area – which had become a veritable no-man's-land – against the indigenous Arab population, who apparently received orders from Damascus. The question of whether to maintain a Jewish presence in northern Galilee in those times of insecurity and confusion or temporarily to evacuate the area in order to avoid loss of life was debated for months among the frontier settlers themselves and among the institutions of the Jewish Zionist community. In both circles, there were those who had called for evacuation for the sake of saving lives. The settlers, however, decided to resist at all costs, and repeatedly petitioned the newly established Jewish institutions, asking for both human and weapon reinforcements.[15]

On 12 December 1919, Tel-Hai suffered its first casualty when one of its members was killed by a stray bullet, while working in the field. At the end of that month, a short while after having arrived in Palestine from Russia, Yosef Trumpeldor went north. Other volunteers went with him. Beginning in January 1920, Galilee was gradually abandoned. Chamara was deserted and destroyed by fire. In mid-January, the Metula settlers too began to leave their homes. In early February another young volunteer, Aaron Sher, was killed in Tel-Hai's field. Trumpeldor and his comrades dispatched increasingly urgent appeals for help to the

---

[15] All these appeals – letters, reports, cables, and personal testimonies to the authorities – are fully documented. See Rogel, *Documents*.

authorities. Most of them were published immediately in *Kuntress*. Thus, the drama was overt and publicly known, and while it was actually unfolding, it became the shared experience of a considerable proportion of the small, emerging Jewish community in Palestine. In these pre-battle appeals, Trumpeldor was already laying the foundations and providing the stuff of the myth that was to evolve around the battle. "A new generation, a generation of free Jews of Eretz Israel, stand at the frontier, prepared to sacrifice their lives for this frontier," he wrote two days after the second death at Tel-Hai. "And there, in the land's interior, they are endlessly negotiating whether to approve the budget or not, in other words whether or not to aid the defenders of the homeland."[16] This primal text, written on the eve of battle, thus established the infrastructure for the conceptual dichotomy, destined to nourish the symbol-making process later applied to the battle: between the new Jew and the old Jew; the new, emergent "Eretz Israel" and the Diaspora spirit in the country's hinterland; the heroic, free frontier, willing and ready to lay down its life, and the self-preserving, hesitant center, ever vacillating and conducting pragmatic, mercantile reckonings.[17] Discernible here on another level was the classic conflict between all that is symbolized by the border – whether physical and external or psychological and conceptual – and by the perpetual reassessment, defiance and border-crossing, versus the secure, conservative center, continually reproducing its centrality, and the nowhereness embodied in the center which is consequently threatened by everything the border represents. Thus, it was not only a specific group of people who were fighting for their lives at Tel-Hai; the very concept of the "new Jew" that was at stake, a concept that by virtue of being such, amounted to more than the sum total of its members' qualities, and which – while it was taking shape in Palestine – was already hanging in the balance.

At the meeting of the Provisional Council of the Jews of Palestine, held on 24 February 1920, in order to address "the situation in Upper Galilee," the debate summed up the two basic, conflicting standpoints in the community regarding the future of the northern Galilee frontier: short- versus long-term considerations; withdrawal versus entrenchment; the fate of the particular group of people at Tel-Hai versus the overall idea of the rebirth of the people of Israel in the land of Israel. The roles played

---

[16] Yosef Trumpeldor to Defence Committee, 9 February 1920, quoted in Rogel, *Documents*, pp. 216–218.
[17] Pinhas Shneourson of Ha'shomer complained that not one of the "great men" had troubled to visit Galilee. "The 'activists' sat at home on their political dais at the Council of Delegates." Quoted in Rogel, *Documents*, p. 256.

by the various speakers at the meeting are of particular interest, since they subverted the self-evident division, later to become so stereotypical, between "right" and "left," extremists and realists, in the Zionist political sphere. Zeev Jabotinsky, the leader of the Zionist Revisionist movement and a guest at the meeting, referred specifically to the young people living in Galilee and to their foreseeable fate, claiming that everything should be done, including abandonment of the sites, to prevent the sacrifice of their lives. He called on his colleagues "to tell the young defenders the bitter truth," and to bring them back to the center of the country. He asked the supposedly pragmatic labor movement leaders, David Ben-Gurion, Berl Katznelson, and Yitzhak Tabenkin, to "tell the comrades: come back from there and build up what exists here."[18] And just as Jabotinsky placed the specific case and its singular circumstances, Ben-Gurion, already the advocate of the great principle overriding the specific historical case, argued that the issue was the Zionist question as a whole, the very status of Zionism in Palestine and the world at large, rather than the specific question of Tel-Hai. "If we flee the robbers there, then by the same token we will soon have to leave not only Upper Galilee but also the whole of Palestine," Ben-Gurion said.[19] "For us there are no frontiers ... if we fall there – we fall all the way down to the desert," said Tabenkin.[20] And Berl Katznelson spoke about rationality and sentiment, defeat and victory, the possible and the impossible, the practicality of the moment versus long-term practicality.

Every strategy can easily provide advance proof of defeat and it is hard to guarantee victory ... we are facing an age-old argument here, an argument which cannot be decided by rational claims. There is a practicality that conducts the reckoning in advance – to leave – and there is another practicality that insists on staying till the very last moment, when it may come to pass that the impossible becomes possible.[21]

Tel-Hai thus became a symbol before a battle had ever taken place there; it was charged with heavy symbolism or bound up with the self-realizing expectation that it would one day become a symbol: of retreat or entrenchment; of surrender or combat. Tel-Hai was perceived not simply as a tiny outpost in the north of Palestine; it became the entire Jewish community in the homeland, the very idea of settling and conquering the land, the soul of the new "Eretz Israel."

The Provisional Council decided to reinforce Tel-Hai and Kfar Giladi. Yet help came all too late. The process of mythologization, however,

[18] Minutes of the tenth session of the Provisional Council of the Jews of Palestine, 24 February 1920. Quoted in Rogel, *Documents*, pp. 238–252.
[19] Ibid., pp. 244–245.   [20] Ibid., p. 246.   [21] Ibid., p. 257.

followed fast in the wake of the disastrous battle.[22] What was it, then, in the Tel-Hai event itself, that invited a mythic story – which is not, according to Ernst Cassirer, a representation concealing some mystery or latent truth, but rather a self-contained form of interpretation of reality.[23] Was it the specific historical and political conjuncture – the post-World War I period of consolidation of political borders and regional power structures, concurrently with the onset of the large-scale third wave of Jewish immigration to Palestine (the Third *Aliyah*) which had become a decisive factor in the formation of a Jewish entity in that land? Was it this specific regional and local reality that had required the creation of a different set of images than those of the actual event that precluded reception, and processing of defeat and retreat, and demanded instead the formulation of a winning and rallying narrative? Was it the searing sense of failure in what had been the first "trial by fire" the Jewish settlement project had faced, as well as the fear of total collapse of the very concept of settling the frontier in order to enhance territorial expansion and conquest of the land? Did it stem from an inordinate awareness of weakness precisely due to the presence of Zionism's most experienced war hero at Tel-Hai? Was the myth-making process somehow affected by the feelings of guilt harbored by the procrastinating, "diasporic" leadership that had dispatched the best of the "new generation" to their futile and foreseen sacrifice? Was it the prior anticipation of sacrifice that accelerated its sanctification? Was it the awe of death?

All these, I would suggest, lay at the basis of the process of symbolization and sublimation of the battle of Tel-Hai, a process set in motion the very instant that word of the defeat had reached the heart of the country. The pragmatic function of myth, Cassirer says in his *Essay on Man*, is to promote social solidarity as well as solidarity with nature as a whole in times of social crises. Mythical thought, he writes, is especially concerned to deny and negate the fact of death and to affirm the unbroken unity and continuity of life.[24] The mythical dimension bestowed on the historical event of Tel-Hai was indeed intended not only to shape the history Zionism "needed" at that given moment, and to repress a defeat which

---

[22] On the mythization of Tel-Hai, the evolvement of the myth, and the collective memory of the battle, see Yael Zerubavel's work, first in articles and later in her book. Inter alia: Yael Zerubavel, "The Politics of Interpretation: Tel-Hai in Israel's Collective Memory," *Association for Jewish Studies Review*, **16** (1–2), 1992, pp. 133–160; Yael Zerubavel, "New Beginnings, Old Past: The Collective Memory of Pioneering in Israeli Culture," in Laurence J. Silberstein (ed.), *New Perspectives on Israeli History: The Early Years of the State*, New York 1991; Yael Zerubavel, *Recovered Roots, Collective Memory and the Making of Israeli National Tradition*, Chicago 1995.

[23] Ernst Cassirer, *Essay on Man*, New Haven 1944, p. 84.   [24] Ibid.

it was unable to confront at such a formative stage; the interpretation assigned that event was not only designed to atone for the perceived sins of the Zionist leaders, to heal the fissure, to compensate for weakness and downfall, or to conceal the sacrifice and make sense of death. It is my contention that it should be perceived as bearing a far-reaching purpose, that is, the obliteration of the experience of death altogether, by suspending the victims over and above their historic death and transforming them into symbolic "dead," eternally living, an immortal "living tel" (*tel hai*), as Jabotinsky phrased it; the living dead integrated in death into the unending cycle of life and nature.

Symbolic suspension of death is vital to the existence of a nascent society, fighting for its territory and inculcating in its sons the ethos of the might and of living on one's sword, a course of "hopeless" battles fought so that "it may come to pass that the impossible becomes possible."[25] The promise of eternal life for the young men and women who fell in battle for the homeland; their sanctification in memorial rituals and the worship of the dead were what George Mosse defined as the creation of a new civil religion in the nation-state of the early twentieth century.[26] They also served as an instrument for mobilization and preservation of a martial, conquering society, and were intended to compensate for the repressed feelings of guilt generated by the "murder" of the sons; continual, self-aware "murder" which sanctified and at the same time justified itself in and through the permanent state of conflict and combat. "They are fallen, and we will yet lay flowers, evergreen wreaths and flowers of eternal spring," wrote the socialist leader Nachman Sirkin of those who died in Tel-Hai.[27] A mere ten days after the event, the farmer-writer, Moshe Smilansky, foresaw, while putting it in motion, the process of the immortalization of the dead, their introduction into the calendar, into the life and memory cycles of the young Jewish collective in Palestine, and formulated an outline of sorts for the new secular liturgy which was to sprout and stem from the graves of the living-dead of Tel-Hai. "Each year," he wrote,

on the 11th of Adar, teachers and students from all the corners of free Palestine will flock to the tip of Upper Galilee, to Tel-Hai and Kfar Giladi. And there, at the foot of the holy graves, the tale will be told in a trembling voice: here is the place where the hallowed ones bowed down and fell; it was here where a tiny, isolated handful of men and women had held out for two and a half months, on their sacred watch. With renewed strength, anointed with the dew of holiness, of

---

[25] Berl Katzmelson at the Provisional Council, quoted in Rogel, *Documents*, p. 257.
[26] George Mosse, *The Fallen Soldiers: Reshaping the Memory of the World Wars*, Oxford 1990.
[27] Nahman Syrkin, "The Defence of Life," *Kuntress*, 30, 19 March 1920.

resurrection, of faith and valor, the teachers and their students will return to their books at school and to their planted rows in the field with pride in their hearts: we are the sons of holy fathers.[28]

Death, territory, and memory

The actual day on which the battle took place, and the site where it occurred, coalesced into what Pierre Nora calls "a realm of memory" (*lieu de mémoire*), a signifier of the twilight zone between the age of memory and the age of history, of the transition from a totem history to a critical history.[29] Following the resettlement of Tel-Hai and Kfar Giladi, at the end of that same year, the site of the hurried burial of the six people killed at Tel-Hai indeed became a "hallowed place." In the course of the first year, the site had become the central locus for the formulation of tokens of worship and of heroism and force, of the social and national longings attributed by Zionism to the ill-starred battle. "But a single year has passed – and already, on the graves … there have sprouted the wondrous buds of a national myth," wrote the editorialist of the labor movement organ on the anniversary of the battle.[30] Contemporary texts regarding Tel-Hai attest to meta-mythical consciousness, to the fact that the people marking out the horizons of the Zionist Jewish collective were not only well aware that a national myth was being woven around that battle, but – being people of profound historical vision who, while making history, also reflected on it, documented it, and took care to represent it in keeping with their views – were the main contributors, out of an ideological standpoint and out of political motives, to the formulation and shaping of the myth.

Very soon, even before the sculptor Avraham Melnikov erected his roaring lion at the site (in 1934), the first "memorial to the fallen" in Palestine, the graves of those killed at Tel-Hai became the model for future cemeteries and memorial sites of those who had died defending the homeland. It is noteworthy that the consolidation of a commemorative place at Tel-Hai paralleled the great European movement of commemoration of the millions of soldiers killed in battle in World War I. European nation-states that had fought the war and had lost huge cohorts of their young men were preoccupied in the post-war years with

[28] Moshe Smilansky, "A Holy Place," *Ha'aretz*, 14 March 1920.
[29] See Pierre Nora's theoretical introduction to the monumental collective study he headed on France's national memory, which he entitled *Les lieux de mémoire*, vol. I: *La République*, Paris 1984.
[30] Moshe Glickson, "The Day of Commemoration," *Ha'poel Ha'tzair*, 28 March 1921.

organizing such commemorative projects. These projects, on a national and local level, which had been born spontaneously and by force of overwhelming popular will, and also resulted from national legislation and action directed from above, were designed to create a social and political channel for the private grief and pain of the families and friends of the fallen sons and fathers, and to share in the mourning. They were intended to give meaning to death for the sake of one's country, to justify the sacrifice, and by this means also to set the national ethos and interests above the personal life of each individual.[31]

However, in addition to the eternal life and everlasting memory granted to those who died for the homeland, their deaths also purchased a living space, a national territory, as it were, and forged the sacred national trinity of death, territory, and memory. Berl Katznelson's *In Memoriam* to the fallen of Tel-Hai, which served as the secular funeral prayer for dead defenders of the country up to the declaration of statehood – and even later in some circles – described "the men of toil and peace, who walked behind the plowshare and risked their lives" for the "usurped lands" of the people of Israel. This is an example representative of the kind of defensive apologetics by means of which – from the onset of the Zionist conquest of the land and consistently afterwards – Zionist discourse cloaked the settlement of and struggle for the territorial expanse.[32] According to the Zionist narrative, history had always begun the moment that Jewish settlers faced attack by Arab marauders; according to this story this moment was not preceded by Jewish settlement in a country inhabited by Arabs, nor by eviction or other kinds of dispossession of the local population. "Tranquil people, cultivating their land in their own country, are suddenly attacked by bandits. What are we to do here in our land?": thus Ben-Gurion described the situation on the eve of the battle at Tel-Hai.[33] Yitzhak Lufban, a little-known yet influential thinker of the labor movement, wrote on the anniversary of the battle: "We do not wish to be bridegrooms of blood. We are not a people of heroes and knights. It is 'good to die' for the homeland rather than for a foreign land, but even better to live for the homeland."[34]

Interestingly enough, he wrote these words at a stage when Palestinian Zionism had just begun developing worship of strength, heroism, and

---

[31] For the case of France, see, Antoine Prost, "Les monuments aux morts," in Nora (ed.), *Les lieux de mémoire*, pp. 195–225.

[32] On the defensive ethos in Zionism see Anita Shapira, *Land and Labor: The Zionist Resort to Force 1881–1948* (trans, William Templer), Stanford 1992, chapters 3, 4, and 5.

[33] Ben-Gurion at a session of the Provisional Council, 24 February 1920, quoted in Rogel, *Documents*, p. 244.

[34] Yitzhak Lufban, "Tel Hai Day," *Ha'poel Ha'tzair*, 28 March 1921.

sacred death. The very use of the phrase "bridegrooms of blood" even if in a derogative sense and in explicit rejection, in the context of the first major battle with another people over the same territory and over national borders, gives one pause to consider the cognitive dissonance, of which the writer was half aware, between word and deed; between a radiant, knightly death for the homeland – which became a basic tenet after the battle of Tel-Hai and was maintained as such, as the Zionist collective took root at the expense of the indigenous population – and the principle of "living for the homeland," which remained a dead letter.

The story of Tel-Hai as related with its dimension of the "few against many," of weak, innocent farmers facing hordes of Arab attackers fitted in aptly with the defensive rhetoric employed by Zionism. Few were aware of the questions which need always be asked when examining a history, in the sense of a given chain of events and their causes; questions such as the starting point for "reading" the history of Jewish–Arab relations in Palestine; was it, as Zionism has claimed, the moment when Jewish settlers, "well-meaning men of peace" (Berl Katznelson), were suddenly attacked by a horde of Arab "bandits" (Ben-Gurion), or did it start in fact earlier, with the Zionist Jewish penetration – which was by virtue of circumstances, invasive, forceful, and conquering, certainly from the standpoint of the country's local population – of areas inhabited by Arabs for generations? The Jewish writer Yosef Haim Brenner, who by 1913, had come to abhor the dissonance between the practical reality of the Zionist penetration and its accompanying rhetoric, spoke out against the false sentimental idealization with which Zionism imbued its deeds. The Arabs, Brenner wrote, had been

de facto masters of the land, and we intentionally come to infiltrate them . . . there is already, must inevitably be – and shall be – hatred between us. They are stronger than we are in all respects . . . but we, the children of Israel, have long been accustomed to living as weaklings among the powerful . . . cursed be the soft and loving! . . . first of all – no sentimentality or idealization![35]

Let there be no mistake. Brenner was not calling for an end to the conquest of the land by force, but was repelled by the fact that this act was accompanied by double-talk, by defensive, apologetic rhetoric. It was not the deed itself that he had wished to abominate but the combination of an act of forceful penetration of the land and timidity and excessive moral scruples "which have no basis in the deepest of man's instincts." This moralistic apologetic stand was coined as "immoral" by him.

[35] Y. H. B. (Brenner), *Revivim*, 3–4, 1913, p. 165.

The join of blood and land, that sustained worship of the farmer-soldier killed at his watch in defense of his homeland, and which constituted fertile ground for the growth of national myths in early twentieth-century Europe, was established at Tel-Hai. On the surface, Tel-Hai may have been characterized as a defensive myth;[36] its deeper message, however, was one of force and conquest, namely that a land is acquired, and its borders expanded and legitimized, by the blood of warriors. The blood of those killed at Tel-Hai simultaneously sanctified and procured the mountains of Galilee. "With their blood they purchased and bequeathed to us the mountains of the Galilee," read an article written on the first anniversary of their death.[37] Over thirty years later, the author of the constitutive text of the defensive myth of Zionism, *History of the Haganah*, wrote explicitly, in his piece on Tel-Hai, that "a spot where Hebrew warriors spilt their blood will never be forsaken by its builders and defenders."[38]

This "marriage of blood," then, which was despicable according to Zionist codes, not only safeguarded and sublimated the given territory; it was delegated symbolic power to expand that territory, to push further both the frontier and the enemies beyond it. For years it was claimed that the northern border of Palestine, as it had eventually been drawn, incorporated large areas of disputed territory by virtue of the "heroic battle" of Tel-Hai. To the various functions and purposes of the myth of Tel-Hai was added yet another, immediate territorial function: the yearned-for borders of the national home are drawn as a result of hopeless heroic battles. Thus the *History of the Haganah* claimed in conclusion that the battle for Tel-Hai had become "a sublime and edifying folk legend." Yet in addition to this comment, the writer added that the memory of Tel-Hai "will stay in the people's hearts for generations," and that Israel's children and warriors would learn from the heroic battle, and would "draw upon it till the end of time."[39]

Initiation into Israeli-ness

Collective memory is a social reality, a political, cultural product that takes shape within the system of social, political variables, and interests of a given community. Transmitted and inculcated, as it is, within distinct

---

[36] This is how a leading historian like Anita Shapira depicts it. See Shapira, *Land and Labor*.
[37] Glickson, "The Day of Commemoration."
[38] Ben-Zion Dinur (chief ed.), *Sefer Toldot Ha'haganah (History of the Haganah)*, vol. II, part 2, Tel Aviv 1964, p. 877.
[39] Ibid., vol. I, part 2, p. 585.

social groups, it is also, according to Maurice Halbwachs,[40] subject to mutations in the degree to which its appropriateness is subject to mutations as times, and with them political structures and climates, change. The territorial expanses conquered by Israel in 1967, with their abundance of old graves and "holy places" of another type, linked to a new Judaism and to a new Zionism, altered the place and meaning of Tel-Hai. From a prominent shrine of memory and pilgrimage, it became a forsaken, half-forgotten, marginal tourist site. However, in the pre-state period and in the first decades of statehood, Tel-Hai and its one-armed hero were ever-present in the public sphere. Their primacy, their association with the historically charged year of 1920, endowed them with a vitality which extended far beyond the event itself. Consequently, Tel-Hai and Trumpeldor endured longer than other, equally momentous events and "heroic battles" that had dropped out of the canon of living national memory.[41] From the early twenties onwards, schools, settlements, organizations and institutions, streets and cemeteries, and children as well were named after Yosef Trumpeldor. The 11th of Adar was marked in schools and youth movements as the day of the newfound physical heroism of the Jews of Palestine; heroism typically distinct from the conduct of Diaspora Jews and directly linked to the myth of the ancient heroism of Massada and Yodfat.[42] Children and adolescents made annual pilgrimages to the graves in northern Galilee, and memorized the "undying" words of Trumpeldor, in a compulsory, inevitable odyssey of initiation into their Israeli-ness. Lyrics, children's books, textbook chapters, pageants, and plays were written about Trumpeldor, and the word of Tel-Hai was spread by all the media channels of the times, not only locally but throughout the Jewish world as well.[43] Both the left and right wings of the Zionist movement appropriated the incident and turned it into an educational symbol, each in keeping with its ideology and its political vision at that particular point in time. The Tel-Hai event was cited in almost every ideological and political struggle which split the

---

[40] See Halbwachs, *Collective Memory*.
[41] See, for example, the bitter fight for Hulda during the Arab uprising of 1929, which ended in yet another Jewish defeat and retreat, and was connected by blood to the battle of Tel-Hai, since Ephraim Chizik, who was killed there, was the brother of Sarah Chizik, killed at Tel-Hai.
[42] Zerubavel, *Recovered Roots*, pp. 68–70, 210–211.
[43] See letters of Yehuda Kopilevitz and Yitzhak Kanievsky (who was injured in Tel-Hai) to He'halutz members in Constantinople, March, April 1920, which include descriptions of the battle and the death of 'the great eagle' Trumpeldor, and encourage them to immigrate and to 'start working'; see also P. Lipovsky, *Yosef Trumpeldor, Ishiyuto, Hayav, Peulotav* (*Yosef Trumpeldor, his Personality, Life and Deeds*), Kovno 1924, Jerusalem 1947 (revised expanded edn.).

Zionist movement and the Zionist collective in the thirties and forties; and as the chasm between the Revisionist and the labor movements widened from the thirties on, the positions adopted by the founding fathers of these movements on the battle's eve were not forgotten.[44] Tel-Hai was an ever-visible presence for every man and woman in Palestine, though not necessarily in the manner anticipated by Brenner when he wrote, on the first anniversary of the death of Trumpeldor and his comrades: "Have we all heard the echo of the exalted and murmured call of the one-armed hero: 'It is good to die for our country?' Good indeed! Blessed is he who dies in such awareness – with Tel-Hai before his eyes."[45]

Theory of death

Twenty-three years after Tel-Hai, in the process of instant appropriation and nationalization of the uprisings in the Jewish ghettos in Nazi-occupied Poland, and in the effort to gain Zionist custody of these acts of heroism, that old "folk tale" of Tel-Hai was not forgotten. Yet only few pondered in awe and humility, alluding to Brenner's words, "from which soil did their bloody struggle emerge? What was their reality, what voice cried out from within them? Tel-Hai lay in some vague, unrelated distance ... Eretz Israel hovered in some remote, blue skies. Tel-Hai was not there right before their eyes. Perhaps nothing was."[46] In contrast, Ben-Gurion instantly and publicly drew the affirmative, binding connection between the two, between Tel-Hai and the Warsaw ghetto, between combatant Zionism in Palestine and the Jewish uprising in Poland. At the annual commemorative ceremony, held at Tel-Hai in 1943, Ben-Gurion conveyed the news of the uprising which had just been received from Poland (the ceremony was held after the first uprising of January 1943, which preceded the major uprising of 19 April): "They have learned the lore of the new death decreed to us by the defenders of Tel-Hai and Sejera – heroic death," he said.[47] This single sentence in fact embodied the ambivalence with which the community in Palestine and, later, the Jewish state related to the ghetto uprisings, as well as the whole spectrum of Jewish armed struggle during the Holocaust: appropriation and exclusion, deference and arrogance. On the one hand, Ben-Gurion perceived the Jewish heroism in the ghettos as inspired by the lessons the rebels had learned from heroic Palestinian Zionism, while on the other hand he

[44] See, inter alia, Yael Zerubavel, "Tel Hai in Israel's Collective Memory."
[45] *Kuntress*, 72, 5th Adar Bet 1921.
[46] Yaakov Eshed, "The War of the Jews," *Mi'bifnim*, June 1943.
[47] Ben-Gurion, "The Tel-Hai Behest," in *Ba'maarakha (In the Battle)*, Tel Aviv 1957, C, 11 Adar 1943, pp. 119–121.

retained the disdainful division between "us" and "them," Eretz Israel, and the Diaspora. "They" had finally learned what "we" had known for a long time – how to die.

This Zionist "theory of death"[48] was projected from afar on to the unprecedented circumstances of both existence and annihilation in the ghettos and the death camps, of which people in Palestine could not have had the slightest understanding. And indeed Berl Katznelson admitted that there was an unbridgeable mental and emotional abyss between the people of Eretz Israel and the dying Diaspora. The young, he wrote, could read about "the attacks and the Arabs or about Trumpeldor ... as something actually concerning him," but as for the present ordeal of the Jews of the Diaspora, "the matter is so deeply foreign to us ... we cannot live the Jewish suffering of the ghetto."[49] The norm was established: the death of the vast majority of the Jewish people, who according to Zionist perceptions, went to their death in passive submission, was an "unsightly" death or a death "which is in no way beautiful," as was written in a major text titled *Theory of Death*. In contrast, the death of the rebels who "took a stand on the walls" was a "beautiful death," through which they achieved "life everlasting."[50] And the commander of the Haganah admitted that "it was of this kind of stand that we were thinking when we discussed the danger of an invasion of Eretz Israel."[51] The ghetto fighters were thus retrospectively "conscripted" into the Haganah's fighting unit, the Palmach, set apart from their brethren in the Diaspora and described as true sons of combatant Zionism. "We fought here and they fought there," said the Palmach commander Yitzhak Sadeh,[52] creating an imaginary equation between the circumstances of the war "here" and "there," thereby trivializing the Jewish condition in Nazi-occupied Europe.

[48] Yitzhak Lufban, "Theory of Death," *Ha'poel Ha'tzair*, 20 May 1943.
[49] Berl Katznelson, "The Common Jewish Destiny as an Educational Element," 6 June 1944, in *Ketavim (Collected Writings)*, vol. XII, Tel Aviv 1950, pp. 219, 222–223.
[50] "Beautiful death" in Greek thought was the exchange of the finite (eschaton) for the infinite (telos), the infinite life resulting from death by choice, the death which liberates from death. "Death in order not to die," as Jean-François Lyotard writes, is the meaning the Athenians gave to the concept of "beautiful death." This concept became a cornerstone in the development of the national idea. Those who die for the sake of a goal greater than themselves, for the sake of the homeland, of an ideal, of the state, of the nation, gain a perpetual name, eternal life. Death in the Holocaust, or "Auschwitz," according to Lyotard, was "the forbiddance of the beautiful death," that is to say, an "ugly death"; see Jean-François Lyotard, *The Differend: Phrases in Dispute*, Minneapolis 1988, pp. 99–101; and Jean Pierre Vernant, *Mortals and Immortals*, Princeton 1991, pp. 50–75.
[51] Eliyahu Golomb, Histadrut Executive Committee, 7 May 1943, Haganah Archives, Golomb, File 52.
[52] Sadeh's remarks were quoted by Surika Braverman in her testimony, in *Sefer Ruzhka (Ruzhka's Book)*, Tel Aviv 1988, p. 245.

In purely military terms, the Warsaw ghetto uprising was not a major operation. It made no contribution towards shortening the war or vanquishing Nazism. It did not save Jewish lives and made no real difference to the process of systematic murder of the Jews of Europe. Several hundred[53] young Jews in the ghetto, at the core of what had formerly been the heart of European Jewry, took up arms and fought back against the Nazi murderers of their people. They held out for about one month, kept a relatively large German force occupied, and caused some damage to troops and equipment. In the end, the ghetto was burned to the ground and turned into a pile of rubble. Most of the Jewish fighters were killed during the battle. Those who survived till the last day of the uprising, including the commander, Mordechai Anielewicz, died in the command bunker of the ŻOB (Jewish Fighting Organization) at 18 Miła Street; some shot themselves and others died when gas was pumped in by the Germans. A mere handful of people escaped the ghetto on the last day, after learning of the deaths of their commander and their comrades, and reached the Aryan side of Warsaw through the sewer pipes. Defeat and death prevailed. And yet, the uprising was a huge, enormously portentous event; its significance, first and foremost for the Jews, but also for the Germans, the Poles, and the entire free world, far exceeded its actual military dimensions. For this was the most extensive and important Jewish military endeavor, and the first mass rebellion in any of the occupied countries, in fact the largest direct rebellion in the annals of Nazi dominion. Moreover, those who launched this great uprising were the weakest, the most persecuted, tortured, and annihilated of the Nazis' victims.

The honor of the remnants

News of the Jewish uprising in Warsaw spread fast throughout the world. The rebellion captured the imagination because it was an utterly exceptional event within the range of responses to Nazi ruthlesness and murderousness. It also captured the imagination because it was an event that could be told, narrated, organized in meaningful words. At the height of a cataclysmic occurrence such as the systematic annihilation of millions of human beings, which existing means of cognition and narration were not only incapable of measuring and relating, but also had themselves been crushed and destroyed in its course, as Jean-François Lyotard

---

[53] There are various estimates by survivors of the uprising, such as Antek Zuckerman, Israel Gutman, and Marek Edelman, which range from 220 fighters (Edelman) to 500 (Zuckerman).

wrote,[54] one particular event stood out. And this event restored to human history its pre-Holocaust concepts, while, at the same time, permitting conceptualization of a humane, comprehensible, meaningful future, by creating a possible human frame of reference, remembrance, and consciousness. A group of people, a mere handful, with distinct faces and histories, each bearing a name – Yurek Vilner and Marek Edelman, Mordechai Anielewicz and Mira Pocherer, Tivia Lubetkin and Tzipora Lerer, Frumka and Hancha Plotnitzka, and Antek Zuckerman – took up meager arms and hurled themselves at the unprecedented murderous might of the Germans, creating an irreversible break in the chain of events generated by the Germans during the war. At a time and place where it seemed that all human concepts were lost forever, they reestablished those concepts. At a time and place when it appeared impossible to rebel, they did so. And at a time and place where no right of free choice was granted to a single individual out of the many millions marked for death,[55] these few made their own choice – even if it was merely choice of the manner and time of their deaths. By their acts, the impossible and inconceivable became both possible and conceivable. The uprising was also an event which allowed a kind of two-fold mental move through time, from an out-of-human-time present, to both a familiar past and a reasonable future. From this stemmed the exceptional power of their story and its extensive dissemination.

Berl Katznelson's comments on the uprising which "rendered" the ghetto inhabitants closer to "us," to "our concepts," and "enabled us to find a certain formula and to adhere to it"[56] were not only a Zionist statement implying that the Jewish ghetto fighter was closer to the idea of Tel-Hai, but also an indication of the limits of the human capacity for absorption and conception of a historical event such as the mass murder of the Jews. However, in addition to the commensurability and humanity of the Jewish uprising, which rendered it easy to remember, verbalize, and narrate amidst the complex of events which could not be told, this uprising – as a realization of Zionist values, as a "beautiful" and worthy death for the homeland – was the history which Zionism "needed" at that

---

[54] Lyotard, *The Differend*, p. 56. See also the post-war remarks of one of the Warsaw ghetto fighters: "I can find no words to express what I feel. The word has been damaged, has lost its value. The same words were used before the war, at its beginning and in its course. And we are obliged to have recourse to the same words now, after it is all over." Tzivia Lubetkin, "The Sorrow of the Meeting," *Yemei Kilion Va'mered* (*Days of Destruction and Rebellion*), Tel Aviv 1979 (unnumbered page).

[55] The death of "Auschwitz," death in the Holocaust, is a death without alternative, without the possibility of choice, in contrast to other types of death which are "death rather than be enslaved …, rather than be defeated …" See Lyotard, *The Differend*, pp. 100–101.

[56] Berl Katznelson, "The Common Jewish Destiny," in *Collected Writings*, vol. XII, p. 223.

moment, and consequently this event – namely, the uprising as a Zionist act – became Zionism's "official" history.

The first word of the uprising reached Palestine through Radio London, via news agencies and Zionist agents stationed on the outskirts of the occupied continent. It was also conveyed in the form of a cablegram dispatched to Palestine which read, "Those members of the movement who are still alive, continue to fight for the honor of the remnants of Israel in Poland." The news caused a storm of emotion in Palestine, but the momentous happenings in the ghetto were colored exclusively by the Zionist perspective. The fighters had rebelled "by force of this home-land," declared Yitzhak Tabenkin at a May Day workers' rally in Haifa, in 1943. And Zalman Rubashov, later to become Israel's President, said: "the flame of rebellion has been ignited in the ghettos in the name of Eretz Israel."[57]

Death for the homeland

There were several reasons why Palestinian Zionism needed to view the ghetto uprisings as Zionist acts: the first and most pressing was that the Zionist collective in Palestine had not lived up to the demands it made of others in the face of the Jewish catastrophe. In contrast to its self-image, it did not risk its all, as did the Polish disciples of the Zionist movement, in order to try and save its fellow Jews from destruction, albeit its ability to do so was strictly limited. It never deviated from the sphere of realism, and calculated what was possible and even what was advantageous and expedient.[58] Despite their rhetoric of lament for Diaspora Jewry, the Jews of Palestine, which was a strategic area for the Allied armies, lived rou-tinely and rather prosperously during those years, particularly after the Nazi threat to the region was lifted at the battle of El Alamein. Not a single emissary from Palestine reached the ghettos of Poland in the war years.

---

[57] Yitzhak Tabenkin, Haifa, 1 May 1943, Kibbutz Ha'meuhad Archives; Shazar (Rubashov), "From Victim to Fighter," *Tav Shin Gimmel*, Tel Aviv 1944, quoted in *Hatzar Ha'matara*, Jerusalem 1975, p. 304.

[58] Even Ben-Gurion's official biographer, Shabtai Tevet, admits that all his life, and particularly in times of crisis, Ben-Gurion acted in the light of utilitarian consideration believing that effort should be invested only in what appeared attainable and not in abortive and fruitless endeavors. And since Ben-Gurion considered the rescue efforts on the part of the Yishuv, which inevitably were aimed at the few and could not fundamentally alter the scope of extermination and the fate of the people, to be hopeless, he avoided them. On the other hand, when attempts were made to transfer money from Palestine to the Jews of Europe, Ben-Gurion took steps to ensure that it would be known "there" that the money and assistance came from Eretz Israel, so as to enhance Zionism's reputation. See Shabtai Tevet, *Kinat David, Ha'karka Ha'boer (David's Zeal, The Burning Ground)*, Tel Aviv 1987, pp. 443–449.

"Our war is here [in Eretz Israel] and not in Radom," Yitzhak Tabenkin explained in early 1943.[59] Ben-Gurion's wording differed only slightly: "While the burning, urgent issue is rescue," he told the secretariat of the Mapai party, "[and while] matters are urgent in Rumania and Bulgaria ... internal action [in the party] is top priority ... party work may be the only route to rescue."[60]

These rebels, raised on the Zionist "theory of death" and model of "beautiful death" more than atoning for the fact that their parents and families – that is, the mass of Diaspora Jews – had gone to their deaths "like sheep to the slaughter," were perceived by the Zionists of Palestine, however unconsciously, as atoning for their own feeble action. What is more, the Jewish community in Palestine had even nursed the a priori expectation that their disciples in the Diaspora would prove their worth, vindicate their Zionist education, and rebel, even if their rebellion was doomed – and all this so that their death would be "beautiful," a Massada-like death, a worthy Zionist death. Near the end of 1942, before the uprisings began, while ceremonies were being held in Palestine in mourning and solidarity for those annihilated in the Diaspora, a socialist youth movement held a ceremony of this kind at Hanukka – the feast commemorating the heroism of the Maccabees – on top of Mount Massada, "the mountain which bears witness to the last heroism of the desperate," thus incorporating both the Maccabees and Massada into its symbol system, transmitting to the Diaspora the message of the "beautiful death" of desperate heroes.[61] A periodical aimed at young people interpreted the acts of the rebels as "a need to resurrect Massada – the symbol of Israel's heroism throughout the generations."[62]

In order to glorify the rebels' "Zionist" heroism and prove the existence of a new, Zionist Jew in the Diaspora, it was first necessary to effect a total conceptual and existential split between the rebels and the rest of the Jewish people who had not taken up arms. It was as if to say that the rebels had not emerged from within this people, had not been raised on its traditions; as if it were not in protest against the outrage to and murder of this very people that they had risen up and died. The split was created by two complementary means: first, by cloaking the rebels in the mantle of Zionism and transforming them into Palmach fighters, accidentally snared in the spheres of Diaspora; and, conversely, by

[59] Yitzhak Tabenkin, Kibbbut Ha'meuhad Council, January 1943, Kibbutz Ha'meuhad Archives.
[60] Ben-Gurion to the Mapai Secretariat, 22 February 1944, Labor Party Archives, 24/44.
[61] Yitzhak Kafkafi, 1943, in Yitzhak Kafkafi (ed.), *Shnot Mahanot Ha'olim*, B (*Mahanot Ha'olim Years*, B), Tel Aviv 1985, p. 332.
[62] *Ba'ma'aleh*, 26 March 1943.

rejecting the conduct of the Jewish masses and their elderly leaders, the heads of the Judenrat, for failing to stand up and rebel, branding those masses, as the poet Nathan Alterman later wrote, as "a dark and beseeching knot of deceived and blinded masses ... led to their death, clinging on with the last vestiges of strength but losing, in the course of this struggle for survival, just as the murderers had plotted, their humanity and the last remnants of human dignity and pride."[63]

The voices judging and denouncing the conduct of Europe's Jews, and praising the uprising, were the rule. Those humble enough to have contemplated the reasons which had moved the rebels to their desperate, heroic deeds, their sense of doom on the eve of the uprising and in its course, and the question of "their reality, the voice crying out from within them"[64] were rather rare. These few individuals within the Zionist collective who questioned the right of those who had not been "there" to pronounce sentence on those who were, were usually people whose positions had brought them into contact with European Jewry. These people had an intimate knowledge of their ways of life and customs, and, hence, did not negate them as an abstract concept, in the way that Zionist ideology did, which thus derived its own justification from this total, conceptual rejection. "We can learn a great deal from it [the Diaspora]. Numerous values have now been created there," said the director of the Jewish Agency's Immigration Department, at the 46th Histadrut Council. By what right, he asked, do we claim leadership of the nation? "Because we are enjoying wartime prosperity and were saved by a miracle from the huge cataclysm? Do they not surpass us in terms of their spiritual and public powers?"[65] And Yosef Sprinzak, later to become the first Speaker of Israel's parliament, pleaded in defense of both the rebels and the Judenräte: "Who is the greater in this chapter of history? We or Frumka? Frumka is the greater," Sprinzak said.[66] Earlier he had warned against a Zionist search for scapegoats in the person of the leaders of the Jewish Councils. "We had no interest in Czerniakow either," he said, "until he committed suicide, and many

[63] Nathan Alterman, "The Uprising and its Times," *Davar*, 1954, quoted in Nathan Alterman, *Ha'tur Ha'shevii* (*The Seventh Column*), B, Tel Aviv 1975, pp. 409–420.
[64] Eshed, "The War of the Jews."
[65] Eliyahu Dobkin at the 46th Histadrut Council, 26 May 1942, Vol. 41; Venya Pomerantz, a Yishuv emissary to Constantinople, said at the Mapai Central Committee in August 1943: "We can learn a great deal from them (the Diaspora), many values have been created there now." Labor Party Archives, 23/43.
[66] Frumka Plotnitzka, one of the central figures in the pioneering Zionist movement in Poland, refused an offer to leave Poland with the aid of a non-Jewish agent, and to flee to Palestine to bring living testimony of the extermination, and was subsequently killed in the rebellion at Bendin.

refrained from eulogizing him, but as it turns out, he should be added to the list of Israel's saints."[67] Even a Haganah leader, a prominent formulator of the ethos of power and with it the heroic image of Palestine youth, was, for a brief moment, appalled at the arrogant attitude towards Diaspora Jews which he had encountered among his disciples. Early in 1943 he posed them the rhetorical question, "Have the Hebrew youth of this country [who consider themselves the heirs of the Maccabees] withstood any tests which are comparable to those thrust upon Jewish youth in the Diaspora?"[68]

Another reason for the process of "Zionization" of the ghetto uprisings, which was set in motion in Palestine, was the need to incorporate the ghetto resistance into the chain of Israel's heroic battles for its homeland and the "Zionist" wars, so as to render the Jews of the Diaspora both worthy of being part of the struggle for a Jewish state, to lend the Zionist fight a global dimension and construe it as a life-and-death struggle, and to establish an uncontestable link between the fate of European Jewry in the war years, and the right to a Jewish state in Palestine after the war. Speaking to the Elected Assembly in October 1943, Ben-Gurion stressed this direct link between the fighting in the ghettos and the relentless struggle for "a right to a homeland," the right to existence, and the right to self-defense. A labor journal claimed that establishment of a "Hebrew homeland" was one of the ghetto rebels' goals, along with "revenge for the spilt blood of Israel" and creation of a new Massada. This kind of discourse eventually led to the Israeli perception that the constitution of the Jewish state was an atonement and compensation of sorts, however partial and belated, for the annihilation of the Jewish people, and to the view that the very existence of this state endowed the death of millions with meaning.

"The human profile of the Jews of Poland and the Jews deported from there was obliterated," said Yitzhak Greenbaum, Chairman of the Yishuv Rescue Committee, who had previously been the leader of that same Polish Jewish community.[69] The expunging of the humanity of European Jews, those who had failed to mount an armed rebellion and to launch physical resistance to the Nazis, and their normative, intentional severance from the minority who rebelled; the immediate appropriation of the fighters by the Zionist collective, which "hushed up" or "obscured"

---

[67] Yosef Sprinzak at the Mapai Secretariat, 15 December 1943, Labor Party Archives, 24/43; Sprinzak at the Histadrut Executive Committee, 11 February 1943, Labor Archives, 5/30.

[68] Israel Galili's speech to "Ha'noar Ha'oved," early 1943, Pinkas Avodah (Working Diary), 1943.

[69] Yitzhak Greenbaum's remarks are cited in *Moznayim*, **16**, p. 250.

the existence of non-Zionist elements within the rebel groups; the obfus-
cation and concealment of the ghetto fighters' sense that the world, their
far-away homeland included, had abandoned them; the reluctance to
detect, or the attempt to muffle the expressions of doubts, despair,
depression, the cry of pain, and the death-wish of the rebels in so hopeless
a situation; and the consequent suppression of the group suicide of the
last survivors besieged in the bunker at Mila 18 – all these were components of the project of nationalization of the ghetto uprisings and the armed
struggle of the agonized Jews facing the extermination. Such, as well,
were the guidelines for organizing the Zionist, national memory of the
uprisings, and for shaping of the narrative of the uprising as a winning
narrative.

The uprisings and their stories

Most of the surviving rebels objected to the distinction drawn in Palestine
between the fighters and the rest of the Jews. They were reluctant to
cooperate in their elevation above the masses. Moreover, they refused to
comply with the – allbeit belated – efforts to save them; efforts initiated in
Palestine after the Zionist leadership panicked at the possibility of "an
overriding psychosis" of suicide among the rebels, of death "to the very
last man." There was fear that Zionist encouragement for the uprisings
could cause "harm by expediting the end," and thus frenzied attempts
were launched to get them out of occupied Europe.[70] "I have a responsibility to my brothers. I can help them. I will not leave them. I have lived
with them and I will die with them," said Frumka Plotnitzka to the non-
Jewish agent dispatched from Slovakia in July 1943 to smuggle her out of
Bendin. And Hayka Klinger, who reached Palestine in March 1944, gave
the Secretariat of the Histadrut Executive Committee a lesson in the
crucial, structural bond between an avant-garde group and the rest of
the people. "Without a people, a people's avant-garde is of no value," she
said. "If rescue it is, then the entire people must be rescued. If it is to
be annihilation – the avant-garde too shall be annihilated ... the movement took the only right path that it could have taken, though it was a
terrible and tragic one: where an entire people dies, its avant-garde must
die with it."[71]

---

[70] Melekh Neustadt demanded that the surviving fighters be rescued, even against their will,
by means of "an order from each movement in this country to its members there that it is
forbidden for them to stay." Neustadt at the Mapai Secretariat, 15 December 1943,
Labor Party Archives, 24/43.
[71] Hayka Klinger at the Histadrut Executive Committee, 15 March 1944, Labor Archives,
6/71; *Yoman Ba'ghetto* (*Diary of the Ghetto*), Tel Aviv and Ha'ogen 1959, p. 95.

The actual motives behind the belated, few, and selective rescue
attempts had connotations to which some strongly objected at the time.
Beyond the immediate, instinctive wish to save the young elite of the
Diaspora, the Zionists' consideration was that they might lose this wondrous youth, this constructive force, and that the tale of their "Zionist"
heroism might die along with them. Once the Warsaw ghetto uprising had
played its part, and proven the soundness of the Zionist revolution, the
Zionist leadership viewed the subsequent uprisings in other ghettos, as
well as escape to the forests to join the partisans, as an act of "forgetting
Zion," a kind of betrayal of the overriding principle of the homeland. "We
received a command at Zaglembie not to organize any more defense
[uprisings]," Hayka Klinger reported in March 1944, "as those who
were still alive were vital to the Yishuv, so they could relate the history
of the [rebel] movement and what happened at its end." She and her
friends, she said, could not accept such a position. "We felt we should not
live by virtue of our Warsaw comrades ... there is nothing to justify why
we rather than anyone else should save ourselves."[72] Indeed, some of the
Zionist emissaries in Constantinople, who for years had borne the brunt
of liaison with the agonizing Diaspora, admitted to the surviving rebels
that the people of the Yishuv regarded them, first and foremost, as
"a precious asset to the nation and the movement, who can at least tell
us everything they endured."[73]

The meaning of the nationalization of the ghetto uprisings was the
nationalization of the narrative of the uprisings as well as the expunging
of its incompatible, non-Zionist components. Early on, while the insurrection was actually taking place, it was convenient to believe in Palestine,
that it was solely borne by the young people of the Zionist youth movements. This glossed over and ignored the fact that the rebel groups
encompassed the entire spectrum of Jewish political parties; that the
Warsaw ghetto uprising was led by a group which did in fact include
representatives of the Zionists, but also members of the anti-Zionist Bund
as well as Communists, and that the Jewish Fighting Organization –
Żydowska Organizacja Bojowa (ŻOB) – received material and moral
support from both community leaders and institutions and representatives of the openly non-Zionist American-Jewish Joint Distribution
Committee (the Joint), without which it could not have operated.

The most striking case of silencing and obscuring was that of Marek
Edelman, one of the leaders of the Warsaw rebellion, a Bund member at

[72] Hayka Klinger, at the Histadrut Executive Committee, 15 March 1944.
[73] Eliyahu Stern, "The Links between the Constantinople Delegation and Polish Jewry,"
Yalkut Moreshet, **39**, May 1985, p. 150.

the time and subsequently a Polish socialist. Edelman persistently refused to view the establishment of the State of Israel as the belated "meaning" of the Holocaust. According to him, the Holocaust could have no meaning, ever, either in Israel or elsewhere. Consequently, his narrative of the uprising was silenced and his role was played down. His book, *The Ghetto Fighting*, published in Warsaw in 1945 by the Bund, was translated into Hebrew only fifty-six years later, in 2001, and after persistent effort on the part of a handful of scholars, who refused to accept the Israeli-national narrative of the uprisings as their sole narrative. Within the flourishing commemoration industry that developed in Israel around the rebellion and its heroes, there was no room for Edelman and his other story. It was not the history that the young Jewish collective in Palestine/Israel needed, and Edelman himself was not a dead and docile hero to be kneaded into shape according to the political demands of the times. On the contrary, he was alive and kicking and recalcitrant, all of which made him highly troublesome and inconvenient material for the creation of a compensating, healing myth of Zionist heroism. Moreover, and perhaps above all, he was not a Zionist. Even after the war, he viewed Poland as his homeland and went on living there, partly, he said, because it was the place where his friends had died and his people been felled, and where hundreds of thousands of its sons and daughters were buried in the ground. Edelman, who was second in command to Mordechai Anielewicz, representing the Bund, and was the commander of the "brush-makers' section" during the fighting, the man whom the resistant Tzivia Lubetkin described as unfamiliar with fear, and whom Antek Zuckerman, also second in command of the resistance organization, called "a man of noble soul," protested at the collective suicide of Anielewicz and his comrades at Mila 18. "Never," he said. "They should never have done it, even though it was a very good symbol. You don't sacrifice a life for a symbol," he told the Polish journalist, Hanna Krall.[74]

After the war he consistently refused to adapt himself to the project of mythologizing and "Zionizing" of the rebels and the uprising, and took no part in it. From the very first moment, he did not choose the right words in order to become the official spokesman of the uprising, Hanna Krall wrote in irony. He said to some representatives of political parties who came to hear his report on the uprising, that it had been possible, in the twenty days of rebellion, "to have killed more Germans and to have saved more of our people," but that the rebels had not been properly trained and were not able to conduct a proper battle. Besides, Edelman said, "the

---

[74] Hanna Krall, *Shielding the Flame: An Intimate Conversation with Dr. Marek Edelman* (trans. Joanna Stasinka and Lawrence Weschler), New York 1986, p. 6.

Germans also knew how to fight." Those who heard him speak nodded and noted, "he is not a normal man. He is a human wreck." So, wrote Krall in her book about Edelman,

from the very beginning he was no good at talking about it, because he was unable to scream. He was no good as a hero, because he lacked grandiloquence. What bad luck. The one, the only one, who'd survived was no good as a hero. Having understood that, he tactfully lapsed into silence. He was silent for quite a long time, for thirty years in fact, and when he finally spoke, it immediately became clear that it would have been better for everybody if he had simply never broken his silence.[75]

For when Edelman spoke, the uprising, as he related it, sounded different than before. "Can you even call that an uprising?" he asked. "All it was about finally, was that we not just let them slaughter us when our turn came. It was only a choice as to the manner of dying." After all, he said, "humanity had agreed that dying with arms was more beautiful than without arms. Therefore we followed this consensus."[76]

The ultimate means of resistance

Edelman did not fit the role of hero, just as his fellow rebels did not fit the bronze and stone monuments erected in their memory in Warsaw and in Israel, the figures of tall, upright, fair and handsome men and women, with grenades clutched in one hand and a rifle in the other. "None of them had ever looked like this," Edelman said. "They didn't have rifles, cartridge pouches or maps; besides, they were dark and dirty. But in the monument they look the way they were ideally supposed to. On the monument, everything is bright and beautiful."[77] Moreover, Edelman's account of Anielewicz, which had given a more human picture, did not fully match the legendary image depicted in Israel by his disciples and friends, an image so badly needed by the Zionist-Israeli discourse of the first decades of statehood. Edelman's Anielewicz broke down and was never again the same person after he first witnessed an *Aktsiya* (Ger.: *Aktion*, operation of deportation) at the *Umschlagplatz* (Tranfer Point), and who had been chosen to command the combat organization and the uprising because he was a "talented guy, well-read, full of energy," but

---

[75] Ibid., pp. 14–15.   [76] Ibid., p. 10.

[77] Ibid., p. 77. In Alterman's conversations with Abba Kovner after publication of the poem "The Day of Memory and the Rebels" in 1954, Kovner too admitted that he had reservations regarding Nathan Rapaport's Warsaw ghetto memorial monument, that he found it discordant and repellent because it was irrelevant, belonging to a different realm." Laor (ed.), *Nathan Alterman's Two Paths*, p. 23.

also because "he very much wanted to be a commander, so we chose him. He was a little childlike in this ambition."[78]

Edelman did not fit the role of hero, just as he was not suited for the role of entrepeneur of the commemoration of the uprising as a singular act severing the continuum of Jewish history in the Diaspora – a role which some of his fellow ghetto fighters who reached Israel took upon themselves. Edelman did not commit suicide after the war, as did his comrades Mordechai Tennenbojm-Tamarof, Franja Beatos and others, who had refused to go on living in a world in which such a human catastrophe had been possible. He stayed alive, but the role of hero and bearer of the torch of rebellion as a heroic and dignified leap out of an environment of submission and self-degradation[79] did not suit him. He himself sank into a deep depression after the war, and depressed heroes who refuse to emerge from under the covers are problematic heroes, certainly as far as ideological missions are concerned. Later he became a renowned cardiologist, a life-saving humanist, capable of transforming inevitable death – he, who had been familiar with appalling forms of death during the war – into a tolerable event, "so that they won't know, won't suffer, won't fear, won't be humiliated."[80] No, he was not suited to the roles of hero or myth-bearer because his sole reproach against the head of the Judenrat in Warsaw, Adam Czerniakow, was that he turned his suicide,

[78] In response to Edelman's remarks on Anielewicz in an interview in a Polish periodical, published in full in *Ha'aretz* (27 April 1976, translated from the German version published in *Die Zeit*), the historian and ghetto survivor Israel Gutman wrote, under the heading "Misrepresentations about the Warsaw Ghetto Uprising," that Edelman had not added to knowledge nor revealed new truths but a "mixture of groundless ponderings and surprising distortions." Gutman goes on to link Edelman's remarks to his non-Zionism. "What impels a man of his stature, who has faced the test, to do this? There is no way of knowing. Why did Marek Edelman remain in Poland as a doctor when almost all his Jewish political colleagues and people close to him personally – left?" *Ha'aretz*, 21 May 1976. In the context of the sublimation of the image of Anielewicz in Israel as part of the nationalized story of the ghetto uprisings, it is of particular interest to examine the memorial site at kibbutz Yad Mordechai (named after Anielewicz before World War II ended), with its semiotic reversal. The mighty figure of Anielewicz, as sculpted by Nathan Rapaport, a symbol of power, heroism, and independence, represents the Holocaust and destruction, while the bullet-pocked water tower, listing to one side, represents the victory of the local fighters in the 1948 war. Moreover, contrary to the chronological order of events, the site is constructed so that it appears to the visitor that Anielewicz's statue, representing the earlier event, grows out of the derstroyed water tower, representing the later event.

[79] In a conversation with Alterman, a week after publication of the column "Memorial Day and the Rebels," Abba Kovner too said that while disagreeing on principle with Alterman, when he had read, shortly after arriving in Eretz Israel, an article claiming that a handful of rebels had erased the shame of that period from the nation, he found this very disturbing. Laor (ed.), *Nathan Alterman's Two Paths*, p. 21.

[80] Edelman was also one of the leaders of "Solidarity." Krall, *Shielding the Flame*, pp. 9–10.

his death, into "his own private business," and died in silence at a time
when "one should die with a bang."[81] He was not suited for the role
because, just as he considered Czerniakow a hero, he considered the
uprising an unexceptional act, the direct outcome of Czerniakow's valiant
attempts to save his community, an additional step in the spectrum of
Jewish response to the systematic Nazi murder machine and the effort to
preserve humanity, demonstrated by the Jewish masses in their "passive"
resistance to the dehumanization forced upon them. His and his friends'
uprising was for him

the logical sequence of four years of resistance on the part of a population
incarcerated in inhuman conditions, a humiliated, degraded population, which
was treated ... as sub-human. In spite of these dramatic circumstances, the
inmates of the ghetto organized their lives, as best they could, according to the
highest of European values. While the criminal occupying regime denied them
their right to education, culture, knowledge, life, in other words – to a dignified
death, they established clandestine universities, schools, welfare institutions and
newspapers. These acts, that generated resistance to whatever threatened the
right to a dignified life, culminated in rebellion. The rebellion was the ultimate
means of resistance in the face of the inhuman conditions of life and death, the
ultimate way to fight barbarism and maintain human dignity.[82]

Shielding the Flame, which tells the story of the uprising as viewed by
Marek Edelman, was translated into many languages immediately after
its publication in 1977, and was adapted for the stage. In Israel, however,
the book could not find a public, established publisher. A small, privately
owned press, Adam Publishers, finally brought out the Hebrew version in
1981. Edelman's arguments and comments in this book regarding the
Warsaw ghetto uprising were verified post factum in Antek Zuckerman's
book, *Those Seven Years*.[83] However, Edelman is still considered by most
Holocaust scholars in Israel as a questionable witness.[84]

Different kinds of death

The evolution of the annual Israeli "Holocaust and Heroism Memorial
Day" and the form it had taken on in the 1950s were inevitably connected

---

[81] Ibid., p. 9.
[82] So he wrote in the introduction to the French translation of his book, quoted in *L'Express*.
[83] Antek Zuckerman, *Sheva Ha'shanim Ha'hen* (*Those Seven Years*) no place and date,
     pp. 194–195.
[84] The editorial note "Marek Edelman's remarks reflect his personal opinion only, for which
     he alone is responsible," accompanying an interview with Edelman by a Polish writer, in
     a special issue of an academic journal issued for the 50th anniversary of the uprising,
     published by the Lochamei Ha'getaot (Ghetto Fighters) Institution – the only one of its
     kind in the issue – is but one example. *Edut*, 9 April 1993, p. 10.

to the question of whether the rebellion was a sequel or a break; a
corollary of Jewish life and Jewish resistance in the Diaspora or an exceptional moment of "Zionist" transcendence in the midst of the degrading
existence in exile; a defeat or a victory. True to his convictions, Edelman
regarded the war and the uprising as an irreparable defeat, and stayed on
to mourn – in his own way – the destruction of his people at the very places
where it had occurred ("People kept asking me, 'Do you want to look at
those walls again, those empty streets?' And I knew that yes, indeed, I had
to come back here and look at them").[85] In contrast, the founders of the
new Israel – supported by the remnants of the rebels who immigrated
after the war, settled, built homes, museums, memorial sites, reconstruc-
tions, and other assorted replacements for what had been, in order to
gather and preserve the memory of their agony and their heroism –
refused to add the national day of Holocaust commemoration to the
traditional cycle of Jewish ritual days, denoting historical tragedies and
cataclysms. From the moment in April 1951 when it was first proposed in
the Knesset that a "Holocaust and Ghetto Uprisings" day be declared,[86]
until the 1959 Holocaust and Heroism Commemoration Day law was
passed, the main purpose was to extol the heroism of the fighters and
rebels who had taken up arms, as opposed to, and at the expense of, all the
other forms of Jewish resistance and survival. As such, the day was
inserted into the national calendar of the nascent Israeli state between
Passover, the festival of freedom, and Independence Day, thus emplot-
ting "the entire story of Israel's national rebirth, drawing on a potent
combination of religious and national mythologies," as James Young put
it. It was a tale of deliverance ritually performed in a repetitive way,
a period of the year commencing, according to Young, "with God's
deliverance of the Jews and concluding with the Jews' deliverance
of themselves in Israel," passing through and doubled by the Jews'
attempted deliverance of themselves in Warsaw.[87] Initially, this commemorative day was two-faced, Janus-like, and both faces were exclusively Zionist in their meanings and functions. On the one hand, it was
meant to remind Jews in Israel and the Diaspora of the fate awaiting those
who failed to choose the Zionist path. On the other, it was intended to
emphasize the direct causal link between the uprising, regardless of its

---

[85] Krall, *Shielding the Flame*, p. 82.
[86] On the formulation of Holocaust and Heroism Day and its historical and political
implications see James E. Young, "When a Day Remembers: A Performative History
of Yom Ha'shoah," *History and Memory*, 2 (2), Winter 1990, pp. 54–75; James E. Young,
The Texture of Memory, Holocaust Memorials and Meaning, New Haven 1993,
pp. 263–281.
[87] Young, *The Texture of Memory*, p. 269.

price,[88] against the oppressive Diaspora existence, that is, between physical heroism and taking up arms and the establishment of a Jewish state in Israel, a modern secular salvation, as it were, and a triumph over the history of the Diaspora.

On Commemoration Day of the year 1954 (30 April; 27 of Nissan according to the Hebrew calendar), the most respected Israeli poet of the time, Nathan Alterman, published his poem, "Memorial Day and the Rebels,"[89] in the daily *Davar*. Speaking for the fighters and rebels, although he was not one of them Alterman wrote: "We are part of the great nation / Part of its dignity and valor and the sound of its bitter weeping / ... Those who fell, weapon in hand, may not accept the barrier / Between them and the death of communities and the heroes who headed them and interceded for them."[90] The true symbol of the Commemoration Day, he wrote, "is not the glorious barricade in flames / Nor the image of the young man and woman who rose up to triumph or to die / As in the immortal pictures of revolts which burn and are never extinguished."[91] These words proposed, much in line with Edelman, a stark antithesis to the lofty ideological structure which Zionism had set up over the uprising – a structure which set apart the few heroes who rebelled from the rest of the people – and called for erasure of the unequivocal, ideological, arrogant segregation of the phenomenon of rebellion from the existential reality of life and death of Diaspora Jewry.

The sweeping counter-reaction to the poem, its almost unanimous denunciation, echoed by representatives of the rebels as well, was deeply significant, making the event of the poem's publication all the more momentous. This denunciation testified to the assimilation of the surviving ghetto fighters into hegemonic Zionist discourse and the view of the uprising as a transcendent Zionist act. It also bore witness to the coercive, engulfing ideologic pressure exerted over newcomers by the prevailing

[88] "The uprising closed in on the entire ghetto and imposed total annihilation while, on the other hand, even the camps left some remnant of hope in the hearts of those transported there," wrote Nathan Alterman in his diaries in April–June 1954, at the time of the public controversy around "Memorial Day and the Rebels." He went on to write: "The uprising was not – and was not intended to be – a shield for the Jews, neither in the clandestine underground movement period nor during the open uprising. In the period of secret preparations, the organization focused only on guarding its own members ... while it was engaged (by necessity) in this task, Jews all around were being executed ... the fighters who waged the rebellion were also the main survivors. The people, on whom the rebellion was imposed, all perished therein." Laor (ed.), *Nathan Alterman's Two Paths*, pp. 22, 18, respectively.
[89] The poem also appears in Alterman, *The Seventh Column*, B, pp. 407–408.
[90] Alterman, "Memorial Day and the Rebels," in Laor (ed.), *Nathan Alterman's Two Paths*, p. 407.
[91] Ibid.

Israeli discourse of the first years of statehood. Yet, the very intensity of
the reactions to Alterman's poem attested also to the width of the already
irreparable, and ever-expanding fissure in the dividing wall which
Zionism had erected between the "rebellion and heroism" and the
"Holocaust."

Alterman's poem triggered so intense an emotional response and such
extreme reactions because it had been written by Alterman, who was
widely regarded as Ben-Gurion's poetic alter-ego; because his poetry
and particularly his major poem "Paupers' Joy" were viewed as the
"epopee of the generation"; and finally, because the poem emanated
from that same exclusive, divisive, haughty Zionism, from within
the hard core of the new pioneering project. In the poem itself, and
in the articles he published in response to his critics, Alterman argued
that the Holocaust period "burns down the dividing wall that we erect
between the heroism of those who fell in armed rebellion and other kinds
of heroism; between the deaths of the rebels and the deaths of the
communities."[92] He denounced the stereotypical divide, promoted
through "speeches, political rhetoric, literature and sculptures," between
"the heroism, the dignity, the light, the justice, the honesty, the national
genius and the emotional strength," on one side, and "the catastrophe,
the darkness, the blindness, the narrow-mindedness, hard-heartedness,
and the complicity," on the other. He criticized the shallow and stereotypical interpretation of the concept of rebellion; the clichés obscuring the
complexity and weight of the act; the verbal banalization that made the
rebellion seem so natural and obvious, thereby deeply wronging "the soul
of the era and the truth of the rebels themselves."[93] He added that all the
phrases employed by a sovereign state could in any way apply to the
Holocaust and the uprisings, "without the awareness that the annihilation
and the rebellion shatter all the frameworks of these concepts like a huge,
heavy uncontainable tangle."[94]

A fascinating debate about history and history telling followed the
publication of Alterman's poem. His critics claimed,[95] each in their
own words, and yet almost in unison, when all was said and done, that
his poems were liable to place the souls of the younger generation at risk,
and that Jewish history, as he viewed and interpreted it, was not the
history that Zionism and the State of Israel needed "now," after independence had been achieved. "The gravest problem of all," it was argued, "is

[92] Alterman, "The Uprising and its Times," in *The Seventh Column*, B, p. 416.
[93] Ibid., p. 415.   [94] Ibid., p. 412.
[95] On Alterman's poems and essays and reactions to them, see Dan Laor, "Afterword,"
in Laor (ed.), *Nathan Alterman's Two Paths*, pp. 114–148.

what lesson this generation will learn."[96] One critic asked: "why was this poem written, for what purpose and whom does it serve, [and] who will avenge the insult to symbols?"[97] Another echoed in asking: "is it not the duty of a people whose sons are led to the slaughter, generation after generation, to hold up as an example to the generations to come, which will yet face arduous trials, manifestations of active heroism?"[98]

Alterman's poem and the scathing reactions it elicited were not published in a political vacuum. The controversy raged at a time when the trial of a certain Malkiel Grunewald for libel, which commenced in the Jerusalem District Court on 1 January 1954, was being transformed by the defense counsel into the indictment of Dr. Israel (Rejo) Kastner, one of the leaders of Hungarian Jewry, for having collaborated with the Nazis, and, by the domino effect, into an indictment against the Jewish leadership during the Holocaust, an indictement against the political leadership of the Zionist collective at the time, the leadership that was still in power in Israel.[99] One cannot, therefore, read Alterman's texts but within the context of the trial and the questions it raised. But like the Grunewald–Kastner trial itself, these texts did not only relate to historical issues concerning the conduct of Jews during the Holocaust; they were part of the struggle for power and political dominance between the various Israeli parties in the 1950s, for whom the Holocaust and its memory were major resources, inexhaustible reservoirs of images, arguments, and assertions.

Alterman was identified with the ruling party and its historic leader, Ben-Gurion. Unlike his critics, who came mostly from the left – parties most identified with the ghetto fighters and the partisans – Mapai and its leadership had no rebel heroes to flaunt, and, conversely, were identified with the Jewish political establishment in the Diaspora, with such people as Kastner, who were involved, by virtue of their standing and positions, in "collaboration" with the Nazis. Now, in the Jerusalem courtroom, at a trial initiated by the Attorney General, that is, the state, the leaders of Mapai, Israel's leadership, found themselves as defendants rather than accusers, entangled in a historical, political, and legal trap, with no

---

[96] Moshe Carmel, in response to Alterman, quoted in Alterman, "On 'The Lesson for the Generation,'" in Alterman, *The Seventh Column*, B, p. 434; "A Generation on the Verge of the Abyss," *La'merhav*, 6 July 1955.

[97] David Cnaani, "Like a Shining Light," *Al Ha'mishmar*, 14 May 1954. Alterman's response, "The Uprising and its Times," in Alterman, *The Seventh Column*, B, pp. 409–420.

[98] Tuvia Buzhikovsky, "The Rebels, the Leaders and the Poet," *Masa*, 27 May 1954.

[99] See chapter 2 of this book; see also Weitz, *The Man who was Murdered Twice*, particularly chapters 3 and 4.

prospect of extricating themselves. Alterman's poem was thus and above all perceived as a political defense of Kastner, and through him also of the ruling party, Mapai. This it indeed was, but it was also much more than that.[100]

Alterman's remarks constituted one of the earliest and most significant discussions of Jewish collaboration with the perpetrators. Using almost identical words as Hannah Arendt after the Eichmann trial,[101] Alterman wrote with regard to the responsibility of the Judenräte that "the agreement to dispatch Jews [to deportation] is one of the murkiest episodes in this dark period."[102] But at the same time, Alterman objected to casting the entire responsibility on the Judenräte while exonerating all other Jewish elements, "including the rebels," and to self-divestment of responsibility, since, as far as he was concerned, that would be "a sin against historical truth and unloading of historical responsibility." Alterman regarded the phenomenon of the Judenräte as the "terrible fruit" of Jewish history. The blind annals of the nation, the blindness of its leaders and its masses had led to a situation where, indirectly or directly, the leaders, the masses, and the Zionist collective, as well as the rebels, in practice consented to this phenomenon. It was not merely morally reprehensible to blame the Judenräte alone, argued Alterman. It was also "an act of contempt for and banalization of history."[103]

Florid phrases and clichés are the greatest enemies of the aspiration for knowledge, said Alterman. Jewish history, he wrote, could not be altered, and should be learned as it was, with its positive and its darker aspects. Those concerned about the lesson and the moral which the nation should draw from those events should object vehemently to the trivialization of history, or to its disregard by force of slogans and phraseology.[104] "It is to be doubted," Alterman wrote, "that the consciousness of the new Jew, particularly a Jew living in his own land today, truly needs such extreme means of proving that self-defense is preferable to surrender, to the point where it is necessary to apply deliberate methods of illuminating and obscuring of the history of the Jews in the last generation." The new, young Israeli, said Alterman, needs "an accurate and alert sense of Jewish

---

[100] After the verdict in the Kastner case, at a meeting of the Mapai Secretariat to discuss the party's response to the verdict, the party Secretary reported that he had met with Alterman, who told him that "he was now occupied in writing an answer" to Kastner's attackers on the left (mainly Ahdut Ha'avoda) "and that it would be the longest column he had ever written." Labor Party Archives, 24/55.

[101] See Hannah Arendt, *Eichmann in Jerusalem: A Report on the Banality of Evil*, New York 1963, p. 117. "To a Jew this role of the Jewish leaders in the destruction of their own people is undoubtedly the darkest chapter of the whole dark story," Arendt wrote.

[102] Laor (ed.), *Nathan Alterman's Two Paths*, p. 105.

[103] Ibid., p. 105.   [104] Ibid.

history as it was," as much as he needs the symbol of the ghetto rebellion. For, he wrote, Jewish history, "is as it is, not otherwise," and it needs no manipulations through "illuminating and obscuring." Moreover, Alterman wrote, Jewish history "has its reasons and justifications for being as it is, not otherwise," and consequently, "we have no right to rob it of its dignity and its heroism, even when it bears no arms and does not man the barricades."[105]

Packages on a quay

Deliberate methods of "illuminating and obscuring" were applied to the *Exodus* affair while it was still ongoing in the summer of 1947, and more pronouncedly after it ended, when it instantly found a place in the saga of suffering and heroism in the years of rift and reconnection between Holocaust and Jewish independence. When compared to the two events discussed above, which also differ significantly from each other, the *Exodus* affair seems a minor and marginal event, rather belonging, in substance and dimensions, or in the memory structure constructed around it, to a different category. Nevertheless, while it was taking place, it reverberated throughout the entire western world, preoccupied heads of state, and had fateful implications for future statehood. More important, the protagonists themselves associated this event with the previous ones, and some of them perceived themselves as successors to the settlers of Tel-Hai and the ghetto fighters.[106] The historical event in itself, to the extent that such a complex and problematic definition is at all possible, was appropriated to serve a purpose beyond it; subjected to the same principles of manipulation and instrumentalization by the Zionist leadership, and depicted in a gloriously winning narrative – much like the other two events – and from these aspects is relevant to the model proposed in this chapter. The *Exodus* affair was undoubtedly triumphal in terms of the immediate political effects that Zionism achieved through it on the eve of statehood. Its human and moral meaning, the role of the Zionist leadership in the saga of the 4,500 Jewish refugee passengers, who were buffeted for months between land and shore and even sent back to Germany, have been expunged from the winning "tale" constructed around the affair.

The British indeed deserved the denunciation uttered by the French-Jewish statesman, Léon Blum, himself a Buchenwald survivor, in his daily

[105] Alterman, "The Uprising and its Times," in *The Seventh Column*, B, p. 419.
[106] See, for example, Mordechai Rozman's Order of the Day to members of Ha'shomer Ha'tzair aboard the ship, in Dror Levi and Israel Rosentzweig (eds.), *Sefer Ha'shomer Ha'tzair (Ha'shomer Ha'tzair Book)*, B, Merhavia 1961 (unnumbered page).

Le Populaire, when the *Exodus* refugees were deported back to Germany aboard British vessels from the small port in southern France where they had been anchored for nearly a month. "The *Exodus* passengers are not packages to be passed from hand to hand by indifferent porters and unloaded on some quay or other," Blum wrote. "They are human beings, free human beings."[107] In no less a fashion, however, his remarks were relevant for the Zionist leadership which transformed the *Exodus* and its wretched passengers into a symbol and an instrument – directed both towards the world at large, and towards the Zionist camp – embodying the ultimate struggle for a Jewish state. The refugees aboard the ship, most of them survivors of the Nazi death camps, have thus become a sort of captives of this struggle. Was this an indispensable sacrifice? Again, it was Alterman who shuffled the cards. Ten days after Léon Blum wrote his diatribe, Alterman, having read of the death of an infant aboard one of the deportation boats en route to Hamburg, wrote: "A nation is allowed to conscript them [the refugee babies] for duty / Only if its heart truly believes / That it will be worthy of looking them in the eye / And justifying itself."[108]

The whole affair only lasted about three months, but it had repercussions for several years. Some 4,500 Jewish survivors, were smuggled across borders from Displaced Persons camps in Germany, to the south of France, and embarked for Palestine, on 11 July 1947, aboard the *President Warfield*, a vessel purchased by the organization in charge of Zionist clandestine immigration (Mossad Le'aliyah Beth). Yet from the moment of its dawn departure from the small French port of Port de Bouc, there was nothing secret about its journey. British warships and planes accompanied the ship, and the whole sailing was a demonstration, a journey of political protest, designed to break the British blockade of Palestine in full view of the world, while the UN committee investigating the Palestine issue (UNSCOP) was still busy on site, carrying out its mandate. At sea, the ship was demonstratively renamed *Exodus 1947*, and this name caught on and became codename for the entire affair. Just off the shore of Palestine the British captured the ship, after a battle between unequal forces, a battle of the type deliberately engineered by the Mossad on its vessels for the world to see, for which purpose Holocaust survivors were the most effective troops.[109]

Three refugees were killed and dozens were wounded in the violent clashes. Instead of sending the refugees to detention camps in Cyprus, as

---

[107] *Le Populaire*, 26 August 1947.
[108] Nathan Alterman, "The Nation and its Emissary," *Davar*, 5 September 1947, reproduced in *The Seventh Column*, A, p. 87.
[109] For an elaboration on this see, Idith Zertal, *From Catastrophe to Power: Holocaust Survivors and the Emergence of Israel*, Berkeley 1998, especially chapter 4 ("Visibility and Resistance").

they had done since August 1946, the British adopted a new policy in this case and returned the refugees to their port of origin, so that that country would pay the price for its complicity in the Zionist endeavor. The socialist-headed French government rejected the British demand to force the Jewish refugees to descend on French shore, while the refugees themselves, encouraged by Zionist agents aboard the ships, refused to do so. The three British naval vessels with their passengers on board waited off the shores of France for nearly a month and none of the parties budged. The whole affair received worldwide press coverage, thus fulfilling the task that Ben-Gurion had assigned to Holocaust survivors in the project of organized clandestine immigration.[110] At the end of the month, the British sent the refugees back to Germany.

While the *Exodus* drama was taking place at sea and off the shores of France, evoking international sympathy for the Zionist cause, the Irgun (ETZEL, the secessionist National Military Organization, headed by Menachem Begin) hanged two British sergeants in reprisal for the execution of three of its members, thus arousing a wave of hostility for the Jewish resistance movement in Palestine. The clash between the two dramas, which indeed undermined the enormous impact of the *Exodus* affair, exposed, among other things, Ben-Gurion's functional and expedient attitude towards the *Exodus* refugees. For the sake of his resolute internal struggle against the secessionist terrorists – whom he called "a gang of hooligans ... worse than the Nazis"[111] – Ben-Gurion elevated the *Exodus* refugees even higher than the ghetto rebels, "because they [the rebels] had no choice, but these Jews [aboard the *Exodus*] had a choice."[112] He described their journey as an unparalleled "epopee of Jewish war in our times." In line with this conviction, Ben-Gurion accused the Irgun of inflicting irreparable harm through their terrorist actions on the focal point of the Zionist struggle – the *Exodus* – by "handing [the British Foreign Minister] Bevin a gift that the whole of his fleet and his entire anti-Semitic establishment could not have brought him." He also blamed Begin's men for "making the world forget the great tragic struggle of the *Exodus*" and removing "from the agenda" "four thousand five hundred Jews like none before them, who have sanctified the name of Israel."[113]

However, while making these statements at various political forums, and denoting the clandestine immigration movement "the most tragic

[110] Ibid., pp. 139, 157–160, 229–235, and more.

[111] "It [the Irgun] displayed Nazi conduct in our midst," said Ben-Gurion at the Histadrut Executive, referring to the hanging of the two sergeants, 6 August 1947, Labor Archives.

[112] Ben-Gurion, ibid.

[113] Ben-Gurion, ibid., and at the Mapai Council, 8 August 1947, Labor Party Archives.

and sublime spectacle in the Zionist struggle of our times," an "enormous, awesomely great spectacle,"[114] Ben-Gurion himself had already removed these Jewish refugee heroes, once they had completed their role, "from the agenda," and had decided on a new scale of priorities. In his new agenda, clandestine immigration and the Holocaust survivors forfeited their importance in the hierarchy of the Zionist struggle, and were replaced by "security issues and the establishment of a Jewish armed force [on which] our entire future, both immediate and distant, depends, and according to which we must devise all Zionist strategy, both externally and internally."[115]

When Haim Weizmann in London, aided by Léon Blum in Paris, attempted to prevent the deportation of the *Exodus* refugees to Germany, and tried, against the odds, to find an agreed, provisional, and more humane solution for them on French soil or in some other European country, so as to spare them the nightmare of returning to Germany, Ben-Gurion intervened to prevent him. The pretext was that any intervention by Weizmann, who no longer held an official role in the Zionist leadership, was undesirable, ineffective, and even dangerous, as it would encourage a new "devils' dance in London of all places," and a "slander and an incitement campaign [conducted] by the propaganda machine of the Foreign Office against the clandestine immigration and the Zionist movement."[116] Moreover, when the Zionist leadership learned that members of the British government were also trying to improvise a solution to the affair and had even appealed to the Danish government to permit thousands of refugees from the deportation vessels to disembark in Denmark, the Jewish Agency Executive cabled the Danish Prime Minister, demanding that his country emulate the French approach and refrain from forcing the refugees to alight anywhere other than their destination of choice, namely, Palestine.[117]

These moves by Ben-Gurion and the Jewish Agency Executive, which eventually frustrated any attempt to prevent the refugees from being returned to Germany, were carried out at the time when Zionist leaders, including Ben-Gurion himself, were attending a meeting of the Zionist Executive in Zurich. There they lauded the awe-inspiring immigration project and the valor of the refugees, while attacking "the cruel folly of the

[114] Ben-Gurion at a reception for the veterans of the First Zionist Congress, 17 August 1947, *In the Battle*, E, pp. 213–215.
[115] Ben-Gurion at a meeting of the Zionist Executive, Zurich, 26 August 1947 (Session 3), Central Zionist Archives, S5/320.
[116] Ben-Gurion to the Jewish Agency Executive in London, Geneva, 7 September 1947, Central Zionist Archives, S25/2630.
[117] Jewish Agency Executive to Danish Premier, Zurich, Central Zionist Archives.

White Paper government, who have banished these victims of the Nazis from the shores of the homeland, and forcibly returned them to the land of the Nazis."[118] The Holocaust survivors aboard the *Exodus*, who for over two years, since the war ended, had been wandering from camp to camp, passed from hand to hand, and "unload[ed] on some quay or other," as Léon Blum had phrased it, were now Zionism's trump card, and the greater their suffering, the greater their political and media effectiveness. Not only did the Zionist leadership make no effort to spare the refugees the apalling return to Germany; it actually took distinct steps towards preventing any solution other than Germany.[119]

A blind encounter

More than any event of those years, it was the plight of the *Exodus* and the tribulations of its passengers that exemplified the "blind encounter" which is the subtext of Alterman's poem, "Michael's Page."[120] It describes a "night of disembarkation," during which Holocaust survivors are borne on the backs of young natives to the shores of the homeland in the dead of night. This encounter of bearers and burdens involved close physical contact, but was totally devoid of concrete eye contact and recognition. The darkness in Alterman's poem was not just the darkness of "nights of disembarkation" when the native sons brought Holocaust survivors to land from boats anchored offshore. This darkness also symbolizes the blindness of this encounter, the absence of a gaze, Zionist lack of recognition, and acknowledgment of the Holocaust survivors as individual human beings, which made their political use, both then and later, not just possible but so highly effective.[121]

Were the *Exodus* passengers indeed "free human beings," capable of deciding their own fate, as Léon Blum believed? Had they "had a choice," as Ben-Gurion claimed when comparing them to the ghetto fighters, who had no such choice? Most of them would appear to have passed the test implied by these questions very well, according to Zionist criteria. When the French government offered them the option of disembarking in French territorial waters, and being granted refuge, the great majority rejected the generous offer. Only a few dozen, most of them ill, did. During their forced landing in Germany, the refugees refused to comply

[118] From Ben-Gurion's closing remarks at the Zionist Executive meeting, Zurich, 2 September 1947, Central Zionist Archives.
[119] On this aspect of the *Exodus* affair, see Zertal, *From Catastrophe to Power*, pp. 245–254.
[120] Nathan Alterman, *Ir Ha'yona* (*City of the Dove*), Tel Aviv 1972, pp. 25–27.
[121] For a wider discussion, see Zertal, *From Catastrophe to Power*, pp. 52–58, 67–79, 135–138, 239–258.

silently and obediently, and opted for resistance. A few months earlier they
had been rounded up hastily from Displaced Persons camps in Germany
by Mossad agents without any prior training. Composed of a random
assortment of people, not necessarily the Zionist "right stuff" – just a
handful were members of Zionist movements – many even registered for
immigration to other countries. A mixed population including the old, the
disabled, pregnant women, and children, they certainly displayed true
heroism, and "appropriate Zionist conduct" in the course of their pro-
tracted and harrowing journey, and deserved all the praise heaped on them.
However, they were not free masters of their fates. From the moment at the
end of June 1947 that they were loaded on to the trucks and trains that
conveyed them from Germany to the south of France, and on to the ship
that would take them to Palestine, they entrusted their lives and their
meagre possessions to the Zionist agents. Moreover, the ground had
collapsed under these people's feet in the course of the war, their families
had been murdered, and their lives utterly destroyed. Two years after the
war ended they were still incarcerated in camps in Germany, living behind
barbed wire. Such a history does not necessarily create "free human
beings." The Zionist emissaries and the Jewish homeland became now
the whole world to them, not because they were free to choose – most of the
countries of the world were barred to them – but because they had no other
choices. Meir Yaari, the leader of the leftist Ha'shomer Ha'tzair movement
in Palestine, a prominent representative of the most rigid sector of pioneering Zionist voluntarism, admitted after a tour of Europe in 1946, that
"there is no more voluntarism in the Diaspora. There is only one way
left ... they haven't come to us of their own free will, and they won't turn
their backs on us on a whim or in a passing mood."[122]

Some of the *Exodus* refugees, particularly the youth movement members, were indeed prepared for any trial and any sacrifice they might face
when they boarded the vessel, "the battleship of the Jewish people's war
for its existence." They viewed the "forbidden" voyage to Palestine as a
continuation, by other means, of the armed struggle of the partisans and
the ghetto fighters.[123] But the great majority of passengers on board had
neither been prepared nor had prepared themselves for the voyage's
unfolding hardships, which were forced upon them or took them by
surprise – a fact which actually accentuates the endurance they displayed,
their quiet, modest heroism. However, neither the heroism of the *Exodus*

[122] Meir Yaari at the Ha'shomer Ha'tzair Council, October 1946, in *Be'derekh Aruka* (*The Long Road*), Merhavia 1947, p. 288.
[123] Rozman's Order of the Day to Ha'shomer Ha'tzair members, Levi and Rosentzweig (eds.), *Sefer Ha'shomer Ha'tzair.*

refugees nor the earlier heroism of the people of Tel-Hai, nor the valor of the ghetto fighters, are the theme of our discussion, but rather the uses to which they were put, during and after the actual events, by people who had not undergone similar trials, either observing them from afar, or activating and interpreting them from an approximate point, devising the stories to fit their own needs.

While the *Exodus* passengers were still in Germany, writer and journalist, Bracha Habas, closely associated with the Zionist leadership, began collecting testimonies of Mossad agents for a book about the journey of the *Exodus*. The book appeared less than two years later, before the last of the *Exodus* passengers had been brought back to Israel, under the title *The Ship that Won*. It was a saga of Zionist heroism and victory of the right kind. The book was followed by a long list of publications of triumph devoted to the affair. In the meantime on the ground, the date of arrival of the *Exodus*, the battle conducted on its deck, and the refugees' resistance to their transfer to deportation vessels, had all been orchestrated to coincide with the presence in Palestine of the UNSCOP. The events were witnessed in person by several committee members who, through no coincidence, were brought to the site. Thus, as soon as the committee submitted its recommendations for the partition of Palestine on 1 September 1947, the *Exodus* refugees were "removed from the agenda" at one fell swoop. Tragically enough it happened at the very time they were being sent back to Germany. The Zionist struggle shifted from the high seas to the UN. When one of the Zionist agents who had accompanied the refugees on their voyages returned and told Ben-Gurion of their "manifestations of Jewish heroism," and "their struggle for the honor of Israel," Ben-Gurion responded impatiently, "It's over, finished. This is the past. Now there is a future."[124] The hour of the refugees deported back to Germany had indeed passed, and they were well aware of it. "Yesterday there were crying front-page headlines about us," one of them wrote, "and today they're silent and we're forgotten as if there had never been an *Exodus* ... we are no longer a sensation."[125]

A nation-building project requires not only memory but also forgetting. Both remembrance and forgetting are a field of cultural negotiations in which different stories compete for territory, for voice, and for a place in history.[126] The dialectical relations between memory and forgetfulness,

---

[124] Elhanan Vinhotzker (Yishai), quoted in Michael Bar-Zohar, *Ben-Gurion*, B, Tel Aviv 1977, p. 656.

[125] Yitzchok Perlov, *The People of Exodus*, Tel Aviv n.d., p. 294.

[126] See Marita Sturken, *Tangled Memories: The Vietnam War, The Aids Epidemic, and the Politics of Remembering*, Berkeley 1997, and in particular the foreword. See also Ernest Renan's classical piece, "What is a Nation?," included in every reader on nationalism.

between "illuminating and obscuring" of specific historical chapters for varying periods of time – which unfailingly stem from the decisions and acts of the elites writing that history – are a function of the goals of a given collective, and of the balance of power between the various groups making up that collective. The objects of the political Zionist clandestine immigration project – the Holocaust survivors – completed their assigned role, in practice, in the autumn of 1947, when combatant Zionism shifted its effort to the UN, and several months later to Palestine itself, where the decisive war for the territory was beginning. And they, the Holocaust survivors, had neither say nor representation, then or for many years after, in Israel's public space because they lacked political power. They were the silent and "anonymous *ma'apilim* [immigrants]" of Zionism, who faithfully played the role that others wrote for them. The intentional and organized visibility of the events of which they were protagonists, orchestrated media-events such as the *Exodus*, did not redeem them from their anonymity, and did not grant them individual faces or stories. And when the fateful 1948 war broke out, orders were transmitted from Palestine to Europe to send over only young men "capable of bearing arms."[127] A few of the *Exodus* refugees, who had been previously returned forcibly to Germany, actually made it back to Palestine in time to "bear arms" and go to war. "Driven, unloaded, called up by name / And by evening they were descending the slopes." Some fell in battle, and remained nameless for ever, "blinded in their darkness."[128] These words were written not by a "new historian" but by the most highly admired poet of the day.

---

[127] Ben-Gurion, *Yoman Ha'milhama (War Diary)*, A, Tel Aviv 1983, 18 March 1948, p. 302; see also message Ben-Gurion and Galili dispatched to Europe, namely: "Immigration which is not entirely aimed – from beginning to end – at our wartime needs, is not beneficial."

[128] Alterman, "Before Day Breaks," in *City of the Dove*, pp. 97–98.

2 Memory without rememberers

The survivor of a man-made catastrophe is one of the signifiers and definers of the twentieth century, the icon of an era of mass horrors. A *survivor* or *survivant* is one who has lived through and beyond; beyond the threshold, beyond the border of life, who went on living after an event which was meant to end his life, after the annihilation of a mass of human beings, of whom he was part. In this sense, the survivor is a remnant from another world, someone who was at the core of the catastrophe, and came back, but left a very significant part of himself behind. The *survivor* or *survivant* is alive therefore, *vivant* in his own specific relation to both the dead and the living; he maintains an intense relationship – defined by an extreme situation and an ultimate trial – with the dead, as well as with ordinary, living human beings, from whom he is set apart because of his bond with the dead and with that event which the dead, unlike him, did not survive.[1]

Survivorship, survival, being a remnant, are extreme situations, whose rarity and improbability define them. Life after a catastrophe is considered an act of grace, a gift, but this grace is two-edged, very often it is poisoned, and sometimes it can turn into a curse. Survivors bear a kind of a lifelong guilt, a guilt both self-imposed and imposed by others, because of the very fact that they have survived; the very quality of survivorship is their offense, the offense of having lived on in a place and time in which they were supposed to be dead. Only dying – that is, joining all the other dead, however late in the day – can absolve them of that guilt. Some are racked by guilt for not having done enough to save the others, or to comfort the dead and render their last hours more endurable. "[More realistic] is self-accusation, or the accusation of having failed in terms of human solidarity," wrote the Auschwitz survivor and its mythical witness Primo Levi.

---

[1] Alain Brossat, "La place du survivant. Une approche arendtienne," *Revue d'histoire de la Shoah*, **164**, September 1998, pp. 79–80.

Few survivors feel guilty about having deliberately damaged, robbed, or beaten a companion ... By contrast, however, almost everybody feels guilty of having omitted to offer help. The presence at your side of a weaker – or less cunning, or older, or too young – companion, hounding you with his demands for help or with his simple presence, in itself an entreaty, is a constant in the life of the Lager. The demand for solidarity, for a human word, advice, even just a listening ear, was permanent and universal but rarely satisfied.[2]

The survivors are condemned to carry forever the weight of memory of the disaster they transversed and the memory of those who were not fortunate enough to survive. Thus, in a way, the survivor is always the "last one left," the "remnant," whose life is prescribed by the impossible task of existing on behalf of others (the dead) among the ordinary living, and of bearing the stamp of his mission of speaking out on behalf of the dead, representing them and attesting to their agony and destruction. The survivor's constituent characteristics which relate him to other survivors do not stem solely from his passage into death and out of death, but also from the dramatic and unique fact that he is a rare being, who has lived beyond probability. Survivors of great catastrophes are united also by something beyond the intensity of the suffering they experienced: they are marked out by their impossible, intolerable isolation, poised as they are between the world of the dead who perished in the catastrophe, who vastly outnumber the survivors, and the world of the ordinary living, who are also immeasurably more numerous than the survivors. By definition, survivors are a tiny minority, living on the edge, on the brink of the abyss separating ordinary individuals from the dead masses annihilated by the catastrophe. The borderline situation, between the dead and the living, and of death within life that the survivor endured, the situation which lends "meaning" to his life and ordains it,[3] also consumes and destroys any form of meaning. "Anyone who has been tortured remains tortured," wrote Jewish philosopher Jean Améry who, more than thirty years after his liberation from Auschwitz, committed suicide. "Anyone who has suffered torture never again will be able to be at ease in the world; the abomination of the annihilation is never extinguished. Faith in humanity, already cracked by the first slap in the face, then demolished by torture, is never acquired again."[4]

---

[2] Primo Levi, *The Drowned and the Saved* (from Italian: Raymond Rosenthal), New York 1988, p. 78.
[3] Brossat, "La place du survivant," p. 80.
[4] Jean Améry, *At the Mind's Limits: Contemplations by a Survivor on Auschwitz and its Realities*, Bloomington, IN, 1980, p. 3, also quoted in Levi, *The Drowned and the Saved*, p. 25.

The inmates of the concentration and extermination camps, even if they happened to keep alive, wrote Hannah Arendt, were more effectively cut off from the world of the living than if they had died. Terror there enforced oblivion. David Rousset, survivor of the camps and one of the first witnesses to testify to the Nazi universe of extermination, called his book *Les jours de notre mort*, in which he described the very permanence of the process of dying itself, a condition in which both death and life were obstructed equally effectively.[5] "Death is not something that we slipped past, as it were, that we brushed against, from which we were rescued ... We lived it. We are not survivors but ghosts ... It is an unbelievable fact, unshareable and inconceivable ... and yet we had this experience of death," wrote Buchenwald survivor Jorge Semprun.[6] The death of "the drowned," as Primo Levi called them, "had begun before that of their body. Weeks and months before being snuffed out, they had already lost the ability to observe, to remember, to compare and express themselves."[7]

We, who are dying here in the face of the world's indifference, an indifference as chilly as the ice of the North Pole, we who have been forgotten by the living, feel the need to leave something behind for the generations to come – if not complete records then at least fragments and remnants; what we thought, what we felt, we the living dead, what we thought and what we wanted.

These words were written by Jewish inmates of Auschwitz, who were apparently planning to produce an anthology entitled *Auschwitz*.

On the graves where we lie, covered with earth while still alive, on our graves the world dances its devil's dance and its dancing feet muffle our groans and our cries for help. When we have suffocated, we will be taken out of our graves, we will be here no longer, only our ashes will be scattered to the seven seas ... some will no doubt emerge from here alive, but not Jews! What will they have to say about our lives, what do they know of our tribulations ... they will have no desire to rummage in the dustbin of memory and to restore to life the pale shadows with dead eyes ... no, we ourselves must tell our story ... words scribbled on the gallows before death, when the rope has been looped around the neck; the hangman is patient and he has time, he toys with his victim ... we will exploit the moment when the hangman is busy swilling his drink, we will use the hanging tree as a writing desk, we will write down what we have to say and to relate.[8]

---

[5] David Rousset, *Les jours de notre mort*, Paris, 1947; see Hannah Arendt, *The Origins of Totalitarianism*, New York (1951) 1972, p. 443.

[6] Jorge Semprun, *L'écriture ou la vie*, Paris 1995, p. 121.

[7] Levi, *The Drowned and the Saved*, p. 84.

[8] This text was quoted by the then Minister of Education and Culture, Ben-Zion Dinur, in his speech in the Knesset during the first reading of the Holocaust and Heroism Law – Yad Vashem, 1953. Knesset Minutes, Vol. 14, Session 227, 12 May 1953, p. 1311. I have not succeeded in locating the text itself or the exact source.

The past belongs to the dead

Whereas the dead, or the living-dead, tried to speak out, mainly mediated by the living, many of the survivors remained silent. This was yet another characteristic of the survivors' condition: the inability to convey their experiences, to utter the unutterable, of death within life. "Torture," wrote Jean Améry,

> whereby the other turns us into a body, obliterates the contradiction inherent in death and allows us to experience our own death ... The pain was what it was. Beyond that fact there is nothing to say. The qualities of feeling are as incomparable as they are inexpressible. They mark the borderline of the ability to share something with others by means of language.[9]

The survivor's condition is also distinguished by his own inability to comprehend what happened to him and to find any meaning in his experience. "Have we – we who have returned – been able to understand and make others understand our experience?" asked Primo Levi.[10] To all this was added the survivor's feeling that if he tried to put his experiences into words and to relate his story, ordinary living people would not only fail to believe him, but would be unable or unwilling to listen. Because what the survivors had to tell about their own living death, and the death of their comrades, was not just testimony to the physical and psychological experiences endured by survivors of some local, contained disaster of conceivable scope which had claimed a handful of victims, known, identifiable, and remembered by name. It was evidence of something entirely different and utterly new to the world; testimony to human inhumanity, to radical, absolute evil as a pure human fact; evidence that "everything is possible," that the "impossible was made possible," as Hannah Arendt wrote in her seminal work on totalitarianism.[11] Many survivors relate that, while still imprisoned in the Nazi camps, and while clinging to any faint prospect of life, above all in order to return to the land of the living and bear witness, it was clear to them that nobody out there was awaiting their testimony or wanted to hear it.[12]

The testimony of the survivors was unacceptable because it was so disquieting and disintegrating the known reality, and because, on returning, the survivor could not but shatter the deceptively normal façade of human existence by virtue of existing and having survived. He had nothing to offer but testimony to the dark, barbaric side of that same

---

[9] Améry, *At the Mind's Limits*, p. 3.   [10] Levi, *The Drowned and the Saved*, p. 36.
[11] Arendt, *The Origins of Totalitarianism*, p. 459.
[12] Levi, *The Drowned and the Saved*, p. 12.

normal life, of civilized existence, of the values and ideals of seemingly enlightened modern society. What the survivors of the camps of totalitarian regimes witnessed and knew, no human being should ever see or know, in the sense Hannah Arendt was referring to when she said that "This ought not to have happened ... This should not have happened. Something happened there, to which we cannot reconcile ourselves."[13]

The Nazi camp survivor, therefore, is a witness to something entirely new, hitherto unknown to mankind; something we cannot grasp, "a phenomenon that nevertheless confronts us with its overpowering reality and breaks down all standards we know."[14] The survivor experienced on his own flesh and gained knowledge of the modus operandi not only of the corpse-manufacturing factories of the Nazis – and of others then and since – but also of the "laboratories where changes in human nature are tested" which these camps were, and therefore their shamefulness is not just the concern of their former inmates and those who controlled the "laboratories"; it is the concern of all human beings.[15] In this respect, the camp survivor should have been regarded as a holy vessel, to be cherished and listened to attentively because of his rarity, because he was a unique human species, and because he was the bearer of new, unprecedented knowledge about the world and mankind. But, conversely, that same survivor was living, breathing proof of the impossibility of testifying on the events he had survived. The total reality of Auschwitz[16] was obliterated by the very impossibility of speaking about it and describing it. "It's not for nothing that Auschwitz is called the 'extermination camp' ... Millions of human beings were exterminated there. Many of the means to prove the crime or its quantity were also exterminated,"[17] wrote the French philosopher Jean-François Lyotard. Elsewhere he said: "With Auschwitz something new has happened in history (which can only be a sign and not a fact), which is that the facts, the testimonies which bore the traces of *here's* and *now's*, the documents which indicated the sense or senses of the facts, and the names, finally the possibility of various kinds of phrases whose conjunction makes reality, all this has been destroyed as much as possible."[18]

Moreover, the unique survivordom essence of the survivors impaired their quality as witnesses, as they themselves, or some of them, have affirmed, since they had not reached the ultimate end of Auschwitzian

---

[13] Hannah Arendt, *Essays in Understanding, 1930–1954*, ed. Jerome Kohn, New York 1994, p. 14.
[14] Arendt, *The Origins of Totalitarianism*, p. 459.   [15] Ibid., p. 458.
[16] "Auschwitz is the most real of realities," writes Lyotard, *The Differend*, p. 58.
[17] Ibid., p. 56.   [18] Ibid., p. 57.

reality, the gas chambers, the place from which nobody returned. "The destruction brought to an end, the job completed, was not told by anyone, just as no one ever returned to describe his own death," wrote Primo Levi.[19] And he added: "There is an additional flaw in any testimony: the witnesses, by definition, are survivors, and all of them benefited, in one sense or another, from some privilege ... nobody related the fate of the ordinary prisoner, since he had no material prospect of survival ... the Mussulmans remained mute."[20] The true witnesses to Auschwitz, according to this argument, are those who are gone, those consumed in the flames or the gas of Auschwitz. "We, the survivors, are not the true witnesses. This is an uncomfortable notion of which I have become conscious little by little," wrote Primo Levi. "We survivors are not only an exiguous but also an anomalous minority: we are those who by their prevarications or abilities or good luck did not touch bottom. Those who did so, those who saw the Gorgon, have not returned to tell about it, or have returned mute."[21] And Elie Wiesel said: "Those who did not undergo the experience will never know, those who experienced it will never speak; neither truly nor completely. The past belongs to the dead."[22]

This muteness, this inability to talk about Auschwitz, was supposed to be breached by the State of Israel. That was one of the roles it was assigned and the justification for its establishment – to give the survivors a voice, to create a space and an echo-chamber for their lives and their stories. According to Lyotard, the State of Israel was supposed to provide the verbal and legal framework for the survivors' cry for help and for their claims and charges.

The shades of those to whom had been refused not only life but also the expression of the wrong done them by the Final Solution continue to wander in their indeterminacy. By forming the State of Israel, the survivors transformed the wrong into damages and the differend[23] into litigation. By beginning to speak in

[19] Levi, *The Drowned and the Saved*, p. 82.
[20] Primo Levi, *Conversazioni e interviste*, Turin 1997: quoted in Giorgio Agamben, *Ce qui reste d'Auschwitz*, Paris 1999, p. 40.
[21] Levi, *The Drowned and the Saved*, pp. 63–64.
[22] See W. Sofsky, *L'organisation de la terreur*, Paris 1995, p. 20, quoted in Agamben, *Ce qui reste*, p. 40. See also Adi Ophir, *Lashon La'Ra (Language of Evil)*, Tel Aviv 2001, pp. 348–350 [Hebrew].
[23] A "differend" is the unbridgeable gap between different genres and heterogeneous frames of reference which causes one of the parties to the conflict to lack the means of citing arguments in order to prevail in the dispute; that party, therefore, becomes the victim. Lyotard also says that "to be a victim means not to be able to prove that one has been done an injustice."

the common idiom of public international law and of authorized politics, they put an end to the silence to which they had been condemned,[24]

wrote Lyotard.

This chapter will examine the process of transformation of wrong into damages and of the unspeakable into litigation, within the framework of the assimilation and absorption of the Holocaust survivors into the state- and nation-building project in the first decade of Israel's statehood. The analysis will be conducted mainly through an examination of the legal and judicial dimension which was part and parcel of the encounter between the survivors and Israeli society, and scrutiny of the construction of Israel's official memory of the Holocaust and the way in which the law and the legal system, and official Israeli memory in the context of the Holocaust and its survivors, functioned for purposes of the constitution and self-definition of the new Israeli nation. I will start by examining the Nazis and Nazi Collaborators (Punishment) Law 1950, and how it was presented and elucidated, in contrast to its sub-text and the real object- ives of its legislation and enactment. Within this framework I will also examine the practical application of the law, at whom it was and was not directed, and what the distinctions drawn by Israel's prosecuting author- ities can tell us about Israeli society which undertook this judicial role. This will lead to the question of the possibility and the right to "bring" the Holocaust to court – who can, and who is entitled to judge – and of the judgeability of such an enormous historical event. Within this context, the chapter concludes with a reexamination of what is known as the Kastner affair, which stirred up a political storm during the 1950s.

From infamy to purge

The legislative assembly and the courtroom are among the major public sites where politics are formulated and practiced: politics in the sense of management of public and community affairs, the affairs of the *polis*, and in the sense of an open and constant exchange of plural, conflicting political and social ideas. There, as in other sites of the public sphere, a community creates for itself a network of discourse and action among its members, recounts its history and itself, and constitutes and legislates itself as a political subject. Israel's legislature and courts, particularly in the first decade of statehood, were also the main stage on which society confronted the memory of the Holocaust and its gruesome specter.

[24] Lyotard, *The Differend*, p. 56.

Through these institutions and other agents of discourse, the Israeli political and cultural establishment tried to establish a new, revolutionary-messianic profile of Israel and "Israeli-ness" by erasing or making selective use of the previous historical Jewish background and recent past.

Historical leaps are possible, asserted Israel's first Prime Minister David Ben-Gurion. He was responding to Hebrew University philosopher Nathan Rottenstreich, who had argued that the distant past alone could not sustain a nation, that it would be left with a shallow past, or none at all, if the recent past were stripped away. "The establishment of the Jewish state was a leap over centuries," Ben-Gurion wrote, "and the War of Independence brought us nearer the days of Joshua ... and our young people nearer ... [his] feats than all the speeches delivered at Zionist congresses. 'The recent past,' sadly, does not exist, because [its] Jewry ... have been annihilated," Ben-Gurion said. He was thus trying to erase not only the century before Israel's establishment, but the entire period of the Jewish Diaspora. "The distant past is closer than the recent past of two thousand years," he wrote.[25]

Israel, like any other state, remembered the past according to its national myths, ideals, and current political needs, claims James Young in his study of Holocaust memory.[26] The act of remembering, that is, of redeeming the victims and the survivors from oblivion and from vanishing altogether from the annals of history, was directed, as always, at the remembering subject: a subject who defined itself through the objects of remembering. Memory itself – preserved, restored, and codified – was Israel's main ideology, a virtual civil religion, its most effective political and greatest "natural" resource. "At times ambivalent, at times shrill, the official approach to Holocaust memory in Israel has long been torn between the simultaneous need to remember and to forget," wrote Young,

between the early founders' enormous state-building task and the reasons why such a state was necessary, between the survivors' memory of victims and the fighters' memory of resistance. On the one hand, early statists like David Ben-Gurion regarded the Holocaust as the ultimate fruit of Jewish life in exile; as such it represented a diaspora that deserved not only to be destroyed but also forgotten. On the other hand, the state also recognized its perverse debt to the Holocaust: it had, after all, seemed to prove the Zionist dictum that without a state and the power to defend themselves, Jews in exile would always be vulnerable to just this kind of destruction. As a result, the early leaders found little reason to recall the Holocaust beyond its direct link to the new state.[27]

[25] Ben-Gurion to Rottenstreich, 9 January 1957, *Hazut*, 3, 1957.
[26] Young, *The Texture of Memory*, p. 210.   [27] Ibid., p. 211.

Like Borges's 'first' Chinese emperor (*The Wall and the Books*), who ordered the erection of the Great Wall of China and the burning of all books prior to his reign so that "history begin with him ... [and] abolish [the] one single memory [of] his mother's infamy,"[28] so the founders of the new Israel strove to begin history anew. By deleting the shame of their mothers and fathers, the shame of Jews, the disgrace of the Jewish Diaspora, they believed they were inaugurating a new era, and reinventing themselves into a new world. However, the drive to delete became also a drive to preserve and exploit the shame as a constant reproach and warning in order to bolster a society that was "ingathering its exiles" and in the throes of consolidation. The deletion project evolved eventually into a purge.

For this was one of the objectives of the Nazis and Nazi Collaborators (Punishment) Law 1950 passed in the second year of statehood. The Knesset debate on the law, which aroused little attention, was the first public reckoning of the Holocaust and essentially an internal Israeli affair. As reflected by the remarks of the Minister of Justice who tabled the bill, it was, from the outset, a matter between Israeli society and the survivors, or among the survivors themselves – not an issue between the survivors or their representative (the state) on the one hand, and the perpetrators of the Final Solution, the Nazis and Nazi Germany. It was certainly not the voice of the survivors that was sought, nor their singular testimony, nor their special, unprecedented knowledge of mankind; nor the transformation of wrong into damages and the unspeakable into litigation against the Nazi murderers in accordance with international law. The law was passed to provide the Jewish state with means to bring to justice a handful of "collaborators" from amidst the Jewish survivors themselves.

"Anyone familiar with the problems [of the survivors]," said Minister of Justice Pinhas Rosen, "knows how painful for them [are] the mutual suspicion and recrimination that, to this day, hover over some of Israel's immigrants who were liberated from camps and ghettos; in some cases, perhaps – because they have not been given an opportunity to prove their innocence before an authorized court."[29] The law thus was not aimed at bringing to trial in Israel Nazi war criminals or their Ukrainian, Latvian, Estonian, French, or other henchmen. "It may be assumed," the Minister acknowledged, "that Nazis guilty of offences under this law will not dare

---

[28] Jorge Luis Borges, *Labyrinths, Selected Stories and Other Writings*, London, 1970, pp. 221–222.
[29] Knesset Minutes, Session 131, 27 March 1950, p. 1148. See also Hanna Yablonka, "The Nazis and Nazi Collaborators (Punishment) Law: An Additional Aspect of the Question of Israelis, Survivors and the Holocaust," *Katedra*, **82**, 1996, pp. 135–152 [Hebrew].

to come to Israel." The law, he elaborated, "also applies to those who carried out the Nazis' orders and, unfortunately, we cannot be sure that some of them are not among us, although the number is undoubtedly small. But even if they number no more than ... the righteous men sought *in vain* in Sodom, even if only a few crimes are concerned, the law is justified."[30]

The State of Israel, more so than any other, had no choice but to introduce into its legal code a law against the Nazis and Nazi crimes, even if it was only symbolic. Following the post-war Nuremberg Charter and Nuremberg trials, which established new principles in international criminal law, various European countries that had suffered under the Nazi dictatorship set up special tribunals to prosecute Nazis who had not been brought before the Nuremberg courts. Elsewhere Nazis and their accomplices were being tried by ordinary courts under the criminal code, or by military tribunals.[31] Israel, which had proclaimed and made itself home to hundreds of thousands of survivors and refugees after World War II; which saw itself as the historical, material, moral, and legal heir of the murdered millions,[32] whom it defined post factum (and unverifiably) as potential Zionists, retroactive future citizens of a State of Israel that did not exist at the time of their death[33] – this state could not permit itself to stand aside. In addition, the Nazis and Nazi Collaborators (Punishment) Law was perceived as the "natural" sequel to the Crime of Genocide (Prevention and Punishment) Law 1950 which was then at an advanced stage of legislation. This law, however, looked to the future with the purpose of precluding Nazi-type crimes, whereas the proposed new law was directed "at the past," at "a specific historical period that began with Hitler's rise to power and ended with his downfall,"[34] at pursuing and punishing the perpetrators of crimes committed before its enactment.

The bill and the accompanying debate were propped by a whole frame of rhetoric designed to project it as a law for the survivors, as if in response to their own demands and desire to disgorge Jewish collaborators who

---

[30] Pinhas Rosen, Knesset Minutes, Session 131, p. 1148 (my italics).   [31] Ibid., p. 1147.
[32] For example "We, Israel, are the heirs," said Ben-Zion Dinur, Knesset Member and professor of history, and shortly after Minister of Education and Culture, in a debate on the Nazis and Nazi Collaborators (Punishment) Law, Knesset Minutes, Session 131, p. 1159.
[33] As early as 1950, and in order to promote the commemoration of the Holocaust, it was proposed to Ben-Gurion that the state bestow symbolic Israeli citizenship on the dead Holocaust victims. The draft "Law for Commemoration of the Holocaust and Heroism – Yad Vashem, 1953", which is discussed below, contained a provision for the bestowal of commemorative Israeli citizenship on all those who perished in the Holocaust.
[34] Rosen, Knesset Minutes, Session 131, p. 1147.

had persecuted them in ghettos and camps at the Nazi behest. Thus, the Minister of Justice emphasized that "the proposed law may contribute to clearing the air among the survivors."[35] True, police stations all over the country registered complaints of "Nazi collaboration" against immigrant survivors, emanating either from "other immigrants" or from "the General Security Service, which passed on information to Police Headquarters on ... former collaborators." As the documentation shows, most of the complaints did come from survivors themselves.[36] The police were under some pressure from survivors – a few dozen all in all – who demanded justice and action against "collaborators." According to this quasi-official narrative, the "predicament" of the survivors is therefore what expedited the legislative process. The Justice and Police Ministries joined forces to draft an appropriate law based on the complaints of a handful (out of more than a quarter of a million) of survivors against other survivors. Thus, a law was promulgated against "war criminals" and the perpetrators of "crimes against humanity,"[37] which, in practice, targeted Jews, themselves Holocaust victims.

The fact that the Minister of Justice had invoked the "righteous men sought in vain in Sodom" in justifying the law[38] to the Knesset indicates his awareness of the moral dilemma posed by the legislation of so pivotal and drastic a law to clarify several cases of dubious, even despicable, behavior of Jews in ghettos or camps under a savage, evil Nazi regime. Unease was also evident in the proceedings of the Knesset Sub-Committee on the Law. The committee which convened thrice wrestled with such issues as the scope of the law (was it restricted to crimes committed against Jews? To crimes perpetrated by Nazis?); the distinction between Nazis and "collaborators"; the types of punishment etc. Knesset members argued that the law was not adequately defined, that a clear division was needed between Nazis and "collaborators". Their comments make it abundantly clear that the committee was well aware that the law was aimed solely at Jews. "In practice," said Zerah Wahrhaftig of the Religious-national party,

[35] Ibid., p. 1148.
[36] National Police HQ Archive, quoted in Yablonka, "The Nazis and Nazi Collaborators (Punishment) Law," pp. 139–140.
[37] There has been little written historical research on The Nazis and Nazi Collaborators (Punishment) Law and its various manifestations in the courts. What has appeared has largely accepted unquestionably the official narrative, which explains the law as stemming from the needs of the survivors. See Yablonka, "The Nazis and Nazi Collaborators (Punishment) Law," pp. 139–140.
[38] Rosen, Knesset Minutes, Session 131, p. 1148.

the law relates to collaborators although, theoretically, it also relates to Nazis. But Nazis won't be coming here so fast. Collaboration, in most cases, was not voluntary but the result of coercion. One can't argue that collaborators and Nazis be [given] the same punishment. They can't all be lumped together. There are people ... who did not hand people over [to others] nor help to do so, and [they] can't be charged with crimes against humanity ... If there is no provision for collaboration, many such people will slip through our fingers ... I do not advise mixing in Nazis and collaborators. I suggest a division, and ... a new scale for collaborators, by degree of offense.[39]

The Justice Ministry representatives who attended all the meetings claimed that, for legislative purposes, it was difficult to distinguish between Nazis and collaborators. "If a Nazi in a concentration camp beat inmates, and a Jewish kapo in the same camp did the same – how can we create a provision for each of them?" asked the Justice Ministry representative. "The Nazi was a murderer and the Jew was forced to act as he did," Wahrhaftig retorted.[40] The formulation was not altered. Justice Ministry officials were in a hurry and urged the legislators to finish the job, to accept the text as proposed by the government, and to vote it through the Knesset.

The plenum debate, too, illustrated the law's complexity and problematics. To sidestep the universally acknowledged difficulty of retroactivity and extra-territoriality of the proposed law, Knesset member Aryeh Sheftel, a survivor of the Vilna ghetto, said that he regarded Nazi crimes "as if ... carried out on Israeli territory."[41] These passionate words, however well intended, contained the germ of what was later to become the ubiquitous use of the Holocaust in Israeli discourse and politics. The implication was that Jews carried the Holocaust or a potential holocaust within them wherever they went, even to Israel – the site of the total revolution in the Jewish condition. The verbal translocation of Nazi crimes from their historical setting to a symbolic site (Israel), their very reproduction and duplication in the act of speech, in themselves already depreciated them, even if unintentionally, and marked the start of a long process of banalization. Yet in the same breath the speaker claimed also the reverse, namely that Israeli or any criminal law was an inadequate instrument to judge Nazi crimes and atrocities because they "exceeded the bounds of normal concepts and even ... of known criminal anomalies." Had Hitler, Himmler, and Goebbels been tried under Israel's criminal laws, Sheftel added, "they would not have been executed, but merely sentenced to life imprisonment."[42]

---

[39] The Sub-Committee on the Nazis and Nazi Collaborators (Punishment) Law 1950, 23 May 1950, Minutes No. a/2.
[40] Ibid.   [41] Aryeh Sheftel, Knesset Minutes, Session 131, p. 1149.   [42] Ibid.

Buried memory

The law aimed high and at the mighty, but was wielded against the lowly and the trivial. What was intended, as Minister of Justice proclaimed to the Knesset, to be "the expression of the revolution which has taken place in the political condition of the Jewish people," and designated as a memorial to the dead and an instrument to bring the past to reckoning ("we will neither forget nor forgive"), for whose sake Israeli legislators deliberately departed from the norms of criminal law, was essentially designed to bring to justice and punish the most marginal perpetrators. Petty "kapos," concentration camp block supervisors who were themselves victims of the Nazis, were the true targets of the law, and they were convicted before they were even charged. "Inmates of this type," police documents claimed, "who enjoyed greater privileges and were appointed block supervisors or kapos, had been recruited from the worst human material."[43]

While the social predicament of survivors who found themselves sharing a new country with former petty tormentors may well have added impetus for devising that law, it seems unlikely that this alone would have set into motion so grave and complex a legislative process. Israel had just emerged from a bloody battle for survival (the first Israeli–Arab war of 1948) in which it had lost thousands of young men and women; it was preoccupied with the awesome task of national reconstruction and state-building; it was also largely indifferent and blind to the survivors of that far-away catastrophe, people who moved like ghosts in their midst,[44] "the absent presentees."[45] How, then, to explain the fact that this society, which negated every aspect of Jewish conduct during the Holocaust (apart from

[43] Yosef Gorsky, Special Section, Criminal Investigation Division of the Police to the Ministry of Justice, Police HQ files, quoted in Yablonka, "The Nazis and Nazi Collaborators (Punishment) Law," p. 140.

[44] "We all knew that people from that world were among us," wrote Nathan Alterman some ten years later, during the Eichmann trial. "We knew that there were men and women from that world among us, but it would seem that only in the course of this terrible and awesome trial, as the witnesses from there went on mounting the witness box, those separate entities of alien and anonymous people whom we have passed by countless times, blended together in our consciousness until we were suddenly and clearly aware that these entities are not only a mass of individuals but a fundamental and forceful essence whose nature and image and horrific memories which are beyond life and nature, are an indelible part of the nature and image of the people to which we belong." See Nathan Alterman, "The Face," *Davar*, 9 June 1961.

[45] This is the opposite of the term "present absentees" applied in relation to the hundreds of thousands of Arab inhabitants of the country, who were expelled or fled their homes, leaving behind all their properties, and whose shadows also filled the country, like the shadows of the survivors.

isolated cases of armed resistance), suddenly proved so sensitive to the emotional needs of a handful of survivors who regarded several of their fellow victims as collaborators? Why did it hasten to conciliate the accusers and bring their brethren to justice for purported "war crimes" and "crimes against humanity"?

"The law is not enacted only for practical purposes," said Knesset Member Yosef Lamm, who was soon to sit on the bench in several of the trials, but "as a teaching device and cultural document. I don't want people in 50–60 years' time to go looking for the text of Section 214 [on the murder of Jews]. This is a unique law which I believe should be studied in every country, and they should know what it refers to."[46] Underlying the legislation, I would suggest, was also the very elementary need for vengeance and, through it, release from the horror and guilt; vengeance which, since it could not be directed at the master perpetrators, and which in any case could not bring relief and bestow some peace of mind, was deflected inward, at the victims themselves. "What is the meaning of all these drastic provisions [of the law]?"[47] asked Supreme Court Justice Shneour Zalman Heshin while presiding at the appeal of the kapo Yaakov Honigman against the District Court's prison sentence: "There can be only one answer ... The stipulated punishments ... were not, in the main, meant to reform the offender or deter potential offenders, but – as the law's name suggests – *to take revenge* on Israel's enemies."[48]

Above all, however, as the early trials demonstrated, the law was meant to appease society's disgust at "Jewish conduct" during the Holocaust. Israel introduced an anomaly into its legal code not in order to confront Nazism, not in order "to clear us of the shame of infamous Germany," as Knesset member Rabbi Mordechai Nurock, himself a survivor, claimed,[49] but to purge the new and "pure" state[50] of Jewish shame. Its main purpose was to "clear the air among the survivor immigrants ... punish

[46] Yosef Lamm, the Sub-Committee on the Nazis and Nazi Collaborators (Punishment) Law 1950, 23 May 1950, Minutes No. a/2.

[47] By "drastic provisions" Justice Heshin was referring to the deviations from the accepted criminal code inserted into the Nazis and Nazi Collaborators (Punishment) Law such as the authority to retry individuals who had already been tried for the same crime, the abolition of the time limitation on crimes, the non-eligibility for pardon of minor offenses, the deviation from the rules of evidence, and, of course, the retroactivity and extra-territoriality of the law.

[48] *Yaakov Honigman* v. *Attorney General*, Criminal Appeal No. 52/22, Legal Verdicts, Vol. 7, 1953, pp. 303–304 (my italics).

[49] Mordechai Nurock, Knesset Minutes, Session 131, p. 1148.

[50] This term was used to describe the young state by the then Attorney General, Haim Cohen in reference to the Kastner affair. Quoted in Weitz, *The Man Who Was Murdered Twice*, p. 102.

[Jewish] criminals," and exonerate "the innocent," as the Minister of Justice solemnly declared, "*and let our home be pure.*"[51] Thus young Israeli society, which faced up to the unprecedented reality of the Holocaust and survivors only by hallowing sporadic resistance or roundly condemning Jewish conduct, sought to purify and be purified, to cast out the Holocaust's malignant specter. To this end, it sacrificed on the court-room altar, a site of higher moral authority and of secular sanctity, the pettiest, most forsaken of Nazi "accomplices." Jews who had not been in Nazi-occupied Europe brought to justice Jews who had been, ostensibly in the name of other Jews "from there," and conducted trials that, in every sense of the word, were purges.

During the 1950s and the early 1960s some forty trials were held under that law. The indictments, evidence and verdicts – whether in direct simple language or dry legal terminology, or inarticulate, halting survivor testimony – presented a picture of everyday human ravages of the Holocaust. They exposed the routine regime of terror, oppression, and abuse in the ghettos and camps, where inmates' human character and moral stamina were obliterated long before their bodies were consumed, and brought to light the existential and moral hell created by the Nazis, the monstrous upside-down world which had transformed persecuted into persecutors, victims into reluctant wrongdoers and accomplices in their own oppression. These harrowing, perplexing memories never made it into Israel's official national memory of the Holocaust.

All those brought to trial under that law (with one minor exception) until the 1961 trial of Adolf Eichmann, were Jewish citizens, new immigrants, miserable, pathetic individuals, themselves Holocaust survivors who, on arrival in Israel, were recognized, sometimes by chance, by other survivors and reported to the police. Israel's legal system had tried them according to the same law under which it would prosecute a decade later senior SS officer Adolf Eichmann, a Nazi who had played a central role in the logistic system of the German dictatorship, the main transporter of European Jewry to the death camps. The irony is that the law, which fitted Eichmann's and his likes' crimes – if any law could be said to fit these crimes' enormity and scope[52] – was not aimed at them. Indeed, practically speaking, the law should have been called the Law for Punishment of Minor Collaborators of the Nazis. Although the court proceedings

[51] Pinhas Rosen, Knesset Minutes, Session 131, pp. 1147–1148 (my italics).
[52] "The Nazi crimes, it seems to me, explode the limits of the law; and that is precisely what constitutes their monstrousness. For these crimes, no punishment is severe enough," wrote Hannah Arendt to Karl Jaspers on 17 August 1946. See Lotte Kohler and Hans Saner (eds.), *Hannah Arendt Karl Jaspers: Correspondence, 1926–1969*, New York 1992, letter 43, p. 54.

against Eichmann turned into an unprecedented, national educational project and a milestone in the Holocaust discourse in western culture, his capture in Argentina and trial in Jerusalem had certainly not been antici- pated, nor was it what the lawmakers had had in mind. As far as Israel was concerned, the Eichmann trial was a quasi-miracle, the outcome of a later Israeli political and historical development, unimaginable at the time the Nazis and Nazi Collaborators (Punishment) Law was passed.

Just how mind-boggling the law's application was in the decade after its enactment is demonstrated by the fact that *not one* of the defendants tried under the law was charged with or found guilty of directly or indirectly causing the death of a single person. Several of the indictments and trials sank to cruelly absurd depths, as in the case of Elsa Trank, tried in the Tel Aviv District Court in August 1950.[53] Her story deserves to be told in detail, like those of other trials, because it embodied Holocaust memory, it was in itself a memory of the Holocaust, but even more so because it illustrates Israel's role-inversion in prosecuting Holocaust victims for whom the Jewish state was supposed to have been a haven. Elsa Trank was charged with "war crimes," "crimes against humanity," and other offenses committed while she was in charge of Block 7 in the women's camp at Auschwitz-Birkenau in the second half of 1944. She was accused of beating and inflicting injury and pain on numerous female block inmates ("a war crime"), of forcing 800–1,000 inmates to kneel for hours at a time, detaining them at length before and after the daily roll calls, withholding aid from those who fainted due to beatings ("crimes against humanity"), and other minor offenses.

At the time of her trial, Elsa Trank was twenty-six years old, that is, accused of crimes committed when she was eighteen. Moreover, accord- ing to transcripts, as block supervisor – a role imposed on her while she herself was "detained and persecuted" – Trank attempted to maintain order and discipline, to assemble the women for roll call as the Germans ordered, and to supervise the fair distribution of food. In so doing, she hit several women "with her hands" and forced recalcitrant prisoners to kneel, a common camp punishment also before her arrival. In general, and irrespective of Trank's conduct, the testimony of the women who suffered at her hands draws a harrowing picture of living conditions in the camp. The matter-of-fact style of the verdict, which recapitulates the evidence, intensifies the horror:

When the women arrived in the camp they were first taken to the washrooms. There clothes and all personal items were confiscated, and after washing, each

---

[53] Verdicts E (District Courts), S. C. [Severe Criminal(Files)], 2/52, pp. 142–152.

was allotted a single dress. Their hair was shorn and numbers tattooed on their arms. From there, they were taken to the various camps where there were large wooden huts known as "blocks," about 800–1,000 women per block. They slept on wooden bunks, 8 to 12 women on each, in appallingly crowded conditions. Discipline was harsh. Before daybreak, a whistle sounded to rouse the inmates of all the blocks and a roll call was held outside of each one. The roll calls lasted for hours. First the prisoner in charge of the block counted the inmates, then the camp commander checked ... followed by a German inspector or other Germans who also made a count. No hour was fixed for the German inspection ... and throughout, the prisoners were forbidden to break rank or relieve themselves in the latrines across the road ... Anyone going for a drink of water was liable to be shot by German guards. At that early hour the prisoners ... suffered from the cold and tried to huddle together for warmth. Because food rations were meager, [they] were weak and found it hard to stand for hours ... Yet they were forbidden to move ... If one prisoner went missing, all the prisoners from all the blocks were forced to stand there until the missing individual was located and collective punishment meted out against the inmates of [that] block ... There was roll call in the afternoon, too, before the order ... to disperse to the huts ... Prisoners slept on their bunks with only a few blankets for all the women on each bunk. Food was distributed soon after roll call. A dark liquid ... called either tea or coffee, a minute bread ration and a fixed amount of liquid known as soup ... In the camp, it was every [individual] for oneself, and everyone tried ... to improve their condition. Anyone able to obtain more bread or food did so. Sometimes, women tried to receive double rations, and each inmate or group of inmates ... tried to secure as many blankets as possible. Quarrels and disruption over ... rations and ... blankets were common. The role of the prisoner in charge of the block was to restore order and maintain discipline ... to assemble [inmates] for roll call, and to supervise the fair distribution of rations.[54]

The loss of reason, the collapse of known, familiar frameworks of life and of meaning, the arbitrary nature of camp procedure, the exposure to the cold and other hardships, systematic starvation, brutality, and daily persecution turned the women of Block 7 at Auschwitz-Birkenau into wretched "she-wolves," debilitated, frozen, famished, sick, and violent, mustering their last remaining resources to survive. "We have heard evidence that the women were not caring towards their sisters or even mothers," declared the judges.[55] Young Elsa Trank was one such prisoner. The Tel Aviv District Court established that "while herself imprisoned as a persecuted individual," Elsa Trank

sometimes hit several prisoners for not climbing down from their bunks and leaving the hut quickly enough when the morning roll-call whistle sounded, for shifting about during roll call, for huddling together for warmth or trying to break rank to relieve themselves or drink water. In one case, a prisoner was beaten for

[54] Ibid., p. 146.   [55] Ibid., p. 151.

wrapping a blanket around herself ... during roll call. Other prisoners were beaten for trying to snatch food from one another. The defendant hit them with her bare [open] hands ... slapping them on the face or the fleshy part of the arm, or with a clenched fist, usually aimed at the head or face ... or the back and shoulder.

The court was pondering whether these actions constituted "war crimes" and "crimes against humanity." A war crime, the court asserted, "refers to ... the murder of a civilian population of an occupied country or within an occupied country, their oppression and deportation for ... forced labor or any other purpose." The judges went on to state that it had been proven "to their satisfaction" that the defendant's misdeeds "do not constitute 'war crimes' in the sense of Section 1 of the law, although each single blow could constitute an offense."[56] As for the charge of "crimes against humanity," the court stated that even if some of the defendant's actions "could be deemed inhuman in the ordinary sense, they did not, under the given circumstances, compare in gravity to the acts that the legislator had intended to include in the definition of 'crimes against humanity'." The court further determined that "the acts proven to have been committed by the defendant" were committed against and inflicted on several individuals as individuals, "rather than against a collective as such." Moreover, these acts were not committed "in premeditation, but mainly out of a desire to maintain order." The court found Elsa Trank guilty of assault and battery, yet it also accepted the defense argument that, in several instances, "the defendant had acted to avert consequences more severe than those of her assault." Noting that the defendant had been imprisoned under much worse conditions since 1942 (prior to being appointed as supervisor), that she had suffered greatly, and that "it has not been proved by any of her actions that [she] identified with the Germans," the judges sentenced Elsa Trank to two years' imprisonment from the date of her arrest. The sentence was not arbitrary. It was exactly two years since her arrest; Elsa Trank was released that same day.

Elsa Trank's trial and the attitude of the judges, like most of the "collaboration" trials, attested to misgivings about the law as interpreted by the state prosecution in pressing suit. The courts not only acted with circumspection in trying Holocaust survivors, but took open issue with the phrasing of several sections of the law and the cases presented under it. Quite a few of the trials ended in acquittals. In others, the judges made do with convictions on lesser charges and with brief, almost nominal, prison sentences that were generally concurrent with pre-trial detention periods.

[56] Ibid., p. 148.

Collapse of the psyche

The following are several brief excerpts from Primo Levi's extensive discussion, in *The Drowned and the Saved*, of the phenomenon of victims' collaboration with their Nazi persecutors, and the various roles played by prisoners in the Nazi extermination system:

The concurrent guilt on the part of individual big and small collaborators ... is always difficult to evaluate. It is a judgment that we would like to entrust only to those who found themselves in similar circumstances and had the opportunity to test for themselves what it means to act in a state of coercion ... The condition of the offended does not exclude culpability, which is often objectively serious, but I know of no human tribunal to which one could delegate the judgment. If it were up to me, if I were forced to judge, I would lightheartedly absolve all those whose concurrence in the guilt was minimal, and for whom coercion was of the highest degree. Around us, prisoners without rank, swarmed low-ranking functionaries, a picturesque fauna ... In general, they were poor devils like ourselves, who worked full time like everyone else but who for an extra half-liter of soup were willing to carry out ... "tertiary" functions: innocuous, sometimes useful, often invented out of the whole cloth. They were rarely violent, but they tended to develop a typically corporate mentality and energetically defended their "job" against anyone from below or above who might covet it. Their privilege, which at any rate entailed supplementary hardships and efforts, gained them very little and did not spare them from the discipline and suffering of everyone else; their hope for life was substantially the same as that of the unprivileged.[57]

And Levi added:

The prisoners of the Lagers, hundreds of thousands of persons of all social classes, from almost all the countries of Europe, represented an average, unselected sample of humanity. Even if one did not want to take into account the infernal environment into which they had been abruptly flung, it is illogical to demand – and rhetorical and false to maintain – that they all and always followed the behavior expected of saints and stoic philosophers. In reality, in the vast majority of cases, their behavior was rigidly preordained. In the space of a few weeks or months the deprivation to which they were subjected led them to a condition of pure survival, a daily struggle against hunger, cold, fatigue and blows in which the room for choices (especially moral choices) was reduced to zero. Among these, very few survived the test.[58]

On the Sonderkommando, whose task it was to remove corpses from the gas chambers, Levi wrote (which is also appropriate for survivors who played lesser roles in the Nazi system):

I believe that no one is authorized to judge them, not those who lived through the experience of the Lager and even less those who did not. I would invite anyone

[57] Levi, *The Drowned and the Saved*, pp. 44–45.   [58] Ibid., pp. 49–50.

who dares pass judgment to carry out upon himself, with sincerity, a conceptual experiment. Let him imagine, if he can, that he has lived for months or years in a ghetto, tormented by chronic hunger, fatigue, promiscuity and humiliation; that he has seen die around him, one by one, his beloved; that he is cut off from the world, unable to receive or transmit news; that, finally, he is loaded onto a train, eighty or a hundred persons to a boxcar; that he travels into the unknown, blindly, for sleepless days and nights; and that he is at last flung inside the walls of an indecipherable inferno. Here he is given survival, one offers to him, nay, he is forced to take upon himself a cruel undefined role ... No one can know how much his soul will hold, how much can it endure before it collapses.[59]

The worst case of abuse of Jews by Jews heard in an Israeli court was that of Yehezkel Anigster.[60] But even here, the court was cautious. The judges were divided on several issues, and criticized both the formulation and application of the law. Yehezkel Anigster had been Chief Kapo in two labor camps, Graeditz and Fauelbruck, in Upper Silesia in 1943–1944. Numerous witnesses from both camps described him as a thickset, red-necked man in boots and leather jacket, who used a rubber-coated wire club to beat anyone who crossed his path. He was charged on five counts: one "war crime," one "crime against humanity," and three counts of "grave ... and deliberate bodily harm ... to a persecuted individual." As in the case of Elsa Trank and other defendants, the court testimony revealed the extreme, devastating hardships of camp life: total detachment from the world, starvation, cold, hard labor, daily long marches from the camp to the workplace and back, beatings, utter exhaustion, and gradual physical deterioration to the point of death. Life was solitary, poor, nasty, brutish, and short, to quote Thomas Hobbes. "Food portions distributed to prisoners have led to starvation ... these living conditions, denial of liberty, forced labor ... few sleeping hours, poor nutrition ... did debilitate the inmates' physical and moral strength and created an alarming death rate," said the court.[61]

In keeping with the Germans' monstrous principle of delegating authority to victims so as to both save on human resources and avoid future accountability, the inmates themselves were responsible for maintaining camp routine. The Germans entered the camps only rarely. Responsible to the Germans for the "proper" management of each camp was one of the prisoners, "the Jewish elder." Beneath him were a number of functionaries such as the "camp steward," "camp gendarme," "room attendants," "chief laborers," heads of labor groups, who were

---

[59] Ibid., p. 59.
[60] Verdicts E (District Courts), S. C., 9/51, pp. 152–180. The name of the defendant appears there in several versions, sometimes Anigster and sometimes Ingster.
[61] Ibid.

known as kapos. All reported directly to the "Jewish elder." The kapos delivered the prisoners to work, supervised them there, and brought them back; they were in charge of food distribution and sleeping hours. The officials were "privileged" inmates, exempt from labor and enjoying larger food rations and other benefits. This multi-layered system of persecutors and persecuted, of brutes and righteous, played havoc with the concepts of good and evil, of decency and villainy.

The camp's objective was to exploit, for the Nazi system's purpose, the body and labor capacity of both inmates and functionaries prior to their killing. However, within the Nazi system, with its distorted boundaries, Anigster – and others in similar positions – enjoyed, for a brief moment, various privileges and benefits. True, as evidence portrays him, Anigster became a persecutor, a particularly sadistic one. "I spent three years in the camps and never encountered a kapo who behaved as badly ... towards Jews," said one witness. "The defendant was one of the worst of the kapos," said another. "I can see his murder machine before my eyes," said a third. "I was in 19 camps and the worst hell was when I was working for the defendant ... On the day that he and 25 kapos ... were sent away from the camp, people danced with joy," related another. "He used to lash with his club at the weak and the fainting ... he severely beat any prisoner whose posture he didn't like."

As soon as he saw someone hurrying or shoving his way into the line, he clouted him with his club, on the head or the face or any other part of the body. If a prisoner happened to be caught red-handed trying to get in line a second time for another plate of soup, this would enrage him and his rubber club would rise and fall on the defendant.

"He used to hit us like a man hitting his enemy ... he would beat us for no reason." "He beat innocent people and caused harm indiscriminately, and [people] because they were so weak ... living on hope of liberation became demoralized and died."[62] Yet, Anigster was also, or primarily, a victim, a persecuted Nazi camp detainee.

All the early Holocaust trials underscored the range of choices and decisions available to prisoners who fulfilled the role of "accomplices," and the extent to which they were coerced. Were the only alternatives to serve the Nazis or face death, to subjugate fellow prisoners or face punitive action? Could a Jewish prisoner refuse a task and stay alive? Did prisoners accept supervisory positions in order to help, rather than persecute, their comrades? Did they accept dubious positions to forestall potentially worse situation? In Anigster's case, prosecution witnesses, in

[62] Ibid., pp. 157–159.

describing the defendant's sadism, said there was no external pressure for the defendant's beatings, since in most cases the Germans were not present. Moreover, several witnesses claimed that no prisoner was forced to accept the position of kapo or Chief Kapo, and that "there were some who refused and were not punished."[63] The law, too, briefly addressed these issues: Section 10 stipulated that a persecuted individual who committed or refrained from committing an act which constituted an offense under the law would be absolved of criminal responsibility if he had acted in order to save himself from immediate mortal danger, and if he had committed the act "with the intention of preventing graver consequences than those caused by the act or the failure to act, thereby preventing these consequences in practice."[64] But the legal definitions were too fluid and open to interpretation. The domain of prisoners' responsibility and choices was never clearly delineated.

Nazis and collaborators

In the Anigster trial as well, the court showed more wisdom and restraint than did the prosecution. It accepted the prosecution's evidence almost entirely, and unanimously found Anigster guilty of grave assault and battery in many instances. As regards the "war crime," however, the judges declared that the defendant had indeed committed acts that fell within the definition of a war crime, but since the defendant and his victims were members "of the same persecuted people," he was acquitted of this graver charge. On the "crime against humanity," however, the judges were divided. Two of them, in a majority decision, stated that "even an individual who is himself persecuted and incarcerated in the same camp as his victims, is capable, legally speaking, of a crime against humanity if he has committed the inhuman acts described above towards his fellow prisoners." In contrast to a war criminal, the judges added, an individual who perpetrates a crime against humanity is not necessarily one who identifies with the persecuting regime and its vicious intentions. "By carrying out these inhuman deeds the defendant allowed himself to become the instrument of the barbarous Nazi regime in its satanic scheme to annihilate the Jewish people, and since he carried out these deeds during the Nazi regime and in an enemy country, he consequently perpetrated a crime against humanity," they said.

---

[63] Ibid., p. 158.
[64] Nazis and Nazi Collaborators (Punishment) Law 1950, Codex 57, 9 August 1950, p. 284.

Judge Yosef Lamm, however, favoured acquitting the defendant on this charge also. It is worth pausing here for a moment to pay close attention to Judge Lamm. Not a survivor, he had nevertheless seen Nazism up close, having been imprisoned in the 1930s at Dachau, the first Nazi concentration camp. Even if the camp was then merely a token of what the future held in store, it may be assumed that his experience there had enriched his knowledge as regards the terror and debasement undergone by camp inmates, and Nazis' exploitation of their victims for keeping their terror machine in motion. As a member of the First Knesset and a legal expert, Lamm had helped formulate the law, although several of his comments and reservations were rejected. "I know of many cases in which these people [kapos] who were themselves persecuted, did every-thing in order to prevent the execution of crimes," said Lamm in the Knesset debate on the law. Often, he said, "there was no choice but to subject the unruly to disciplinary action in order to avert mortal danger from the entire group."[65] In his minority opinion in the Anigster case, he declared that since the defendant had not intended to exterminate the civilian population to which his prisoner victims belonged, he had not, in effect, intended to exterminate a single prisoner. And since the defendant had not "collaborated" with the Nazis – in not a single case did he cause "the Nazi controllers themselves to personally intervene" – but merely "made it easier for the Nazis to execute their plan to annihilate the Jewish people, thereby playing a terrible and heinous role, but with intentions utterly different from those of the Nazis," he was merely a Nazi "accom-plice." Lamm adjudged that in no way could Anigster be regarded as guilty of crimes against humanity.

All three judges opposed the death sentence even in Anigster's case. But the conviction of a crime against humanity, the majority judges declared, left them no other choice. It would have been better had "the legislator left sentencing to the courts," they stated, and for two reasons: first because there could be no comparison between a Nazi criminal or one aligned with the barbarous Nazi regime and a criminal such as the defendant, who was himself persecuted and who himself suffered the same inhuman conditions as his victims; secondly, not all crimes against humanity were equal: the evidence had shown that some kapos had acted in even crueller fashion than the defendant. Consequently, they would

---

[65] Yosef Lamm, Knesset Minutes, Vol. 6, 1 August 1950, p. 2395. Lamm, who had a doctorate in law from Vienna University, was arrested by the Nazis, sent to Dachau, released, and immigrated to Palestine in 1939. He served in the British Army in World War II, and was elected as First Knesset member on Mapai's list. In May 1951 he resigned from the Knesset and was appointed a district judge. In this capacity he sat as judge in several early Holocaust trials.

have preferred a sentence of ten years' imprisonment for crimes against humanity, and briefer concurrent prison terms for the other offenses. Judge Lamm, who had objected to defining the defendant's crimes as "crimes against humanity," proposed also that the defendant be sentenced to ten years in jail.[66] As the defendant was suffering from a malignant disease and had "been severely punished from on high," and was unlikely to live much longer, the judges agreed unanimously to recommend to the President of Israel that the sentence be mitigated.[67] The Supreme Court, which heard Anigster's appeal, sentenced him to two years' imprisonment from the day of his arrest. Anigster died shortly afterwards.

The leniency displayed by the courts in even the gravest abuse cases stemmed, one would assume, from the impact of the ghastly picture that emerged from the testimony of both prosecution and defense witnesses: the extreme, borderline conditions in which people, robbed of their humanity, were essentially dead while still alive. Among those living dead there were decent individuals and there were brutes like Anigster. In the first place, however, they were all victims, total victims, "totally innocent," as Hannah Arendt wrote, since they were there not for any act committed but because they were who they were,[68] because they were Jews.

Two major points arose with regard to the indictments and trials under the Nazis and Nazi Collaborators (Punishment) Law. The legal process did not make the essential distinction between Nazi criminals and Nazi victims defined as "collaborators," many of whom did not survive the Holocaust. Nor did it relate to the role of the Judenräte (the Jewish Councils) and other Jewish community leaders either prior to deportation or within the ghettos and the camps – the single most acute issue in the tragedy of Jewish "collaboration." The trials (resulting from the prosecution's decisions) ignored the mightier even among the Jews and went for the lowly, whose additional sin was that they had survived the Holocaust and could be charged. Moreover, by coming to Israel they put themselves within reach of the state arm.

---

[66] Verdicts E (District Courts), S. C., 9/51, pp. 178–180.   [67] Ibid., p. 180.
[68] Arendt, *The Origins of Totalitarianism*, p. 448. Arendt drew a clear distinction between the situation of the Jewish leaders in their communities and hometowns under Nazi terror, and that of the prisoners in the camps. She discussed it in her book on the Eichmann trial, arguing that however harsh was Nazi terror, they could still have refused to serve as leaders and to collaborate with the Nazi death machine. In contrast, the situation of the prisoners in concentration and death camps made their span of choice, under conditions of total oppression, terror, and violence, in fact non-existent.

In contrast, the "privileged," as Hannah Arendt called them – whose very existence, definition, and acceptance as such in Diaspora communities had been "the beginning of the moral collapse of respectable Jewish society"[69] – were not included in the profile of "Nazi collaborators." Even though they, too, had had to work with the Nazis under a reign of oppression and terror, their situation had been infinitely better than that of the non-privileged "collaborators" in forced labor, concentration, and death camps. Yet, they were not indicted for their acts, decisions, and choices. They were spared according to Israel's legal code. The most senior "collaborators" to be prosecuted were the highly despised Jewish commanders and members of police in the ghettos.

Hirsch Berenblatt, Jewish police commander in the Polish town of Bendin, was brought before the Tel Aviv District Court in the early 1960s.[70] It was one of the last cases to be heard, just after the Eichmann trial (Berenblatt's file was transferred from the police to the prosecution between Eichmann's apprehension and court appearance),[71] that is, in a totally different political and social atmosphere to what had prevailed during the first trials. He was convicted in early 1963 of having "rounded up and arrested, together with others, dozens of Jewish children from the municipal orphanage ... and [of having] handed them over to the Gestapo." Berenblatt was also found guilty of having assisted the Nazis in rounding up the town's Jews for a "selection" (*selektzia*), preventing Jews marked for extermination from escaping to other groups, and of other lesser offenses. The conviction was based on the testimony of a single witness, whom the court found reliable, and Berenblatt was sentenced to five years' imprisonment.

But while convicting the defendant, the court was already conscious of the total unprecedentedness of the Holocaust and was referring to the utter "otherness" of its daily reality and the difficulty, even impossibility, of judging it. Distance in time, and the impact of the Eichmann trial produced new insights and new sensibilities. The District Court also stated that under the unprecedented pressures of the Holocaust period, "Moral concepts and values were adjusted, and ordinary, educated, pleasant people did not reject any life-belt offered, even if it obliged them to hand over fellow Jews to the Nazi murderers." Aiming at the 1950 law, the judges declared that in light of the enormity of the

---

[69] Arendt, *Eichmann in Jerusalem*, p. 131.

[70] *Hirsch Berenblatt v. Attorney General*, Criminal Appeal No. 77/64, Legal Verdicts, Vol. 18, 1964, pp. 70–108.

[71] Ibid., p. 77. I note this in order to demonstrate that at a time when preparations were underway for staging the Eichmann trial, the State of Israel continued to try Jewish survivors on the basis of the same law under which Eichmann was brought to trial.

Holocaust, in which a third of the Jewish people were annihilated by the Nazi persecutor and the main centers of its national existence totally eradicated, "the Israeli legislator of 1950, speaking on behalf of the entire nation, was unwilling to pardon those ordinary, pleasant people, who, normal in normal times, selfishly sinned against others in that abnormal period."[72]

The Supreme Court heard Berenblatt's appeal in April and May 1964 and acquitted him. The composition of the court was of particular interest. Two of the justices had prior experience of Holocaust trials: Moshe Landau had been Court President at the Eichmann trial. Haim Cohen had been involved in the Nazis and Nazi Collaborators (Punishment) Law's legislation as Attorney General, and had been State Attorney, Chief Legal Adviser to the Government during the Grunewald–Kastner trial (see below) and its chief prosecutor. Their previous experience may be assumed to have influenced the two when they sat at Berenblatt's appeal. Cohen, a far different man now, focused in his verdict mainly on undermining the sole testimony at the basis of the convictionon, not touching on the nature or moral validity of the law itself. Moshe Landau, on the other hand, dwelt on the period of the Holocaust, the individuals involved, the law, the competence of Israeli courts in such cases, and the difficulty of distinguishing "between acts that may have been morally despicable and the conduct for which he [the appellant] deserved the sanctions of the criminal law."[73] It would be both arrogant and hypocritical on our part, wrote Justice Landau,

on the part of those who never stood in the place of [the victims and survivors] and those who managed to escape from there, like the prosecution witnesses ... to condemn the "ordinary people" who did not rise to exalted moral heights because they were being oppressed by a regime whose prime aim was to wipe their human image off the face of the earth; nor must we measure the fundamentals of the unique offenses defined under the Nazis and Nazi Collaborators (Punishment) Law according to some yardstick of moral behavior that only few were able to live up to. We must not attribute to the legislator the intention of demanding a standard of conduct that the public is unable to meet, especially as we are dealing with rules ... established *post factum*. Let us not delude ourselves into thinking that if deeds committed there by our persecuted brethren are judged in criminal courts according to a yardstick of pure morality, this will ease our anguish at the catastrophe that befell our people.[74]

Landau also disagreed with the District Court regarding the appellant's "selfish motives" in joining the Jewish militia and serving in it. "A person is close to himself and takes care of his own interests and those of his

---

[72] Ibid., p. 101.   [73] Ibid., p. 103.   [74] Ibid., p. 101.

family," he stated. "The interdictions in criminal law, including the Nazis and Nazi Collaborators (Punishment) Law, were not formulated for rare, unique heroes, but for ordinary mortals with ordinary weaknesses."[75] Of all the survivors brought to trial in Israel, Berenblatt, a member of the Judenrat, came closest to being a "Jewish leader." Both his senior position and the late date of his trial saw a new attitude towards Jewish conduct during the Holocaust. Both courts discussed the role and dilemmas of the Judenrat members, and the boundaries of culpability. The District Court's verdict stated that

> the defendant was not at all a lawbreaker, but blended into an apparatus ... guided and directed by people ... known before the war as officials and spokesmen in the Jewish community, and it would have been difficult for him to adopt an independent stance [or] ... moral considerations that clashed with [their] guidance, particularly since the Judenrat ... example matched his own interests and his natural desire to save himself.[76]

In the Supreme Court, President Yitzhak Olshan, who presided over Berenblatt's appeal, deliberated at length on the Judenräte's insoluble dilemmas. "*The very existence* of the Judenräte and Jewish police was helpful to the Nazis, Olshan argued, otherwise the Nazis would not have been interested in establishing and maintaining them." These organizations, he said, assisted the Nazis by collecting and handing over Jewish belongings and assets, registering Jews, maintaining order in the ghettos, and "supplying" Jews for forced labor and extermination. Olshan's pages-long judgment included a bewildering oxymoronic statement: "Even if they served *the interests of the Jewish community* – they were also *advantageous to the Nazis*, since this made it easier for them to locate the victims for persecution or extermination, particularly when extermination was accelerated and the Nazis frequently exploited this organization by employing deceit and various ruses."[77] Was he not trying this way to square the circle? Could "Jewish interests" during the war, in any way, under any circumstances, be congruent with "Nazi advantages"? Were they not mutually exclusive? Indeed, Olshan seems to have been straining towards the twilight zone of Jewish aporias engendered by the Final Solution, namely that anything which, even momentarily, served certain Jewish interests, was done at a price which ran counter to other Jewish interests.

Olshan was writing his ruling in 1964, after the Eichmann trial, after the publication of Hannah Arendt's *Eichmann in Jerusalem*, and the more distant impact of the Grunewald–Kastner trial. Referring to the "ongoing

---

[75] Ibid.   [76] Ibid., p. 91.   [77] Ibid., pp. 93–94.

controversy" in the Jewish and Israeli world "which, so it seems, will never end," on how the "Jewish community and its leaders" should have behaved under the Nazis, Olshan wrote:

A certain view was expressed, though it was not widely held, that it was the Jewish leadership and the Jewish organizations in the countries of the massacre, that were responsible for the appalling dimensions of the catastrophe, and that had it not been for them the Germans would have been unable to carry out extermination on such a scale.[78]

Olshan's phrasing seems to indicate disagreement with this assertion, which is strikingly reminiscent of Arendt. Yet his own statement on the Judenräte's assistance to the Nazis, by collecting and handing over Jewish assets, maintaining order in the ghettos, and "supplying" Jews for forced labour and extermination, echoed Arendt, almost word for word.[79]

   Olshan stressed the different shades of opinion about the Judenräte. Speaking about those who argued that, due to considerations of "national honor" or the principle that "one should not cause the loss of a single Jewish life even in order to save numerous Jewish lives," the Judenräte should be punished, versus the more lenient opinion; in regard of the "terribly tragic situation of the Jewish leaders whose hearts were torn," Olshan concluded that it was not "a question for the courts, but for history," since the legislator had not specified that the court must take a stand nor what stand it should take.[80] Judge Landau echoed his senior colleague's judgment in stating that

it is universally agreed that the court should not rule in the great controversy now raging – largely as a result of hindsight – on the Judenräte's role ... [on] whether, by collaborating to one degree or another with the Germans they infringed moral principles ... [or] whether the benefits of their action and their very existence outwighed the harm that they did.[81]

Doubt and understanding

Thus, the benefit of the doubt and the understanding that the immense Jewish tragedy was not a matter for the courts, that no court could take it in, was reserved for Judenrat members, the senior accomplices with the Nazis, those who organized, rounded up, registered, collected, and

[78] Ibid., p. 95.   [79] Arendt, *Eichmann in Jerusalem*, p. 125
[80] *Berenblatt* v. *Attorney General*, Criminal Appeal No. 77/64, Legal Verdicts, Vol. 18, 1964, pp. 95–96. Olshan added that "even the most extreme critics never claimed that the Judenräte or the Jewish police set themselves the aim of assisting the Nazis in the extermination of the Jews." Ibid., p. 96.
[81] Ibid., p. 100.

handled the Jews en route to the trains which transported them to Auschwitz and Treblinka, and withheld from the minor Jewish "aides" in the camps, who slapped or hit other victims in the food allocation line, in the bunks, or during roll call. The law itself seemed a bit vague and exempted the Judenräte from indictment; by failing to instruct the courts to adopt a stand on the issue, it appeared to preclude discussion of Judenräte behavior. Several legislators had tried to raise the question of the Judenräte during the legislative process. "Every Judenrat member who sat there ... not because he was sent there, is a criminal, a Nazi collaborator," said a Knesset member, who belonged to the leftist political movement that saw itself as the representative of the ghetto rebels. "Every man knows that there comes a time to die rather than cross the line." On the suicide of the head of the Warsaw ghetto Judenrat, this kibbutz member commented that Adam Czerniakow had sentenced himself justly because "had he not committed suicide it would have been necessary to prosecute him."[82] The argument that the failure to distinguish between the different Judenräte or between "a Jewish accomplice, even one who did beat prisoners, and a Nazi in Auschwitz,"[83] was an insult to the memory of the Holocaust was rejected. Early 1950s Israel was a place of no nuances.

Judenrat members, only a few of whom survived to reach Israel, were often closely associated with the establishment and major political parties. Some, a handful, later held public and political positions in the young state. They were not targeted by the law, not perceived as Nazi "accomplices." In fact they were granted a kind of immunity. This perspective puts an entire new complexion on what is known as the Kastner affair. The affair, concurrent with the trials of kapos and other small "collaborators" in the fifties, stirred up Israeli society and unveiled the specter of the Holocaust as no previous Holocaust trial had done. It began in exactly the same way: somebody accused somebody else of collaboration and demanded justice. In this case, however, the State of Israel tried not the suspected collaborator, but his accuser. The accused and the accuser were so paradigmatic both to our argument and to the uncanny moral play in which they were becoming entangled, and to Israeli national discourse, that had they not existed, it would have been necessary to create them. This is exactly what the court did.

The accuser, Malkiel Grunewald, turned by the state prosecution into the accused party, had immigrated to Palestine before the Nazi occupation

---

[82] Sub-Committee on the Nazis and Nazi Collaborators (Punishment) Law 1950, 23 May 1950.
[83] Ibid.

and owned a small hotel in Jerusalem. Hungarian by birth, he had lost
many of his relatives in the Holocaust.[84] He had also lost a son in the 1948
War of Independence, who had fought with the Irgun (ETZEL), the
military wing of the Revisionist movement, the historic opposition to the
ruling socialist party, Mapai. Back in Europe, Grunewald had already
waged a vociferous battle against Jewish political functionaries, particularly
those aligned with Mapai and the Jewish Agency. He continued this
campaign in the early 1950s, by printing and distributing leaflets to mail-
boxes in Jerusalem: a determined one-man opposition. His targets were
usually the larger parties' institutions and personalities. In the summer of
1952, he went after Dr. Israel Kastner, the Trade and Industry Ministry
spokesman, accusing him of a long list of crimes during World War II,
including collaboration with the Nazis in Hungary; testifying on behalf of
SS officer Kurt Becher at the Nuremberg trials, which led to Becher's
acquittal; rescuing his own family and close friends and associates by
organizing a train that took 1,685 Jews out of Hungary while abandoning
many others to their fate in "the valley of the shadow of death"; pocketing
funds and "lulling Hungary's Jews" about their impending fate.
Grunewald also emphasized Kastner's political connections, his Mapai
membership and candidacy for the Knesset. His language was distasteful,
even in a society not known for verbal restraint: "The stink of a corpse
irritates my nostrils!" Grunewald wrote, "Dr. Rudolf Kastner should be
exterminated!"[85]

Kastner, the accused, was his total antithesis: a Jewish socialist party
leader in Hungary, a man of the world according to the standards of
1950s Israel, an establishment figure all his life, educated, successful, an
admired journalist, self-assured, and with great personal charm and the
right connections. On the eve of the affair, he was looking at a political
career in the ruling party. But his conduct during the Holocaust haunted
him. In a way, Grunewald's pamphlet came as no surprise to him and its
contents held more than a grain of truth. Nor was Grunewald alone in his
charges. Complaints, accusations, and rumors had dogged Kastner since
the end of the war, in Hungary and later in Israel, but they had not
gathered sufficient momentum to justify legal charges, investigation, or
even to check Kastner's political and social ascent in Israel. One can only
imagine what would have happened had the state, i.e., Attorney General
Haim Cohen, ignored Grunewald's charges, which at the time were

[84] The informative details on the affair quoted below are largely based on Weitz, *The Man
Who Was Murdered Twice*, and on Tom Segev, *The Seventh Million: Israelis and the
Holocaust* (trans. Haim Watzman), New York 1992.
[85] Weitz, *The Man Who Was Murdered Twice*, pp. 93–96.

confined to his insignificant pamphlet, and done nothing. Cohen, however, then all-powerful in the legal system, chose not to ignore them. "We
cannot remain silent in the face of this publication," Cohen – then also
Acting Minister of Justice – wrote in a confidential memorandum to the
Minister of Trade and Industry, under whom Kastner served. "If, as
I presume, there is no truth in the accusations, the man who published
them must be brought to trial,"[86] Cohen added. Many years later, when
he was a Supreme Court justice, Cohen said on television: "I simply could
not conceive that somebody tainted by the grave suspicion of 'Nazi collaborator' could serve in a senior position in our *new, pure, ideal* state."[87]

Of the many defeated "heroes" of the gloomy affair, the role of Haim
Cohen, who was chiefly responsible for its development, was the most
puzzling. This shrewd German-born jurist, educated in both German and
Jewish institutions, went on to become one of the most liberal, enlightened justices to serve on the Israeli Supreme Court. In the Kastner affair,
however, not only was he not liberal at all, but he overturned the law he
had helped devise for the sake of the establishment, party considerations,
and of what he perceived as *raison d'état*. At the time Cohen was regarded
as Ben-Gurion's right-hand man, a jurist who, by his own admission, put
state and security considerations first. Since 1947 Cohen had placed his
legal skills at the disposal of the emergent state: first as Secretary of the
Legal Council to the Situation Committee; from 1948 to 1950 as State
Attorney and Director General of the Justice Ministry, and in the decade
of most of the Holocaust trials, as Attorney General, responsible for all
the executive legal aspects.

When the Kastner affair began, Cohen was in an outstanding position
of influence and deaf to all those who urged him to abandon, and let it be
forgotten, the potentially explosive political and emotional issue. Was it
the arrogance of prolonged power, shared by many members of Israel's
ruling elite, that led one even to consider employing such powerful means
in the defense of a supreme end, the idea of a "pure" state? In any case,
Cohen pressed ahead with the trial, even against Kastner's own wishes,
who apparently was not anxious to see the story of Hungarian Jewry and
his own role in it dragged through the courts, although there are various
versions on this point.[88] Cohen's move also showed that the legal code
could provide the suitable law for almost any political action.

---

[86] The Minister of Justice to the Minister of Trade and Industry, "Re Rudolf Kastner,"
confidential, quoted in ibid., p. 103.
[87] Quoted in ibid., p. 102 (my italics).
[88] Weitz cites several versions of Kastner's views on the possibility that the matter would be
brought to court. Ibid., pp. 104–107.

To clarify Grunewald's charges and clear Kastner, the Attorney General did not invoke the Nazis and Nazi Collaborators (Punishment) Law 1950 that he, himself, had helped draft. Cohen could certainly have charged Kastner under Section 5 of the Law, which stated that "an individual who, under Nazi rule, in a hostile country, aided in the handing over of a persecuted individual to a hostile regime – shall be sentenced to up to ten years imprisonment,"[89] thus offering him the public stage to exonerate himself. It will be recalled that the Minister of Justice at the time had tabled the bill with the declaration that those under suspicion might welcome investigation for they "have not been given the opportunity to prove their innocence before an authorized court."[90] For this was the declared intention of the law and the spirit of the law: to enable Holocaust survivors suspected of collaboration to clear themselves, and thereby "clear" the atmosphere among them. Instead, and unlike any of the "collaborator" trials, the state ranged itself on the side of the suspect against the accuser. Grunewald was charged with libel. Attorney General Cohen thus reversed the roles of accused and accuser, of defendant and plaintiff. The maneuver backfired: the trial was a disaster for both the Attorney General and the political establishment, a perverse form of poetic – if not legal and historic – justice.

Kapos and Judenräte

Why was Kastner not tried under the Nazis and Nazi Collaborators (Punishment) Law 1950, to enable him to exonerate himself of false charges as the law stated, and as was done in other cases at the time? Did the Attorney General act as he did because Kastner had been a senior government official, Mapai's candidate for the Knesset, well connected in high places? Could not the nature of his cooperation with the Nazis – political and organizational assistance at the bureaucratic level, negotiations and bargaining, rescuing the few while forgoing the many – be perceived as such by the Attorney General or according to Israeli criteria at the time? Was such collaboration more elusive and deceptive than the unequivocal blows and physical harm inflicted by petty functionaries in the camps, less vicious or judgable than the kapos' concrete, tangible deeds? Was it the potential similarity between the Judenrat behavior and the conduct of the political leadership in Palestine which rendered the affair so explosive and threatening that there was a need to suppress and banish it from

---

[89] The Nazis and Nazi Collaborators (Punishment) Law 1950, Codex 57, 9 August 1950, p. 283.
[90] Pinhas Rosen, Knesset Minutes, Session 131, pp. 1147–1148.

public discourse by means of a charge of libel? Political haughtiness of the powers that be; a sincere desire "to purge the camp"; simple professional negligence in examination of Grunewald's accusations, which would have revealed their firmness; shortsightedness regarding the explosive potential of such a sensitive case; the thought that one can, by the state's power, legal procedure in this case, suppress for long trauma's memories or the story of a minority, however weak and wretched?

There is no way to determine the relative role of each factor in Cohen's decision to launch the libel trial. Historically speaking, these were the first years of statehood, in which great efforts were being made to consolidate a new national identity for the numerous ethnic, social, and cultural groups "ingathered" into Israel, to transform "an artificial assembly of varied and conflicting forces into an organic body with a single collective consciousness," as a Knesset member said in debate on the contemporary State Education Law.[91] Grunewald's trial was intended to still subversive voices, marginal as they were, that appeared to undermine the Holocaust national historical narrative in its exclusive link to the state. Grunewald's bill of indictment was submitted in May 1953. On 12 May, the Minister of Education and Culture, Ben-Zion Dinur, submitted the Holocaust and Heroism Remembrance Law – Yad Vashem, 1953, to the Knesset for a first reading.[92] On that day, ten years after the outbreak of the Warsaw ghetto uprising, after lengthy postponements and delays, the State of Israel formally began to create its official national memory of the annihilation of European Jewry in World War II.[93] Concomitantly, the State Education Law, 1953, was drafted and being debated in the Knesset.[94] The two, politically interconnected,[95] were presented by Ben-Zion Dinur, a Hebrew University professor of history and one of

---

[91] Haim Boger, Knesset Minutes, Vol. 14, Session 252, 22 June 1953, p. 1679.

[92] Knesset Minutes, Vol. 14, Session 227, 12 May 1953, pp. 1310–1314.

[93] Ben-Gurion was in no hurry to nationalize the Holocaust commemoration projects and to appropriate them. "The one fitting tombstone in memory of European Jewry exterminated by the Nazi beasts is the State of Israel," wrote Ben-Gurion to a memorial rally to which he was invited. *Davar*, 22 April 1952. Noteworthy is Ben-Gurion's use of the word *matzeva* (tombstone) instead of monument or memorial – with all its connotations, including the cemetery, as a definition of the State of Israel, which, according to Ben-Gurion himself on other occasions, and even in the same text, represented rebirth, renewal, independence, and life. "The state in which the hopes of generations of the Jewish people are embodied and which serves as a free and loyal refuge for any Jew in the world who wants to live a free and independent *life*." Ibid. (my italics)

[94] Knesset Minutes, Vol. 14, Session 252, 22 June 1953.

[95] Ben-Gurion who did not consider the Holocaust commemoration law to be particularly urgent, was, on the other hand, very interested in the State Education Law, which evoked criticism and opposition in various circles in Israel. Dinur helped him to pass the law and won his gratitude and also his agreement to pass a Holocaust commemoration law.

the most interesting and influential intellectuals of his time. Each law, in its own way, was to fuse the mass of immigrants from more than a hundred countries into a national collective, driven by a common memory and sharing a single vision of the present and future.

Scholar and statesman, Dinur had interesting, original insights about collective memory and nation-building. In the 1920s and 1930s, long before the theoretical and political study of collective memory became fashionable, Dinur was already writing about memory and historiography as key instruments for nation-building. For him, writing Jewish history was not merely a profession but a historical and political mission.[96] He knew all about the role that knowledge of the past played in shaping the present, and to no less a degree about the shaping of the past for needs of the present – and, thus, about the historian's role in creating and imparting a national narrative. The historian's task, he had written in 1926, is not only to know the national past but to enlist it for national objectives, to achieve the supreme goal of merging the individual self with the nation's collective self.[97] Decades later, on 18 May 1953, in the Knesset debate on the Holocaust and Heroism Remembrance Law – Yad Vashem, he used almost identical words:

There can be no doubt that memory, in the life of an individual, is one's self, because the individual self exists only to the extent that it integrates all its life's events and experiences into a single continuum. The same is true of a nation's memory. A nation's self exists only to the extent that it has a memory, to the extent that it manages to integrate its past experiences into a single whole, and only when this condition is met, does it exist as a nation, as a single entity.[98]

The draft of the Holocaust and Heroism Remembrance Law – Yad Vashem was accompanied by Dinur's long, impressive historiographical essay on the systematic destruction of European Jewry "by a legally established regime" before the eyes of the entire world and the nations among whom they had lived for centuries.[99] The law, said Dinur, was aimed at "the 'ingathering' of memory into the homeland," at establishing a memorial for each and every Jew slain.

If we manage to collect the names of all those who perished, those who were murdered and slaughtered, and create a ledger in which each and every name is

---

[96] See Uri Ram, "Then and Now: Zionist Historiography and the Invention of the Jewish National Narrative: Ben-Zion Dinur and his Times," *Iyunim Bitekumat Israel*, 1996, p. 131 [Hebrew].

[97] Ben-Zion Dinur, *Israel Ba'gola: Mekorot U'teudot* (*Israel in the Diaspora: Sources and Documents*), Tel Aviv 1926, p. 31. Quoted in Ram, "Then and Now," p. 132.

[98] Ben-Zion Dinur, Knesset Minutes, Vol. 14, Session 230, 18 May 1953, p. 1352.

[99] Dinur, Knesset Minutes, Session 227, 12 May 1953, p. 1310.

recorded ... such a ledger will resurrect the images and likenesses of millions of our brethren from "the depths of miles-long pits filled to overflowing, layer by layer, drowned and burnt." On behalf of future generations, this ledger will resurrect our murdered brethren from Treblinka, Sobibor, Auschwitz, Belzec, Ponar, Babi Yar and elsewhere. It will reveal our "desiccated, pulverized and crushed" brethren to both generations to come and ourselves, it will resurrect them, old men and women, fathers and mothers with babes in their arms – the millions who were turned into living torches – they will stand there and cry out for vengeance till the end of time.[100]

The law also made the crucial, exclusive link between Holocaust memory and the State of Israel, between the Holocaust and Jerusalem, the only place that could house this memory, according to the official Israeli narrative.

This name [Yad Vashem (Isaiah 56:5)] also implies that *Israel our country and Jerusalem our city are the proper place for them and their commemoration* ... the name of the project – Yad Vashem – does not only refer to a place, it embodies the significant fact that the place is Jerusalem. This is the heart of the nation, the heart of Israel, everything must be concentrated here.[101]

Dinur mentioned them all: the dead, the destroyed Jewish communities, the heroes, the partisans, and ghetto rebels. Only one category was not mentioned by the minister responsible for the Holocaust commemoration law: the survivors. They, those who had experienced the horrors directly, who were living in Israel in their hundreds of thousands, the most immediate, direct bearers of the unprecedented memory, the prime source, the most valuable asset of Holocaust memory – were discounted in the state where they were picking up the pieces of their shattered lives. Dinur spoke with reverence about every scrap of "dead" evidence that had remained and been brought to Israel, "every document, every memory, every vestige." But not a word about the living; their previous lives, their culture; not a word about their rescue, their heroic role in Zionism's struggle for statehood, nothing about their rehabilitation, heritage, and memories. Holocaust commemoration, which the State of Israel instated in law, was a memory without rememberers.

---

[100] Ibid., pp. 1311–1312
[101] Ibid., pp. 1311, 1314. Dinur also said that "Israel, the scattered nation whose sons were annihilated, must establish just one central memorial authority, in its homeland." Ibid., p. 1313. The marking out of the memorial territory, the naming of Israel and Jerusalem as the only fitting place for commemoration of the Holocaust, and the demand for exclusive jurisdiction over memory expressed by Dinur were a response to the memorial projects which were beginning to be established elsewhere in the world, and particularly in Paris. See Eliezer Don-Yehiya, "Memory and Political Culture: Israeli Society and the Holocaust," *Studies in Contemporary Jewry*, 4, 1993, pp. 139–162.

On the other hand, the Knesset debate on the draft of Holocaust and Heroism Commemoration Law, as did the earlier debate on the Nazis and Nazi Collaborators (Punishment) Law, raised, again, questions about collaboration and the Judenräte in juxtaposition with the heroism of the resistance fighters who had redeemed the "national honour." Dinur himself noted that the Nazis had intended "to break the people's spirit, to seek out and cultivate its worst and most corrupt elements, and put them in charge of their fellows; [and that] the promotion of these elements marked the beginning of the Holocaust."[102] The debate was acrid, the views tainted by political convictions and affiliations. Avraham Berman of the Left, who had been in the Warsaw ghetto underground, spoke of "the damned Jewish ghetto police" and the Judenräte as "willing slaves of the Hitlerist murderers," the rotten fruit of the Jewish political *reaktzia*.[103] Zerah Wahrhaftig of the Zionist religious party objected to the cleaving of memory resisters in arms and non-combatants, arguing that not all the Judenrat members were traitors. "Many of them sacrificed their lives by joining the Judenräte ... those who managed to hide ... should not slander these victims ... I know how many traitors there were, but the great majority of the people were 'pure and holy.'"[104]

By the same token, it is no accident that the "collaborator" trials being held at that time in Israeli courts were not mentioned in the Knesset, or that the tragic accounts being exposed there, living, bitter, contemporary tales of the devastation, were never incorporated into Israel's Holocaust memory; to this day, they lie like corpses in the obscurity of Israel's legal archives. These tales were not recounted then (press reports were very brief) nor have they been recounted since. They were not given life, not passed on from generation to generation,[105] nor taught in schools. This Holocaust literature, this record of the complexity of human existence and its negation in the cataclysmic situation in the camps was not handed down because it embodied – and still does – a vast threat, emanating from the very triviality of the "crimes" exposed and the banality of the people who committed them; ordinary Jews, everyday people, who might well

---

[102] Ibid. It is noteworthy that similar remarks, though less extreme, of Hannah Arendt in her book on the Eichmann trial, created a furor, while the reactions to Dinur's remarks in the Knesset were local in scope, part of the debate and no more.

[103] Avraham Berman, Knesset Minutes, Vol. 14, Session 230, 18 May 1953, p. 1339.

[104] Zerah Wahrhaftig, ibid., 18 May 1953, pp. 1345–1346.

[105] As noted, few articles have been written on this subject, and they do not quote at length the testimony given at the trials: Tom Segev refers briefly to the trials in his book *The Seventh Million*; also of interest is the documentary by Danny Siton and Tor Ben Mayor, *Kapo*, 2000, in which former Justice Haim Cohen says, among other things, that those who were not interned in the Nazi camps have no right to judge the actions and conduct of the Jews who have been there.

have been us; individuals trapped in insoluble dilemmas with no way out except suicide; who, for one brief moment outside of "normal" time, turned into persecutors, beating, slapping, whipping, and torturing other people for more food, less work, less suffering, to save themselves – thereby forfeiting their place in the world. And because these accounts deal with ordinary, normal people, and expose the fragility and imperceptibility of the line between good and evil, right and wrong, and the leakage – invisible at the time – from one side of the line to the other – their troubling message could not be compulsory material for a nation establishing and defining itself as absolute good against the Holocaust's absolute evil. This message could not be tolerated by a nation that teaches its children about the Holocaust only through "its direct link with the state,"[106] and sends its sons and daughters on death camp pilgrimage so that they will return as fortified Jews and Israelis with a reinforced national identity, and readiness to face imminent holocausts and the evil they themselves will have to commit in defence of the state and to ward off a future Holocaust or a ghost of a Holocaust.

The court versus the state

Nor did the Knesset mention the Kastner affair at a time when the trial of his accuser, Grunewald, later to become a Judenrat trial of a sort (Kastner's), was being prepared by the Attorney General. Was there an inherent connection between the early Holocaust trials and the Grunewald–Kastner trial, on the one hand, and between the two major laws, the Holocaust and Heroism Remembrance Law and State Education Law, on the other? Were these two parallel processes inherently interwoven or, on the contrary, totally detached from one another? There is no way to be certain. What is certain is that the trials and the laws both reflected and helped mold the "spirit of the times." A distinct group of people, all members of the ruling elite and closely interrelated socially, politically, and personally, formulated laws, made decisions, and acted on them through various agencies of government.

The same factors that led the Attorney General to try Grunewald also influenced the course of the trial. A secondary member of the Attorney General's staff – not he himself – represented the prosecution, and was sent into the arena unprepared. His very juniority, it may be argued, shows that the decision to prosecute was not a major political move. Perhaps. Or, perhaps, the prime mover, Haim Cohen, preferred to pull the strings from

---

[106] Young, *The Texture of Memory*, p. 211.

behind scenes (as Ben-Gurion did, a decade later, in the Eichmann trial). Perhaps, too, being confident of his ability to control totally the course of the trial, Cohen was blind to potential directions the trial would take. All one had to do was look back at the comments made three years earlier by Grunewald's young and ambitious attorney, Shmuel Tamir, on Palestine's Jewish leadership during the Holocaust to know that Grunewald was secondary to him, and that beyond Kastner, his larger target would be the Mapai ruling party and his leader, Ben-Gurion. Referring to the issue of the German reparations, Tamir had written: "And now, they want to protect their lying, parasitical regime by accepting 'reparations' for [the] extermination – in which they played a part – 'reparations' for the flesh and blood of members of the Jewish people ... maybe even ... for the flesh and blood of their own fathers and mothers."[107]

In Tamir's untrammelled hands, what was supposed to have been a marginal and well-contained trial, a pre-emptive measure to silence opposition to the organized, national discourse on the Holocaust fostered by the national leadership or the "idyll of forgetfulness," as Tamir termed it,[108] became a platform for denouncing not only the hegemonic Holocaust narrative, but the regime that had created it. To dull the sorry impression left by the prosecution witness Kastner's muddled, evasive testimony, the prosecution called to the stand a battery of political "privileged" which only enhanced the trial's political tint. And to counter the testimony of the "privileged," the defence attorney summoned a long list of survivors, anonymous individuals snatched from the shadows of Israeli society and deposited on center stage to deliver their painful accusations. In this sense, the trial replicated the tragic dichotomy of the Holocaust era between the privileged, represented by Kastner, and the nameless, between the few who made it out on Kastner's rescue train and the many who were trapped on trains to Auschwitz.[109] By the time the prosecution grasped that the trial had been "re-reversed" and the Attorney General bestirred himself to appear in court, it was too late – if there had ever been a chance – for such a political project in court. The trial had slipped away from the prosecution and, with the help of the court, had taken on a life of its own. Ironically enough, at this juncture, the defence availed itself of the procedural concessions granted by the Nazis and Nazi Collaborators (Punishment) Law, such as the exemption from proving its case beyond

---

[107] Shmuel Tamir, "To the Graveyard, Beggars," *Herut*, 16 March 1951.
[108] *Attorney General* v. *Malkiel Grunewald*, Criminal File 124/53, 1965. Quoted in Shalom Rosenfeld, *Tik Pelili 124 (Criminal Case 124)*, Tel Aviv 1955, p. 310 [Hebrew].
[109] See Leora Bilsky, "The Kastner Trial," in Adi Ophir (ed.), *50to48: Momentim Bikortiim Be'toldot Medinat Israel (Critical Moments in the History of the State of Israel)*, Jerusalem and Tel Aviv 1999, pp. 125–133.

a reasonable doubt.[110] With the help of a sympathetic judge, Benyamin Halevi, the defense attorney Tamir was able to present his own, unambiguous truth about Kastner's culpability and that of the Jewish leadership in general; to establish a connection between it and Palestine's "collaborationist" Jewish leadership; to argue that their offense had been one and the same – and to do so in plain, bloodthirsty parlance.[111]

There was no lack of politics in this affair, from the primal motives of the trial to Tamir's defense to Mapai's crying "foul" for using the "sacred" courtroom as yet another arena to denounce the regime – a stance echoed to this day by the dominant, national, ideological historiography. Nor was there lack of politics in the trial's immediate and long-term consequences. Judge Halevi's acquittal of Grunewald of the charge of libel, was handed down – by chance? – on the eve of the general elections to the Third Knesset in which the right-wing opposition party, Herut, doubled its strength and Mapai lost more than 10 percent of its seats – the first chinks in the seemingly invincible labor movement's political and social edifice since the beginning of the twentieth century.

The court did not clear Kastner, as the Attorney General had hoped, Israel was not exorcized of the Holocaust dybbuk, and the question of the Judenräte was not resolved. Nor apparently will it ever be, as the President of the Supreme Court subsequently declared.[112] Out of the ravages of the trial emerged the hand that pressed the trigger that killed Kastner on a Tel Aviv street in March 1957, before his acquittal by the Supreme Court in 1958. Out of the same trial was born the Eichmann trial, which was intended as, and indeed became, the great redress for the Kastner affair, the show of power of the new and "another"[113] Israel prosecuting now, not Jewish victims, but a Nazi criminal for war crimes and crimes against humanity – Ben-Gurion's last great national undertaking.

---

[110] Ibid., p. 131.
[111] Tamir, "To the Graveyard, Beggars." An extensive discussion of Halevi's verdict in this trial appears in chapter 4 in the present book.
[112] *Hirsch Berenblatt* v. *Attorney General*, Criminal Appeal No. 77/64, Legal Verdicts, Vol. 18, 1964, pp. 95–96.
[113] This is how Ben-Gurion defined Konrad Adenauer's post-war Germany in order to legitimize his contested claim for German reparations.

3   From the People's Hall to the Wailing Wall

Great humiliation never ends, said Auschwitz inmate Primo Levi, an authoritative witness to the subject, in *The Reawakening*.[1] The memory of the offense engenders evil and hatred, which break the body and the spirit and mark both survivors and oppressors. This insight is, in a way, Primo Levi's legacy, expressed after his liberation from the death camp. The nature, effects, and functions of traumatic memory, especially memory of an immense human catastrophe such as the Holocaust, and more specifically the impact of this memory on the Israeli–Arab conflict, will be at the heart of this chapter. It deals with the mobilization of the memory of the Holocaust in the service of Israeli politics, beginning with the capture and trial of Adolf Eichmann in 1960–1962. A line is drawn from this event, and the specific Holocaust discourse it generated, to the Six Day War (June 1967) with its own existential Holocaust discourse.

Hence the cryptic title of the chapter which delineates its time frame: the People's Hall (in Hebrew, *Bet Ha'am*) was the site in Jerusalem where Israel held the trial of the Nazi criminal. The Wailing Wall (or Western Wall) of the title, which is considered a remnant of the outer wall of the Second Temple in Jerusalem, has become a national symbol and a major Jewish religious site. It was captured by Israeli forces sweeping through East Jerusalem during the 1967 war and immediately appropriated by Israeli authorities, to be transformed into the largest outdoor Orthodox synagogue in the world. It became the symbol of this "holy war" in its dual meaning: the deliverance war of the ancient and sacred regions of the homeland, and the war which miraculously saved Israel from a new holocaust. Beyond that, the title, as does the chapter, reflects the course Israel has taken along this time frame, from a secular, nationally mobilized and collectivist society into a messianic-like entity displaying religious and meta-historic features.

---

[1] Primo Levi, *The Reawakening*, trans. Stuart Woolf, New York 1986, pp. 182–183.

This chapter, which analyzes the first stage of the Holocaust's presence in Israel's collective mind and the use of this presence in the state's existential discourse, will not deal with the respective historical events themselves – topics already extensively researched and discussed. It is devoted rather to their discursive dimension, to their role in the shaping of the Israeli and Jewish collective memory of the massacre of European Jewry in World War II, and to the dialectics of the reciprocal influence of this construed memory on events through its incorporation into the context of Israel's existence. It will be argued here that, while the Eichmann trial was a turning point in creating and shaping a specific Israeli memory and political narrative concerning the Holocaust, the 1967 war – and especially what is known as the "waiting period" immediately preceding its outbreak – was the first test and application of this discourse in the context of Israel's wars.

The judgment of Adolf Eichmann in Jerusalem by an Israeli court was an extraordinary event by any measure. The trial, the full sessions of which were broadcast live on national radio, changed the face of Israel, psychologically binding the pastless young Israelis with their recent history and revolutionizing their self-perception. "Not one of us will leave here as he was before," wrote the poet Haim Guri, who covered the trial for a Tel Aviv paper.[2] It was also a major step in the shaping of western post-Holocaust culture and the effort to grapple with the history and memory of the Holocaust. Susan Sontag expressed the fundamentally paradoxical essence of this event, claiming in a 1964 text that the trial was the "most interesting and moving work of art in the past ten years," and that it was "primarily a great act of commitment through memory and the renewal of grief, [which] clothed itself in the forms of legality and scientific objectivity."[3]

"Renewal of grief" is indeed the right phrase, because for years mourning for the Holocaust and its victims had been, as it were, suspended. The psychological and political repercussions of the Jewish catastrophe had certainly been simmering, at least subliminally. Yet the decade and a half that preceded the capture and trial of Eichmann were marked, in Israel and in other countries such as France and the United States, by public silence and some sort of statist denial regarding the Holocaust.[4] The devastating burden of the catastrophe and its unprecedented nature could not coexist with the general effort to

---

[2] Haim Guri, *Mul Ta Ha'zekhukhit* (*Facing the Glass Booth*), Tel Aviv 1963, p. 73 [Hebrew].
[3] Susan Sontag, "Reflection on the Deputy," in Eric Bentley (ed.), *The Storm over the Deputy*, New York 1964, pp. 118–123.
[4] Alain Finkielkraut, *La mémoire vaine*, Paris 1989; Deborah Lipstadt, "America and the Memory of the Holocaust, 1950–1965," *Modern Judaism*, **16** (3), October 1996, pp. 195–214.

renew some semblance of life and a kind of normalcy after the war. The enormity of the experience precluded any normal conversation about the event, and mere survival, which was crucial for the survivors especially, meant suppression of emotion. Young societies in the process of becoming often try to suspend the very idea of death. Such suspension is particularly vital to the survival of a society fighting over territory and demanding from its young the willingness to sacrifice their lives for the homeland. Thus, there was an almost concerted effort to "disremember" the recent, unbearable past.[5]

Years of organized silence

From the moment the State of Israel was proclaimed, after a political and diplomatic campaign in which the Holocaust and Holocaust survivors played a prominent role, came an organized and quasi-official divorce from this close past, combined with an effort to extract the newborn state from history and endow it with a transcendental and meta-historical character. For Ben-Gurion, the state he created was the prefiguration of a millennial future and, at the same time, the resurrection of a distant, glorious past. "From the conquest by Joshua son of Nun, there never was such a formidable event," he said.[6] The other critical events in Jewish history, according to Ben-Gurion, were the Exodus from Egypt and the assembly at Mount Sinai. The Holocaust was not equal to any of them, nor was any other event relating to the Jews of the Diaspora.

Ben-Gurion dismissed the history of two millennia of Jewish life outside of the Land of Israel. The Zionist revolution excelled in erasing entire eras from the annals of the Jewish people and strove to disconnect itself from, and therefore to forget, the diasporic chapter of Jewish history. Already in 1917, the year of the Balfour Declaration, Ben-Gurion wrote that from the time of the Jewish people's last national disaster, the Bar-Kochba rebellion,

we had no more Jewish history, because the history of a nation is only the history which creates the nation as a single whole, as a national unit, and not that which happens to individuals and groups within the nation ... For 1,800 years ... we have been excluded from world history which is composed of the chronicles of peoples.[7]

[5] I borrow the term "disremember" from Ignes Sodre in her conversation with A. S. Byatt about Toni Morrison's *Beloved*, in A. S. Byatt and Ignes Sodre, *Imagining Characters*, New York 1995, p. 196.
[6] David Ben-Gurion, "Concepts and Values," *Hazut*, **3**, 1957, p. 11 [Hebrew].
[7] David Ben-Gurion, "The Redemption," *Der Yiddisher Kempfer*, **39**, 16 November 1917.

The State of Israel, the culmination of this revolution, was, in its first, formative decade, a monument to selective amnesia and erasure of certain chapters in Jewish history that would have hindered its constituting effort and contradicted the state's narrative of power and renewal.[8]

In such a nascent or renascent society, connected to a mythified, distant past yet deprived of its closer past, there was no space in the public sphere for the history of the Holocaust or for the bearers of its direct memory – the survivors. And although almost 300,000 such survivors reached Israel between 1945 and 1955 and changed the visage and the fabric of the society,[9] they were the "absent presentees"[10] of the country. It was heroes', not victims', time.[11] Acts of commemoration of the Holocaust were few and sporadic. State commemoration, official publications, literature and historiography, and school manuals, celebrated, if at all, only the very few ghetto fighters and partisans. In a 220-page textbook of Jewish history published in 1948, only one page was devoted to the Holocaust, compared to ten pages on the Napoleonic wars.[12] Remembrance Day itself, later to become the grand leveler and unifier of Israel's political culture, had a long history of postponements.[13]

Not only was the memory of the Holocaust repressed, but even its uniqueness was questioned. Normalcy, the long-yearned-for aim of Zionism, and *Realpolitik* were the idioms of the time. The notion of revenge, although mentioned, was largely excluded from public discussion.[14] After short-lived and semi-clandestine efforts immediately after the war to pursue and liquidate Nazi officers, Israel made a point of not being involved in Nazi hunts that would demand all sorts of illegal activities. Such involvement also would have collided with the state's efforts to become a "nation among the nations" and to establish full-fledged diplomatic relations

[8] Charles Liebman and Eliezer Don-Yehiya, *Civil Religion in Israel,* Berkeley 1983, p. 105.
[9] Idith Zertal, "The Bearers and the Burdens: Holocaust Survivors in Zionist Discourse," *Constellations*, 5 (2), June 1998, pp. 283–295; see also previous chapter. Statistically and for a certain period of time in the early 1950s, Holocaust survivors constituted almost half of Israel's population.
[10] A reversed term, "present absentees," was given to the Palestinian inhabitants who fled or were expelled from their homes and villages in the 1948 war and became "displaced persons" in their native country.
[11] Finkielkraut, *La mémoire vaine*, p. 37.
[12] Ruth Firer, *Sokhnei Ha'lekakh (Agents of Zionist Education)*, Tel Aviv 1985, p. 70 [Hebrew].
[13] Young, "When a Day Remembers."
[14] In response to the opponents of the Reparations Agreement with Germany who claimed, among other things, that Germany, like the Amalekites, should be eradicated from the face of the earth, Ben-Gurion said: "'Blot out the remembrance of Amalek' is a meaningless verse for us." David Ben-Gurion at the Mapai Central Committee, 13 December 1951, Labor Party Archive, 23/51; see also Segev, *The Seventh Million*, pp. 189–226.

with the international community. The Nazis and Nazi Collaborators (Punishment) Law 1950, solemnly adopted by the Israeli Knesset, was actually aimed at Jewish "collaborators."[15] Spontaneous, sometimes quasi-clandestine gestures of commemoration were performed, especially by the survivors themselves, individually or in groups, in order to preserve their heritage and erect humble monuments to the memory of their families.[16] The state, however, repeatedly postponed the establishment of an official, government-sponsored institution to cultivate the memory of the Holocaust and its victims. "Not just the world forgets, we do too," declared a Knesset member in a debate in 1950.[17]

Facing the horror

This was why Ben-Gurion's short, unexpected announcement to the Knesset, on 23 May 1960, about the capture of Adolf Eichmann, his imprisonment in Israel, and his future trial under the Nazis and Nazi Collaborators (Punishment) Law, fell like a bombshell on Israel and the world. Indeed, from its inception, with Ben-Gurion's declaration in the Israeli parliament, it became a consciousness-changing event. Finally the Holocaust could be faced, looked at, but from a very specific perspective – from a position of power, sovereignty, and control. Just as the project of Israeli nation-building first required "forgetting" the past or some parts of it, to borrow Renan's dictum, or some "collective amnesia," in Benedict Anderson's words,[18] Ben-Gurion's nationalism needed now to forge new memories according to its own specific profile and goals. Since memories of defeat and death, transformed in the national sphere through various discursive strategies, can grow into vital, mythified national rites of passage and be celebrated as feats of test and rebirth, the Eichmann case was now to become, under Ben-Gurion's supervision, the perfect vehicle for his grand national pedagogy. The total helplessness of European Jewry in World War II could now directly serve as the "counter metaphor" to the discourse of Israeli omnipotence and also as its ultimate justification. "Only the Jewish state can now defend Jewish blood and thus shatter the basis of the total pogrom and send it a very serious warning," declared the daily *Yedioth Aharonoth*'s editorial in a special edition of the paper published a few hours after Ben-Gurion's announcement:

[15] See previous chapter.
[16] Judith Tidor Baumel, "'In Everlasting Memory': Individual and Communal Holocaust Commemoration in Israel," in Wistrich and Ohana (eds.), *The Shaping of Israeli Identity*, pp. 146–170.
[17] Knesset Minutes, 5713 (1952/1953), 1313.
[18] See Anderson, *Imagined Communities*, pp. 187–206.

Hitler almost succeeded in proving that Jewish blood is valueless. The evidence: he murdered millions of Jews whose blood was never avenged ... The capture of the Nazi exterminator by the remnants of the exterminated people and his judgment by a Jewish tribunal according to Jewish justice is meant to prove to terrorists of all kinds, Germans and non-Germans, brown, white, red, black and all those who have already prepared themselves for the role of future exterminators of Jews, that Jewish blood will never be defenseless again. It also declares that however powerful all the pogromchiks under the sun may be – they will be caught by us and judged by a Jewish tribunal.[19]

The other Israeli evening paper, *Ma'ariv*, made an even tighter connection between the devastation of the Jews of Europe and Israeli power: "From the abyss of Jewish bereavement," wrote its editorialist,

from the mounds of ashes of the burned, from all the anonymous, nameless buried, rose the silent cry that shattered Israel: The greatest nations on earth could not catch him. The young men of Israel – did. In the battle with the Jewish mind, with our strong will to catch him, with the courage of Israeli security men – he failed [for all his satanic cunning] ... And justice will be done now. Justice befitting a lawful country and a Jewish state, millions of whose potential builders and soldiers were butchered on Eichmann's order.[20]

The entire Eichmann case, that is, his capture, the preparations for the trial, and later the trial itself, was transformed in Israeli conversation into a symbol of Israel's asserted sovereignty and power, even of a new kind of Israeli manliness, masculinity. "The panicky and primitive sentiment of the urge for revenge is the weapon of the weak," wrote one commentator. "The tireless striving for justice, however, the patience applied in the realization of all the legal procedures – are all evidence of psychological heroism, moral robustness, and even masculine character."[21]

The tone was set: the Holocaust, along with its victims, was not to be remembered for itself but rather as a metaphor, a terrible, sublime lesson to Israeli youth and the world that Jewish blood would never be abandoned or defenseless again. "Commitment through memory," as Susan Sontag put it; memory in the service of politics, of the nation. Control, of this memory and of the pursuant events related to the Eichmann project, was a key word. Ben-Gurion, who ordered the capture of Eichmann, who almost single-handedly and without the knowledge of his closest colleagues, supported the planning and implementation of the abduction scheme, and who was the architect, director, and stage manager of the preparations for the trial and the trial itself, was also the guiding spirit in

---

[19] Editorial, *Yedioth Aharonoth*, 23 May 1960 (special edition).
[20] "The Day of the Great Shock," *Ma'ariv*, 24 May 1960.
[21] Moshe Prager, "Interim Reckoning of the Eichmann Trial," *Davar*, 12 May 1961.

the process of creating the new Israeli discourse of the Holocaust from the perspective of power.[22] It was his finest hour. Only two weeks prior to his announcement in the Knesset, he had been the embattled, worn-out, and much criticized political leader, angrily greeted in the press upon his return from the historic meeting with Konrad Adenauer, from whom he demanded more money and weapons for Israel's defense.[23] Now, once again, as in the first years of statehood, he was hailed as the great, historic Zionist leader.

Although he expressed himself publicly in a measured and calculated way, his fingerprints could be detected everywhere. Articles, editorials, and op-ed pieces by various writers in different newspapers bore his imprint. Sometimes he would talk to the Israeli public through the world press. In his first interview after the announcement in the Knesset, given to a British newspaper and reproduced in the Israeli press, Ben-Gurion outlined his views on the main questions regarding the capture and trial of Eichmann. To those who argued that Israel had not existed when Eichmann's crimes were committed, that the crimes had been committed in Europe, and that therefore it was not for the State of Israel to judge Eichmann, he retorted in a general and scornful manner that "Jews in England and in Israel, who object to putting Eichmann on trial in Israel, suffer from an inferiority complex [a trait usually attributed by the Zionist–Israeli discourse to Diaspora Jews], if they do not believe that Jews and Israel have the same rights as other nations." Repeating this charge, Ben-Gurion claimed that in Israel, the juridical power is independent of the government. "The trial will be open, and every state, Argentina included, desiring to send observers to the trial, can do so. There is no punishment great enough for Eichmann's deeds," Ben-Gurion added, "but we want the trial to educate our youth. In addition, this trial is needed because the world has started to forget the Nazi horrors."[24]

Yet right from the outset he added another dimension to the planned trial. Asked by the interviewer what he meant when he said that the trial would be important because it would expose facts regarding Israel's Arab

[22] When Hannah Arendt wrote of Ben-Gurion's role in the Eichmann case in her controversial book *Eichmann in Jerusalem*, she was harshly criticized. This is, however, exactly what Hugh Trevor-Roper wrote in his *Sunday Times* article, written from Ben-Gurion's perspective, and praising Ben-Gurion for being wholly responsible for the Eichmann capture and trial. See Hugh Trevor-Roper, "Behind the Eichmann Trial," *Sunday Times* (London), 9 April 1961.

[23] Segev, *Seventh Million*, pp. 318–320.

[24] David Ben-Gurion, "Ben-Gurion: When I Listen to Nasser, it Seems that Hitler Is Talking," *Yedioth Aharonoth*, 6 June 1960.

neighbors, Ben-Gurion responded: "I was referring especially to Egypt, where many Nazis are hiding. When I listen to the speeches of the Egyptian president on world Jewry controlling America and the West, it seems to me that Hitler is talking."[25] In an interview with the *New York Times*, Ben-Gurion talked about his expectations for the forthcoming trial: "It may be," he said,

that the Eichmann trial will help to ferret out other Nazis – for example, the connection between Nazis and some Arab rulers. From what we hear on the Egyptian radio, some Egyptian propaganda is conducted on purely Nazi lines. The Egyptians charge that Jews – they usually say "Zionists" but they mean Jews – dominate the United States, Jews dominate England, Jews dominate France, and that they must be fought. I have no doubt that the Egyptian dictatorship is being instructed by the large number of Nazis who are there.[26]

Arabs = Nazis

It was not the first time that Ben-Gurion had drawn the equation "Arabs equal Nazis" or compared Arab leaders with the incarnation of absolute evil, Adolf Hitler. But he usually used this kind of rhetoric in closed talks to the political leadership of the country, to the military, or in his private correspondence. He did it mostly in times of political and personal crisis, when he felt he had to use the ultimate weapon in his political battles, either to save his regime or to impose his will on his colleagues. Even before the 1948 war, Ben-Gurion had suggested the possibility of yet another Jewish devastation, this time in the Land of Israel. At the Zionist General Council held in Zurich in late August 1947, Ben-Gurion confronted his colleagues with gloomy forecasts of an imminent war in Palestine, presenting the local enemy as the reincarnation of the Nazis.[27] The wish, undoubtedly real, that he ascribed to the Arabs, namely, total destruction of the Zionist enterprise, would hence become a recurring card in Ben-Gurion's political deck. He played this card again a few years later, when he decided, almost alone and against strong opposition from both the Right and the Left, that the State of Israel should accept financial reparations from Germany. He then justified his bold and controversial decision before his party's Central Committee, by stressing once again the existential threat the Arabs represented to the

[25] Ibid.
[26] David Ben-Gurion, "The Eichmann Case as Seen by Ben-Gurion," *New York Times Magazine*, 18 December 1960.
[27] Ben-Gurion to the Zionist General Council, 26 August 1947, Central Zionist Archive, S5/320, cited in Zertal, *From Catastrophe to Power*, p. 242.

young and precarious state. "They [the Arabs] could slaughter us tomorrow in this country ... We don't want to relive the situation that you [Holocaust survivors] endured. We don't want the Arab Nazis to come and slaughter us."[28]

The Holocaust also served him in his secret drive for the development of the ultimate weapon – an Israeli nuclear bomb – starting in the early 1950s. In this weapon he saw the only tool that could counter the fateful imbalance of numbers and power between Israel and the Arab world. His correspondence on the subject in the spring of 1963 with President John F. Kennedy is of great interest because he so directly harnessed the Holocaust in his plea for Israel's right to define its own security needs and to develop the bomb. After the 17 April 1963 proclamation of an Arab Federation, signed by Egypt, Syria, and Iraq, whose official goal was to form a military union to bring about the "liberation of Palestine"– a recurrent rhetoric in Arab leaders' summit meetings – Ben-Gurion wrote a seven-page letter to President Kennedy. This unique document, the content of which was not known at the time even to Ben-Gurion's closest colleagues, can indeed tell us more about the psychology of the old leader (he was then seventy-six, on the verge of his final, definite resignation from the premiership) than about the actual state of affairs and balance of power between Israel and the Arab world. The "liberation of Palestine" meant for him the total destruction of Israel – a new Holocaust. "[It] is impossible without the total destruction of the people in Israel," he wrote,

but the people of Israel are not in the hapless situation of the six million defenseless Jews who were wiped out by Nazi Germany ... I recall Hitler's declaration to the world about forty years ago that one of his objectives was the destruction of the entire Jewish people. The civilized world, in Europe and America, treated this declaration with indifference and equanimity. A Holocaust unequalled in human history was the result. Six million Jews in all the countries under Nazi occupation, men and women, old and young, infants and babies, were burned, strangled, buried alive.[29]

Yet it was the Eichmann event, which preceded this correspondence, that turned out to be a landmark in the process of the organized, explicit mobilization of the Holocaust in the service of Israeli politics and state policy, especially in the context of the Israeli–Arab conflict. Hannah Arendt's prophetic words, written in a letter to the German philosopher Karl Jaspers not long before she went to Jerusalem to cover the trial for the

---

[28] Ben-Gurion at the Mapai Central Committee, 13 December 1951, Labor Party Archive, 23/51, quoted in Segev, *Seventh Million*, p. 369.
[29] Ben-Gurion to John F. Kennedy, 1963, quoted in Avner Cohen, *Israel and the Bomb*, New York 1998, p. 120.

New Yorker and in response to her correspondent's fears about the way Israel would conduct the trial for its political purposes, were but a pale shadow of what actually occurred:

It's a pretty sure bet that there'll be an effort to show Israeli youth and (worse yet) the whole world certain things. Among others, that Jews who aren't Israelis will wind up in situations where they will let themselves be slaughtered like sheep. Also: that the Arabs were hand in glove with the Nazis. There are other possibilities for distorting the issue itself.[30]

The transference of the Holocaust situation on to the Middle East reality, which harsh and hostile to Israel as it was, was of a totally different kind, not only created a false sense of the imminent danger of mass destruction. It also immensely distorted the image of the Holocaust, dwarfing the magnitude of the atrocities committed by the Nazis, trivializing the unique agony of the victims and the survivors, and utterly demonizing the Arabs and their leaders. The transplanting of one situation into the other was done, before and during the trial, in two distinctive ways: first, by massive references to the presence of Nazi scientists and advisers in Egypt and other Arab countries, to the ongoing connections between Arab and Nazi leaders, and to the Nazi-like intentions and plans of the Arabs to annihilate Israel. The second means was systematic references – in the press, on the radio, and in political speeches – to the former Mufti of Jerusalem, Haj Amin El-Husseini, his connections with the Nazi regime in general and with Eichmann and his office in particular. In those references he was depicted as a prominent designer of the Final Solution and a major Nazi criminal. The deeds of Eichmann – and other Nazi criminals – were rarely mentioned without addition of the Arab–Nazi dimension.

Hugh Trevor-Roper, the British historian who was sent to Jerusalem by the London *Sunday Times* to write about the trial, also stressed its actual meaning in the context of the Israeli–Arab feud. In a long article published on the eve of the trial and written from Ben-Gurion's perspective, Trevor-Roper wrote that

Nazis are far more alive to Israel than to us. Like the Jews, their enemies too have now gone east. If several Nazi war-criminals escaped to South America, to lie low, many more have escaped to the Arab countries, to put their Nazi anti-Semitism and their German efficiency at the disposal of the new nationalist rulers of the Near East, who also have their "Final Solution" for the Jews who have settled in their midst.[31]

[30] Hannah Arendt to Karl Jaspers, 23 December 1960, quoted in Kohler and Saner (eds.), *Correspondence*, p. 416.
[31] Trevor-Roper, "Behind the Eichmann Trial."

Trevor-Roper's article was fully reprinted in the Israeli press.[32] Although he received the information about the Arab–Nazi relationships from Israeli sources – this topic did not exist as a historical issue in the nascent studies of the Holocaust – a word on the matter from this authoritative scholar of Nazism carried special weight.

As for the building of the case against the Mufti of Jerusalem as a major Nazi criminal, the hammering started during the preparations for the trial. Israeli papers, reporting on Eichmann's interrogation by the special police unit established for the case, repeatedly stressed his ties with El-Husseini, "a fanatic Jew hater, who belongs among the biggest Nazi war criminals."[33] Eichmann's testimony at the trial, Israeli journalists could foresee, would reveal the Mufti's real role in processing the plan physically to annihilate the Jews of Europe; how he prevented the rescue of the Jews; and how he urged Eichmann to exterminate the Jews of Europe in order "to solve the problem of Palestine." The link created between the Mufti and the Jewish catastrophe was unambiguous. One Israeli newspaper subliminally suggested that the Nazi order for the mass murder of European Jewry was actually inspired by the Mufti. "Various certificates and documents found in archives in Europe after the Nazi defeat," said the paper, "have proven that El-Husseini, the most extreme leader the Israeli Arabs have ever had, was one of the most important collaborators of Adolf Eichmann. Those documents indicate that the physical annihilation of the Jews of Europe began at the end of 1941, close to the Mufti's visit to Berlin in November 1941."[34]

At his party's leadership rally on the occasion of the official inauguration of the coming election campaign, which coincided with the opening of the trial, Ben-Gurion parried an opposition call on him, by a university professor, to resign so that a new government could be constituted without him, or to adopt a less belligerent Israeli policy towards the Arab countries, by saying:

Has the distinguished professor coordinated his call with the tyrant of Egypt who has just declared that Israel is an "element which must be eradicated . . . "? Would the distinguished professor dare to blame the six million Jews of Europe annihilated by the Nazis – claiming that the fault was theirs for not acquiring the love and friendship of Hitler? The danger of the Egyptian tyrant [is] like that which afflicted European Jewry . . . Is he [the professor] not aware that the Mufti was a counselor and a partner in the extermination schemes, and that, in all Arab countries, the popularity of Hitler rose during World War II? Is the distinguished professor

---

[32] *Davar*, 11 April 1961; the evening paper *Yedioth Aharonoth* also published large excerpts of the article.
[33] Shmuel Segev, "Eichmann on the Mufti," *Ma'ariv*, 10 March 1961.   [34] Ibid.

confident that, without the deterrent force of the Israeli army, which he sees as an "anti-security" and "harmful" factor, we would not be facing similar annihilation?[35]

During the trial itself, where proper legal procedures and the law of evidence were to be followed, the Mufti of Jerusalem, Haj Amin El-Husseini, appeared in more correct proportions, as a fanatic nationalist-religious Palestinian leader who, in the context of the "sacred" war he waged against the Zionist enterprise, sought help and advice from the Nazi leadership and found solace in their murderous actions during World War II. The question of the Mufti was raised right at the first sessions of the trial. In his speech for the prosecution, the State Attorney, Gideon Hausner, stressed the impression Eichmann and the Mufti made on each other, and noted that El-Husseini asked Himmler to provide him, when he entered Jerusalem at the head of the Axis troops, with a special adviser from Eichmann's department to help him solve the Jewish question. On the eve of the evidence phase of the trial, the press filled in the details, and stressed the "role" of the Mufti in the murder of Europe's Jews, and his contacts with the Nazi leadership were elaborated. After the Mufti's visits to Eichmann's bureau in Berlin and to Himmler's, Eichmann told Dieter Wisliceny that he had lectured the Mufti in detail about the solution of the Jewish problem in Europe, and that the highly impressed Mufti told him about his request that Himmler appoint a personal adviser from Eichmann's staff after the occupation of Palestine by the Germans. "In the wake of the Mufti's intervention, Himmler issued a general ban on the emigration of Jews from the occupied countries to Palestine. Himmler's stand, resulting from the Mufti's intercession, influenced later negotiations for rescue of Jews, and particularly the Jews of Hungary," said the prosecutor[36]

Documents presented to the court indeed showed that the Mufti had tried to interfere with plans to transfer Jewish children out of Bulgaria and Hungary.[37] These were acts of total evil, yet none of the documents proved that it was the Mufti's interference that prevented the rescue of the children, nor could they sustain the claim that he was a major contributor to the Final Solution. Despite this lack of evidence, the Israeli prosecutor insisted on inflating the Mufti's role in the planning and implementation of the Nazi crimes, devoting precious hours in court to the issue. The Israeli press followed suit. Regardless of the dubious legality of dragging the specter of the Mufti into the Jerusalem courtroom where Eichmann and the Nazi

[35] Ben-Gurion to Mapai activists, 4 April 1961, fully reproduced in *Ma'ariv*, 19 April 1961.
[36] See for example, *Davar*, 25 May 1961; *Ma'ariv*, 5 June 1961.   [37] Ibid.

system were being prosecuted, this move could certainly contribute, even if inadvertently, to the distortion and minimization of the exceptional, unprecedented scope and meaning of the Nazi crimes, and the responsibility of the true perpetrators.[38]

It was, however, very much in line with the specific political and pedagogical aspect that Ben-Gurion wanted to assign to the trial. The inflation of the Mufti's image and his role in the extermination of European Jewry was not confined to the educational and political act of the Eichmann trial. It also seeped into serious historiography of the Holocaust, and found a place, both overtly and by implication, even in a publication which was supposed to be an indisputable and authoritative source of knowledge of the Holocaust. I am referring to the *Encyclopedia of the Holocaust*, a Yad Vashem international project, which was completed in the 1980s. In his book on the presence of the Holocaust in American life, the American historian Peter Novick noted the astounding fact that the Mufti was depicted by the *Encyclopedia*'s editors as one of the great designers and perpetrators of the Final Solution: his entry is twice as long as each of the entries devoted to Goebbels and Goering, longer than the two combined entries for Heydrich and Himmler and longer than the entry on Eichmann.[39] One might add that in the Hebrew edition of the *Encyclopedia*, the entry on El-Husseini is almost as long as that on Hitler.

National pedagogy

Why now? Why did Ben-Gurion maintain relative silence on the issue of the Holocaust for more than a decade and launch his spectacular educational display so late? What had changed since he told his colleagues at his party's (Mapai) Central Committee, up in arms on the question of reparations from Germany, that "what we have to say on the things they [the Nazis] did to us we will say if we need to say it . . . we will speak out, when opportunity comes, but preferably not too early neither too often, because if you do, this will arouse contempt . . . if a new Jeremiah arises – he will have his say"?[40] Was this the proper "opportunity" he had been awaiting? Had a new Jeremiah arisen? The fact that Eichmann was captured only in the spring of 1960 does not explain everything. As

---

[38] For the elaboration of this claim, see Arendt, *Eichmann in Jerusalem*, pp. 223–225, 230 and passim.
[39] Peter Novick, *The Holocaust in American Life*, New York 1999, p. 158.
[40] Ben-Gurion at the Mapai Central Committee, 13 December 1951, Labor Party Archive, 23/51, quoted in Segev, *Seventh Million*, p. 209.

mentioned earlier, Israel had willfully abstained from Nazi hunting during the 1950s and only in 1957 did Ben-Gurion give the Israeli Mossad the green light to launch its pursuit of Eichmann, who had for some time been in the agency's sights.[41]

Ben-Gurion himself did not believe in conducting historical reckonings with former enemies or in retribution, and was aware of the pointlessness of thoughts and declarations of revenge of many of his associates. If Israel had been capable of punishing countries, Ben-Gurion would have chosen first and foremost to take revenge on real, contemporary enemies, whom he regarded as substantial threats to Israel's existence and welfare. "Even if I could do it [take revenge], I would act first against Iraq," he declared at his party meeting in December 1951 regarding the Reparations. As a pragmatic, voluntarist leader, Ben-Gurion always concentrated on achieving one large goal at a time. The 1950s were for him the decade of building and fortifying the infrastructure of the state, with German money as it was; of the "ingathering of the exiles"; of creating an army; and of securing Israel's standing as a legitimate state among other states. Now that this formative stage was coming to its close, now that Israeli society was more diversified and divided, now that Ben-Gurion was coming to the end of his tenure, and his regime was increasingly contested, the time had come for a great project of national consciousness building.

The Eichmann trial was, from this point of view, a most adequate occasion for the establishment of renewed national unity through memory. It achieved this by mobilizing the utter political power of the Holocaust and its victims to create that "common city (*cité commune*) between the living and the dead," in the words of Jules Michelet, by "exhuming the dead," and by giving them "a second life" and a new meaning, "the real meaning of their sayings and deeds [and their lives and deaths] that they themselves did not understand."[42] The trial would also become Ben-Gurion's belated answer to his many opponents' claims, relating to the German reparations money and the Kastner affair, that he had "forgotten" the Holocaust, had "sold" the memory of the victims for German money, and had not done enough, as the leader of the Jewish community in Palestine during World War II, to come to the aid of his brethren in Europe.[43] The Eichmann trial would

---

[41] Segev, *Seventh Million*, pp. 324–325.

[42] Jules Michelet, "Histoire du xix siècle," in *Oeuvres complètes*, Paris 1982, vol. XXI, p. 268; Roland Barthes (ed.), *Michelet par lui-même*, Bourges 1954, p. 92; both are cited in White, *Metahistory*, pp. 158–159.

[43] See chapter 2 of the present book.

thus provide Ben-Gurion with a means of expressing his own overall version of history and memory, his own legacy concerning the way things happened and the way things ought to have happened.

All these evidently contributed to the reconstruction of the waning narrative of Ben-Gurion as "father of the nation," the architect and founder of the state, just as he was now the designer of the show trial which was aimed at reconstructing the mythical discourse of redemption out of destruction under the leadership of the prophet-leader. These were the messages, explicit or latent, which were attributed to the Eichmann trial by its shaper and organizer, and which were conveyed through dozens of statements made by him and by his associates in the interval between the announcement of Eichmann's capture and the opening of the trial, at which Ben-Gurion, as a rule, would not be present, leaving the arena solely to legal deliberations.

The most characteristic and focused Ben-Gurionic statement about the trial was voiced, by no accident, obliquely, by a foreign authority, supposedly alien to the local scene, and hence of particular validity. This was the above-mentioned lengthy article, by the renowned British historian, Hugh Trevor-Roper. Indeed, Ben-Gurion could not have found himself and his vision a more eloquent and authoritative formulator than the historian of Nazism, whose article in the *Sunday Times* was written entirely from Ben-Gurion's perspective, sometimes even in Ben-Gurion's own words. As such this text should be reproduced here extensively:

To Mr. Ben-Gurion, Eichmann is a symbol, and his trial is to be symbolic, too, symbolic not merely of slow-footed retribution, not merely of world Jewry's martyrdom in Hitler's Europe, but even of a longer struggle. It will commemorate at its highest crisis the struggle which has lasted all Mr. Ben-Gurion's own lifetime and out of which the present State of Israel was born. For the whole Eichmann policy is, in a particular way, *personal to Mr. Ben-Gurion. He and he alone* authorized and ordered the entire process: the long, patient trial, the bold defiant capture in a distant land, the skilful, secret abduction across half the globe. So *personally*, so *privately* did the Prime Minister act that all Israeli officialdom was taken by surprise . . . such a coup perhaps had to be personal; for whoever ordered it, with all its calculable and incalculable consequences, took enormous risks. And even at home, or at least within the Jewish world, there was the possibility of disapproval. Jews would certainly not deny the justice of revenge on Eichmann, but some of them might well deny the expediency, in the long run, of so belated a trial. This in fact is what many Jews outside Israel (and some within it) do feel. They feel that the trial may be misinterpreted, and that the Prime Minister of Israel has unnecessarily committed the whole of world Jewry to a policy from whose unpredictable consequences there is now no escape. However, in all these respects, Mr. Ben-Gurion has triumphed at least in Israel . . . *the personal policy of Mr. Ben-Gurion has led to a personal triumph.* In spite of great risks at every stage, he has brought it to its logical climax. And in doing so, *he has re-created, for a time at least, his own original image as the Joshua* who finally established his people in their Promised Land. For that image, it must be admitted, has recently *lost some of its old radiance.* There have been deep internal rifts in Israel, many of them caused by *the powerful personality of the Prime Minister himself* – or at least by the problem of finding a successor to him in a new State whose institutions are not yet firm and whose enemies are so many and so close. But now, on the eve of this great *ceremonial trial,* such rifts are closed, or at least temporarily papered over, by public agreement with the Prime Minister's aims and admiration of his skill. Outwardly, all Israeli parties, from extreme Right to extreme Left, are one in this. Even the Prime Minister's severest critics and opponents have congratulated him on the imagination and bold decision which have led, through such hazards, to such success [my italics].

According to Trevor-Roper, Ben-Gurion's rivals and critics supported his move because, like him, they were aware of the long historical chain, in which the destruction of European Jewry was only one link, and because they understood the need to inculcate its meanings and the justification for the establishment and existence of Israel in Israelis and in the rest of the world, particularly since "a new generation is growing up which knew not Hitler, to which the old persecution is not a personal memory and which takes the State of Israel, born out of so much blood and anguish and idealism, for granted," and also for that "large minority of Israelis who, having come to the new State from the Middle East and Africa, never felt the impact of Nazism at close quarters," and who were now a majority of the population of Israel. Everybody sees now "the need to remind a new generation, as forcefully as possible, of the days of wandering, of persecution and tribulation in the wilderness, of the grim Pharaoh in the monolithic Reich-Chancellery, and, beyond that, of the pioneers, the old Founding Fathers: the tradition and the Patriarchs." The beginning, the dynamism and idealism of the pioneers, the tiny besieged, boycotted social Jewish experiment, squeezed between the Arabs and the sea, as Trevor-Roper described it, derived their meaning and justification from the Nazis' evil acts and could no longer be merely "the last form of European imperialism" as many considered them to be. On the other hand, the new state which arose on the ruins of the Jewish people and was depicted as its antithesis, while perceived as the avenger of the blood of millions of murdered Jews ("We, the sovereign Jewish people in Israel, are the redeemers of the blood of six million Jews," said Ben-Gurion), this state construed the Holocaust into the great, teleological process of Israeli redemption, since for Ben-Gurion "the trial is not so much the punishment of a particularly odious criminal, as the exposure of a *sacred experience* in the history of Israel" (my italics).

In order to preserve and cherish such memories what better way is there than to hold a "public trial," which not only

revives the memory of past agony, but also, in a dramatic manner, gives notice of present strength, telling the whole world and the soft Jews of the Dispersion, that Jewry, once so cowed, now has the power, through its only effective representative, the Middle-Eastern State of Israel, to trace and seize and try its persecutors, wherever they may have hidden?

Who can protect world Jewry against a new Hitler, a new Eichmann, if that state should fail, asked Trevor-Roper.[44]

The Israeli judges made every effort to follow legal procedure during the trial's sessions.[45] Yet it was Ben-Gurion's trial, and it was a show trial by design. Three months before the trial opened, on 10 January 1961, the government submitted to the Knesset a bill amending the Courts (Offenses Punishable by Death) Law. The amended law suggested major changes in trials whose only possible verdict was the death penalty. According to the Israeli legal procedure, which adopted British tradition, a defendant who pleaded guilty was automatically convicted, and the court could only debate the sentence. Yet the State of Israel would not let Eichmann set the rules of the planned trial. In order to prevent the trial from being cut short, in case Eichmann pleaded guilty, the new law, unofficially called "the Eichmann law," stated that "when the accused pleads guilty in answer to the information, the court may continue the proceedings as if the accused had not pleaded gilty."[46] The intention behind the problematic "ad-hominem" amendment was transparent to most parliamentarians, and to representatives of the press, and yet everybody went along with the legislation.[47] Ben-Gurion himself declared a few days before the solemn opening of the trial that "the fate of Eichmann, the person, has no interest for me whatsoever. What is important is the spectacle."[48] As Trevor-Roper knowingly wrote, to Ben-Gurion the trial was not so much about the punishment of a particularly

---

[44] Trevor-Roper, "Behind the Eichmann Trial."

[45] See among others, Pnina Lahav, *Judgement in Jerusalem: Chief Justice Simon Agranat and the Zionist Century*, Berkeley 1997, pp. 145–148.

[46] Courts (Offences Punishable by Death) Law, 5721–1961, passed by the Knesset on 31 January 1961, and published in *Sefer Ha'khukim*, **325** (6 February 1961), p. 24. The Bill and an Explanatory Note were published in *Hatza'ot Khok*, 445 of 5721, p. 72; see also Y. Rosenthal, "Eichmann Law No. 1 Presented to the Knesset," *Ha'aretz*, 11 January 1961.

[47] Rosenthal, "Eichmann Law No. 1 Presented to the Knesset." The amendment was extracted from Israel's book of laws in 1965, not long after the Eichamnn affair was concluded and done with.

[48] Ben-Gurion, "Interview with Prime Minister David Ben-Gurion," *Yedioth Aharonoth*, 31 March 1961.

odious criminal as it was about the "exposure of a sacred experience in the history of Israel."

In praising Ben-Gurion for the "spectacular" achievement of the capture of Eichmann, "which has led to this *spectacular* trial," Trevor-Roper also expressed some fears, thus exposing the innate paradox of the trial, and also its not so hidden connection to the Kastner tragedy: "If long enough to prove justice," he wrote,

[the trial] may be too long to be effective as *propaganda*: the solemn act of historical vindication may be submerged in legal questions of procedure or competence ... The world, however unfairly, may refuse to believe that Israeli judges can, in such a case, be humanly objective, and a new anti-Semitism may be stirred to life by a single, inadequate act of revenge. And who can tell what compromising revelations of Nazi–Jewish collaboration may not be exposed by a resourceful defence? The recent Kastner case, which rose out of such revelations, and led to others, did nobody any good. These are the real dangers which still lie ahead. Because of them, Mr. Ben-Gurion's personal triumph, though it may still be completed, is at present only half-won. The active, *spectacular* part is over; the more difficult part is to come. The trial, to some extent, is his trial too.[49]

To prove Eichmann's guilt there was no need for the "spectacular trial" Ben-Gurion staged. In order to render justice and punish the criminal, "it was sufficient for the prosecution to prove Eichmann's responsibility for one death-transport only, which he planned and ordered," wrote Nathan Alterman, Israel's poet laureate and a close associate of Ben-Gurion, in his prestigious weekly column.[50] Yet the trial aimed at other goals: it aimed to be a well-targeted course in history for his countrypeople and the international community as well. "I want them to know," Ben-Gurion repeatedly said in his interviews. The main lesson he wanted to bequeath concerned Israel's legitimate striving for power. The desire to legitimize the will to power was the sub-text of the entire trial and of the discourse which grew out of it. "It is necessary that our youth remember what happened to the Jewish people ... They should be taught the lesson that Jews are not sheep to be slaughtered but a people who can hit back – as Jews did in the War of Independence."[51] In his radio speech that year on Independence Day, which fell close to the opening of the trial, Ben-Gurion established the mythical link between Israel and the heroism of

[49] Trevor-Roper, "Behind the Eichmann Trial" (my italics).
[50] Nathan Alterman, "The Seventh Column," *Davar*, 12 May 1961. Later, Alterman would write quite the opposite, saying that the "Jerusalem trial was a historic trial because it was anti-historic, which, for the first time bound the massacre of the Jews not in history volumes but in a Jewish legal-criminal file, marked 'Criminal File 41/60'," *Davar*, 7 June 1961.
[51] Ben-Gurion, "The Eichmann Case."

military might, and between the heroism of ancient times and of modern Israel 2,000 years later. The ancient heroism of Bar-Kochba's men and the modern courage of the Israeli army's fighters and of the young, "in whose ears the cry of the blood of the six million constantly echoed, and they spared no effort or risk or stratagem till they discovered [Eichmann's] hiding place and brought him to the only country worthy of trying him," this unique kind of courage and heroism, ancient and newly found, had the power to redeem the blood of the six million victims.[52] Moshe Dayan, then Minister of Agriculture in Ben-Gurion's government, for his part added a new element to the objectives of the trial, which was to prove long-lived: the sanctification of every square inch of the soil of Israel for Jewish settlement. Speaking of the Arab refugees, and welcoming the fact that the Arabs had fled the country during the 1948 war, Dayan said that "what is becoming clear at the Eichmann trial is the active passivity of the world in the face of the murder of the six million. There can be no doubt that only this country and only this people can protect the Jews against a second Holocaust. And hence every inch of Israeli soil is intended only for Jews."[53]

Gratuitous sentiments

The mentality of a given group, its self-image and conceptual discourse, is to be detected not necessarily in the conversation of its leaders but rather in the language used by its secondary elites or common people. The Eichmann trial swept through Israel's language and images. Everything was now discussed anew in relation to the trial: Israeli politics, Israeli youth, world Jewry, Holocaust Remembrance Day, lessons of the Holocaust, the security of Israel, and the Arabs. Committees for the study of the relevant issues were established. The trial was ever-present, hovering over the country from end to end, like a living organism, as if it had taken on entity, character of its own, even if not always in conscious and formulated fashion. "The country continues its life and its movement day and night," wrote Haim Guri two weeks after the trial opened,

and *it*, this trial, accompanies it. The life of the country continues and *it* accompanies it. One cannot sense it outwardly far from Bet Ha'am. But it seems to be in the air and the water and in the dust on the trees. And when *it* is abandoned, forgotten, behind people's backs, *it* returns without warning and is reflected in their eyes.[54]

---

[52] Ben-Gurion in a radio speech for 1961 Independence Day, *Davar*, 22 April 1961.
[53] Moshe Dayan, *Davar*, 1 July 1961.
[54] Haim Guri, "Facing the Glass Booth," *Lamer'hav*, 24 April 1961, reproduced in *Facing the Glass Booth*, p. 25 (my italics).

Eichmann's "lessons" were also sucked into the election campaign, which was launched almost simultaneously with the trial, and the Nazi criminal was on every party apparatchik's lips, serving many purposes. The Holocaust was thus dragged into intraparty quarrels and served daily political issues. In his own, dominant party, Ben-Gurion had his epigones, and as is the rule with epigones, their use of the Holocaust often carried a note of farce. "The Eichmann trial is the trial of the Jewish people against eternal anti-Semitism in all nations and through all generations," said Mapai's Secretary General in an electoral speech. "It is also the trial of the future. 150 meters from the courtroom there is a border, and behind that border *thousands of Eichmanns* lie in wait, proclaiming explicitly, 'what Eichmann has not completed, we will.'"[55] At a political rally in the Negev town of Dimona, another of Mapai's bureaucrats claimed that "the Nasserite policy of 'throwing the Jews into the sea,' is essentially no different from Eichmann's Final Solution. The events that have been revealed in this case [the Eichmann trial] must become a warning of what can happen when a nation does not have a defense force."[56] At a meeting of women members of Mapai, convened just after the opening of the trial, the "lesson" was formulated clearly: "In light of the Eichmann trial, and the annals of the Holocaust," one should know that "Tzahal [IDF, the Israeli army] is not a function in the reality of our lives: it is a value."[57]

Israeli militarism and security consciousness were boosted by the trial and the new narrative it produced. The trial stressed the "sanctity" of the army, conceived of now as the venerated, holy executor of the last will and testament of the six million. The military parade on Independence Day during the year of the trial became an occasion for many writers to mix time, space, and realities, the "here" and the "there," in hazy images overloaded with heavy metaphors and sentimentality, juxtaposing the unjuxtaposable, using multiple repetitions, aiming at evoking low and gratuitous sentiments. The following is but one example:

In the march of the soldiers of Israel on the outskirts of Jerusalem, I have seen columns of a million empty shoes . . . shoes opening their dark interiors, like the dark and bleak opening of an empty shelter which has lost its dwellers, like the valley of death of the blackened ovens of Auschwitz . . . and slowly they walk, quietly, clinging like shadows to the march of the columns and, in a mute voice that tears the

---

[55] Yosef Almogi, "There are Thousands of Eichmanns near the Borders of Israel," *Davar*, 12 June 1961 (my italics).
[56] "The Eichmann Trial – A Warning against Absence of Defence Force," *Davar*, 29 May 1961.
[57] "Y. Simhoni: The Eichmann Trial's Conclusions: Security is the Key to our Existence," *Davar*, 11 May 1961.

heavens, they say: We are here! To the captivating and delightful clatter of the shoes
of Israel's women-soldiers attach the marching sounds of the shoes of those who
are no more ... the shoes of the slaughtered daughters of Israel, whose footsteps
echo the cry and mourning of their youth in the woods of Poland and the graveyards
of Ponar ... On this day, a never-ending column of the shoes of the murdered, baby
shoes, shoes of women, women in bloom ... shoes with no flesh or foot or body in
them, but shoes with eyes and souls. And their tread echoes from the ground ...
The day will come and our marching feet will thunder: "we are here!" How they
thunder, those marching feet, awesome and terrible ... they rose up from the walls
of the courtroom – the hall of the people in Zion. They emerged from the blood-
stained scorched parchments brandished by Gideon the prosecutor in their name
and in the name of Israel everywhere, the reckoning for the spilt blood of six million
... six millions of shoes, from out of which there plead and scream the eyes of
children and their mothers ... a million pure innocent souls crying for restitution ...
they are marching, and their terrible voice mingles with the blast of the trumpets
and the song of hope: "We are here!"[58]

In organizing the trial as a historic, continuous morality play, not only
did Ben-Gurion establish the belated link between pastless Israeli youth,
and their murdered grandparents; he also created the teleological, indispensable connection between the agony and death of the Jewish Diaspora
and the establishment and the right to exist of the State of Israel, including its daily practices, especially the military ones. Thus, the trial gave
new meaning to the fight against the Arab enemy and to the possibility of
death in this fight – the belated vindication of the fathers' helplessness in
the face of the Nazi enemy. One enemy was combined with the other.
Defense of one's country became a sacred mission endowed with the
weight of the ultimate catastrophe. And the lesson was learned and
memorized by an entire generation of Israeli youth for whom the trial
was their first, stunning encounter with the Holocaust, an encounter
which was to shape them for years to come.[59] The life and death of
Ofer Feniger, one of many, sensitive young "children of the dream,"
one of the golden youths of the Israeli Zionist utopia, were the very stuff
of which this atoning and redemptive discourse was made. "I feel it in the
devastation and terror of the wise Jewish eyes behind the electrified
barbed wire, which saw all the sufferings," he wrote in the wake of the
Eichmann trial.

---

[58] Haim Taharlev, "The Double March," *Davar*, 10 May 1961.
[59] I can testify for myself, a high school student at the time, and for my friends: the trial was
an event of major influence for us. Although my father served as a soldier in Europe in
World War II, worked with Jewish survivors after the war, and published a book about his
war experiences; and although his entire family perished in the Holocaust, he never talked
about it at home. The trial was thus my first encounter with the horrors, brought to us by
the trial witnesses' testimonies that were broadcast live.

And I know that out of this total helplessness the terrible need grows within me to be strong; tearfully strong, strong and ferocious like a sword; serene and cruel. I want to know that these eyes will never again stare from behind barbed wire. For this I need to be strong! If we are all strong! Strong, proud Jews! Never again to be led to the slaughter.[60]

Four years after this letter was written Ofer Feniger was killed during the 1967 war, in the battle for Jerusalem.

A beleaguered nation

"Human beings," writes Michel-Rolph Trouillot, "participate in history both as actors and narrators."[61] They make things happen, they relate in their own ways the things that have happened, and their lives themselves could be read as texts, as history. In his life and premature death in the battle of East Jerusalem, the good Israeli soldier-boy Ofer Feniger, like many other young Israelis killed in the war, narrated the teleological story of *Hurban U'geulah* (Devastation and Redemption), forged by Ben-Gurion by means of the Eichmann trial. By "rescuing" Israel from the allegedly imminent, Holocaust-like devastation it faced on the eve of the war, while at the same time "liberating" the sacred, ancient heart of Eretz Israel including the Wailing Wall in Jerusalem, Ofer Feniger enacted with his own body the recurring Jewish historical pattern of national revival as the outcome of destruction. His death, like that of hundreds of other Israeli soldiers in the war, was thought to have saved the millions who might have been annihilated had Israel not gone to war and won as spectacularly as it did. "There would have been no Jewish refugees had Israel lost the war," declared Israel's Foreign Minister Abba Eban at the United Nations Special Assembly after Israel's victory: "There would have been two million corpses added to the six million Holocaust victims." And he added that "no individual who lived in Israel in the days between 25 May and 5 June can ever forget the atmosphere of devastation which hovered over our stressed and pressured country ... surrounded and besieged ... bombarded day and night with prophecies of the approaching end."[62]

---

[60] Ofer Feniger to Yael, *Ha'olam Haia Betokhi* (*The World Was Inside Me*), Tel Aviv 1972, pp. 52–53.

[61] Michel-Rolph Trouillot, *Silencing the Past: Power and the Production of History*, Boston 1994, p. 2.

[62] Abba Eban responding at the UN to King Hussein's complaints over Isarel's actions in the war, reproduced in *Ma'ariv*, 27 June 1967. The quotation from Eban's speech, delivered in English, was translated here from Hebrew.

Through this kind of discourse, which prevailed in the wake of the war and Israel's sweeping victory, the deaths of Feniger and other young soldiers and the war itself were endowed with two-fold sanctity – as a war of rescue from great catastrophe and a war of redemption of the ancient land – and were thus elevated to the sphere of sacred war and "beautiful death," the bricks and mortar of nation-building and maintenance.[63] In a speech to the Knesset shortly after the war, Prime Minister Levi Eshkol said that the Israeli army was a mighty fighting force, as the world had learned, not only because its soldiers and commanders were excellent fighters but also, and above all, "because in the heart of each and every soldier beats the sense of the nation's mission in its land ... When he fights, he embodies the significance of the unique, age-old Jewish history. He fights not only for the life of the nation but also for its redemption."[64]

The capture of the holy sites of the Jewish scriptures and the ancestors' mythified graves – located in the conquered territories – transformed the 1967 war into a religious transcendental experience and turned land and stones into sacred entities. "Even the free thinkers among us talk about an experience that is in its essence religious," wrote Eliezer (Elie) Wiesel upon his return from the "liberated" Wailing Wall in the eastern, Arab sector of Jerusalem:

They say to me: here is the Wall. I don't believe. I don't and I can't believe ... Deep inside I somehow know that it is true, that this Wall is that Wall. What kind of Jew will not immediately recognize it, even if he never saw it before? ... It is me standing and looking at it, as if struck by a dream. Looking at it, holding my breath, is like looking at a living body, omnipotent and almighty. A human entity which has transcended itself – and those observing it – beyond and above time. An entity that transferred me to a far-away and uncanny place, in which stones too, have their own will, their own fate and memory.[65]

Yet, as already mentioned, the war was understood in another dimension, even by some prominent Holocaust survivors such as Elie Wiesel, who should have known better. Here is what Wiesel, the former inmate of Auschwitz and Buchenwald, wrote right after the war. Although it was written in the euphoric days of the victory it projects and represents the atmosphere of the days preceding it:

The enemy predicted but did not grasp his own prediction. The war became total. He was defeated not only by the soldiers and commanders of the Israeli army,

---

[63] For the elaboration of the term "beautiful death," see Lyotard, *The Differend, Phrases in Dispute*, pp. 99–101; Vernant, *Mortals and Immortals*, pp. 50–75.
[64] Levi Eshkol's speech was reproduced in *Davar*, 13 June 1967.
[65] Eliezer (Elie) Wiesel, *Yedioth Aharonoth*, 16 June 1967.

but by Jewish history. Two thousand years of sufferings, expectations, and hope were *mobilized in the battle*, as well as the *millions of Holocaust victims*. As clouds of fire they came and protected their inheritors. And no enemy can ever overcome them ... The enemy lost the war also because of the Holocaust, that is, because of some expressions he employed. Not knowing that there are words that cannot be expressed in our generation, in regard to the Jewish people; not imagining that one can destroy one's world not only in one hour but also in a word. He was too quick to threaten the annihilation of Israel, and that was one of his biggest mistakes ... A few words from Nasser sufficed to turn this event into a war of the entire Jewish people.[66]

How Israel could have perceived itself – to the point of collective, if subdued, hysteria, and in disturbing detachment from reality – to be in imminent danger of mass destruction on the eve of June 1967 is worthy of analysis here, since this has much to do with the political, collective memory called up by the Eichmann case and cultivated since then in Israel. Ben-Gurion's legacy to his people by means of the Eichmann trial was two-fold: eternal hatred of the Jews still endured despite the existence of the State of Israel, and the Nazi-like enemy was still rallied at the gates of the nation-in-siege. "The hatred is still seething," he said in his nation-wide broadcast for Independence Day in 1961, the year of the trial:

On this holiday it is our obligation to warn the people of Israel that the independence we gained thirteen years ago is neither complete nor guaranteed. The hatred for Israel that brought about, twenty years ago, the extermination of two-thirds of European Jewry, who had not sinned or done wrong; this hatred is still simmering among the rulers of our neighboring countries, plotting to eradicate us, and dozens of Nazi experts are their tutors and advisers in their hatred for Israel and the Jews of the world.[67]

This was the legacy of the trial: the dangers which Israel confronted and still confronts are Nazi in essence and scope, and any military threat or apparent threat to Israel means a new holocaust. Statements of this kind were commonplace after the Eichmann trial at all levels of Israeli discourse, and Auschwitz was at its center. "Peace," explained one of the prominent members of Israel's security establishment, "peace does not depend upon us, but it does depend upon us to ensure that Auschwitz will not recur."[68] These endlessly repeated expressions in Israel's public life evoked an older, more traditional symbol system, which seemed to express more adequately the perpetual Israeli condition: that of a lone,

[66] Ibid. (my italics).
[67] David Ben-Gurion, broadcast for Independence Day, reproduced in *Davar*, 22 May 1961.
[68] Israel Galili at Kibbutz Lohamei Ha'Getaot (The Ghetto Fighters' Kibbutz), 27 April 1967, quoted in Liebman and Don-Yehiya, *Civil Religion in Israel*, p. 184.

beleaguered nation surrounded by an antagonistic, anti-Semitic world, and that of the eternal victim.[69]

History as a weapon

Wars, like other great "hot" events, eventually generate fierce historiographical battles. The transition from totemic to critical history of the "Six Day War" (1967) – which, although the shortest war in Israel's history, continues by other means to this day – is in its infancy, due to the gradual opening of archives and the growing impact of processes of "demystification" of the relevant historical organizations or protagonists, and by force of changes in concepts of writing history and the self-conceptions of the societies involved. The narrative of the averted catastrophe or the redemption of the ancient land created by the June 1967 war is now confronted by critical versions of the question of the inevitability of the war: was this war the inexorable outcome of the constraints of the Israel–Arab dispute or of internal Israeli economic, social, and political interests, which contributed to the exacerbation of hostile acts on the eve of the war, and exaggerated the claim that Israel was under existential threat in order to justify the early launching of a pre-emptive strike?

It is not my intention to propose here a new version of the events which led to the outbreak of war, but rather to discuss the Holocaust dimension which was inserted systematically into the collective talk and imagination in Israel on the eve of war, its roots, motives, and aims. It should also be noted that the historical sequence briefly presented here is accepted nowadays by most historians of the war. A series of accelerating developments along Israel's borders in April and May 1967, in Arab capitals and within Israel, eventually led to the outbreak of the war, which in the final analysis was the outcome of a chain of misjudgments and miscalculations on both sides.[70] In most of the events that preceded the war, it is generally acknowledged that Israel played the active part. To go back a bit, tension between Israel and Syria over the issue of the Jordan River's water distribution had already started to escalate by 1964. In September 1966, Israeli Chief of Staff Yitzhak Rabin sent a warning to Syria, implying that Israel intended to overthrow the Ba'ath regime. On 4 November

---

[69] Liebman and Don-Yehiya, *Civil Religion in Israel*, p. 142.
[70] This summary of the events preceding the outbreak of the war is based on standard works on the subject, such as Richard B. Parker, *The Politics of Miscalculation in the Middle East*, Bloomington, IN, 1993; William Quandt, *Peace Process: American Diplomacy and the Arab–Israeli Conflict since 1967*, Berkeley 1993; for the Israeli side I based my sequence of events mainly on David Shaham, *Israel: 50 Ha'shanim* (*Israel: Fifty Years*), Tel Aviv 1998, pp. 242–262.

1966, Egypt and Syria signed a mutual defense agreement. The same month, after a land mine placed by the Palestinian organization PLO had killed three Israeli soldiers, the Israeli army retaliated in broad daylight in the Palestinian village of Samu, destroying houses and inflicting heavy casualties on the Jordanian army which intervened. The scale of the operation, which extended beyond authorized parameters, outraged moderate Prime Minister Levi Eshkol.

On 7 April 1967, following an exchange of provocations on both sides of the border, the Israeli air force shot down six Syrian aircraft over Syria, one of them over the capital, and, on 11 May Chief of Staff Rabin again declared that Israel's aim in a future conflict with Syria would be to occupy Damascus and topple the Ba'ath regime. The next day, the Soviet Union announced that Israel was mobilizing to attack Syria; in response, the Egyptian leader, Gamal Abdel Nasser, ordered Egyptian troops into the demilitarized Sinai. On 17 May, Israel began to mobilize its reserve forces and by 20 May completed its mobilization, straining the economy and increasing pressure to end the crisis quickly. On 21–22 May the Egyptian Commander in Chief ordered two actions that caused a rapid deterioration in the already tense situation, and for which, some historians argue, he did not have Nasser's approval: reconnaissance flights over the Israeli nuclear installation in Dimona and the removal of the United Nations Emergency Forces (UNEF), which served as a buffer on the border between Israel and Egypt. Nasser, it is now agreed, wanted the UN forces only redeployed, not removed, but Abdel Ammar's more sweeping demands and the obtuseness of UN Secretary General U Thant brought about the UNEF withdrawal. The crisis escalated on 23 May when Egypt declared the closing of the Tiran Straits to Israeli vessels.

Yet the specific position of the Egyptian troops in the Sinai desert and, as two Egyptian generals acknowledged in their memoirs, the general confusion, lack of supplies, and absence of battle plans, are evidence of Nasser's plan to retain the Egyptian forces in the Sinai in a defensive posture over a long period and not for offensive purposes. The Egyptian moves, however, were accompanied by Nasser's harsh rhetoric and blunt threats to annihilate Israel, which were broadcast daily on the Hebrew programs of Egyptian national radio, heard in Israel, and reproduced in its press. Nasser's threats undoubtedly played a crucial role in intensifying the anxiety of Israel's population. These wild speeches of the Egyptian leader also served those on the Israeli side who, for their own reasons, urged the launching of an Israeli pre-emptive strike. In any case, in the absence of means of judging Nasser's and other Arab leaders' plans for Israel's Jewish population in the event of a military victory over Israel, it is nonetheless possible to accept the assertion that they indeed did mean to destroy it. The relevant question, however, is not so much Nasser's intentions or desires, but the capabilities of the Arab world in June 1967 and Egypt's specific military operational plans aimed at realizing these desires.

In Israel the relative complacency that characterized the first week of the crisis was replaced by mounting tension and anxiety even among elite circles and decision makers. They were familiar with the facts and had no reason to doubt Israel's military ability to defend itself and win any war. According to army intelligence evaluations at the time, Egypt would not be ready to wage a war against Israel until 1970–1971 at the earliest. Nasser himself acknowledged time and again that Egypt was not yet ready for what he called the decisive battle.[71] On 28 February 1968, Rabin said in an interview with the French paper Le Monde, that he did not "believe that Nasser wanted the war. The two divisions he dispatched to Sinai were not sufficient to wage a war. He knew it and we knew it." It should also be noted here that, a few days before the outbreak of the war, Israel secretly completed the production of its first two nuclear bombs, which were ready for launching if necessary.[72] Yet despite all this, from a certain point in time during the crisis, the threat of destruction began to be broached, and many were deluded into believing in the danger of mass annihilation or were gripped by real dread at such a possibility. Nasser's brutal threats and the announcements of his intention to destroy Israel and to cast its population into the sea, the rhetoric of hatred of other Arab leaders, the sight of deserted streets in the cities after Israel's reserve forces were mobilized and the almost total absence of young men from the civilian landscape – contributed to the growing anxiety, but they alone could not explain the hysteria. By 20 May the Israeli army (regular and reserve units) was mobilized and positioned along the borders. It totaled some 300,000 soldiers, the lion's share of Israel's working population. The economy was literally paralyzed, a state of affairs that no country can tolerate for a substantial period of time. Almost every civilian activity was suspended; people emptied supermarket shelves, and some fled the country.[73]

[71] After the war, Chief of Staff Yitzhak Rabin said that, if anything, Israeli intelligence overestimated the strength of the Egyptian army; see Yitzhak Rabin, interview in Yedioth Aharonoth, 4 October 1967, quoted in David Kimche and Dan Bawli, The Sandstorm, London 1968, pp. 135–136.

[72] My claim regarding Israel's nuclear capabilities at the time of the 1967 war is based on the published testimony of the director of Rafael (Israel Council for the Development of Military Means); see Munia Mardor, Personal Diary, 28 May 1967, quoted in Rafael: Research and Development for Israel's Future, Tel Aviv 1981, pp. 498–499. I am grateful to Avner Cohen for this reference.

[73] News item printed in Ma'ariv, 29 May 1967.

A unit of Hevra Kadisha (the burial authority) located large sites for mass graves.[74]

On the assumption that collective consciousness and collective memory are not natural, given objects, but are the arena of constant exchange and tussles between orientations and interests in a given society as part of the struggle over its image; and on the assumption that they are cultural constructs, products of shifting socio-political realities which reflect power struggles and political motivations existing within that society, which shapes itself through them – one should regard the Holocaust discourse of May–June 1967 as a complex, non-random product of all these. Tracing the growth and development of a certain discourse and the scope of its dissemination and impact is not an easy task since we are not dealing with an immutable, material, substantial entity. Notwithstanding, the Holocaust discourse of the period is certainly traceable, and the sites in which it was formulated and from which it was marketed, the kind of places in which collective memory is usually shaped and national meaning is created, have political names and faces.

Published on 22 May 1967, at the beginning of the second week of the crisis, an article entitled "From the Rhine to Erez [an Israeli settlement on Israel's border with Egypt]," written by a prominent editorialist of *Ha'aretz*, insinuated that, although Erez was far away from the Rhine, and although the Egyptians were no Germans and therefore Nasser was no Hitler, there was a clear similarity between the "two obsessed dictators." These two dictators shared "the obsession of encirclement, the obsession of a Judeo-Bolshevist conspiracy to be crushed, and that of the Zionist cancer and the Israeli-imperialist connection meant to humiliate the Arab nation." The author of this text, a member of the Ben-Gurion's circle, then scornfully added, targeting the current Israeli government:

Government circles in Israel have detected a sense of détente in the last 24 hours. This is the same détente, well remembered by those who lived in Europe before the war, that descended on its capitals after each one of Hitler's usurpations ... and Hitler encouraged this feeling, because it served his goals. Israel's leaders, who cooperate in producing that lulling notion, have forgotten the past; they may find themselves condemned to live it for the second time.[75]

This was the first allusion to Nazism and the Holocaust, And even if no explicit comparison was drawn, the subliminal messages were clear. Israel's political leadership at that time, like the Chamberlains in their

[74] *Ha'aretz*, 2 June 1967.
[75] A. Schweitzer, *Ha'aretz*, 22 May 1967. It should be noted that Schweitzer was a member of Ben-Gurion's new political party, and close to Israel's leaders of the security establishment.

day, was short-sighted, weak, favored appeasement, and was destined to bring down on itself and on its people a catastrophe of similar scope to World War II, a new Holocaust. Armed with insubstantial historical lessons, reproducing the Holocaust discourse formulated during the Eichmann trial, the article was aimed, above all, at undermining the legitimacy of Levi Eshkol's government and causing its downfall, this being the political objective of Ben-Gurion and his associates.

The West's stand of non-intervention raised the specter of Munich and enhanced the sense of another betrayal by the world. What *Ha'aretz* had stated rather subtly erupted in its full coarseness in the popular evening papers: "For the time being," wrote *Yedioth Aharonoth*'s editorialist, "everything is proceeding according to the Munich pattern: encouraging the strong at the expense of the weak . . . and the absence of a warning to muzzle Nasser. And on the horizon a Chamberlain-like declaration of 'peace in our time' once we are erased off the map."[76] Three days later, the same editorialist wrote:

Oh, how we have sinned against the holy and pure memory of the deceased Chamberlain! How we attacked him, how we ridiculed him and how we slandered him – and all for what? For speaking softly to the loud Hitler! While Hitler had power, those facing him were physically powerless, but those crawling on their bellies today are armed to their teeth! Well? . . . Chamberlain's western critics nowadays are . . . are . . . no, I would not like to wash their underwear now . . . Chamberlain? He was a spiritual hero compared to them.[77]

A few days later, Munich was cited again in the same writer's column:

America is somewhat panicked by the Holocaust that might befall it and with it on the whole world if the Munich affair recurs *here* . . . Thanks to our decision, thanks to our intention to drown any Munich-like solution in the blood of those who aspire to achieve that solution, a new picture has suddenly appeared on the horizon.[78]

In his turn, Ben-Gurion himself, now in the opposition and a ferocious rival of his former friend and colleague Prime Minister Eshkol (and hence not innocent of political motivations), warned that Israel faced a trial more severe than ever:

A war of annihilation. None of us can forget the Holocaust that the Nazis inflicted on us. And if some Arab rulers declare day and night that Israel must be annihilated – this time referring not to the entire Jewish people in the world,

[76] Herzl Rosenblum, Editorial, *Yedioth Aharonoth*, 23 May 1967.
[77] Herzl Rosenblum, Editorial, *Yedioth Aharonoth*, 26 May 1967.
[78] Herzl Rosenblum, Editorial, "With Warm Congratulations to IDF," *Yedioth Aharonoth*, 29 May 1967 (italics in the original).

but to the Jews living in their land – it is our duty not to take these severe statements lightly.[79]

It was, however, the usually rational and moderate paper, *Ha'aretz*, that led the campaign of substituting one historical situation for another and transplanting the Holocaust's terms and images into the current political context of the Middle East. The paper had a clear political agenda – to replace the moderate Eshkol as Israel's Prime Minister with either Ben-Gurion or General Moshe Dayan – and its use of the Holocaust served that agenda well. In a series of articles, op-ed pieces, and news items written and published day after day by different correspondents and essayists, the sense of an impending existential danger of Holocaust proportions was accumulating. Following the first article, previously mentioned, another article, written by the paper's military correspondent, claimed bluntly that Nasser's intentions were the same as Hitler's.

It is bewildering to what degree a people that experienced the Holocaust in World War II, is willing to believe and take risks a second time . . . Nasser has declared his intentions to annihilate Israel [the professional peaceniks ridiculed this declaration in the past], and he will try to realize his plans. Is there anyone who still doubts it?"[80]

Another text in that series, written by a noted Labor intellectual, was entitled "The Return of the Hitlerite Danger." In the article, the writer pleaded the need to learn from past mistakes and take the Arab threats most seriously:

The Jewish people cannot sustain another blow. We can accept no consoling and comforting advice. We shall pay the full price. The others will express sorrow for our disappearance. The sincerity of his [Nasser's] repetitive and emphatic declarations, that he wishes to annihilate Israel, cannot be doubted. It would be irresponsible folly not to believe what Nasser has been writing and saying for the last twelve years.[81]

Israel must therefore "crush the machinations of the new Hitler right away, while it is still possible to do so," said the commentator. "For us, Abdel Nasser *is* Hitler."[82] A revered, old-guard author close to Ben-Gurion followed this line and called on the world to pay attention to Nasser's Hitlerite intentions to liquidate Israel: "That is the plan by which he wages war against Israel."[83] A few days later, on the morning the Israeli

[79] Ben-Gurion, quoted in "Ben-Gurion Declared: Our Behaviour and Leadership will Determine Our Fate," *Yedioth Aharonoth*, 30 May 1967.
[80] Zeev Schiff, "The Sand Clock," *Ha'aretz*, 29 May 1967.
[81] Eliezer Livneh, *Ha'aretz*, 31 May 1967.   [82] Ibid.
[83] Haim Hazaz, "Facing the World," *Ma'ariv*, 2 June 1967.

air force simultaneously attacked Egypt and Syria, *Ha'aretz* provided a detailed comparison between the statements of the two leaders – Hitler and Nasser.[84]

Organized authentic anxiety

Waging war is an enormous endeavor of general mobilization, political, economic, as well as cultural and educational. It would be unwise to try to trace a simple, linear, tangible link between the Holocaust discourse developed on the eve of the war, and the decision to engage in a military preemptive strike. One cannot ignore, however, the omnipresence of that discourse, its initiators, and its accumulative effect in the context of the 1967 war. Collective anxiety or hysteria is a complex phenomenon that is hard to define and delineate.[85] Feelings of persecution, combined with a peculiar angry sensitivity and irritability towards those regarded, once and forever, as enemies, are the most striking traits of the inner life of a crowd, said Elias Canetti. "These enemies can behave in any manner," he writes, "harsh or conciliatory, cold or pathetic, severe or mild – whatever they do will be interpreted as springing from an unshakeable malevolence, a premeditated intention to destroy the crowd, openly or by stealth."[86] Canetti's observations concerning crowd mentality can also be attributed to an "imagined community" such as a nation, which, at certain points in history may adopt the emotions or anxieties of the crowd.

The American historian Murray Levin argues that there may be certain events in a nation's history that are generally regarded as peripheral or weird, yet may reveal profound forces that lie below the surface of society.[87] Analyzing the case of the Red Scare of 1919–1920, Levin maintains that the almost universal belief in the imminent destruction

[84] "Between Hitler and Nasser," *Ha'aretz*, 5 June 1967.
[85] Sigmund Freud's discussion of hysteria can be of use to us here: "No hysterical symptom can arise from real existence alone," he wrote. "In every case the memory of earlier experiences awakened in association with it plays a part in causing the symptom." See Sigmund Freud, "The Aetiology of Hysteria," in James Strachey (ed.), *The Standard Edition of the Complete Psychological Works of Sigmund Freud*, 24 vols., London 1953–1974, vol. III, pp. 193, 198. While referring in this case to experiences of the individual, Freud himself claimed that these concepts were also valid for group psychology. "The contrast between individual psychology and social or group psychology which at first glance may seem to be full of significance, loses a great deal of its sharpness when it is examined more closely." See Sigmund Freud, "Group Psychology and the Analysis of the Ego," in Strachey (ed.), *Standard Edition*, vol. XVIII, p. 62. See also Michel de Certeau, "Psychoanalysis and Its History," in *Heterologies: Discourse on the Other*, trans. Briar Massumi, Minneapolis 1986, pp. 5–7.
[86] Elias Canetti, *Crowds and Power*, trans. Carol Stewart, London 1962, p. 22.
[87] Murray B. Levin, *Political Hysteria in America: The Democratic Capacity for Repression*, New York 1971.

of American civilization by a highly organized and financed Bolshevik conspiracy was baseless and that such danger never really existed. "Political hysteria," he writes, involves "an extreme loss of customary political self-control and a very high degree of misperception – a passionate crusade to eliminate an imaginary threat." This kind of threat, he argues, is usually fabricated by elites, and mainly by elites fearing that their hegemony is weakened or threatened.[88] The threat is constructed out of bits and pieces of reality that never add up to a whole. Anxiety is induced among the masses, which anticipate a danger and yearn for its elimination. Political hysteria, therefore, is a "peculiar combination of conscious elite contrivance and spontaneous and largely unconscious mass response."[89] Among those who promote hysteria, there are some who actually believe in the threat, while for others it is a manipulation designed to achieve certain ends such as managing and maintaining an existing political system or, on the contrary, overthrowing an existing system.

Collective anxiety can never be solely the product of invention or manipulation by the elites. Discursive maneuvers of this kind become effective only when they respond to deep and genuine social concerns, and in time of general malaise. Israeli society in the spring of 1967 was a divided, orphaned society. After Ben-Gurion's stormy, pioneering, and goal-oriented era came the normal, more easygoing, and lackluster days of the lenient, compromising Eshkol, and with them, economic recession, high unemployment, social unrest, and a prevailing sense of depression. This period was also marked by substantial emigration – the opposite of the Zionist grand design of ingathering the exiles.[90] It was a climate receptive to the manipulations of hysteria. It was also easy ground for the popular, spontaneous, and undiscriminating reception of Nasser's threats to annihilate Israel, enhanced and disseminated by interested groups within Israel. Many contradicting forces – political parties, individuals, army commanders, and the press – and a variety of motivations were active behind the scenes. The Eshkol government, which, with Abba Eban as Foreign Minister, was considered weak, "diasporic" more than Israeli in its make-up and diplomatic, lobbying practices, sought a political solution to the crisis at almost any price. Eban's efforts prior to the war to solicit mediation by France, Great Britain, and the United States were viewed by the government's opponents as old, exilic, obsequious

---

[88] Ibid., p. 136.   [89] Ibid., p. 4.

[90] A bitter popular joke at the time was about a big sign hanging at the national airport that said, "The last to leave will please switch off the lights," alluding to the feeling that the Israeli experience was in its final chapter.

ways, a government which does not elevate itself to the demands of the hour.[91] General Ariel Sharon described the government as servile, asserting that "we are presenting ourselves as empty vessels, as an impotent country."[92]

So discredited were the rather positive, optimistic reports of the Foreign Minister from his diplomatic voyages that the head of the Mossad was secretly sent to the United States to check up on Eban's talks there. "The impression given in Paris after the meeting of the [foreign] minister with the president [de Gaulle] was depressing," reported the *Yedioth Aharonoth* correspondent in the French capital, who was close to Ben-Gurion and to the security establishment.

Eban, instead of issuing an unequivocal, clear and forceful warning to the *General* about Israel's resolute decision to defend its rights by taking up arms ... gave de Gaulle the pathetic impression of being an *intercessor*. Israel does not want war, Israel will not initiate a war, Israel is recruiting the aid of the world, this is what Minister Eban said to *General* de Gaulle while tens of thousands of Israeli soldiers had already deployed armor along the Sinai border.[93]

The proponents of action (who advocated a preventive, imminent military strike) consisted of the army command, three cabinet ministers, right-wing parties, and, as already mentioned, the evening papers and especially the daily *Ha'aretz*, whose main motive was not so much war as the replacement of Eshkol at the head of the government and the Ministry of Defense. With General Moshe Dayan as the paper's choice to succeed Eshkol, the organ's editorialists relentlessly fought for this political coup, using the inflated Holocaust discourse for this purpose. The army, which ironically enough was experiencing – under the moderate Eshkol – unprecedented renewal and expansion and was more prepared than ever for a preventive strike, also demanded immediate action to break the stalemate. Army commanders claimed that Israeli hesitation to act would damage the army's deterrence capacity and its

---

[91] On 25 May, *Ha'aretz* wrote that "the personal make-up of the government and its combined choice of talents" were inadequate for taking the necessary decisions. On 29 May, the paper openly called for the replacement of Eshkol by Ben-Gurion as Prime Minister and Dayan as Defense Minister. Other major newspapers joined in this call.

[92] Ethan Haber, *Hayom Tifrotz Milhama* (*A War Will Break Out Today: Memoirs of General Israel Lior, Military Secretary of Premiers Levi Eshkol and Golda Meir*), Tel Aviv 1987, pp. 195–196.

[93] Article by Yeshayahu Ben-Porat on moves prior to the war, *Yedioth Aharonoth*, 23 June 1967 (my italics). Noteworthy is the loaded and deliberate depiction of the frightened, pathetic Israeli "gabai" (synagogue clerk), bearing the message of Israel's unwillingness to go to war, confronted with the French "general," the standard-bearer of the uprising of Free France against the collaborationist French government in World War II. Ben-Porat goes on to claim that it was not the fault of Eban but of the entire Eshkol government.

effectiveness, and that a delay in launching the first strike would place Israel under the threat of annihilation. Yet it is clear that other motivations, such as the inner need and drive of any such organization to test its capabilities to the full, as well as the ambition of its leaders to impose their views and vindicate them, were also clearly playing their roles and impelling the army to adopt its offensive, belligerent stance. To this was added the feeling within army ranks – a feeling that quickly spread in the country, fueled and manipulated by the interested groups – that Israel was being held back by a group of elderly people, members of the Eshkol exilic-oriented circle, Jewish rather than Israeli in their manners and thinking, who were not capable of making crucial, existential decisions.[94]

The 28th of May 1967 was a decisive day both for the war and for Premier Eshkol. After an unfortunate, live radio broadcast to the nation in which he stuttered and fumbled (due to last-minute hand-written changes his aide had inserted into the text), a broadcast that had a devastating effect on the country, the shaky Prime Minister met with the army command. The meeting was unprecedentedly stormy, the generals having openly expressed their lack of confidence in the incumbent government and its head, in a kind of cold military putsch. Eshkol who valiantly retorted left angrily before the meeting was formally concluded. A growing political coalition against the Prime Minister, composed even of some of Eshkol's friends and colleagues, and spontaneous as well as organized street demonstrations demanding that Eshkol be replaced by Dayan, finally led Eshkol to resign on 1 June as Minister of Defense, ceding his place to Dayan and thus paving the way for the establishment of a unified national government. The political upheaval calmed the country immediately. Just as the hysteria had erupted, abruptly and quite mysteriously so, it subsided in a moment – a fact which testified to its (if only partially) manipulated nature and superficiality. The ground for a first, "preventive" strike had been prepared. The war could now be perceived both as a war of defense and as a war of redemption, the victory miraculous, the alternative – total destruction.

Memory on-call

"From Auschwitz to Sinai," exclaimed the French academician Thierry Maulnier in *Le Figaro*.

---

[94] The wise bon vivant Eshkol was known for his Jewish humor and mild manners – his style was the emblematic opposite of Ben-Gurion's adversarial, belligerent approach to life and politics.

The struggle was as if crowned by the light of a great miracle, receiving its significance, at least partially, from the depth of history and the great legends of mankind ... In one generation only, almost at one stroke, the Hebrew people have completed the journey from the Warsaw Ghetto to the praised Zion, from Auschwitz to Sinai.[95]

The war itself and Israel's swift military victory – additional evidence that the image devised for the Israeli people and the world just a short time earlier was inaccurate – did not undermine the notion of recent, impending doom. To the contrary, it further enhanced and fueled the legend of the averted holocaust, as if in a closed self-nurturing circle of logic, as clear-cut proof: the greater the victory the greater the averted catastrophe. The victory, the new conquered territories were the alternative to the crematoria. "To our joy – and the Arab states' sorrow," wrote *Yedioth Aharonoth,*

the State of Israel was not annihilated and its inhabitants not slaughtered and not sent to the gas chambers and the ovens. The Arab states had such plans ... they had declared that they would annihilate us, burn our towns and villages and destroy us ... The world knew but did not believe the Arabs would execute their threats; we were the only ones to believe. We knew what our fate would be had the Arabs won the war. We knew that if we surrendered, we would be annihilated.[96]

This kind of discourse did not stop at the columns of the popular evening papers. It also infected the best and the brightest. "In light of your lengthy knowledge, do not confront this nation with 'no alternative'," wrote the poet and essayist Haim Guri.

At a time like this [this people] becomes another and irrevocably disrupts the "intelligence assessment" amassed in your minds, hearts and files. The poison of "no alternative" is transformed in their veins, by no miracle, into a wondrous draught. It generates surprises. It breaks records in weight lifting and sprinting. The full weight of its history is borne on its back along the paths of fire.[97]

And Israeli poet and former World War II partisan, Abba Kovner, said after the war, "This home, this home of mine ... together with all its inhabitants and all its deeds, had been doomed to slaughter before the end of this month."[98] On the same occasion, Guri declared that "ours is the generation which saw the furnaces, and our children have taken the lesson of the Holocaust to heart. All of a sudden many Jews understood

---

[95] Thierry Maulnier, *Le Figaro*, reproduced in Hebrew in *Yedioth Aharonoth*, 26 June 1967.
[96] Aharon Shamir, *Yedioth Aharonoth*, 23 June 1967.
[97] Haim Guri, "Forthright Words, Fitting Words," *Ma'ariv*, 7 July 1967.
[98] Abba Kovner in a writers' and intellectuals' meeting, Jerusalem, 10 July 1967; "In these great days," published in English by the Hebrew Writers' Association.

what was involved, and believed in words which suddenly came alive, pierced the heart and wrought havoc there."[99]

Because "Auschwitz" as history, as past reality, as a symbol, and as a metaphor was so unimaginable and indescribable, it could now become, in a most distorted way, a figure of speech, an easy commodity. Its very unrepresentability rendered it exchangeable with all sorts of utterly different historical instances. If Auschwitz could be perceived as "the price paid for Israel's resurrection," as Thierry Maulnier put it, it could also be exploited to define the pre-1967 borders of Israel, borders that, for two decades, had proved defensible and viable.[100] And fifteen years later, it would also become, in Premier Menachem Begin's words, the sole alternative to the Israeli invasion of Lebanon.[101] Thus the memory of Auschwitz as a constitutive myth, healing and all-justifying, the commitment through memory as Susan Sontag put it, would be transformed into a memory on-call, an all-purpose memory, a memory for all seasons. The belated victory over "Auschwitz" in the battles of Sinai, the West Bank, and the Golan Heights made possible the fateful transformation of the State of Israel, a modern, rational, political manifestation, into the Land of Israel, the primordial, sanctified, and ahistorical concept of Israel, and endowed the land with the added sanctity of the averted destruction.

This miraculous transformation also mesmerized the Israeli government. The West Bank, that ancient home of Israel and the present home of the Palestinians, was excluded from its historic, if short-lived 19 June 1967 decision, stating its willingness to withdraw from the Sinai and the Golan Heights, if Egypt and Syria agreed to direct negotiations, peace treaties, and mutual security arrangements. This area was immediately extracted from the government's decision and from politics in general, that is, from the possible, from the present, from people's times, choices, and decisions. "The State of Israel has suddenly become the Land of Israel ... It means living according to the laws of a different hour, being sensitive and strong in order to stand up to these trials; and understanding that all paths of retreat are blocked," said Haim Guri.[102] A piece of land thus became non-negotiable, beyond the realm of politics, "a living body – beyond and above time," as Elie Wiesel had phrased it.[103]

---

[99] Guri, "Forthright Words."

[100] The first to utter these words was Abba Eban, who later tried to dissociate himself from them. The phrase was appropriated, however, never to be returned by the Israeli political Right.

[101] Menachem Begin, Cabinet Meeting, 4 June 1967, reproduced in the Israeli press.

[102] See Guri, in a writers' and intellectuals' meeting, Jerusalem, 10 July 1967.

[103] Wiesel, in *Yedioth Aharonoth*, 16 June 1967.

In a kind of echo of Primo Levi's words about "the incurable nature of the offense, that spreads like a contagion,"[104] and from a perspective of twenty years of Israeli occupation of the West Bank, the Israeli-Palestinian writer Emile Habibi reflected in the mid-1980s on the devastating effect the Holocaust, and the memory of the degradation inflicted on the Jews in the Holocaust, had had on the Israeli psyche. In an essay entitled "Your Holocaust, Our Catastrophe," published in the Israeli journal *Politika*, Habibi wrote:

I cannot imagine that, had the Holocaust not happened, the brothers of Heinrich Heine and Maimonides, Bertolt Brecht and Stefan Zweig, Albert Einstein and the immortal Arab-Jewish poet Shlomo Ben Ovadia would have permitted a Jewish government to expel another Semite people out of its home ... Indeed, the horrifying suffering inflicted on the Jews by the Nazi beast can be measured not only by the six million annihilated in the concentration camps and by other means of mass killing. It is measured also by the terrible price the Jewish people have paid in losing their glorious Jewish tradition and in the damage it has caused to what is called the "Jewish heart."[105]

[104] Levi, *The Reawakening*, pp. 182–183.
[105] Emile Habibi, "Your Holocaust, Our Catastrophe," *Politika*, 5, 1986, p. 28.

Few are the texts which mold a generation's thinking and discourse instantly and lastingly, and create conceptual breakthroughs. If the 1961 Eichmann trial in Jerusalem elevated talk of the Holocaust to the public sphere and granted it the legitimacy and circulation it had not previously had, then the report of the trial by Hannah Arendt in her book *Eichmann in Jerusalem* (1963) transformed this speech and revolutionized its language and meanings. Thus the two events, the trial and the book, and subsequently the fierce controversy around the book as well, became inextricably connected and of one piece. Not only did the trial take on mythological dimensions as a restorative and expiatory event, summing up a historical chapter and, as it were, "rendering justice" to the victims of the Holocaust, the Jewish people, and the State of Israel, as if justice could be rendered; Arendt's book itself, which endeavored to deconstruct the redemptive mythical discourse of the trial – and the maelstrom which engulfed the book and its author – also assumed mythical dimensions. It is therefore no longer possible to discuss the Eichmann trial and its significance separately from Arendt's analysis of it; or to discuss the meaning of the book without referring to its reception and perception.

The Arendt polemic jolted the Jewish world to such extent because it was related to the two central and identity-constituting events in the Jewish history of the twentieth century – the destruction of European Jewry and the establishment of the State of Israel; because it touched on the complex connection between those two events, and because it contained within it the struggle for control of Jewish memory, its language, meanings, bearers, and custodians. The eye of the storm was the United States, where Arendt's articles first appeared – and were immediately published in book form – and where many prominent intellectuals, both Jewish and non-Jewish, took part in the polemic. The controversy raged for three years in the mid-1960s, in fact, it has not died down to this day, and so far has brought forth more than one thousand publications, articles, and books.[1] In the past decade numerous works have been devoted to the polemic itself.

The present chapter, too, deals with Arendt's book and the controversy it provoked; it does so, inter alia, through analysis of two major relevant documents: the public letters[2] exchanged by the renowned Kabbala scholar Gershom Scholem and Hannah Arendt after her book appeared. It focuses in particular, as the controversy did, on the issue of Arendt's Jewishness, her attitude and "loyalty" towards Judaism and the Jewish people, Zionism, and Israel. It was Scholem, in his letter to Arendt, who, in his ostensibly friendly manner, raised these issues. Her profound and emphatic reply, however, was accessible only to those fluent in English, French, German, and a number of other languages, into which the correspondence was translated: to the Israeli public only Scholem's accusatory document was available. Contrary to the agreement between the two, Arendt's reply was not translated into Hebrew, and thus was never printed side by side with Scholem's letter.

Scholem was neither the only scholar nor the first to dwell on Arendt's "Jewishness" or "loyalty" to her people after the publication of her book. This was the main weapon in a campaign directed against her which, as is the case with quasi-pathological events of this kind, rapidly deteriorated into character smear and arbitrary branding. The labels affixed to Arendt ranged from the banal and predictable to the deranged and delirious: she was suspected, inter alia, of latent and overt sympathy for Nazism, of a demonstratively favorable attitude to Eichmann himself, and of depicting him as a "Zionist" and denying the evil and atrocity of his actions. The then President of the American Jewish Congress, Rabbi Joachim Printz, accused Arendt of having described Eichmann as a "sweet and misguided man,"[3] while the historian Barbara Tuchman wrote that Arendt had been

---

[1] See Walter Laqueur, "The Arendt Cult – Hannah Arendt as Political Commentator," in Steven A. Ascheim (ed.), *Hannah Arendt in Jerusalem*, Berkeley 2001, pp. 47–48.
[2] The public nature of the letters is highly problematic in the Israeli context. Gershom Scholem responded to Arendt's book by writing her a personal letter, which was intended from the outset for publication and asked her permission to publish it. Arendt concluded her reply by acceding to Scholem's request, on condition that the two letters be published together, side by side. This was done everywhere and in all languages, except (in Hebrew) in Israel. Scholem did not keep his promise. While Scholem's letter appeared in Hebrew twice in his lifetime – first on 31 January 1964 in *Davar*, and the second time in Scholem's collection of essays, *Dvarim Be'go* (*Explications and Implications*), Tel Aviv 1975, pp. 91–95 – undoubtedly with his knowledge and under his auspices – Arendt's reply was translated into Hebrew and published for the first time in that language, in the original version of my book in September 2002. Excerpts from Scholem's letter have reappeared in Hebrew several times over the years, even in scholarly publications, without ever mentioning the existence of Arendt's response.
[3] Joachim Prinz, *Arendt Nonsense*, New York 1963, quoted in Novick, *The Holocaust in American Life*, p. 135.

inspired by a conscious desire "to support Eichmann's defense"[4] (a doubly weird claim both because of its content and because Arendt published her report after Eichmann's execution in 1962). The Jewish Anti-Defamation League publicly campaigned against the "evil book," and the Jewish Publication Society of America distributed, as Peter Novick recorded, a 400-page attack on Arendt's book.[5] Finally, the title of a discussion of Arendt's book in a French weekly, was the not necessarily rhetorical question "Is Hannah Arendt a Nazi?"[6]

While the general polemic around Arendt's book has already been studied in depth,[7] its pale shadow, namely the Israeli polemic, whose intensity never approximated that of the New York "civil war," as Irving Howe described it,[8] still awaits thorough investigation.[9] Although most of the criticism leveled against Arendt in Israel was cloaked in the guise of historical debate, dealt with the details of the facts and was aimed at questioning her erudition and skills in her field of research, the tone, the sub-text and the overt wording of many of the critiques and references to the book and its author charged her with "anti-Zionism," with "exilic self-hatred," and with hostility towards the great Israeli Zionist endeavor at a moment of cathartic national unity. Both the professor of philosophy Ernst Simon and the historian Israel Gutman, who wrote the weightier of the Israeli articles about Arendt's book,[10] emphasized, in almost identical words, her abandonment of Zionism. Both wrote that when she left France in 1940 (having escaped Nazi Germany several years previously) Arendt did not "follow her former students to Eretz Israel" (Simon) or "her path did not lead to Eretz Israel" (Gutman), and that she chose the United States where she developed her career, as if this primal choice of hers had forever faulted her judgments and shaped – and distorted – her intellectual insight and achievements. And whereas Simon referred to Arendt's "assimilation process," to the fact that "she never found time for serious study of Hebrew or Yiddish," and to her

[4] Barbara Tuchman, "The Final Solution," New York Times Book Review, 29 May 1966, pp. 3, 12, quoted in Novick, Holocaust in American Life, p. 135.
[5] Novick, Holocaust in American Life, pp. 134–135.   [6] Ibid.
[7] Noteworthy in this context is Richard I. Cohen's comprehensive study, "Breaking the Code: Hannah Arendt's Eichmann in Jerusalem and the Public Polemic: Myth, Memory and Historical Imagination," Michael: On the History of the Jews in the Diaspora, 13, 1993, pp. 46–60.
[8] Irving Howe, A Margin of Hope: An Intellectual Autobiography, New York 1982, p. 290.
[9] A preliminary investigation can be found in Idith Zertal, "Hannah Arendt versus the State of Israel," in Ophir (ed.), Critical Moments, pp. 158–167.
[10] See Akiva Ernst Simon, "Hannah Arendt: An Attempt at Analysis," Molad, 21 (179–180), July–August 1963, pp. 239–256; Israel Gutman, "Arendt-style Self-Hatred," Yalkut Moreshet, 4 (6), December 1966, pp. 111–134.

abandonment of Zionism because of her "attitude towards the Arab question,"[11] Gutman noted Arendt's "untrammelled self-hatred," her "delicacy and great consideration" towards Eichmann, her blindness towards "the new Israel," and the striking absence in her book of "any description of an Israeli house, street or individual."[12] The editor of the intellectual and highly influential periodical, *Amot*, attacked Arendt and her book in a lengthy article in the daily *Davar*, using such epithets as "strange creature," "Prussian Jewess," "Jewish-Prussian soul," or "disintegrated emotional elements." Expressing openly his distaste, he wrote: "How varied and mixed are the components of malignant evil in Jews of Miss Arendt's kind," and added, "It is the source that is crucial: the poison which consumes its very bearer, so that he takes it with him wherever he goes – to Auschwitz, to Jerusalem – everywhere."[13]

Yet the Arendt polemic in Israel was conducted as if in a sealed room, mainly within a small scholarly community, without reaching the general public, and without giving Arendt a voice. Not only Arendt's reply to Scholem, but her other answers to her critics in Israel as well were never published in Hebrew;[14] and some forty years were to pass before her book on the trial, the object of the controversy, appeared in Hebrew (previous attempts, from the mid-sixties on, to publish a Hebrew translation proved fruitless).[15] Arendt was never again invited by an Israeli academic institution to have her say after the publication of her book, either on the book or on any other subject. Although this was never stated formally, she was persona non grata in the Israeli academic establishment. The voice which was cardinal to any meaningful debate in Israel on Arendt's arguments was silenced and never heard there. Hers was the missing voice in the polemic about her. Arendt was like a black hole, unseen and unheard, but still acting as a focus of gravity – perhaps precisely because of its absence and its immense power – and generating movement and upheavals in

---

[11] Simon, "Hannah Arendt: An Attempt at Analysis," pp. 246, 239, and 245 respectively.
[12] Gutman, "Arendt-style Self-Hatred," pp. 111, 116, 118 respectively.
[13] Shlomo Grodzensky, "Miss Arendt among the Perfume Flasks," *Davar*, 3 May 1963, p. 3.
[14] See, for example, her response to Yaakov Robinson's book, *And the Crooked Shall Be Made Straight: The Eichmann Trial, the Jewish Catastrophe and Hannah Arendt's Narrative*, New York 1965, published in January 1966, cited in Ron H. Feldman (ed.), *Hannah Arendt: The Jew as Pariah, Jewish Identity and Politics in the Modern Age*, New York 1978, pp. 252–259.
[15] The rights to Hebrew publication were owned by Shocken, in whose American branch Arendt worked as a senior editor. The Israeli publishing house, Amikam, bought the rights from Shocken and commissioned the publiscist, Boaz Evron, to translate it, and he in fact completed the task and received payment. However, the book was never published. The "hidden hand" as Evron called it, may have acted. Conversation with Boaz Evron, 2000, and Boaz Evron, *Ha'aretz*, 6 October 2000.

Israeli discourse. Only gradually, in recent years, more Israeli scholars from various disciplines have had recourse to Arendt's writings.[16]

An obligation towards the past

When she set out, on her own initiative, to cover the Eichmann trial in Jerusalem for the *New Yorker*, Hannah Arendt was already a distinguished and esteemed political philosopher, author of a seminal work on the twentieth-century phenomenon of totalitarianism, which, like her many other books, has never been translated into Hebrew. As recorded in her letters, she wanted to be present at the trial and to observe the defendant, Adolf Eichmann, at close quarters, as part of her continual interest in and study of totalitarianism. Arendt felt that she had missed an opportunity by not being present at the Nuremberg trials, which tried the heads of the Nazi dictatorship and the individuals responsible for the atrocities perpetrated by Germany in the Second World War, and she believed that Eichmann's trial would be the last of the trials of Nazi arch-criminals. "I missed the Nuremberg Trials," she wrote. "I never saw these people in the flesh, and this is probably my only chance."[17] She also considered her presence at the trial as a kind of obligation towards herself and her past as a Jewish refugee from Germany, who had endured the early days of Nazism, experienced persecution, and conducted research on the subject.[18] She spent time in Jerusalem and followed Eichmann's trial for two periods,[19] several weeks in all. After the trial, the verdict of the District

[16] In the last decade two conferences on Arendt's work were held in Israel. The first took place in December 1997 in Jerusalem and the contributions were published in Ascheim (ed.), *Hannah Arendt in Jerusalem*; the second conference, gathering Israeli scholars, was held at Tel Aviv University in April 2003. Its contributions were published in Idith Zertal and Moshe Zuckerman (eds.), *Hannah Arendt: Hatzi Mea shel Pulmus* (*Hannah Arendt: A Half-Century of Polemics*), Tel Aviv 2004.

[17] Arendt to the Rockefeller Foundation, 20 December 1960, quoted in Elisabeth Young-Bruehl, *Hannah Arendt: For Love of the World*, New Haven and London 1982, p. 329.

[18] "I would never be able to forgive myself if I didn't go and look at this walking disaster face to face in all his bizarre vacuousness, without the mediation of the printed word. Don't forget how early I left Germany and how little of all this I really experienced directly," wrote Arendt on 2 December 1960 to her mentor and friend, the German philosopher, Karl Jaspers. See Kohler and Saner (eds.), Correspondence, Letter 271, pp. 409–410. Since the publication of the book it was brought to my attention that the English version of this letter is wrong and misleading. The original reads: "I would never forgive myself if I didn't go and see with my own eyes this real-life disaster unfolding in all *its* uncanny vacuousness." This means that Arendt was referring to the trial itself, not to the defendant.

[19] Ibid., Letters 285, 287 and more, pp. 434–441. It should be noted that Arendt came to the trial with firm views, and the preliminary outline of her book is discernible in the letters, particularly where Eichmann's character is concerned: "Eichmann is no eagle; rather, a ghost who has a cold on top of that and minute by minute fades in substance, as it were, in his glass box." Of the Presiding Judge, Moshe Landau, she wrote: "Marvellous man!" It is worth noting that this letter to Jaspers, in which she expresses herself without

Court, the appeal by the defense counsel, the Supreme Court ruling, and Eichmann's execution, Arendt wrote her series of articles for the New York weekly, which were published in five installments in early spring of 1963.[20] The articles appeared in book form in the early summer of that year, with the disquieting sub-heading, "A Report on the Banality of Evil." This term, "banality of evil," mentioned only once in the book, right at the end,[21] became a major ingredient in the debate on Nazism and its crimes, Arendt's identifying mark, and a primary target of attack, which often took on the dimensions of a personal defamation campaign or a dybbuk-exorcising ritual.

Arendt's report of the trial was not a reassuring or consoling document. It was neither a self-satisfied conclusion to a historical reckoning, nor a celebration of the new Jewish nationalism, born according to Zionist discourse, in an inevitable, predestined, and teleological drive out of the ashes of the murdered European Jewry, thereby endowing it with retro-spective, redemptive significance. The report is both an angry and a chilling analysis – emotional and ironic, penetrating and subversive – of the way in which the trial was conducted, its aims and lessons. By means of the trial Arendt also formulated an original and innovative discussion, though in the spirit of her previous writings, of the kind of personality and crime represented by the defendant, the nature of the regime which dispatched him to perpetrate his crimes, and the conduct of the Jews, the object of those crimes, while they were taking place.

The book, therefore, revolved around three central issues, unequal in scope and importance: Eichmann and Nazism, namely the murderers; the Jews, namely the victims; Israel and the court it established in order to judge the "Final Solution" and Eichmann, namely the "heirs." The murderers were murderers, the victims were victims, the judges were judges, and Arendt's heart was in the right place, the only place where it could have been. And yet the picture of the Holocaust which emerged from her disturbing report was not simple; it was complex and marked by paradox and ambivalence. And the adversarial, sometimes provocative narrative proposed by Arendt turned out to be intolerable in that

restraint, also includes a disturbing section about the Israeli police and crowd, tainted with a note of racism and with subliminal allusions to what the trial was about: "Everything is organized by a police force that gives me the creeps, speaks only Hebrew, and looks Arabic. Some downright brutal types among them. They would *obey any order*. And outside the doors, the oriental mob, as if one were in Istanbul or some other half-Asiatic country." Ibid., Letter 285, p. 435 (my italics).

20   Arendt's report was published in weekly installments in the *New Yorker* from 16 February 1963 under the heading *Eichmann in Jerusalem* in the section the weekly allotted to its major stories: "A Reporter at Large."

21   "It was as though, in those last minutes he [Eichmann] was summing up the lesson that this long course in human wickedness had taught us – the lesson of the fearsome, word-and-thought-defying *banality of evil*." These are the concluding words of Arendt's book, before the epilogue. See Arendt, *Eichmann in Jerusalem*, p. 252.

particular place and time – the early 1960s – when Jewish pain and sensitivity were only capable of absorbing a tale of absolute evil versus absolute good. And the fact that this narrative stemmed from within, from the family, that is to say, from a Jewish woman who was well acquainted with the Jewish story and knew the profoundest Jewish "secrets,"[22] rendered the whole affair even more intolerable.

A "respectable" citizen

The central and crucial innovation in Arendt's book was her discussion of Eichmann's personality, and through him, of the nature of the Nazi regime and the Nazi individual as SS man. Arendt loathed Eichmann and despised him from the depths of her being and convictions and these emotions[23] were reflected in all her personal and public statements, and throughout the book. Eichmann, to her mind, was the personification of the new type of bureaucratic mass criminal, the desk-murderer, whose hands were "clean" in the direct physical sense; the kind of unprecedented murderer created by the totalitarian regimes of the twentieth century. Eichmann was neither a monster nor a pathological sadist; he never killed a single human being directly. And, consequently, Arendt was severely critical of the prosecution's hopeless attempt to prove that Eichmann had murdered a Jew with his own hands (the court pointed out the prosecution's failure to prove this point).[24] She believed that this was not the point, and that efforts to prove Eichmann's "monstrosity" devalued the meaning and unique nature of Nazi crimes. It was Eichmann's "normalcy" which called for attention, and this "normalcy" had been confirmed by the numerous psychiatrists who examined him. "The man was 'normal'," declared one of them, "more normal, at any rate, than I am after having examined him."[25] The discrepancy between the horror of the crimes and the normalcy of their perpetrators, she asserted, should have been the core of the discussion of Nazism and of Eichmann. "The law-abiding good citizen" Eichmann, obeying orders (he left no doubt, wrote Arendt, that he would have killed his own father if ordered to do so),[26] the man of "conscience," who "would have had a bad conscience only if he had not done what he was ordered to do: to ship millions of men, women and children, to their death with great

---

[22] On Arendt as the "bearer of secrets" and, consequently, as one whose words create an effect of Freudian *unheimlich*, see Zertal, "Arendt versus the State of Israel." Arendt herself employed the term "bearers of secrets" with regard to the Jewish leaders during the Holocaust.

[23] See, among others, Arendt's letter from 13 April 1961, in Kohler and Saner (eds.), *Correspondence.*

[24] Arendt, *Eichmann in Jerusalem*, p. 246.   [25] Ibid., p. 48.   [26] Ibid., p. 42.

zeal and the most meticulous care,"[27] this Eichmann was the phenomenon which caught Arendt's interest and which should have been debated in court, she argued. It was the question of how to establish the connection between the "unspeakable" atrocities and "the undeniable ludicrousness of the man who perpetrated them" which should have been under discussion.[28]

Eichmann's ludicrousness found expression in the nullity, the total emptiness of his personality ("a walking human catastrophe," as she denoted him) and in the depressing banality of his language, namely his thinking. "Despite his rather bad memory, [he] repeated word for word the same stock phrases and self-invented clichés (when he did succeed in constructing a sentence of his own, he repeated it until it became a cliché) each time he referred to an incident or event of importance to him."[29] His incapacity to speak attested, according to Arendt, to his inability to think, namely, to think from the standpoint of somebody else. "No communication was possible with him, not because he lied but because he was surrounded by the most reliable of safeguards against the words and the presence of others, and hence against reality as such."[30] In Arendt's eyes, Eichmann was the exemplary product of a regime which destroyed in its citizens the faculty of thinking and judging, and the ability to distinguish between good and evil, right and wrong, namely, everything that makes up a human being. By omitting to address these questions, by assuming that the defendant, like all "normal people" must have been aware of the criminal nature of his actions, and by failing to take into account that Eichmann was by no means exceptional within the framework of the Nazi regime, and that under the conditions of the Third Reich only "exceptional" individuals in fact reacted in "normal fashion" the court had "missed the greatest moral and even legal challenge of the whole case," Arendt wrote.[31]

In employing the term "banality of evil" Arendt had no intention of arguing, nor did she do so, that there was anything banal about the crimes perpetrated by the Nazi regime and its emissary Adolf Eichmann, as many of her critics claimed. She argued repeatedly that these crimes were unprecedented in their horror – not only in scope but also in essence. Indeed, she was the very first to grasp – before all her moral censors – already in the second half of the 1940s, in her chapter on the concentration and extermination camps,[32] the radical evil and total novelty of the

[27] Ibid., p. 25.   [28] Ibid., p. 54.   [29] Ibid., p. 49   [30] Ibid.
[31] Ibid., p. 26. See also the discussion of Richard J. Bernstein, *Hannah Arendt and the Jewish Question*, Cambridge, MA, 1996, pp. 137–178.
[32] Arendt, *Origins of Totalitarianism*, pp. 437–459.

totalitarian system, in which "all men have become equally superfluous,"[33] and whose aim was the destruction of the concept of humanity itself. It was not the Nazi atrocities which were banal. "Banal" in the sense of being common, accepted, all-pervasive and regarded as innocuous, was the quality – the product of the totalitarian system – of the great majority of the perpetrators of the Final Solution, namely, lack of consciousness, extensive destruction of thought, incapability to discriminate between right and wrong. Indeed, Arendt could not detect "any diabolical or demonic profundity" in Eichmann,[34] and his SS colleagues, who epitomized for her the "word-and-thought-defying banality of evil."[35] Arguing against any "satanic greatness" in the Nazi crimes, she was to eventually define evil as something which "possesses neither depth nor any demonic dimension," and which "can overgrow and lay waste the whole world because it spreads like a fungus on the surface."[36] Yet the shallowness and thoughtlessness of Eichmann and his like did not absolve them in the eyes of Arendt, on the contrary. Thus, in blatant contrast to several of those who accused her of sympathy for Eichmann, but conversely were opposed to his execution,[37] Arendt vehemently supported the death sentence because of the totally non-banal crimes he had committed. She thought that this man, even if incapable of distinguishing between good and evil, did not deserve to live because he carried out a policy of mass murder, of refusal to share the earth with the Jewish people and the people of other nations, and therefore "no member of the human race can be expected to want to share the earth" with him.[38]

Moral collapse

The other subject in Arendt's book, which stirred up emotions more than any other issue, was the conduct of the Jews – in particular the Jewish leadership – during the Holocaust, that is, the cooperation of the Jews with their murderers in the process of extermination. Arendt devoted no more than a couple of dozen out of 300 pages to this subject, but this was to become the searing, scorching core of the book. The incisiveness and

---

[33] Ibid., pp. 457–459.   [34] Arendt, *Eichmann in Jerusalem*, p. 288.   [35] Ibid., p. 252.
[36] See inter alia, her letter to Gershom Scholem, in Feldman, *Jew as Pariah*, pp. 250–251. Both letters, Scholem's and hers, were first published in *Commentary*, 22, 1964.
[37] Gershom Scholem, to take one example, wrote that "Eichmann's execution is **not the right ending**. It distorts the historical meaning of the trial by creating the illusion that something can be settled in regard to this affair by hanging this worthless individual." See Scholem, *Explications and Implications*, p. 119 (bold in the original).
[38] Arendt, *Eichmann in Jerusalem*, p. 279.

acuity of Arendt's arguments were interpreted as lack of compassion in a place and circumstances in which compassion towards those who had been confronted with a phenomenon she herself described as unprecedented in the history of mankind was not only appropriate but essential. Indeed, Arendt performed her dissection of Jewish conduct and the structure of Jewish society without analgesics. Citing the seminal study by Raul Hilberg on the destruction of European Jewry, published shortly before,[39] Arendt asserted that the extensive cooperation of the Jews with the Nazis in all the countries of Europe, and the fact that they were organized within community frameworks and led by community heads, facilitated their murder and magnified the destruction.[40]

In Amsterdam as in Warsaw, in Berlin as in Budapest, there was no difference between the assimilated Jewish communities of Central and Western Europe and the Yiddish-speaking masses of Eastern Europe in regard to cooperation. All over Europe "Jewish officials could be trusted to compile the lists of persons and of their property, to secure money from the deportees to defray the expenses of their deportation and extermination, to keep track of vacated apartments, to supply police forces to help seize Jews and get them on trains."[41] And the Jews registered, filled out innumerable forms and pages of questionnaires about their property, thereby making the task of the looters and persecutors easier; then they gathered at the assembly points and boarded the trains. "Day in day out the people here leave for their own funeral," commented a Berlin Jew in 1943.[42] The Germans themselves were surprised at the degree of Jewish cooperation. In several cases they examined the area and the conditions in order to ascertain "whether Jews could be made to walk to their doom on their own feet, carrying their own little valises, in the middle of the night, without any previous notification."[43]

Had the Jews not been organized throughout Europe and had they been leaderless "There would have been chaos and plenty of misery," Arendt wrote, but the total number of victims of the Nazis would never have reached "four and a half to six million" (these were the figures Arendt cited, based on Gerald Reitlinger and the prevailing estimate at the time she wrote).[44] Citing Hilberg, Arendt brought evidence and calculations to prove that wherever the Jews did not cooperate, wherever

---

[39] Raul Hilberg, *The Destruction of European Jews*, Chicago 1961 (2nd and expanded edition in 3 volumes, New York 1985). Hilberg's book too has never been translated into Hebrew.

[40] It should be noted that Arendt uses the word "cooperation" and not the more loaded "collaboration."

[41] Arendt, *Eichmann in Jerusalem*, p. 118.   [42] Ibid., p. 115.   [43] Ibid., pp. 155–156.

[44] Ibid., p. 125.

they fled the Nazis or went underground, the number of victims was halved. The story of two Greek communities does corrobarate this claim. Rabbi Dr. Zvi Koretz was the head of the Judenrat in Salonika. Compliant with Eichmann's team orders to organize the community for its collective dispatch for "resettlement" in Cracow, he became a tragic link in the apparatus of Nazi extermination of its own community. He himself was not spared. Along with other Judenrat members he was deported towards the end of the war to Bergen-Belsen and died there of typhus. In contrast to Koretz the Athenian rabbi Eliyahu Barzilai rebelled and did not cooperate. He refused to give the lists of Athens's Jews, mislaid the community archive, and with help from the Greek resistance and a large sum of money succeded in hiding the entire community in the mountains and in churches and monasteries, and thus saved it.[45] The case of the small Danish Jewish community, all of whom were rescued in an operation of the Danish underground, was exceptional even according to this conception.

It is noteworthy that Arendt's argument about the cooperation of the Jewish leadership with the Nazis, and the singling out of a selected few for rescue as part of that cooperation, bears a striking resemblance to the judgment of Justice Benyamin at the Grunewald–Kastner trial, and was similar in spirit. This similarity may explain, even if only partially, the fury evoked by Arendt's remarks, particularly within the Jewish-Zionist estab-lishment, which believed that the Eichmann trial was making amends for the political disaster of the Kastner case, for its subversion of the organ-ized memory of the Holocaust and, on another, unspoken plane, for the catastrophe of the Judeocide. Both Arendt and Halevi took issue with the view of the Jewish masses in the Diaspora as an anonymous, passive, powerless object, lacking will or decision-making capacity of their own, "who had no legs to escape with" and "had no spirit left," which was how they were described by the prosecutor at the Grunewald–Kastner trial, the then State Attorney, Haim Cohen, in his concluding speech.[46]

Halevi did indeed refuse to regard those Jews as "lambs led to the slaughter," as State Attorney Cohen defined them, quoting what he claimed was the "ancient curse."[47] It was the duty of the Jewish leadership,

[45] See for this, Michael Burleigh, *The Third Reich: A New History*, New York 2000, pp. 654–655.
[46] Rosenfeld, *Criminal Case 124*, p. 281. See also chapter 2 of this book.
[47] Ibid. Rosenfeld quotes Cohen as follows: "And they were considered to be but lambs led to the slaughter, to be killed and annihilated, afflicted and oppressed." There is no such verse in the Bible and this quotation is a combination of verses from Isaiah 53, 7; Psalms 44, 24; the Scroll of Esther; and also alludes to the curse in Deuteronomy 28, 15 on. I am grateful to Dan Michman for this comment.

Halevi argued, to arm the people, if not with weapons then with knowledge of the truth about what was occurring in Auschwitz and other death sites, and to enable them to decide for themselves and their families, to grant them the freedom to make choices and decisions with regard to their fate. Halevi, like Arendt, saw the Jews as subjects, sovereign individuals, capable of thinking for themselves and taking decisions, even if only as to the manner and timing of their deaths. In his verdict, Halevi wrote:

The dissemination of the substantial information among the Jewish leaders, and in particular the Zionists in the provincial towns, and through them among the masses, could have ... acquainted those leaders and the people with the real dangers and fortified them against the Nazi lies and deceits ... In light of the alternative of Auschwitz, the Jews as leaders or as ordinary people were capable of full and thoughtful deliberation on the ways and means of defending or rescuing themselves in accordance with circumstances.[48]

Like Arendt several years later, Halevi did not speak of rebels or heroes, of those who took up arms, but of the refusal of ordinary men to obey orders and to cooperate, which held out at least a chance – though no guarantee – of restricting the destruction:

Any disruption, temporary halt or slowdown in the general pace could have considerably reduced the final number of victims. It is impossible and unnecessary to launch into surmise as to how matters would have developed without Kastner's cooperation with Eichmann ... There can be no doubt that this path – the method of free rescue independent of the Nazis – was dangerous for all those who took it and its outcome was not guaranteed; it was impossible to know how many would be saved and how many lost in this way, or to establish in advance who would be saved and who would fall victim.

Thus, the refusal to collaborate was not an absolute guarantee but this mode of action might have held out some hope of rescue, might have created some barrier to total destruction. In light of her own principles and conceptions, and though not familiar with Halevi's judgment, Arendt said the same in almost identical words.[49] Like Halevi before her, and certainly contrary to the claims of her critics, Arendt explicitly took the side of the Diaspora Jews, victims of the massacre. Moreover, it was the rank-and-file she sided with, the simple, "ordinary" Jews, those who were nameless and had no particular standing or connections, either in their

[48] District Court Verdict, pp. 110–115. It is quoted almost in full in Rosenfeld, *Criminal Case 124*, pp. 407–449.
[49] Ibid. Hannah Arendt was acquainted in general with the details of the Kastner case. She writes in her book with great acrimony about Kastner and quotes Halevi's famous statement that Kastner "sold his soul to the Devil," namely to Eichmann, but she almost certainly never read the entire verdict, published only in Hebrew, either directly or through a mediator.

communities or elsewhere in the world, whom nobody was concerned to rescue from their hell. And her position, even in retrospect, contained a great moral message. Arendt's argument (in the context of the Kastner case) was that the acceptance of distinctions between the more and the less privileged among the Jews marked the beginning of "the moral collapse of respectable Jewish society."[50] The moral damage entailed in acceptance of these categories, she argued, stemmed from the fact that all those who sought to include someone among the "exemptions from the rule" were thereby acknowledging the rule, that is the existence of the negligible, murderable mass. In other words, even the Jewish victims had accepted the yardsticks of the Nazi Final Solution, the conviction that a distinguished Jew was more deserving of survival than an ordinary Jew (she mentioned in this respect Himmler's complaint that there were eighty million good Germans, each of whom had "a decent Jew" of his own, and noted that it was said even of Hitler that he knew 340 "first-rate" Jews, and granted them the status of Germans or the privileges of half-Jews).[51]

In Germany today, this notion of "prominent" Jews has not yet been forgotten ... the fate of "famous" Jews is still deplored at the expense of all the others. There are more than a few people ... who still publicly regret the fact that Germany sent Einstein packing, without realizing that it was a much greater crime to kill little Hans Cohn from around the corner, even though he was no genius,

wrote Arendt.[52] Be that as it may, she did not sweepingly "negate"[53] the Diaspora Jews and their way of life as did the Zionist ideology, and as did the prosecution at the Grunewald–Kastner trial. She conducted a reckoning for their cooperation with the Jewish leaders, with the functionaries, those who set themselves apart from the community, whether for purposes of self-preservation and preservation of their relatives or for other reasons.

Nor did Arendt consecrate the militant heroism lauded by Israeli Zionism. Unlike her Israeli-Zionist critics, she had not expected the Jews of occupied Europe to take up arms and revolt; armed uprising was, at best, rare, confined to a tiny minority, solely young people, and under the prevailing circumstances, could be nothing but a "miracle." And although the proper legal procedure could not – and was not supposed to – permit testimony of the ghetto fighters in court, since this testimony was not directly relevant to the actions of the defendant,

---

[50] Arendt, *Eichmann in Jerusalem*, p. 131.   [51] Ibid., p. 133.   [52] Ibid., p. 134.
[53] The concept and ideology of "negation of the Diaspora," the total rebellion against what the Jewish Diaspora represented, its way of life, and what was called "the Diasporic soul," were central to the activist revolutionary Zionism in Palestine/Israel.

usually strict Arendt welcomed their appearance on the witness stand. This testimony, she asserted, "dissipated the haunting specter of universal cooperation, the stifling, poisoned atmosphere which had surrounded the Final Solution."[54] And since rebellion was so far beyond the realm of the possible for most people, the rhetorical question asked by the prosecutor, Gideon Hausner, "Why did you not rebel?" which was repeated over and over again, appeared to her as obtuse and rude, and mainly a smokescreen camouflaging the more vital question, which was asked only twice in court, despite the prosecutor's effort to avert it, namely the question of Jewish cooperation.[55] But, while the path of rebellion was taken by few, the option of refusal, of passive refusal, was within the bounds of possibility to all. "In order to do nothing," Arendt wrote in her letter to Scholem, "one did not need to be a saint, one needed only to say: 'I am just a simple Jew, and I have no desire to play any other role.'"[56] Refusal to conform, to obey, the act of autonomous thinking, of deliberating with and for oneself, and of choosing not to take part in wrongdoing, both on the part of the murderers and of the victims were according to Arendt the essence of humanity.[57]

The Jew as parvenu

Arendt's discussion of "the role of the Jewish leaders in the destruction of their own people," which she described as "undoubtedly the darkest chapter of the whole dark story"[58] – a chapter which the trial in

---

[54] Arendt, *Eichmann in Jerusalem*, p. 123.   [55] Ibid., p. 124–125.

[56] Arendt to Scholem, 24 July 1963, in Feldman (ed.), *Jew as Pariah*, p. 248.

[57] The shining moment at the trial, according to Arendt, was the testimony of Abba Kovner, who referred to the German soldier, Anton Schmidt, who for six months helped the Jewish underground and partisans until he was arrested and executed. A hush settled over the courtroom at that moment, wrote Arendt, as if the audience had decided spontaneously to honor the memory of a man named Anton Schmidt, "And in those two minutes, which were like a sudden burst of light in the midst of impenetrable, unfathomable darkness, a single thought stood out clearly, irrefutably, beyond question – how utterly different everything would be today in this courtroom, in Israel, in Germany, in all of Europe, and perhaps in all countries of the world, if only more such stories could have been told." Arendt, *Eichamnn in Jerusalem*, p. 231.

[58] Ibid., p. 117. It is noteworthy that the Israeli poet Nathan Alterman, as early as the mid-fifties, during the Grunewald–Kastner trial, used almost identical words in the context of collaboration by the Judenräte: "This issue of consent to the deportation of Jews is one of the darkest chapters in this dark period." See Laor (ed.), *Nathan Alterman's Two Paths*, p. 105. Despite the similarity between them, Alterman's remarks on the Judenräte, which were also fiercely criticized by the "rebels" and those who considered themselves their political representatives, were aimed, unlike Arendt's stand, at defending the Judenräte and championing their cause, by citing the insoluble dilemma entailed in the functioning of the Judenräte and the overall Jewish responsibility for the phenomenon. "This

Jerusalem had failed to tackle, so she claimed – did not derive from a preconceived decision to include it in her book; she wrote about it because the question of the Jewish leadership emerged during the trial, the efforts of the prosecutor to prevent it notwithstanding, and because her report was intended from the outset to be a detailed and full survey of the trial. More important, however: she touched on this question also because it supplied the most profound insight into the moral collapse caused by Nazism, among the persecuted as well as the persecutors.[59] There was one major villain in this story – Eichmann. But in order to ascertain the scope of the crime he had perpetrated on behalf of a perverted and murderous regime, it was essential to demonstrate that any cooperation with this system, whether with good or malicious intent, was devastating.

The roots of Arendt's criticism of cooperation of the Jewish leadership with the Nazi regime – in her research, in her intellectual world, in her personality and biography – call for separate analysis. In the present context, I would like to offer, in brief, an additional dimension for possible elucidation of Arendt's uncompromising attitude to the conduct of Jewish leaders and their organizations. Although she never said this explicitly, nor did her various interpreters note this fact, I would suggest that her extremely judgmental characterization of the Judenräte – many, if not all, of them – in the few but sulphurous pages dedicated to them, was neither arbitrary nor capricious, but rather the product of her continuous, profoundly committed reflections on Jewish behavior in history. The mold of the Jewish parvenu, namely, the privileged, prominent Jew, who tries to play by the rules imposed by others, by the very society which brands and outcasts him, and who struggles to win special treatment for himself and his own kind, tragically fitted most of the Judenräte's cases, at least as she understood them. This Jewish parvenu, a central concept in her analysis of Jewish history in the past two centuries, was, in her eyes, the product of abortive attempts at assimilation. This was a new Jewish figure produced by the Emancipation, characterized on the surface by economic ambition, and deep down by a denial of its Jewish roots. To those who aspired to find their identity by "losing" it through assimilation and a place in society were added the "privileged" Jews. They belonged, according to Arendt, to a variety of sub-categories. While some did

---

phenomenon is a terrible fruit and there is perhaps no element in Judaism which is entitled to deny its responsibility, including the rebels," wrote Alterman. "The blind annals of the nation, the blindness of its leaders and its masses, have created a situation whereby, obliquely or directly, leaders and masses as well as the Yishuv and the rebels acquiesced in this phenomenon." Ibid. See also chapters 1 and 2 of this book.
[59] Arendt, *Eichmann in Jerusalem*, pp. 125–126.

everything in their power personally to enjoy and exploit their exceptional, "privileged" status, totally detaching themselves from any public Jewish activity, there were others, usually Jewish community leaders, who, while tending their flock in their own way, not only tried to accommodate themselves to existing social and political conditions, but even inhibited and actively suppressed any impulse for genuine political action on the part of the Jewish community. Many of these prominent, usually wealthy, Jews, even some who were involved in charity activities, the philanthropists or heads of communities, betrayed their fellow Jews, according to Arendt who followed Bernard Lazare in that matter,[60] and exhibited parvenu characteristics. Since while alleviating Jewish suffering in the short run, they nevertheless contributed to the deepening and perpetuation of social and political persecution of their fellow Jews. They were, in Arendt's eyes, "coresponsible" for the existent state of affairs.

There were exceptions among the Jewish community leaders. Adam Czerniakow of Warsaw, "who was not a rabbi but an unbeliever ... who must still have remembered the rabbinical saying: 'Let them kill you but don't cross the line,'"[61] chose to take his own life rather than assist in the shipment of his fellow ghetto dwellers to Treblinka. The Athenian rabbi Eliyahu Barzilai, as already mentioned, saved his community by not complying with Dieter Wisliceny's orders. But most of the Jewish leaders during the Holocaust adopted, if only subconsciously, the stereotypes of their persecutors about themselves and their brethren; they tried to be "good Jews," "respectable" and obedient, and behaved as they were ordered to, sometimes even beyond the "call of duty": "No one bothered to swear the Jewish officials to secrecy; they were voluntary 'bearers of secrets', either in order to ensure quiet and prevent panic, as in Dr. Kastner's case," wrote Arendt, "or out of 'humane' considerations, such as that 'living in the expectation of death by gassing would only be harder,' as in the case of Dr. Leo Baeck."[62] They acted that way because that was what they had traditionnaly been taught to do, and because this had always been their way of acting; and they did it in order to

---

[60] Arendt who edited the English translation of Bernard Lazare's writings and wrote the foreword, "discovered" the Dreyfus Affair through Lazare's writings, and adopted many of his concepts. Bernard Lazare, *Job's Dungheap*, New York 1949; she uses the terms "parvenu" and "pariah" extensively in her book *Rahel Varnhagen: The Life of a Jewish Woman*, New York (rev. edn.) 1974; see also the discussion in Bernstein, *Hannah Arendt and the Jewish Question*, pp. 14–45.

[61] Arendt mentions the fact that Czerniakow "was not a rabbi" in order to emphasize the contrast between him and the leader of German Jewry, Rabbi Leo Baeck, whom she had mentioned several sentences before. Arendt, *Eichmann in Jerusalem*, p. 119.

[62] Ibid., pp. 118–119.

accommodate their persecutors and gain in exchange some alleviation, maybe even the lives of some Jews, "prominent" Jews, perhaps their own lives. "Even after the end of the war, Kastner was proud of his success in saving 'prominent Jews,' a category officially introduced by the Nazis in 1942, as though in his view too, it went without saying that a famous Jew had more right to stay alive than an ordinary one," Arendt wrote.[63] By doing what they did, the Jewish leaders actually mobilized themselves, even if unwillingly, in the service of the realization of their persecutors' ideology and policy, and became accomplices, a crucial component in the Nazi machine of the destruction of European Jewry, of their own communities, and at the end of the day, also of themselves, of their own bodies.

It was the other trend of Jewish tradition – a "hidden tradition," that of a minority of Jews, who preferred the status of "conscious pariah," who, by their very existence and refusal to accept the world as it was, and their effort to transform it into something else, made it a better place to live in, not just for themselves, or for some "privileged" individuals but for everybody – which not only fascinated Arendt but to which she would have liked to think she belonged. Her admiration for that whole new breed of people, which "modern Jewish history was apt to forget," could perhaps explain why she was incapable of moderation when discussing the grim, tragic case of the Jewish leaders, and the Jewish traditional social structures, which facilitated destruction in such a catastrophic way. At the same time, it is evident that her standpoint was by no means a fleeting whim, nor was it inspired by deliberate malice or latent sympathy for Nazism, as many of her critics claimed, because of their misunderstanding of her text, unfamiliarity with her previous writings and unwillingness to study them in depth and face up to their significance. It was a conclusive stand, rooted deep in the patterns of her political philosophical thought.

It was from the very same perspective, as noted, that she regarded the actions of the tiny minority of ghetto rebels, as a "miracle" when set against the poisoned atmosphere of moral collapse and universal cooperation which had surrounded the Final Solution.[64] She aimed at establishing as an ideal of humanity the refusal to comply, to take part in wrongdoing, to rebel, both among Jews and non-Jews, whether militant or expressed in "doing nothing," and in passive non-cooperation. Thus she defined the refusal of the Danish people to cooperate with the Nazi scheme to exterminate their Jewish community, and the shipment of the entire community to the Swedish shore by the Danish resistance

[63] Ibid., p. 132. See also chapter 2 of this book.   [64] Ibid., pp. 122–123.

movement, one of the few cases of resistance to the Nazis during the Holocaust, as "required reading in political science for all students who wish to learn something about the enormous potential inherent in non-violent action and in resistance to an opponent possessing vastly superior means of violence."[65]

Concepts of Jewish history

The overall framework of Arendt's book was discussion of the trial itself, Israel's right to hold it, the way it was conducted, and the lessons it taught. Here too Arendt was brilliantly erudite, uncompromising, and unexpected in the paradoxical nature of her arguments. Although she believed, like many of her colleagues abroad (and several in Israel), that it would have been advisable to conduct the trial in an international tribunal, she acknowledged Israel's right to try Eichmann, both because such a tribunal did not exist and there was no prospect of establishing one, but mainly because some 300,000 survivors had immigrated to Israel and made it their home.[66] On the other hand, she was critical of the political, educational, and propaganda nature which Ben-Gurion – the "invisible stage manager" of the trial[67] – had imparted to the event, as he himself attested.[68] She openly disliked the way in which the State Attorney conducted the prosecution case which caused the trial itself and Israel in general to fail a great moral, intellectual, and political challenge. The objectives Ben-Gurion set for the trial, Arendt argued, however noble and historically understandable, exceeded the bounds of law and legal procedure. It was incumbent on a court to weigh the charges against the accused, to arrive at a verdict, and to sentence him. All other extra-legal aims were therefore the source of the innumerable "irregularities and anomalies at the trial," until the court itself, trying to stem the flood, was forced to declare that it could not "allow itself to be enticed into provinces which are outside its sphere ... the judicial process has ways of its own, which are laid down by law, and which do not change, whatever the subject of the trial may be."[69]

However, the greatest weakness of the trial, according to Arendt, was the fact that all the participants in the project, inside the courtroom and elsewhere, and the general public as well, grasped and understood the

---

[65] Ibid., p. 171

[66] Arendt to Jaspers, 23 December 1960, Kohler and Saner (eds.), *Correspondence*, pp. 414–418.

[67] Arendt, *Eichmann in Jerusalem*, p. 5.

[68] For elaboration of this theme and numerous examples, see chapter 3 in the present book.

[69] From the judgment, as quoted in Arendt, *Eichmann in Jerusalem*, p. 253.

phenomenon of the mass murder of Europe's Jews by the Nazi regime in terms which were not compatible with the unprecedented character of the atrocities and their utterly new nature. And since they considered "Eichmann" and "Auschwitz," Nazism and the Holocaust solely in terms of their own history, Jewish history, Arendt claimed, they (those who conducted the trial and its audience) viewed these phenomena in terms of the oldest crime they knew and remembered, "the most horrible pogrom in Jewish history," and therefore could not understand "Auschwitz" in terms of the new twentieth-century phenomenon of murderous totalitarianism, a crime of a new kind, unprecedented not only in scope but, primarily, in essence. In this fashion, Arendt asserted, "none of the participants ever arrived at a clear understanding of the actual horror of Auschwitz."[70]

On 23 June 1963, six weeks after receiving a copy of her book, Gershom Scholem wrote a letter to his old friend, Hannah Arendt. Their ties went back to the early thirties and had evolved, at first at least, around their profound esteem and friendship (of each separately) for the philosopher Walter Benjamin.[71] They also shared sympathy for the views of the small but prestigious Brit Shalom movement on the way in which the two peoples fighting over Palestine should share the land (Scholem had been among the founders of the movement in the mid-1920s). In the 1940s and 1950s, she in New York and he in Jerusalem, they took a close interest in one another's work. Arendt was also involved in the publication of Scholem's work in the United States. While literary editor of Shocken Books in New York, she edited Scholem's writings, along with those of Kafka, Bernard Lazare, and Benjamin's posthumous manuscripts. In 1948, she published an enthusiastic review of Scholem's book, *Major Trends in Jewish Mysticism*, of which she wrote that his research had changed "the whole picture of Jewish history."[72] But unlike Scholem, who dealt, to a large extent, with the religious dimensions of the Sabbatian movement, Arendt, the political philosopher whose thinking

---

[70] Ibid., p. 267.

[71] Gershom Scholem, *Walter Benyamin, Sipura shel Yedidut*, Tel Aviv 1987, pp. 208–209; *Walter Benjamin, the Story of a Friendship*, Philadelphia 1981, pp. 213–214. According to Scholem, they became acquainted in 1932, in Berlin. When she left Berlin and ran the Paris office of Youth *Aliyah*, Arendt visited Palestine on several occasions, "and we had formed a closer relationship there" (Scholem). In the late thirties, on the eve of the war, they met several times in Paris, and were involved together in efforts to help Benjamin support himself and publish his writings. Scholem, *Walter Benjamin*, pp. 188, 208–209, 211. A slightly different story is to be found in the Hebrew version of the same book. See also Hannah Arendt, *Men in Dark Times*, Harmondsworth 1973, pp. 165, 167.

[72] "Jewish History, Revised," *Jewish Frontier*, 15 (March 1948), reproduced in Feldman (ed.), *Jew as Pariah*, p. 96.

core and main message was people's responsibility for politics and for being full active citizens,[73] longed to find in Jewish mystical thought and the messianic drive a vast potential for concrete political action. In the sense of its active role in history, and not only victimhood, in its urge to change the Jewish condition, Arendt regarded the Sabbatian movement as the precursor of the Zionist national movement.[74]

The first exchange of polemical letters between Scholem and Arendt followed her series of articles in the 1940s on Zionism and the evolving political and cultural image of the Palestinian Jewish community, in which she formulated her oppositionary approach to hegemonic Zionism and its demand for a Jewish state in Palestine. In these letters, Scholem, like others (such as her close friend, the German-born Zionist leader, Kurt Blumenfeld), took issue with Arendt not only for her "anti-Zionist" outlook but also for the tone of her remarks, which already seemed to him unnecessarily caustic, arrogant, and cynical. "What upsets me in your anti-Zionist arguments, more than their content, which is open to argument, is the tone of your discussion," wrote Scholem to Arendt after reading her article "Zionism Reconsidered." In Arendt's "anti-Zionism," as he phrased it, Scholem discerned "communist inspiration, mixed with vague residues of *Galuth* [exilic] nationalism and something indefinably American."[75]

In this respect, there was nothing new in either the content or the tone of Scholem's letter to Arendt after her book on the Eichmann trial appeared. What is more, despite the friendship between them, Scholem had long since appeared to Arendt, to be "more difficult than ever," developing what she regarded with concern as "an increasingly nationalist orientation" and the type of "fanaticism" associated with it. But, she commented, "old friends are old friends, despite that."[76] Nonetheless, and also because of her heightened sensitivity in light of the attacks on her

---

[73] See Margaret Canovan, *Hannah Arendt: A Reinterpretation of her Political Thought*, Cambridge, MA, 1992, p. 276.

[74] See an excellent discussion in Bernstein, *Hannah Arendt and the Jewish Question*, pp. 58–62.

[75] The Scholem–Arendt correspondence is part of the Scholem archive in the National Library, Jerusalem. The quotation is from Martine Leibovici, *Hannah Arendt, une Juive, expérience, politique et histoire*, Paris 1998, p. 366. Raymond Aron, too, in his critique of Arendt's book on the origins of totalitarianism, referred to her "note of arrogant superiority with reference to individuals and human beings," a comment which impelled the French-Jewish philosopher, Martine Leibovici, to ask whether Aron had ever passed similar comments on Sartre's tone. See ibid., p. 367. Most of Arendt's articles on questions of Zionism and Judaism, originally published in various Jewish and Zionist periodicals, are to be found in Feldman (ed.), *Jewas Pariah*. See also Hannah Arendt, *The Jewish Writings*, Jerome Kohn and Ron H. Feldman (eds.), New York, 2007.

[76] Arendt writes this in a letter to Karl Jaspers, on 11 March 1949. See Kohler and Saner (eds.), *Correspondence*, p. 133.

book, Scholem's reproving letter came as a surprise to her.[77] The things said there, the way in which they were phrased, the tone, and in particular the overt urge of the author to expose his supposedly personal criticism, and thereby to denounce her in public, came as a disappointment to her, although by nature she usually relished a good fight. It may be assumed that this was the personal and emotional background to the acerbic reply she wrote to Scholem.[78]

It was because she regarded Scholem as a personal friend, and because she was, in contrast to Scholem, scrupulously exigent about friendship,[79] and less about issues of ethnic, religious, or national affiliations, that the correspondence between them became so paradigmatic, representing different, almost diametrically opposed types of human commitment and "belonging" and self-positioning in the world: on one hand, love of mankind as individual human beings, irrespective of their religious or national affiliation or, in other words, *her* "love of the world,"[80] on the other hand, religious, national affiliation, and collective loyalty, in other words, *his* "love of the people" or "love of Israel (*Ahavat Israel*)."

[77] In a letter to Karl Jaspers, dated 20 July 1963, four days before she wrote her reply to Scholem, Arendt wrote that she was stunned by the uproar caused by her book and had not expected anything of the kind. She described the storm raging around her as "a smear campaign," being conducted "on the lowest level," and based on the claim "that I said the exact opposite of what I did in fact write. The Jewish press reported that Hausner, the State Prosecutor, came to America at the government's urging and for the express purpose of heating things up. At the moment three or four large organizations, along with whole regiments of 'scholarly' assistants and secretaries, are busying themselves with ferreting out mistakes I made. It is quite instructive to see what can be achieved by manipulating public opinion and how many people, often of a high intellectual level, can be manipulated." *Ibid.*, Letter 331, pp. 510–511. In this letter, Arendt did not refer to Scholem by name but it seems very likely, especially when one reads her reply to him, that she was referring to him as well.

[78] One can learn about Arendt's somber mood at the time (also caused by her husband's illness) and her militant nature from an excerpt from a letter she wrote to her friend, the writer Mary McCarthy, on 16 September 1963: "generally, one can say that the mob – intellectual or otherwise – has been successfully mobilized. I just heard that the Anti-Defamation League has sent out a circular letter to all rabbis to preach against me on New Year's Day. Well, I suppose this would not disturb me unduly if everything else were all right. But worried as I am, I can no longer trust myself to keep my head and not to explode. What a risky business to tell the truth on a factual level without theoretical and scholarly embroidery. This side of it, I admit, I do enjoy; it taught me a few lessons about truth and politics." Carol Brightman (ed.), *Between Friends: The Correspondence of Hannah Arendt and Mary McCarthy 1949–1975*, New York 1995, pp. 145–146.

[79] A supreme value for her, Arendt found in friendship the support of her existence. Speaking about herself while lauding Lessing, she said that Lessing "considered friendship ... to be the central phenomenon in which alone true humanity can prove itself." Arendt, *Men in Dark Times*, p. 20. This is but one example.

[80] See the title of the best-known biography of Arendt: Young-Bruehl, *Hannah Arendt: For Love of the World*.

The issue of "group belonging" and loyalty to the collective lay at the heart of Scholem's admonishment of his friend, and from it stemmed all his other arguments. This issue, which also captured the imagination of her many critics, evoked Arendt's anger more than anything else. Although the whole theme has already been extensively discussed, we ought to dwell on it in our own turn, as it is a crucial component of this book's argument. As Scholem put it, "in the Jewish tradition there is a concept, hard to define and yet concrete enough, which we know as *Ahavat Israel*, 'love of the Jewish people'. In you, dear Hannah, as in so many intellectuals who came from the German Left, I find little trace of this." To this Scholem added, in an ostensibly conciliatory tone, the following sentence: "I see you wholly as a daughter of our people, and in no other way."[81] This sentence which became the trademark of Scholem's admonition concealed his patronizing attempt to appropriate Arendt and claim custody of her (an attempt which was not innocent of genderic attitude), both a kind of scolding and an arrogant effort to dam Arendt's own critical spirit, her most precious asset and characteristic. Arendt's Jewishness, her place and citizenship in the world, the territory of her belonging, from which were deduced the contours of her loyalties and her thought, all of these were submitted to Scholem's judgmental and categorizing gaze ("I see you wholly as a daughter of our people, and in no other way"), and from this scrutiny was derived her offense, the guilt of having crossed the line, the guilt inherent in her independent, untameable personality.

In her long, emphatic, and sometimes ironic reply to Scholem, written on 24 July 1963,[82] Arendt was more than ever loyal to herself, both in content and form, non-compliant and radiantly self-assured, which leads one to ponder in retrospect not only on Scholem's hasty, superficial reading of Arendt's book, but on his misjudgment of her possible reaction to his rebuke as well. Indeed, Scholem's pride was deeply hurt by Arendt's response, and their relationship never recovered.[83]

On love and politics

One by one, from the minor to the more substantial, Arendt deconstructed Scholem's conceited, all-knowing claims. She was not, she said, "one of the

[81] Feldman (ed.), *Jew as Pariah*, pp. 241–242.
[82] "Dear Gerhard", Arendt's letter to Scholem, in ibid., pp. 245–251. See also *Jewish Writings*, p. 466. All following quotes from Arendt's letter to Scholem may be found in ibid., pp. 465–471.
[83] "In his old age, he felt the dispute to have been 'one of the most bitter controversies of my life,'" writes Cynthia Ozick in her review of Scholem's collection of letters published in the United States. See Ozick, "The Heretic," *New Yorker*, 2 September 2002.

'intellectuals who come from the German Left,'"[84] a fact of which she was not particularly proud, she said, especially since the McCarthy era. "If I can be said to 'have come from anywhere,' it is from the tradition of German philosophy," she wrote in her response. His statement, however, about her being "a daughter of our people," left her stunned, even though not speechless: "I found it puzzling that you should write 'I regard you wholly as a daughter of our people, and in no other way,'" she retorted.

The truth is I have never pretended to be anything else or to be in any way other than I am, and I have never even felt tempted in that direction. It would have been like saying that I was a man and not a woman – that is to say, kind of insane. I know, of course, that there is a "Jewish problem." I have always regarded my Jewishness as one of the indisputable factual data of my life, and I have never had the wish to change or disclaim facts of this kind. There is such a thing as a basic gratitude for everything that is as it is ... To be sure, such an attitude is pre-political, but in exceptional circumstances – such as the circumstances of Jewish politics – it is bound to have also political consequences though, as it were, in a negative way.[85]

As to Scholem's claim that there was little trace of "*Ahavat Israel*" (love of the Jewish people) in her, Arendt corrected him and put him in his place, launching into more fundamental discussion of the connections between politics and love, and the issue of politics and compassion. What was written in her book, she said, had no connection to "self-hatred" or "self-love" because there was no room for love in a discussion of that type:

I am not moved by any "love" of this sort, and for two reasons: I have never in my life "loved" any people or collective – neither the German people, nor the French, nor the American, nor the working class or anything of that sort. I indeed love "only" my friends and the only kind of love I know of and believe in is the love of persons.

She went on claiming that this "love of the Jews" seemed to her, since she was herself Jewish, as something rather suspect. "I cannot love myself or anything which I know is part and parcel of my own person." She then told Scholem of a conversation she had in Israel with a prominent political personality, Golda Meir,[86] who was defending the "disastrous" – according to Arendt – non-separation of religion and state in Israel. Meir said to

---

[84] Noteworthy is Scholem's recurrent need to tag Arendt and ascribe her to a collective or ideology. See his letter after the publication of her article "Zionism Reconsidered." Arendt herself protested against this act: "It is incomprehensible to me why you should wish to stick a label on me which never fitted in the past and does not fit now." Feldman (ed.), *Jew as Pariah*, p. 246.

[85] Feldman (ed.), *Jew as Pariah*, pp. 245–246.

[86] At Scholem's request, when the letters were about to be published, Arendt did not reveal which personality she meant, and even disguised the fact that it was a woman.

Arendt, that as a socialist, she "of course" did not believe in God; she believed in the Jewish people. Too shocked by this statement, Arendt did not reply at the time. She did belatedly in her letter to Scholem:

> The greatness of this people was once that it believed in God, and believed in Him in such a way that its trust and love towards Him was greater than its fear. And now this people believes only in itself? What good can come out of that? – Well, in this sense, I do not "love" the Jews, nor do I "believe" in them; I merely belong to them as a matter of course, beyond dispute or argument.[87]

To discuss the same issue in political terms, Arendt continued, would lead to a consideration of patriotism, and she believed that both she and Scholem shared the view that there can be no patriotism without permanent opposition and criticism. More than that, she admitted something which was mostly ignored by her critics, namely, that wrong done by her own people naturally grieved her more than wrong done by others. This grief, however, she said, is not for display, even if it should be the innermost motive for certain actions or attitudes.

> Generally speaking, she wrote, the role of the "heart" in politics seems to me altogether questionable. You know as well as I how often those who merely report certain unpleasant facts are accused of lack of soul, lack of heart, or lack of what you call *Herzenstakt*. We both know, in other words, how often these emotions are used in order to conceal factual truths.[88]

Before assailing her book's analysis of Jewish conduct during the Holocaust, Scholem segregated Jewish history as a whole within a sacred delineated space. This had been his own area of research for four decades, as he was careful to note in his letter – superfluously, unless his words were directed at an audience beyond Arendt since she had been acquainted with his work for thirty years.[89] This sanctification implied that Jewish history differed fundamentally and essentially from non-Jewish history – a conception which Arendt vehemently criticized, claiming that it was the source of the ahistorical conduct of Jews throughout history – and that this sacred Jewish historical space was barred to all except the certified "priests," like Scholem himself, they who had

---

[87] Feldman (ed.) *Jew as Pariah*, p. 247. It is interesting to note that even most recently Arendt's statement about "love" of her people has been distorted. In her review of Scholem's collection of letters, Cynthia Ozick quoted only part of Arendt's response to Scholem. "In this sense I do not 'love' the Jews," she cited, omitting the following: "nor do I 'believe' in them [the Jews]; I merely belong to them as a matter of course, beyond dispute or argument," which gives Arendt's position a different meaning altogether. Ozick, "The Heretic."
[88] Feldman (ed.), *Jew as Pariah*, p. 247.
[89] This rhetorical addition and other statements by Scholem in his letter create the impression that he was writing, from the outset, for publication more than as a personal appeal to Arendt.

proclaimed their priesthood and marked out the sacred territory. Without saying so explicitly Scholem let it be understood that Jewish history was a kind of mystic entity, whose depths could not be plumbed and whose full meaning was beyond human comprehension, and hence any attempt at analytical and rational examination was sacrilege. "I am aware that there are aspects of Jewish history (and for more than forty years I have concerned myself with little else) which are beyond our comprehension," he wrote. "On the one hand, a devotion to the things of this world which is near-demonic; on the other, a fundamental uncertainty of orientation in this world – an uncertainty which must be contrasted with that certainty of the believer concerning which, alas, your book has so little to report."[90] In this context, Scholem attempted to establish, in convoluted fashion, Arendt's entitlement or more exactly her non-entitlement to deal with these matters, especially with the issue of the Jewish behavior during World War II, not to say to exercise judgment: "The discussion of these matters is, I believe, both legitimate and unavoidable – although I do not believe that our generation is in a position to pass any kind of historical judgment. We lack the necessary perspective, which alone makes some sort of objectivity possible."[91] Elsewhere in his letter he added:

> I have not read less than you have about these matters, and I am still not certain; but your analysis does not give me confidence that your certainty is better founded than my uncertainty. There were the Judenräte, for example; some among them were swine others were saints ... There were among them also many people in no way different from ourselves, who were compelled to make terrible decisions in circumstances that we cannot even begin to reproduce or reconstruct. I do not know whether they were right or wrong. Nor do I presume to judge. I was not there.[92]

After posing the question of Arendt's authority and right to judge on such issues as the Holocaust, and particularly on the conduct and role of the Jews in it, an authority and right that the Israeli establishment and many Israelis, including Scholem himself even in his letter to Arendt, and elsewhere, had adopted unreservedly,[93] Scholem went on to express open and sharp reproof of the tone of her discussion of these matters, which he perceived as intolerable, "sneering and malicious." In this respect, Scholem was representing the opinion of the great majority of Arendt's readers, even of her most ardent advocates in the controversy around her book. They too agreed that her tone in a number of sections of the book was not only discordant, but also unwise and rather unnecessary for conveyance of her message; it did rather undermine the credibility of

---

[90] Feldman (ed.), *Jew as Pariah*, pp. 240–241.   [91] Ibid., p. 241.   [92] Ibid., p. 243.
[93] See chapters 1, 2, and 3 of this book.

her valid arguments. But beyond Arendt's sometimes hasty choice of words and formulations which were insufficiently subtle, there can be no question that her secular, rational, critical, sometimes ironic sometimes aloof, and wholly modern style was perceived by Scholem and other critics as evidence of her lack of awe, her contempt for the sublimity, the numinous sanctity of the Holocaust, the mystical, religious dimension attributed to the events, namely her contempt for all that was sacred to the nation, of which the Holocaust was now becoming a part.

It is that heartless, frequently almost sneering and malicious tone with which these matters, touching the very quick of our life, are treated in your book to which I take exception ... To the matter of which you speak it is unimaginably inappropriate ... I detect, often enough, in place of balanced judgment, a kind of demagogic will-to-overstatement,

Scholem wrote to Arendt.[94] From here the distance was short to the charge, which borders on the pathological, that she, Arendt, was guilty of a warped kind of sympathy for Eichmann, inspired, according to Scholem, by her open "dislike" for Zionism.

Your description of Eichmann as a "convert to Zionism" could only come from somebody who had a profound dislike of everything to do with Zionism. These passages in your book I find quite impossible to take seriously. They amount to a mockery of Zionism; and I am forced to the conclusion that this was, indeed, your intention. Let us not pursue the point,

he wrote.[95]

Self thought (*Selbstdenken*)

Deeply disappointed by Scholem's narrow-minded, parochial reading of her text, influenced by the "present campaign of misrepresentation" launched against it by the Jewish "establishment" in Israel and America, Arendt deplored Scholem's lack of what she considered to be the most precious human quality, namely, independent thinking, Lessing's famous *Selbstdenken*, "another mode of moving freely in the world."[96] Unfortunately, she wrote to Scholem, there are very few people who are able to withstand the influence of such campaigns. "Public opinion," she said, "especially when it has been carefully manipulated, as in this case, is a very powerful thing. Thus, I never made Eichmann out to be a 'Zionist.' If you missed the irony of the sentence – which was plainly in *oratio obliqua*, reporting Eichmann's own words – I really can't

---

[94] Feldman (ed.), *Jew as Pariah*, pp. 241–243.　　[95] Ibid., p. 245.
[96] Arendt, *Men in Dark Times*, p. 16.

help it." She went further saying that she never asked why the Jews "let themselves be killed," unlike the prosecutor Hausner, who had posed this question to witness after witness. There were no people and no group in Europe which reacted differently under the immediate pressure of terror, she said.

The question I raised was that of the cooperation of Jewish functionaries during the "Final Solution," and this question is so very uncomfortable because one cannot claim that they were traitors. (There were traitors, too, but that is irrelevant.) In other words, until 1939 and even until 1941, whatever Jewish functionaries did or did not do is understandable and excusable. Only later does it become highly problematic ... This constitutes our part of the so-called "unmastered past," and although you may be right that it is too early for a "balanced judgment" (though I doubt this), I do believe that we shall only come to terms with this past if we begin to judge and to be frank about it.[97]

Arendt claimed that Scholem obviously did not understand her position, although she made it quite plain. "I said that there was no possibility of resistance, but there exists the possibility of *doing nothing*. And in order to do nothing, one did not need to be a saint, one needed only to say: 'I am only a simple Jew, and I have no desire to play any other role.'" What needed to be discussed, according to her, were not the people so much as the arguments with which they justified themselves in their own eyes and in those of others.

Concerning these arguments we are entitled to pass judgment. Moreover, we should not forget that we are dealing here with conditions which were terrible and desperate enough but which were not the conditions of concentration camps. These decisions were made in an atmosphere of terror but not under the immediate pressure and impact of terror. These are important differences in degree, which every student of totalitarianism must know and take into account. These people had still a certain, limited freedom of decision and of action. Just as the SS murderers also possessed, as we now know, a limited choice of alternatives. They could say: "I wish to be relieved of my murderous duties," and nothing happened to them. Since we are dealing in politics with men, and not with heroes or saints, it is this possibility of "*nonparticipation*" that is decisive if we begin to judge, not the system, but the individual, his choices and his arguments.[98]

And the Eichmann trial was concerned with an individual, she said. And as she spoke in her report only of things which came up during the trial itself, she could not mention the "saints" about whom Scholem was speaking in his letter. She had to limit herself, instead, to the resistance fighters whose behavior, according to her, "was the more admirable because it occurred under circumstances in which resistance had really

[97] Feldman (ed.), *Jew as Pariah*, p. 248 (italics in the original).
[98] Ibid., pp. 248–249 (italics in the original).

ceased to be possible." There were no saints among the witnesses for the prosecution, but there was one utterly pure human being, old Grynszpan, whose testimony she reported at some length. On the German side, one could also have mentioned more than the single case of Sergeant Anton Schmidt. But since his was the only case mentioned in the trial, she had restricted herself to it. "That the distinction between victims and persecutors was blurred in the concentration camps, deliberately and with calculation, is well known, and I as well as others have insisted on this aspect of totalitarian methods," she wrote. But, she repeated, this was not what she meant by a "Jewish share in the guilt," or by the totality of the collapse of all standards. "This was part of the system and had indeed nothing to do with Jews."[99]

Finally, Arendt tackled the Zionist chapter in Scholem's letter, stating that the fact that Scholem could believe that her book was a "mockery of Zionism" would have been "a complete mystery" to her had she not known that many people in Zionist circles have become "incapable of listening to opinions or arguments which are off the beaten track and not consonant with their ideology." There were exceptions, she said, who regarded the book, the last chapter in particular (her recognition of the competence of the court, the justification of Eichmann kidnapping), as very pro-Israel. "What confuses you," she wrote to Scholem,

is that my arguments and my approach are different from what you are used to; in other words, the trouble is that I am independent. By this I mean, on the one hand, that I do not belong to any organization, and always speak only for myself, and on the other hand, that I have great confidence in Lessing's *Selbstdenken* for which, I think, no ideology, no public opinion, and no "convictions" can ever be a substitute. Whatever objections you may have to the results, you won't understand them unless you realize that they are really my own and nobody else's.[100]

Arendt concluded her letter by reacting to Scholem's comment on the phrase she had coined, "the banality of evil." Scholem regarded this term as no more than verbal provocation, "a catchword," which was not the fruit of profound research such as that invested in her previous book, on the origins of totalitarianism. "At the time," he wrote to her, "you had not yet made your discovery, apparently, that evil is banal. Of that 'radical evil,' to which your then analysis bore such eloquent and erudite witness, nothing remains but this slogan."[101] This was, as Arendt put it, the only matter where Scholem had not misunderstood her, and where he was

---

[99] See for this also chapter 2 in the present book.
[100] Feldman (ed.), *Jew as Pariah*, pp. 249–250.   [101] Ibid., p. 245.

quite right: "I changed my mind and do no longer speak of 'radical evil,'" she wrote.

It is indeed my opinion now that evil is never "radical," that it is only extreme and that it possesses neither depth nor demonic dimension. It can overgrow and lay waste the whole world precisely because it spreads like a fungus on the surface. It is "thought-defying," as I said, because thought tries to reach some depth, to go to the roots, and the moment it concerns itself with evil, it is frustrated because there is nothing. That is its "banality." Only the good has depth and can be radical.[102]

This banal, prevailing evil, being intrinsically and profoundly linked to the inability to think independently, or to the prevalent abdication of autonomous thought, could also take the form of a smear campaign, an organized "witch hunt" against those who dare to take a stand, outside of the crowd, to cling to their own independent thought and tell the masses unsettling truths about themselves. The crowd, or, as Arendt called it, the "mob,"[103] had sweeping, infectious, enticing power, and it did not take much for the "respectable society," including educated, well-meaning people, to turn into an inflamed mob. The principle of the mindless mob did not necessarily apply to an extreme phenomenon such as Nazism or its unprecedented crimes. The moral questions it raised related rather to the conduct of ordinary, respectable people in their everyday lives. She regarded Scholem's letter as proof of his lack of independent thinking in relation to the Eichmann trial and her critical report of it, and of his being part of the organized incitement campaign both in Jerusalem and in New York. In letters she wrote at the time to her friends Karl Jaspers and Mary McCarthy, she reiterated the term "mob" in relation to the storm roused by her book, and the "character assassination" it entailed.[104]

---

[102] Ibid., pp. 250–251. In a letter to Arendt dated 31 January 1956, written after reading her book on the origins of totalitarianism, Karl Jaspers used the image of the fungus spreading and consuming everything in its path, in reference to totalitarianism. "Every politician active today ought to read it and understand it. It's like the diagnosis and symptomatology of a fungal disease that spreads and eats up everything in its path. The carriers of the disease are intelligent the way fungi are because they do instinctively what is required of them; that they are capable of what is required is also a consequence of their basic nihilism, which overcomes all human resistance." Kohler and Saner (eds.), *Correspondence*, Letter 180, p. 273.

[103] Arendt's interest in the "crowd" or "mob" was not new. In her seminal work on totalitarianism, she included a lengthy discussion of this phenomenon of modern times. See Arendt, *Origins of Totalitarianism*, pp. 186–243. See also Elias Canetti's deliberation on the "crowd" in his *Crowds and Power*, p. 22.

[104] "Nobody on my side dares to publish his views anymore, and with good reason. It's extremely dangerous because a whole very well-organized mob immediately pounces on anyone who dares to say anything. Finally, everyone believes what everyone else believes – as we have often experienced in life," wrote Arendt to Jaspers. Kohler and Saner (eds.), *Correspondence*, Letter 336, 20 October 1963, p. 523. She expressed herself very similarly to other correspondents in the same period.

"Public opinion," she had written to Scholem, "especially when it has been carefully manipulated, as in this case, is a very powerful thing."[105] From her pertinent and pessimistic analysis of modern nationalist societies and states, let alone totalitarian regimes, she knew that only few people were capable of standing firm in the midst of the storm. It is no accident that the most moving pages of her book dealt with those singular human beings who had the personal spiritual robustness to set themselves apart from the crowd, to be utterly alone, to remain true to themselves and think independently, which in itself was perceived by Arendt as a moral political action, and a great, noble endeavor.[106] She believed that these individuals – in writing about them she was undoubtedly writing about and at the same time constituting herself – illuminated "that space which reason creates and preserves between men," and brought salvation to the world and made it a better and worthier place to live in. As far as she was concerned, Scholem had not passed this hard yet elementary test, that of autonomous, independent acts of thinking, and of the readiness to sustain and fight for such thinking, which was, in her eyes, the supreme test, the very essence and definition of humanity.[107]

The conscious pariah

The fact that Arendt was critical of certain aspects of the new Zionist, national religion and the substitution of the cult of the state for the cult of God, did not make her a self-hating Jew, an anti-Zionist or an enemy of the State of Israel, as her critics claimed. The following lines can be read as a kind of substantiation and reification of the way in which Arendt was labeled and her loyalty submitted to meticulous scrutiny, and as a reverse contribution of a sort to that dubious political-intellectual move. And yet they are a vital conclusion to the discussion. As she wrote to Scholem, Arendt regarded her Jewishness as one of the indisputable facts of her life, and was grateful for this, in her own fashion. She wrote these words in an incomparably natural and noble manner,[108] bringing to mind what

---

[105] Feldman (ed.), *Jew as Pariah*, p. 248.

[106] See the story of Sergeant Anton Schmidt related by Abba Kovner in his testimony at the trial. See also Richard Bernstein's discussion in *Hannah Arendt and the Jewish Question*, pp. 173–178.

[107] See, for example, what Arendt wrote about the personal "inviolability" of her friend, the German, anti-Nazi philosopher Karl Jaspers: "It was self-evident that he would remain firm in the midst of catastrophe… an assurance that in times in which everything could happen one thing could not happen." Arendt, *Men in Dark Times*, pp. 78, 79.

[108] Feldman (ed.), *Jew as Pariah*, p. 246.

Sigmund Freud wrote in 1930 in the foreword to the Hebrew edition of *Totem and Tabu*:

The reader of this book [in its Hebrew version] will not easily find himself in the emotional standpoint of the author, who is ignorant of the holy tongue and scriptures, who has moved away completely from the religion of his forefathers – as from every other religion – and who cannot share national ideals, and yet at the same time has never kept his brethren at a distance nor moved away from them, and who feels that he is a Jew in the essence of his being and has no desire to change that being.[109]

In total contrast to the charges of self-hatred, anti-Semitism, and Nazi sympathies leveled against her, Hannah Arendt demonstrated her natural, unquestionable loyalty to her Jewish selfhood through her actions and her life, in both trivial and substantial ways. Thus, for example, she never changed her surname to that of her German husband, whom she married during the dark days of 1940, when both were refugees in occupied France. "I continue to use my old name. That's quite common here in America when a woman works, and I gladly adopted this custom out of conservatism (and also because I wanted my name to identify me as a Jew)," she wrote to Karl Jaspers, in 1946, in a private letter when they renewed their correspondence at the end of World War II, and many years before she became embroiled in the controversy on her loyalty to Judaism.[110] Her Jewishness was manifested not in membership of various Zionist-Jewish organizations and fraternities, but in her loyalty to what she considered to be Jewish sensitivities and commitments, from active assistance and contributions to refugee aid associations, both Jewish and non-Jewish, throughout her life, to the intellectual responsibilities and "roles" she undertook for which she paid a heavy personal price within her community.

Because she believed, as has been noted, that the role of the Jew, according to the "hidden tradition" of the conscious pariah, was to remain outside the ranks, not to belong, to become an outcast by choice, a rebel, and from this singular vantage point to make a contribution to mankind, and to enter its midst as a Jew.[111] Her self-positioning "outside the camp" was both principled and conceptual, two-folded and of dual meaning. Her perception of her duty to be both "solidaire et solitaire"[112]

[109] Quoted in Yosef Hayim Yerushalmi, *Freud's Moses: Judaism Terminable and Interminable*, New Haven and London 1991, p. 14.
[110] Kohler and Saner (eds.), *Correspondence*, Letter 34, 29 January 1946, p. 29.
[111] Hannah Arendt, "The Jew as Pariah: A Hidden Tradition", in Feldman (ed.), *Jew as Pariah*, pp. 67–68. See *Jewish Writings*, pp. 275, 282.
[112] This is how Albert Camus defined the ideal stand of the intellectual in his own society.

within her own people, and to think for herself in the political sphere and within the world, informed her analysis of Jewish history and the Jewish assimilation project. Indeed, Arendt could not have been more acerbic and severe in her treatment of assimilation. Assimilation, or emancipation from that perspective, she claimed, meant total, active self-abdication, and, "in a society on the whole hostile to the Jews ... it [was] possible to assimilate only by assimilating to antisemitism also."[113] "Assimilated" Jews always had to pay "with political misery for social glory and with social insult for political success," she wrote.[114] The Jewish parvenu who opted for the Gentile rules of the social game not only lost his humanity, his Jewishness, and any spontaneity in his choices on his way up, but worse even, became the very evidence of the anti-Semitic caricature of the Jew.[115] The consequences of this denial of one's own origin and of cutting oneself off from those who have not, or have not yet done it were that one became "a scoundrel."[116]

And yet, on a personal level, while being "solidaire" she rejected any organizational affiliation or collective "mobilization" so as to be able to adopt the role of "observer" outside the crowd. Only such an observer, she believed, could sustain "the activity of thinking as such, the habit of examining and reflecting upon whatever happens to come to pass, regardless of specific content and quite independent of results," as she put it,[117] and be able to judge, to tell right from wrong in particular concrete circumstances. Examining, reflecting independently, making deliberate moral choices: this was the conditio sine qua non for transforming judgment into effective action. The role of thoughtful observer was inseparable from the tasks of documenting and protest. A central dimension of her Jewishness, as she saw it, was her role as witness and recorder. She had been trained for this role from an early age – as Julia Kristeva commented – by her mother, who used to bear witness, to protest, who never failed to write angry letters and dispatch them by registered post whenever young Hannah's high school teachers in Germany voiced anti-Semitic comments. "It is not enough to say that what was clearly being formulated here was a secular, non-religious definition of Jewish identity," wrote Kristeva. It was self-definition by means of writing and documentation, namely "I define myself not as someone who shares a religion, as a partner in faith, but rather realize my identity by defending myself alone, and I write – we write

---

[113] Arendt, *Rahel Varnhagen*, p. 224. For a wider discussion of this issue see Bernstein, *Hannah Arendt and the Jewish Question*, pp. 14–45.
[114] Arendt, *Origins of Totalitarianism*, p. 56.
[115] Arendt, *Rahel Varnhagen*, p. 208.   [116] Ibid., p. 224.
[117] Arendt, "Thinking and Moral Consideration," p. 418, quoted in Bernstein, *Hannah Arendt and the Jewish Question*, p. 171.

[mother and daughter] – to whoever necessary because I believe – we believe – that one can and should record and judge wrongs."[118]

Opposition was Arendt's domain of thought and action, since without it, as she wrote to Scholem, there can be no patriotism or democracy. But she herself defined it as "loyal opposition." And, in fact, according to her perception, the same was true of her attitude to Zionism, even after she severed her organizational connections with it having realized that her views and those of her cothinkers in Brit Shalom regarding a binational state had been defeated, and Ben-Gurion's drive for separation and power was now the hegemonic policy. Her articles on Zionism – which she regarded as a political movement of major importance, since it was essentially an act of national self-determination by Jews, who thereby became active subjects in history; but was, at the same time, taking on disquieting apolitical and ahistorical characteristics – were clear manifestations of that same "loyal opposition." Her writing was inspired by a sense of deep emotional and intellectual involvement and of sincere apprehension for the future of the Zionist project.

She argued that a "Jewish state" would not only destroy the Palestinian entity, but also, as a result, endanger the very existence of the Jewish community in Palestine. A nation-state which derived its legitimacy from a distant, foreign power was, to her mind, a recipe for disaster.

Nationalism is bad enough when it trusts in nothing but the rude force of the nation. A nationalism that necessarily and admittedly depends upon the force of a foreign nation is certainly worse. This is the threatened fate of Jewish nationalism and the proposed Jewish State, surrounded inevitably by Arab states and Arab peoples. Even a Jewish majority in Palestine – nay, even a transfer of all Palestine Arabs, which is openly demanded by [Zionist] Revisionists – would not substantially change a situation in which Jews must either ask protection from an outside power against their neighbors or effect a working agreement with their neighbors ... The Zionists, if they continue to ignore the Mediterranean people and watch out only for the big faraway powers, will appear only as their tools, the agents of foreign and hostile interests. Jews who know their own history should be aware that such a state of affairs will inevitably lead to a new wave of Jew-hatred, the anti-Semitism of tomorrow.[119]

A Jewish nation-state, she also wrote, would gradually turn into a homogeneous Jewish state, its Arab population would be "driven" outside its borders, and thus a new stateless people would be created, the Palestinian Arab refugees. "After the war it turned out that the Jewish

---

[118] Julia Kristeva, *Le génie féminin, Hannah Arendt*, Paris 1999, pp. 174–175; see also interview of Arendt with Gunther Gauss.

[119] Hannah Arendt, "Zionism Reconsidered," in Feldman (ed.), *Jew as Pariah*, pp. 132–133. See *Jewish Writings*, pp. 344–345.

question, which was considered the only insoluble one, was indeed solved –
namely, by means of a colonized and then conquered territory – but this
solved neither the problem of the minorities nor the stateless ... The
solution of the Jewish question merely produced a new category of
refugees, the Arabs," she wrote.[120] In her article "To Save the Jewish
Homeland: There Is Still Time," written in 1948, at the height of the
conflict between the two national communities which claimed title to the
territory, she foresaw a gloomy future for the Jewish state if it did not
succeed in establishing cooperative and peaceful relations with the Arabs
within and outside its borders, and in granting full freedom, equal rights,
and human dignity to both Palestinians and Jews. Without these, she
argued, neither the Jews nor the others could survive.

And even if the Jews were to win the war, its end would find the unique possibilities and the unique achievements of Zionism in Palestine destroyed ... The
"victorious" Jews would live surrounded by an entirely hostile Arab population,
secluded inside ever-threatened borders, absorbed with physical self-defense to a
degree that would submerge all other interests and activities. The growth of a
Jewish culture would cease to be the concern of the whole people; special experiments would have to be discarded as impractical luxuries; political thought would
center around military strategy; economic development would be determined
exclusively by the needs of war. And all this would be the fate of a nation that –
no matter how many immigrants it could still absorb and how far it extended its
boundaries ... would still remain a very small people greatly outnumbered by
hostile neighbors.[121]

Once Israel was an established fact, Arendt followed events there
systematically and with concern. She was highly critical of Israel, the
nationalistic trends prevailing there, the insensitivity of its political leaders towards the Palestinian Arabs, the failure of the Israelis to launch
direct negotiations with their neighbors, the "theocratic rule of the rabbis," and the readiness of secular politicians to compromise on basic civil
rights in order to win the political support of the orthodox religious
parties. In the article above quoted, "To Save the Jewish Homeland,"
she also wrote that "every believer in a democratic government knows the
importance of a loyal opposition. The tragedy of Jewish politics at this
moment is that it is wholly determined by the Jewish Agency and that no
opposition to it of any significance exists either in Palestine or
America."[122]

[120] Arendt, *Origins of Totalitarianism*, p. 290.
[121] Arendt, "To Save the Jewish Homeland: There Is Still Time," in Feldman (ed.), *Jew as Pariah*, p. 187. See *Jewish Writings*, pp. 396–397.
[122] Ibid., p. 184.

But, to the day of her death, Israel was close to her heart and played an important role in her life, although, as was her wont, she did not often proclaim this fact. Together with her criticism of Israel's policy, she was also highly impressed with the state, particularly in its first years, with the prevailing social equality and the phenomenon of the kibbutzim which she perceived as a new aristocracy that had succeeded in creating a new individual. It was precisely her constantly critical stand towards Israel, tinged with strong emotion, which could attest to her inability, perhaps even unwillingness, to cut herself off from Israel and dissociate herself from it, though the new state often caused her disappointment and grief. And precisely because she was so critical of the state's political leadership and its political stands, she never ceased to be anxious for its fate, its very existence, and lived with the sense of the fragility of that existence, which was by no means self-evident. After the 1967 war she wrote to her friend Mary McCarthy that "any real catastrophe in Israel would affect me more deeply than almost anything else."[123]

"Solidaire et solitaire," involved and detached, present yet distant, family-member yet alien, Hannah Arendt was all these things, and this was how she saw herself, "the girl from another land" in Friedrich Schiller's words: a refugee,[124] a stateless émigrée, rebel by choice, without national affiliations, unless the whole world is a homeland, rootless, except for the roots of her thought and intellectual activity. "Thinking and Remembering ... is the human way of striking roots, of taking one's place in the world into which we all arrive as strangers," she said.[125] In this respect, one might say that the way in which she was cast out in almost ritual fashion by her community after the publication of her disturbing report on the Eichmann trial and the attempts to disown her reproduced in both content and form her existential condition. The

---

[123] Arendt to McCarthy, 17 October 1969, in Brightman (ed.), *Between Friends*, p. 249. For a more extensive discussion of Arendt's links to Israel, see also Bernstein, *Hannah Arendt and the Jewish Question*, pp. 154–157.

[124] In 1943 Arendt published an article entitled "We Refugees" in the Jewish periodical *Menorah Journal*, and although the United States had become her country, she continued to see herself as identified with the fate of the refugee everywhere, and was actively involved with and assisted political refugees. To be a refugee, for her, was also a chosen existential political stance towards the world and one's own community. "Those few refugees who insist on telling the truth, even to the point of 'indecency', get in exchange for their unpopularity, one priceless advantage: history is no longer a closed book to them and politics is no longer the privilege of Gentiles ... Refugees driven from country to country represent the vanguard of their peoples – if they keep their identity," she wrote in the same essay. See Feldman (ed.), *Jew as Pariah*, p. 66. See *Jewish Writings*, p. 274.

[125] See her lecture series, "Some Questions of Moral Philosophy," in 1965. Arendt Archives in the Library of Congress, Washington, quoted in Bernstein, *Hannah Arendt and the Jewish Question*, p. 211.

campaign to expel Arendt, which was nothing but a bitter and desperate attempt by her compatriots to exorcize the dybbuk of the Holocaust from their own bodies; the dybbuk of sober numinous testimony on what had occurred there; of the total powerlessness of the Jews during the Holocaust; of the tragic role of the Jews themselves in their own extermination; the dybbuk of the guilt of those who had not been there and had not done all they could to try to extend aid to their brethren; of the agonizing knowledge that such a human catastrophe was possible; of the malignant, identifying, constituting, and restorative memory of that catastrophe – this banishment campaign whose target was Hannah Arendt reified in some way her own personal choice and located her in the place where she wanted – and would have chosen – to be.

5   Yellow territories

The Jewish catastrophe in World War II, and the hundreds of thousands of Jewish refugees it left in its wake, rendered more urgent than ever the Jewish need for a homeland. The vision of that homeland was wholeheartedly supported even by as critical a Jewish philosopher as Hannah Arendt. The post-Holocaust world provided, she said, a rare opportunity for Jewish rehabilitation. However, while she had welcomed the foundation of a Jewish homeland, Arendt remained critical of many aspects of this vision, as conceived by the Zionist leadership, as well as the national myths at the basis of this vision, particularly those that were, in her eyes, thwarting the possibility of peaceful coexistence with the Palestinians and the Arab world. The most powerful myth, according to Arendt, was that throughout history the Jews, in contrast to all other nations, "were not history-makers but history-sufferers, preserving a kind of eternal identity of goodness whose monotony was disturbed only by the equally monotonous chronicle of persecutions and pogroms."[1] Arendt believed that this view was an attempt to discharge the victim of responsibility, and that it extracted problems of Jewish identity and suffering from history, from their very historicity by essentializing Jewish victimhood. Such a view, Arendt said, cut off Jewish history from European and world history, and created a state of mind that she defined as "worldlessness."

Involvement, responsibility, and historicity are key concepts in Arendt's political thought. Despite their grim history, the Jews have always been and remain still one group of people among other groups, "all of which are involved in the business of this world. And it does not simply cease to be coresponsible because it became the victim of the world's injustice and cruelty," she wrote.[2] Because of its history, and the fact of it having avoided all political action for two thousand years, the political history of the Jewish people became, according to Arendt, even more dependent upon unforeseen, accidental factors than the

---

[1] Hannah Arendt, "Jewish History Revised," in Feldman (ed.), *Jew as Pariah*, p. 96. See *Jewish Writings*, p. 303.
[2] Arendt, *Origins of Totalitarianism*, p. 6.

history of other nations, "so that the Jews stumbled from one role to the other and accepted responsibility for none."[3] In history and politics, however, people are never merely "sufferers" but always at the same time "doers." Their actions have consequences; they start a chain of occurrences which, because of its infinity, is boundless. The smallest act in the most limited circumstances bears the seal of the same boundlessness, she wrote, "because one deed, and sometimes one word, suffices to change every constellation." That is why, she said, "the old virtue of moderation, of keeping within bounds, is indeed one of the political virtues par excellence, just as the political temptation par excellence is indeed *hubris.*"[4]

Humans are limited beings among other limited beings, who are all the same, that is, human, yet at the same time utterly different from each other, because "nobody is ever the same as anyone else who ever lived, lives, or will live."[5] Humans are limited first by birth and death, then by the fact that they are not alone, they all live on the earth and inhabit the world, and thus they are affected and conditioned by both their own actions and those of all other human beings, and because each and every one of them is endowed with the capacity to instill reality with meaning and to create a social and political world, according to one's own vision. Therefore, writes Arendt, plurality is *the* condition of human action and of all political life.[6] To act, Arendt says, is to insert oneself into a public sphere whereby one's acts are defined and judged by others; it is to thrust oneself into an intangible and unpredictable "web of human relationships," which exist wherever men live together; a web that both constrains activity and empowers it, makes it possible. Yet, because of this already existing web of human relationship, "with its innumerable, conflicting wills and intentions, that action almost never achieves its purpose" in full.[7] The role of politics, therefore, is to create a common sphere, in which different human beings with different, often conflicting, visions and wills can act and speak confidently and freely as equal participants and be involved in "the business of this world."

Extreme realism

Zionism's innovation and its inital strength were its willingness to assume political responsibility for Jewish life, its desire to act within history and to do something in regard to the Jewish question, and its claim for the historical reintegration of the Jews in political terms. Yet from its inception, Herzlian Zionism was anti-political as much as it was political.

---

[3] Ibid., p. 8.   [4] Hannah Arendt, *The Human Condition*, Chicago 1958, pp. 190, 191.
[5] Ibid., p. 8.   [6] Ibid.   [7] Ibid., p. 184.

Zionism's determination to solve the problem of anti-Semitism through the establishment of a Jewish state, and by the deployment of organizational, diplomatic, economic, and eventually military means, was utterly political. However, the Zionist perception itself of anti-Semitism was deeply apolitical. Herzl saw anti-Semitism as a constant, a given phenomenon of nature, and the world a hostile space, where there are only Jews and anti-Semites.[8] For Herzl there had always been anti-Semitism and there always would be; anti-Semitism being also the definer of the Jewish people as such: all through history the Jews have been forced to be one people by their enemies, he said. In its extreme form, this view was reduced, in Arendt's words, "to the assumption, as arbitrary as it is absurd, that every Gentile living with Jews must become a conscious or subconscious Jew-hater."[9] This conviction reflected, paradoxically enough, a form of adoption, by the Jews, of that same outlook, namely the anti-Semitic view of Jews, an issue which preoccupied Arendt in all her writings on Jewish questions. Furthermore, such an attitude, she said, gave rise to cynicism and a type of political nihilism which, by its definition, devalues the present at the expense of a mythical and archetypal future, frustrates the possibility of devising and seeking political solutions to historical problems, and consequently encourages political irresponsibility.[10]

Zionism's nationalistic ideology has undermined its original rebellious political impulses. In its pursuit of a Jewish state, the be-all and end-all of Jewish/Zionist politics, the Zionist movement was blindly utopian, Arendt thought, because of its failure to acknowledge its own as well as the other party's limitations, or relative strength, and to take into consideration the historical circumstances within which it operated. Arendt saw in Zionist ideology and leadership from Herzl on a definite tendency of evading questions of political consequences, and an unspoken, hidden streak of political messianism. On the eve of the establishment of the State of Israel, Arendt observed with growing anxiety the intransigent positions of both belligerent parties, the Palestinians and the Jews, leading inevitably to a double tragedy, of both peoples. She deplored the Jewish bellicose and triumphal state of mind, mixed with what she saw as a suicidal messianism, and the Jewish unanimous consensus concerning the road (map) to be taken, consensus that accepts no criticism, no dissenting voices or differences of opinion; attitudes that were enhanced by the

---

[8] "The peoples among whom Jews live are one and all shamefully and shamelessly anti-semitic," wrote Herzl in *Der Judenstaat*, quoted in Hannah Arendt, "Herzl and Lazare," in Feldman (ed.), *Jew as Pariah*, p. 127. See *Jewish Writings*, p. 341.

[9] Hannah Arendt, "Zionism Reconsidered," in Feldman (ed.), *Jew as Pariah*, p. 147. See *Jewish Writings*, p. 358.

[10] For a wider discussion, see Jeffrey C. Isaac, *Arendt, Camus, and Modern Rebellion*, New Haven 1992, pp. 206–216.

pressure and conflicts in Palestine and the enormous catastrophe in
Europe. Of this state of mind she wrote:

The moment has now come to get everything or nothing, victory or death; Arab
and Jewish claims are irreconcilable and only a military decision can settle the
issue; the Arabs – all Arabs – are our enemies ... only outmoded liberals believe in
compromise, only philistines believe in justice, and only *schlemiels* prefer truth and
negotiation to propaganda and machine gun; Jewish experience in the last decades ... has finally awakened us and taught us to look out for ourselves; this alone
is reality ... We are ready to go down fighting.[11]

The historical proximity between the Holocaust and the establishment
of the State of Israel, and the decisive role of the former in achieving and
shaping the latter, yielded this kind of catastrophic messianism, and a new,
or new-old, myth of destruction and redemption; of powerlessness and
empowerment that was removed from both the historical and the political.
The connection of Israeli power and power practices of the new, Jewish
state with the history of total powerlessness and victimhood of the
Holocaust had began to be forged while the war was still raging, and
developed in gradual fashion and at various levels. It was not born out of
a formal, explicit decision, but was rather part of the continuous effort
invested in the political and educational endeavor of nation-building by the
dominant cultural and political elites in Israel. This connection had gathered momentum and evolved into a self-evident presence, expounding
itself as part of the great narrative of Israeli redemption, until it became
the narrative itself. From the partisan-poet Abba Kovner to the right-wing
leader Menachem Begin, from the Palmach commander Yitzhak Sadeh to
the soldier-general Ariel Sharon, from Ben-Gurion and Nathan Alterman
to the song writer Haim Hefer and the politician Benjamin Netanyahu,
through right, left, center, and fringe politics, the Israeli discourse of power
was perceived not only as a vital necessity in the context of the Israeli-Arab
conflict, but also as a form of atonement, endowing the Holocaust and the
history of the Diaspora with retroactive, belated meaning.

The process was dialectic. Memory of the Holocaust invested the local
conflict with significance, and extracted it from its political and historical
dimensions, while the discourse of the conflict consolidated and reinforced
the role of the Holocaust as the constituent myth of the Zionist-Israeli
meta-narrative. Both the Holocaust and the ongoing conflict were thus
detached from their specific historical contexts, from their complexities
and inner contradictions as historical events; borders between them

---

[11] Hannah Arendt, "To Save the Jewish Homeland: There Is Still Time," in Feldman (ed.),
   Jew as Pariah, p. 181. See *Jewish Writings*, p. 391.

became blurred, turning them into closed, critique-proof mythical realities, bound together and sustaining one another. The Jewish Holocaust, and the Israeli power, had thus become a central factor in consolidating the Israeli identity and in fortifying social cohesion and solidarity within Israel.

Tracing this discourse and its various components – the sanctification of Israeli military power, of the homeland and its borders, and of death for the sake of the homeland and its sacred borders – when linked with the Holocaust, along with the political implications of that discourse, is the subject of the closing chapter of this book. Power, justification of power, land and borders, and "beautiful death" for their sake will be discussed here, as well as their expropriation from the political context and their translocation to the sacred and the absolute. The way in which they were conjoined, fatefully and mythically, with the Holocaust and its nationalized, political memory, which played a critical part in constituting the consciousness of their sanctity, will be part of the argument.

The victim and the power

The central, hegemonic, though not exclusive, wellspring for discourse related to the Holocaust and to power in the pre-state stage was the dominant, active, and organized bloc in the Jewish community in Palestine, namely the labor movement. The discourse was created jointly by political leaders, the military, artists, poets, and teachers, most of whom had not been in Europe during the war and had no close-range experience of Nazism and the destruction it had inflicted on European Jewry. This remoteness from the historical actuality, and the infinite complexity of that human catastrophe generated the alienation which, from the outset, made possible the adoption of the Zionist and Israeli view of the Holocaust, its victims and survivors, and their conversion into ideological and political arguments in the service of the state. However, from the very beginning, there were fundamental differences between the use the left-wing sector made of Holocaust discourse and its use by the other large sector, namely the right wing. Whereas the central, hegemonic Holocaust discourse of the labor movement applied the images of the Holocaust and Nazism in particular to external enemies – mainly for purposes of fostering Israeli power and the ethos of its justice – Holocaust images employed by the opposing right wing were applied to the adversary within, the political rival,[12] in particular in the context of

[12] See, for example, Begin's remarks on the 1947 partition scheme: "If the scheme is criminal, what can we say of Jewish assent to this scheme? What can be said of Jews, of Jewish 'leaders,' who are ready to assent to a liquidation plan? What can be said of a

the borders of the land and the state, and in order to distinguish between the state (whose borders are deemed provisional) and the (eternal) land.

The role fulfilled by the Holocaust in the discourse of the local conflict has, for many years, had a direct impact on the way in which people imagine their present condition and their lives. The Holocaust is inserted directly and metaphorically into everyday life in Israel, which is loaded, in this fashion, with meaning beyond itself, as are power and the ideology of power. A quality beyond the secular and the historical has been attributed to this power; the transcendental, inexpressible quality, drawn from the depths of Jewish experience and charged by Jewish victimhood – by absolute Jewish guiltlessness and justice on the one hand and the eternal hostility of a Gentile world on the other – all of which reached their apotheosis in the Holocaust.

"Whence did this nation derive its strength?" asked the poet Haim Guri rhetorically after the 1967 war, which transformed the link between Israeli power and the Holocaust into a fateful mutation. "From there," was his answer, a "there" that is introduced time and again into Israeli existence and is always defined as "here"; it also came from a never-ending past, which was a perpetual, immobile present, a present without a past or a future. "Take note of this lesson," wrote Guri to his native-born Israeli audience, young soldiers destined to carry forever the burden of war:

Those who were liquidated there had no homeland and nobody cared about their lives, neither their neighbors nor the strong and remote people in the capital cities of the West and the East. Take note of this lesson! *All of the past is but the present,* and between you and your annihilation lies only *your sword.* Do not despise your battered and dead forefathers ... You, who have a country, do not pass judgment on those damned people! If you have the strength to read the history books without being stupefied by fury and pity, go to the books and learn whence this nation gained its strength ... You too come from the ashes, you who have a land beneath your feet.[13]

This text contains all the needed elements: eternal, unchanging super-fluousness and murderability of Jews with no country; the ashes of "there" that constitute the power of "here"; the sword, the last sole barrier to total annihilation; and the blood-link between Israel's young natives and the battered, exterminated fathers in Europe.

leadership ready to profiteer with the blood of tens of thousands, ready to become – despite their 'patriotic' prattle – a Judenrat? If splitting the country is a crime, then consent to that splitting is a two-fold crime." Menachem Begin, *Ba'mahteret (Underground)*, Tel Aviv 1976, vol. II, p. 250, quoted in Aryeh Naor, *Eretz Israel Ha'shlema, Emuna U'mediniyut (Greater Israel, Belief and Policy)*, Haifa and Lod 2001, p. 92.

[13] Haim Guri, "You Who Have a Country," *Zot Ha'aretz*, 18 April 1969, pp. 4–5 (my italics).

Twenty years before the older Guri wrote "Whence does this nation derive its strength?" the young Guri provided the answer to his own rhetorical question, declaring that Israeli power emanated "from that conflagration which consumed your tortured and blackened bodies." In Guri's words, the new Israelis, Israeli power, and Israel's war in the Middle East are forever stoked by the flames of the great conflagration which raged through Europe, consuming most of its Jews, and derive their meaning and self-justification from there. "With [that conflagration] we went to battle on our land … we transformed your insult into guns … your song, stifled in the flames, rose up from the throats of the commando units like a vow … we avenged your bitter and solitary death with our fist, which is heavy and hot."[14] According to Guri, the Children of Israel come out of Egypt and of other places of servitude, and continue to do so from generation to generation, emerging "from the ashes" in a never-ending cycle, converting the insult inflicted on the Jews into guns and avenging, with their fists, the continuing death of those who perished, as if military victory elsewhere, in another war, could resurrect those dead. Guri, the poet and journalist who saw the ruins of post-war Europe with his own eyes, nevertheless appointed himself the spokesman of that quasi-material, fixed, mythical, ahistorical essence. By its nature, this essence could not be the object of historical perception and denouement. For years, as might have been expected, this earlier text has had an autonomous, rich life, being, among other things, the main text declaimed at Yad Vashem commemoration ceremonies in Jerusalem for many years.[15]

In texts less direct than Guri's, the Holocaust also plays a major role in constructing the logic of Israeli power, its signification and justification. Yitzhak Sadeh, mythical commander and mentor of the Zionist Striking Units, the Palmach, a central member of the state-building elite, speaks in his homily "My Sister on the Beach" – written in the late forties – about the direct encounter between Holocaust survivors and native-born Israelis. The wretched, violated, and sterilized Diaspora personified by the girl survivor reaching the shores of the homeland serves Sadeh in the validation and sanctification of power; the new masculine Israeli power, avenging and atoning, in contrast to the feminine Diaspora Jewish wretchedness:

> For these sisters – I am *strong*.
> For these sisters – I am *brave*.

[14] Haim Guri, "From that Conflagration," in Yitzhak Zuckerman and Moshe Basok (eds.), *Sefer Milhamot Ha'getaot, Bein Ha'homot, Ba'mahanot, Ba'ya'arot* (*The Book of the Battles in the Ghettos, between Walls, in Camps, in Forests*), Tel Aviv 1954, p. 696.
[15] Author's conversation with Haim Guri, Jerusalem, July 2001.

For these sisters – I will also be *cruel*.
For you everything – everything.[16]

The Holocaust licensed heirs

In Sadeh's early text, the Holocaust and its appropriated survivors had become the supreme sanction for the deployment of Israeli power, its interpreters, apologists, and justifiers. But since the Holocaust had been positioned as all-embracing ultimate authority, lending significance to Israeli existence and the continuing conflict, and since discourse formulators cannot exercise full control over the uses made of it and on its behalf, Holocaust discourse too was turned upside down; it brought out and exposed a repressed, threatening, and muffled truth about the nature of Israeli power and its victims, the troubling insight that perpetrators and victims, the humane and inhumane, exist side by side and finally, that evil is not the exclusive trait of one group or another, as Romain Gary said: "It concerns not only the Germans. It follows humanity everywhere, and always ... and the moment it gets too close, it penetrates you, you become a German."[17] Yosef Nahmani, a member of the early paramilitary groupHa'shomer (the guardian), senior officer in the Haganah, and later Director of the Jewish National Fund in Eastern Galilee, was stunned by the cruelty of Israeli soldiers towards Arab villagers in late 1948, and the model he cited to describe it was that of Nazi troops during World War II. He wrote in his diary after having seen the devastation wrought by young Israelis in Galilee:

In Safsaf, after ... the inhabitants raised the white flag, they assembled the men and women separately, bound the hands of fifty or sixty villagers, shot and killed them and buried them in a single pit. They also raped several of the village women. Near the thicket, he [Friedman?] saw several dead women, among them a woman clutching her dead child. In Ilabun and Faradia, they greeted the soldiers with white flags ... and then ... [the soldiers] opened fire and after thirty people had been killed they started moving the rest on foot ... [towards] Lebanon. In Salha, which raised the white flag, there was a real massacre. They killed men and women, about 60–70. *Where did they learn cruel conduct such as that of the Nazis* [?] ... One officer told me that the most eager were those who had come

---

[16] Y. Noded (Yitzhak Sadeh), "My Sister on the Beach," in Zerubavel Gilad (ed.), *Sefer Ha'palmach* (*The Book of the Palmach*), A, Tel Aviv 1953, p. 725 (my italics). See Zertal, *From Catastrophe to Power*, pp. 263–9.

[17] "Il n'y a pas que les Allemands. Ça rôde partout, depuis toujours, autour de l'humanité ... Dès que ça se rapproche trop, dès que ça pénètre en vous, l'homme se fait allemand." Romain Gary, *Éducation Européenne*, Paris 1945, p. 76.

from the camps ... Is there no more humane way than sending these inhabitants away by such means and then looting their property [?][18]

Meir Yaari, a radical left-wing leader, said in response to the conduct of Israeli troops in Arab villages during the 1948 war (and to the claim of one soldier that he had wanted to avenge the "six million Jews"): "What a lie and atrocity to say it was revenge for the six million ... Are we going to permit the villains to hide behind the six million, to murder a single defenseless Arab without compunction."[19]

Several years later, in the massacre of Arab civilians in the village of Kafar Kassem, the Holocaust again served as yardstick for Israeli soldiers' conduct, cut from their own perspective. "We acted like Germans, automatically, we didn't think,"[20] said Shalom Ofer after he, together with several of his men, had killed forty-one Arab villagers, men, women, and children, in October 1956. Not all Israeli soldiers acted like Ofer, "like Germans." Some of them openly refused to obey the order, whose vague phrasing and tone made it possible to liquidate Arab civilians on their way back from work because they had not observed the curfew. These soldiers actively evaded the order and did not take part in the massacre. But there were some, as there always are – Shalom Ofer and his like – who, even if they had not heard with their own ears the rhetoric of Holocaust and power of Israel's ruling elite, had regarded themselves as standard-bearers of the mission of total warfare against the Arab-Nazi threat. Shalom Ofer expressed no remorse over his actions, neither at his trial nor subsequently.[21]

He and his troops did not perpetrate the killing on a momentary impulse or as a defensive act. Lucidly and deliberately, they awaited their victims at Kafar Kassem and when these helpless laborers, who were ignorant of the new curfew regulations imposed in their absence,

[18] Diary of Yosef Nahmani, 6 November 1948, quoted in Benny Morris, *Tikun Ta'ut, Yehudim Ve'aravim Be'Eretz Israel, 1936–1956 (Correcting an Error: Jews and Arabs in Eretz Israel, 1936–1956)*, Tel Aviv 2000, pp. 131–132 (my italics).
[19] Meir Yaari at the Mapam Political Committee, 11 November 1948, Kibbutz Artzi Archives, 10.95.10 (6), Aharon Cohen's notes, quoted in Morris, *Correcting an Error*, pp. 138–139.
[20] Quoted in Ruvik Rosenthal, *Kafar Kassem, Iru'im U'mitos (Kafar Kassem, Events and Myth)*, Tel Aviv 2000, p. 32, 47. Some of the reactions to the massacre linked it in one way or another to the deeds of the Nazis. "Soon we shall resemble Nazis and pogromists," wrote Rabbi Benyamin in *The Candle*, (November–December 1956), while Yeshayahu Leibovitz wrote in a letter to *Ha'aretz*, on 28 October 1956: "We must organize a mass petition ... and demand a revision of the Nuremberg trials and the rehabilitation of the officers, troops and bureaucrats who were sentenced to death there and hanged, because they all acted only in accordance with the explicit orders of their legal commanders."
[21] Rosenthal, *Kafar Kassem*, p. 32.

reached the village's outskirts, Ofer gave the order "to mow them down."[22] Following this "mowing down," the soldiers went further and carried out a "killing verification" procedure. The role reversal had now been completed. The licensed heirs of the Holocaust had transformed themselves into efficient and murderous "Germans," while the "reincarnation" of the Nazis, according to Israeli Holocaust discourse, simple Arab villagers, became by this deed the total victims of the misdeed of transposing the Holocaust into the local conflict.[23]

The politics of Holocaust representation, its recounting and construing into local politics is older than the State of Israel. And it seems to have known no limits. An initial move had been the transformation of the Arabs into Nazis, initially adopted by Ben-Gurion in the pre-state period, when he equated the conflict to a confrontation of Holocaust-like potential and dimensions. Speaking of the imminent war in Palestine, Ben-Gurion warned that the opponents in this struggle would not be political but "the disciples and even teachers of Hitler, who know only one way of solving the Jewish problem: total destruction."[24] While this statement could have been seen as a one-time slip of the tongue, a rare comment delivered in a closed forum, a statement Ben-Gurion made a few years later in his party's Central Committee during the debate on the German reparations reinforced the equation of Arabs and Nazis. Justifying the need for German funds to consolidate the state and build up the country and its military might, Ben-Gurion said: "We do not want to return to the ghetto ... We do not want the Arab Nazis to come and slaughter us!"[25]

---

[22] Ibid., p. 28.

[23] Yael Mishali, a settler in Efrat in the Etzion Bloc, writes in the seventeenth month of the second Palestinian Intifada: "As a Jewish Israeli woman, located on the less sympathetic side of the conflict, I teach my children that from day to day we become less right, less moral, less strong and less triumphant. The choices we made and the paths we followed not too many years ago are becoming irrelevant ... Yes, occupation corrupts. It forces our soldiers (our children, brothers, husbands) to wrestle with a Nazi style of soldiery. Even if only a few of them fail, we cannot permit it." Yael Mishali, "Losing the Way," Y-net, 17 February 2002.

[24] Ben-Gurion at the Zionist Executive meeting, Zurich, 26 August 1947 (Session 3), Central Zionist Archives S5/320.

[25] Ben-Gurion at the Mapai Central Committee, 13 December 1951, Labor Party Archives, 23/51; in his preface to the book *Gvilei Esh* (*Scrolls of Fire*) which commemorated those killed in the 1948 War of Independence, Ben-Gurion wrote: "Only a few years ago six million Jews were liquidated in Europe by the Nazi murderers. One of Hitler's close associates in this genocide ... was Haj Amin Husseini, then Mufti of Jerusalem. This Nazi leader of the Arabs was now one of the leaders of the attempt to annihilate the Jewish Yishuv in Eretz Israel." In Reuven Avinoam (ed.), *Gvilei Esh* (*Scrolls of Fire*), Tel Aviv 1952, p. 12; the first issue of the IDF weekly, *Ba'mahaneh*, also drew an

The Nazification of the enemy, whoever that enemy may be, and the transformation of security threats into danger of total annihilation of the state, seem to have characterized the way of speech of Israel's political, social, and cultural elites, with very few exceptions. However, whereas the translocation of Israel's 1948 military struggle back to the psychological sphere of World War II Europe by a man like Abba Kovner, who had been there and was still immersed in the vanished Jewish world, was understandable, the systematic analogy drawn by Benjamin Netanyahu fifty years later, in his speeches and book, *A Place Among the Nations*, between Arafat (and Haj Amin El-Husseini) and Hitler, was a calculated political move. Kovner, a leader of the Jewish underground in Vilna – a partisan who, on his own admission, abandoned his mother in the ghetto when he went to the forests to fight; who witnessed the murder and disappearance of his family and friends and saw his Jewish world collapsing around him; who had just emerged from the dark period in his life and from his post-Holocaust involvement in attempts to wreak revenge on surviving Nazis – served during the 1948 war as cultural and information officer of the Givati Brigade on the southern front. In his daily "Battle Page" which he wrote for the Brigade troops in July–November 1948, he compared the battle against the Egyptian army to the fighting in Europe a few years earlier, and perceived it as the continuation of the ultimate, total struggle against the Nazis.

These "pages" are replete with highflown "Soviet" rhetoric and phraseology from World War II reality. In the first issue Kovner equated the logic of the Egyptian fighting and "the Egyptian invaders" with "the logic of insanity, the insanity of the illusion, that same illusion which impelled Hitler." Revenge against the "[Egyptian] brutal invaders" must not be "too cheap," he wrote, and compared kibbutz Negba's stand against the Egyptians to the battle for Stalingrad. In other "pages" he employed bloodthirsty and hate-filled fascist images in referring to the enemy, such as "murderous dogs," "bloodhounds," "corpses, corpses, corpses," "pools of blood," or "stinking heaps of Egyptians," "all around you gleam the stupid eyes of the Nile's dogs – into the Nile, dogs!" "for they came to exterminate us … This soil cannot tolerate their unclean jackboots, vipers," "the body of the Egyptian snake writhes fragment by fragment," "how great is the night of revenge, invaders, the night of revenge." Finally, Kovner compared the fleeing Egyptians to "a blind … herd of sheep," a reverse allusion to the image of Jews going to their death "like

analogy between Arabs and Nazis, in Order of the Day No. 4 of the Chief of Staff, Yaakov Dori: "The allies and disciples of Nazism joined forces against us, against our rebirth, against our independence." *Ba'mahaneh*, 16 April 1948.

sheep to the slaughter," a phrase Kovner himself had first written in his January 1942 call to resistance in Vilna.[26]

Benjamin Netanyahu's discussions of the conflict from a perspective of half a century after the fact were deliberate experiments in cloning, conducted in the discourse laboratory of Israeli right-wing politics. They could be understood as part of his campaign against the peace agreements Israel had signed with the Palestinians or as his own struggle for prominence within the Israeli right, or both. Netanyahu's remarks implied that those who negotiate with the Palestinians and sign political agreements with them are not different from those who did, or would have done the same with Hitler. Arafat and his organization, says Netanyahu, are spiritual and political descendants of the Mufti of Jerusalem,[27] and the demonization of the Mufti serves to magnify the Arafatian threat. Netanyahu is not content, therefore, with a prosaic and precise description – dubious and despicable enough in itself – of the Mufti's ties with Nazi Germany, nor even with stating that the Mufti "played a part in the decision to exterminate the Jews of Europe," and that he "repeatedly proposed ... primarily to Hitler, Ribbentrop and Himmler the extermination of the Jews of Europe." He adds what, in the past, was just implied, namely that the Mufti was "one of *the initiators of the systematic extermination of European Jewry ... collaborator and advisor* of Eichmann and Himmler in the execution of the plan,"[28] a claim that has no – and never had – historical substantiation, and that removes a large part of the responsibility from the true initiators and perpetrators of the Final Solution.

To strengthen his argument about the Nazi–Palestinian link, Netanyahu was not shy in drawing the fascist and Nazi tendencies of the Palestinian national movement in the 1920s and 1930s, the establishment of its own National-Socialist cells, and its activity in disseminating Nazi and anti-Semitic literature.[29] The Nazi annexation of the Sudetenland,

[26] First page undated; page No. 2, 9 July; No. 5, 13 July; No. 6, 14 July; No. 8, 16 July; No. 9, 17 July; No. 11, undated; No. 15, 19 October; No. 16, 20 October; page of 11 November, respectively.
[27] Benjamin Netanyahu, *A Place Among the Nations*, New York 1993, p. 195. It is noteworthy that not long after having written this, Netanyahu, while in power, negotiated with Arafat and signed agreements with him.
[28] Ibid. p. 193 (my italics).
[29] Ibid., pp. 190–191. There were no National-Socialist trends in Palestinian society, despite Netanyahu's assertion. However, in the 1930s there were in fact groups in Palestinian-Arab society which were attracted to fascist ideologies, and were drawn to ideologies of national liberation, power, and strong leadership, just as such groups, e.g. the Revisionist movement, existed in Jewish society in Palestine during that period, which Netanyahu does not mention. Nor does he refer to the numerous denunciations of Nazism in Palestinian Arab society, the censoring of pro-German proclamations, and

first stage in Czechoslovakia's occupation, is then compared by Netanyahu to the gouging "of Judea and Samaria out of the body of Israel."[30] Last but not least, the UN is depicted as a proto-Nazi organization. Its November 1975 resolution defining Zionism as "a racist movement" is an achievement that "had eluded even the greatest anti-Semitic propagandists like Torquemada and *Goebbels*,"[31] while what Jew haters "failed to do in the Inquisition and in *the darkest days of the Holocaust* had at long last been achieved by the General Assembly of the United Nations."[32]

From the ashes of history

Two major texts of the 1950s, written by two of the most influential figures and identity-builders in Israel, established, each in its own way, the construed link between the Holocaust and Israeli power in the context of the Israeli–Arab conflict. The first, chronologically, was Ben-Gurion's radio address to the nation on 19 October 1953, after the Kibbya massacre. The second was Chief of Staff Moshe Dayan's eulogy over the grave of Ro'i Rothberg. The Kibbya story began with the murder of a woman and her two small children in the village of Yahud, on the night of 12–13 October 1953, by Palestinian border-infiltrators from Jordan. The decision to retaliate was taken at the highest level, at a meeting attended by Prime Minister Ben-Gurion (then on vacation), Acting Minister of Defense, the Chief of Staff, and the Head of the Operations Moshe Dayan. Army units were dispatched to the Palestinian village of Kibbya to mount a "reprisal operation," the aim being "destruction and maximum casualties in order to drive the villagers out of their homes."[33] In the course of the military operation carried out two nights after the Yahud murder by soldiers of Unit 101 and a parachute battalion commanded by Ariel Sharon, some sixty people were killed, most of them women and children, and forty-five houses were destroyed. A worldwide outrage, unprecedented since Israel's establishment, erupted in the wake of the operation. Britain and the United States threatened to take action against Israel. Foreign Minister Moshe Sharett confessed in his diary his shock at

the support in the Arab media in 1939 for the Allies in the war against Germany, in contrast, as noted, to the Mufti's stand. See Azmi Bisahra, "The Arabs and the Holocaust: The Problem of the Word And," *Zmanim*, 53, Summer 1995.
[30] Netanyahu, *A Place Among the Nations*, p. 158.   [31] Ibid. (my italics).
[32] Ibid., p. 84 (my italics).
[33] IDF Archives 644/56/207, quoted in Morris, *Correcting an Error*, p. 176; see also Shabtai Tevet's article, "The Mysteries of Kibbya," in two parts – Part A: "Was the Operational Order Forged?"; Part B: "Who Altered the HQ Order?" *Ha'aretz*, 2 and 9 September 1994 respectively.

the scope of the slaughter. In order to "reduce the political damage," Ben-Gurion made the following statement to the nation:

> For more than four years armed forces from Transjordan and other Arab countries have been breaking into frontier Jewish settlements ... for purpose of murder and robbery ... hundreds of Israeli citizens, woman and men, old people and infants, have been murdered and severely injured ... the frontier dwellers, most of them Jewish refugees from Arab countries or *survivors of Nazi concentration camps*, have been for years the target of these murderous assaults ... The Israeli government justifiably allotted them weapons and trained them to defend themselves. However, the armed forces from Transjordan did not cease their criminal attacks until the patience of some frontier settlements was exhausted, and after the murder of a mother and her two children in the village of Yahud, they attacked this week the village of Kibbya across the border ... The Israeli government strongly rejects the absurd claim that six hundred soldiers of Israel's Defense Forces took part [in the operation] against Kibbya. Having conducted a thorough investigation, we certify beyond a doubt that not a single military unit, however small, was absent from camp on the night of the attack on Kibbya.[34]

The veracity of the speech and the political-media manipulation by the Prime Minister had already been deliberated.[35] What is important in the context of our discussion is the two-fold use made by Ben-Gurion of Holocaust survivors living in border settlements, to whom he added at this opportunity "Jewish refugees from the Arab countries." While rhetorically magnifying the crime of the Palestinian infiltrators by defining the objects of their crime as ultimate Jewish victims, survivors of Nazi concentration camps, Ben-Gurion did the almost inconceivable, not so much by lying to Israeli citizens (in itself no rare phenomenon in politics), but by pointing to those same victims and singling them out as having "justifiably" taken up arms and perpetrated the Kibbya massacre. Through this political-rhetorical act, by means of his story, Ben-Gurion recast the entire pack of participants. While concealing the role of the army in the affair, either for *raison d'état* or out of internal political calculations, he moved the Jewish frontier dwellers, many of them in fact Holocaust survivors, immigrants to a new country still foreign to them, Israel's weakest and most forsaken people, to center stage, equipped them with weapons, and transformed them into avengers who had taken the law into their own hands. By so doing, he also exposed them to possible retaliatory acts on the part of Palestinians across the border. He allowed himself to do it – something he would never have considered doing to veteran Israelis – because these marginal, new immigrants, living on the

---

[34] Ben-Gurion on Kol Israel, 19 October 1953 (The Voice of Israel: Israeli, national radio), quoted in Morris, *Correcting an Error*, p. 286 (my italics).
[35] See, inter alia, Morris's discussion in ibid., p. 186.

borderline of Israeliness, in every possible sense, had no voice, no representation, and no political power, and, consequently, could be discounted. Just as they had been sent, without being consulted, to those border villages, many of them recently abandoned Arab villages converted to immigrant settlements, to become the living barrier of the new state, so they could also be given an identity and molded to fit any propaganda need or political contingency.

The Zionist revolution which, according to Zionist discourse, represented a break and a new beginning in Jewish history, did not constitute a barrier to the infiltration of Holocaust images into the concept of heroic death on the country's borders in the 1950s. Whereas Ben-Gurion recruited living Holocaust survivors to meet the needs of the state as he perceived them at that given moment, Chief of Staff Moshe Dayan harnessed the Holocaust dead who gave meaning to Israel's "border wars," to its justified use of the sword and the inevitable death for the land. Death always brought out the best in Moshe Dayan. "Cemeteries provide him with the inspiration for his best speeches, and it is in his eulogies that he almost becomes a poet," wrote Amos Oz of Dayan.[36] Delivered on 30 April 1956, Dayan's eulogy for the slain Ro'i Rothberg, was indeed the best funeral oration he ever delivered, a masterpiece of national rhetoric of death, which draws its energies from the depths of the Jewish destruction.

In charge of the security of his kibbutz on the Gaza Strip border, Ro'i Rothberg was shot and killed on the morning of 29 April 1956, while patrolling the fields on horseback. A chain of events in the few months preceding the murder had exacerbated tensions along all of Israel's borders. Israel reacted to the frequent border-infiltrations and the murder of Israelis in border settlements by mounting larger reprisal attacks. The Kinneret Operation under Ariel Sharon's command (December 1955), aimed at Syrian positions across the border without having been "preceded by any specific provocation by the Syrians,"[37] which claimed more than fifty Syrian lives, including civilians, provoked criticism within cabinet circles, against Israel's excessive use of power and Ben-Gurion's decision-making process without consulting his colleagues. Cabinet members argued that Dayan had deliberately "heated up" the borders to draw Israel into a pre-emptive war.[38] In early April 1956, three Israeli

---

[36] Amos Oz, *Be'or Ha'tkhelet Ha'aza* (*In the Fierce Blue Light*), Jerusalem 1990, p. 284.
[37] "Report of Investigation of Operation 'Olive Leaves,'" IDF HQ, undated, quoted in Benny Morris, *Israel's Border Wars, 1949–1956: Arab Infiltration, Israeli Retaliation and the Countdown to the Suez War*, Oxford 1993, p. 381.
[38] Moshe Sharett, *Yoman Ishi* (*Personal Diary*), Vol. 5, p. 1313, entry for 23 December 1955. Sharett quotes others who said the same.

soldiers on motorized patrol along the Egyptian border in the Gaza Strip were killed. In reaction, Israeli guns shelled Egyptian positions, and the Egyptians, in their turn, shelled the kibbutzim along the border. Israel again reacted more drastically with shelling at Gaza town itself.[39] Fifty–eight Egyptian and Palestinian civilians were killed, including fifteen women and ten children. About one hundred were injured. Five Israeli civilians were killed in the exchange of fire, two soldiers were injured.[40] In retaliation, the Egyptians renewed the *fedayun* infiltrations into the Gaza Strip, and in the second week of April, in a series of terrorist acts in Israel's hinterland, ten Israeli civilians were killed, including children and teachers. Israel mobilized reserve units and was on the verge of war. UN Secretary Dag Hammarskjöld's intervention achieved a ceasefire, which led to a certain relaxation of tension, but did not stop the infiltrations into kibbutz Nahal Oz fields.

The ambush murder of Ro'i Rothberg was not incidental. It was planned and particularly shocking. Ro'i's body was savagely mutilated. Several days earlier, during a tour of the area, Dayan had met Ro'i, the blond Israeli youth from Tel Aviv who had settled on the border on his own volition, and had been captivated by everything this boy represented. He was personally touched by the murder, beyond its national and military implications. He returned to Nahal Oz to eulogize Ro'i Rothberg, and through his oration, the words he chose with great skill, he performed the Homerian act of elevating the dead young man from ordinary on to a more sublime plane; pulling Rothberg out from the anonymity of the ordinary living and dead, transforming his death, the sacrifice on the nation's altar, into a "beautiful" and glorious death in classic Greek terms, a death, which bestows life after death, eternal life.[41] Dayan's eulogy appeared in every newspaper the following day and was reprinted many times in weeklies and contemporary texts, and broadcast frequently.[42] It had an immediate, stunning impact. The Israeli

---

[39] This was Mordechai Bar-On's, Dayan's bureau chief, testimony.

[40] All these details are based on Morris, *Israel's Border Wars*, pp. 387–389. Mordechai Bar-On wrote similarly in his books *Etgar Ve'tigra: Ha'derekh Le'mivtza Kadesh – 1956* (*Challenge and Dispute: The Road to the Sinai Campaign – 1956*), Be'er Sheva 1991, p. 88, and *Sha'arei Aza: Mediniyut Ha'bitahon Veha'hutz shel Medinat Israel 1955–1957* (*The Gates of Gaza: Israel's Security and Foreign Policy 1955–1957*), Tel Aviv 1992, p. 144. Morris, who usually avoids loaded statements, adds in his cautious way: "The Israeli response was swift and massive. Perhaps Dayan sought to provoke war." Morris, *Israel's Border Wars*, p. 388.

[41] On the term "beautiful death," see Vernant, *Mortals and Immortals*, pp. 50–75; Lyotard, *The Differend*, pp. 99–101.

[42] Moshe Dayan, *Avnei Derekh, Autobiografia* (*Milestones, Autobiography*), Tel Aviv 1976, pp. 190–191. See also Amos Lev, "They Murdered Ro'i," *Ba'mahaneh*, 34, 2 May 1956.

collective, the members of the young Israeli elites, saw themselves as represented and defined by this text, which had become the voice of a generation. Dayan's oration is so suggestive and paradigmatic in the context of the present discussion and so rich in itself that it deserves to be quoted in full:

Yesterday morning Ro'i was murdered. The quiet of a spring morning blinded him, and he failed to see those who lurked in wait for him behind the furrow. Let us not, today, hurl accusations at the killers. Why should we complain at their fierce hatred of us? For eight years they have been dwelling in refugee camps in Gaza, and before their very eyes we are turning the land and the villages where they and their forefathers dwelt into our home.

It is not from the Arabs in Gaza, but among ourselves that we should seek Ro'i's blood. How could we have failed to look our fate in the eye, to see the destiny of our generation in all its brutality? Have we forgotten that this group of young people, living in Nahal Oz, bear on their shoulders the heavy gates of Gaza, gates beyond which are crowded hundreds of thousands of eyes and hands, praying for our weakness, so as to tear us to pieces – have we forgotten this? For we know that, in order for their hope of annihilating us to die away, it is incumbent on us – morning and night – to be armed and ready. We are the generation of settlement, and without the steel helmet and the cannon's mouth we cannot plant a tree nor build a house. There will be no life for our children if we do not dig shelters, and without barbed wire fences and machineguns we cannot pave roads nor drill for water. *Millions of Jews, who were exterminated because they had no country, are watching us from the ashes of Israeli history and exhorting us to settle and to build up a land for our people.*[43]

But beyond the furrows of the border surges a sea of hatred and dreams of vengeance, awaiting the day when the calm dulls our alertness, when we lend an ear to the ambassadors of scheming hypocrisy, who exhort us to lay down our arms. Ro'i's blood cries out to us from his mangled body. For we swore a thousand times that our blood would not be spilled in vain and yesterday we were beguiled once more, we listened and we believed. Let us conduct a reckoning with ourselves today. Let us not shrink from seeing the enmity, which attends and fills the lives of hundreds of thousands of Arabs, who dwell around us and await the moment when they can spill our blood. Let us not lower our gaze lest our arm be weakened. This is the decree of our generation. This is our only choice – to be ready and armed, strong and hardy, for if the sword slips from our fists – our lives will be cut short.

Ro'i Rothberg, the lean blond youth, who left Tel Aviv to build a home at the gates of Gaza, to be a wall for us all; Ro'i – the light in his heart dazzled his eyes, and he did not see the glint of the knife. The yearning for peace dulled his hearing,

---

[43] (My italics.) During one of the blackest and bloodiest weeks of the second Intifada, Chief of Staff Shaul Mofaz, in a live TV speech, quoted excerpts from Dayan's eulogy, including the section on the Holocaust dead "watching us from the ashes of Israeli history and exhorting us to settle and to build up a land for our people," 10 March 2002.

and he did not hear the sound of lurking murder. The gates of Gaza weighed too heavily on him and undid him.[44]

Dayan's lament, the narrative fabric he wove over Ro'i Rothberg's grave, its beauty and rhetorical richness aside, was a complete and self-contained story, and all its preordained protagonists – Ro'i Rothberg, the Arab killers, the dead of the Holocaust and Jewish history, the United Nations ("the ambassadors of scheming hypocrisy, who call on us to lay down our arms"[45]) – played their parts in perfect, paradigmatic fashion. In this story Dayan constructed a personal and collective allegory for an entire generation, the "decree of our generation," the "only choice," to be "ready and armed, strong and hardy." Ro'i Rothberg, to whom and of whom Dayan spoke, addressing him by his first name, was both the personal, individual boy-soldier, whose death and its manner were heart-breaking, and the collective, national representative of a generation "condemned" to wield the sword, who undertook to bear on his shoulders the heavy gates of Gaza. But while Ro'i Rothberg was the new ideal Israeli, fair-haired and light-eyed, he was also the timeless, ahistorical Israeli Jew, embodied in different form in each generation, sacrificing himself over and over again, in endless recurrence, for the sake of the nation, "to be a wall for us." And death came each time anew as a surprise to that young soldier, man of peace and of labor, defending his land with his body, because it was extricated from the historical sequel of events. His yearning for peace, his guilelessness and innocence ("the light in his heart dazzled his eyes") blinded him to the sight of the schemers.

In contrast, the Arab murderers in Dayan's eulogy are nameless and faceless. Yet, unlike naive Ro'i Rothberg, dazzled and blinded, the Arabs have "hundreds of thousands of eyes" gazing in hatred, their "hands, praying for our weakness" in order "to tear us to pieces." Dayan's dichotomous presentation was only to be expected. However, in his case, the expected was unexpected. His second sentence already contained a surprising reversal of meaning, rare indeed in that period, in effect exonerating the murderers themselves from the charge of murder. While referring to the historical chain of events, to the ousting of the Arabs from their

---

[44] The text quoted here is taken from Dayan, *Milestones*, p. 191.

[45] Dayan was referring to the UN Secretary, Dag Hammarskjöld and the West in general for having had, in effect, imposed a ceasefire on Israel. On another, latent plane, he was undoubtedly referring to his critics inside Israel, in particular Foreign Ministry officials, who claimed that he was trigger-happy and was heating up the borders unnecessarily. According to Morris, Ben-Gurion was angered by the expression "ambassadors of scheming hypocrisy" and ordered that it be erased from all rebroadcasts of Dayan's eulogy. In his autobiography, Dayan restored the full version of the speech. See ibid., p. 190.

lands and homes for purposes of Jewish settlement, Dayan established forcefully the reason for and justification of their hatred, the tragic battle for the land, and its historical reasons: "For eight years they have been dwelling in refugee camps in Gaza, and before their very eyes we are turning the land and the villages where they and their forefathers dwelt into our home." Yet the conclusion Dayan drew from his historical insight, so rare at the time, recalled the conclusion drawn by Yosef Haim Brenner in 1913[46] – not the need to render justice to the robbed, even if only for utilitarian reasons, for allaying their animosity, but the deterministic ahistorical perception of the generation's "decree" and its fate to bear the sword and be "strong and hardy." For this was the supreme imperative, "from the ashes of history," of the Holocaust dead to Israel's youth. The unique nature of their annihilation made the Holocaust victims into supreme, lasting, and indisputable moral sanction, yet at the same time, they were recruited as active players in Israeli politics of that time, of all times.

Eternal present

The 1967 Six Day War elevated the rhetoric of holocaust and power to new heights, and restored to it an additional, central component – the state's – and the land's – borders.[47] Israel's swift military victory, rather than checking discourse on a holocaust threat and relieving Israeli society of it, was perceived instead as total salvation from absolute destruction, "the unique transformation which turned the danger of annihilation into unparallelled salvation," as Nathan Alterman wrote immediately after the war.[48] This cyclic destruction–redemption perception both generated numerous texts about the divine intervention and miracle wrought for Israel, and was shaped by these texts, whose authors were otherwise secular Israelis. Israel's soldiers did not fight alone in that war. Shoulder

---

[46] The Arabs, wrote Brenner, were "de facto masters of the land, and we intentionally come to infiltrate them ... there is already, must inevitably be – and shall be – hatred between us. They are stronger than we are in all respects ... but we, the children of Israel, have long been accustomed to living as weaklings among the powerful ... cursed be the soft and loving! ... first of all – no idealization!" Y. H. B. (Brenner), *Revivim*, 3–4, 1913, p. 165.

[47] This component was part and parcel of the right-wing discourse on the borders and Greater Israel, and of the kibbutz Ha'meuhad and its leader, Yitzhak Tabenkin, within the labor movement. It peaked during the partition controversy in the late 1930s, over the 29 November 1947 resolution, the establishment of Israel, and the 1956 war, and was then dormant to a certain extent until the 1967 victory. On this see below in the present chapter.

[48] Nathan Alterman, "Facing the Unparalleled Reality," *Ha'hut Ha'meshulash* (*The Triple Thread*), Tel Aviv 1971, p. 26.

to shoulder with them stood Jewish fighters throughout history, from Massada suiciders through Bar Kochba and his rebels to Europe ghetto fighters. The history of the Jewish people from ancient times and up to the State of Israel thus became a single, a priori, and constant essence, shaping not only national consciousness but also national being and practices.

Periods, events, and images far apart from one another are pasted together into a viscous mythical-national mass in Haim Hefer's makamma "We were like dreamers." In this very popular text, recited in public ceremonies, Chief of Staff of the 1967 war, Yitzhak Rabin, the personification of Israel-Jewish warrior from the heroic days of the Palmach, meets his ancient counterpart, King David, across thousands of years, in a time outside of time. His well-known taciturnity and avoidance of grandiloquent language notwithstanding, Yitzhak Rabin of the poem tells King David about the great victory:

It was not we alone who liberated the mount ... with them [the fighters] marched / A whole brigade of Massada fighters / And Bar Kochba's men, brave and true / Fought at their side with bows and arrows / And alongside them could be heard loud and clear the footsteps / Of all those murdered and slaughtered and plundered / All those who died because they were Jews.[49]

Everything is in the present tense in Jewish martyrology, nourished and sustained over and over again by a Zionist project that aimed at putting, once and for all, an end to it.

During the War of Attrition along the Suez Canal, which was the direct consequence of the 1967 "war of redemption," and evidence of the spuriousness of the salvation aspect attributed to that war – Menachem Begin said that Israel should not trust mankind but only its own power, since that power alone makes the distinction between the smoke rising over the bombarded Suez Canal and "the darkest smoke of the crematoria." The Holocaust, Begin said, would never return due to the change in the power of the Jewish people. "Eretz Israel is in our hands now, and never again will there be a Massada,"[50] said Begin, juxtaposing remote incidents, telescoping the entire Jewish annals into a single, ahistorical, never-ending present. And the prominent ideologist of the Greater Israel movement, once a labor movement intellectual, Eliezer Livneh, said it bluntly after the murder of Israeli athletes at the Olympic Games in Munich: "Memory of the Holocaust is a central stronghold in our security

[49] Haim Hefer and Marcel Yanko, *Misdar Ha'noflim (The Parade of the Fallen)*, Tel Aviv 1968, first makamma.
[50] Menachem Begin, "The Welfare of the People and the Indivisibility of the Country," speech at the National Council of the Herut movement, 23 April 1970.

deployment and a major element in our everyday self-defence ... the more we feel the Holocaust the more we will understand present events; the more we remember its horrors, the more we will succeed in withstanding the horrors around us." And he added that this is not a reference to the past but, as always, "to the present."[51]

The border is the soul

The clearly demarcated and secure border that separates the inside from the outside, the familiar from the foreign, the friendly from the hostile, has been a central aspect of the concept of order and of instilling order, which are of the essence of modernity. However, the modern, secular Zionist project refrained unequivocally from defining its territorial borders. Whereas in their imagining or platforms, political groups and bodies within Zionism delineated what they regarded as the ideal borders of the land, the Zionist movement as representative of Jewish national aspirations, and subsequently all of Israel's governments, evaded debate and decisions on the issue of the state's borders. At no stage has the State of Israel defined its own borders – optimal, official, secured – nor acted to constitute these borders and win international recognition for them. The porous, fragile border, never agreed upon either internally or internationally, of the Israeli-Jewish nation-state's territorial container, and Israel's deliberate policy of territorial vagueness, also found expression in repeated acts of breaching that border by both the state and radical groups, with open or covert support of the state. By speaking in several voices with regard to the border, permitting various bodies, whether semi-official or ostensibly subversive, "to move outside the fence,"[52] and establish facts in the territories beyond, the sovereign state of Israel was to pursue the policy of vagueness and double-talk in the spheres of security, settlement, and immigration that had characterized the pre-state period of struggle for that same sovereignty. In this respect, Israel continued to act as a community, not as a political sovereign.

---

[51] Eliezer Livneh, "The Security Debacles and their Source," *Zot Ha'aretz*, 29 September 1972, p. 2.
[52] The "move outside the fence" was the conceptual and practical revolution in the security conception of the organized Jewish community (Yishuv) which occurred at the height of the 1936–1939 Arab Rebellion. The strategy of defensive alignment within security fences of the settlements was found to be ineffective in the face of the partisan warfare of the Arab insurgents, and was replaced by the conception of nationwide, mobile, offensive, pre-emptive warfare, outside the boundaries of the settlements, that was carried out at night as well. This new modus operandi also engendered a new type of fighter and ethos.

From the across-the-border "reprisal operations" in the 1950s to the aggressive, massive settlement of the occupied territories, populated by another people, with the "land of the forefathers" for pretext, and annexations of territory since 1967, Israel did more than any other power to blur and breach its own borders. This did not rule out the conversion of the border as such into a national icon, the object of sanctifying national rituals.[53] The deliberate transience of the political border, and the blurred spheres around it, as established by Israel's governments, also left ample space for the emergence of a mythology of the true, promised, sacred "other" border, and the existence of unspecified, borderless "yearned-for realms," such as Ben-Gurion referred to when – for want of a better alternative – he adopted the 1947 Partition Plan. "We must return to the starting point: strive to achieve the indivisibility of the land by peaceful means, but if we are attacked we will not regard the borders as sacred,"[54] said in 1950 Israel Galili, subsequently one of the formulators of Israel's settlement policy in the territories occupied in 1967. The absence of an agreed-upon border thus served to stimulate the delusion of Greater Israel, which was actualized resolutely and inflexibly in the territories, diverted Israel's historical course, and finally led to the assassination of a Prime Minister.[55]

The term "Greater Israel," relating to the borders of the land, is a contemporary term, and fruit of the 1930s controversy over the various ideas and plans of dividing Palestine. From its first stages, however, the internal Zionist debate on the borders of the National Home, the rhetoric of all parties was rich in expressions related to human body and soul. In the spirit of Frederick Hertz's analysis, the homeland was perceived to be a living body, whose borders are sacred, and renunciation of any part of it was likened to limb amputation, a threat of total destruction.[56] The Holocaust heightened this discourse and endowed the concept of the indivisible and sacred national body with the added value of being a

---

[53] Adriana Kemp, "The Janus-faced Border: National Space and Consciousness in Israel," *Teoria U'vikoret (Theory and Criticism)*, 16, 2000, pp. 13–43.

[54] Israel Galili, quoted in Yossi Beilin, *Mehiro shel Ihud: Mifleget Ha'avodah ad Yom Ha'kippurim (The Price of Unity: The Labor Party up to the Yom Kippur War)*, Tel Aviv 1988, p. 25.

[55] "Like a specter, the old Jew arose from among us [in the wake of the Six Day War]. The border-crosser reverted to his historical ways as in the days when he settled all over the world in a milieu which was not his own. Thus there commenced the truly anti-Zionist act of settlement without sovereignty and without the hope of full sovereignty within the fabric of another national entity," wrote A. B. Yehoshua in "The Obligation of the Border," *Ha'aretz Supplement*, 8 February 2002, pp. 18–20.

[56] Frederick Hertz, *Nationality in History and Politics: A Psychology and Sociology of National Sentiment and Nationalism*, London 1944, pp. 28, 150–151.

guarantor of redemption, meaning that only the territorial body as a whole could prevent a new holocaust.

The connection between the dismembering of the body of the Jewish homeland and the threat of a new holocaust was first made in the summer of 1946, when the idea of partitioning Palestine was mooted again. An expanded conference of the Jewish Agency Executive held in Paris decided, on 5 August 1946, to "discuss" an American proposal for the establishment of a viable Jewish state in "part" of Palestine.[57] "It is a crime to rob a nation of the most precious ... the holiest of holies: the homeland," was Menachem Begin's reaction to that resolution. "It is a crime to turn wretched Jewish rulers ... into haters of their people, hated by their people ... and all these are the inevitable outcome of the 'partition plan,' the establishment of a Jewish *reservat* on the coastal strip, whether it be called a district or a 'state'."[58] Begin's speech was saturated with Holocaust images and allusions. Wretched Jewish leaders, Jewish "reservat," and other terms, borrowed from another historical instance, were already serving, in this early text, to establish the analogy between the partition of the "Land of Israel" and the Nazi horrors. Consequently, partition's advocates were likened to the Judenräte, the "wretched Jewish leaders ... hated by their people," and the envisioned state to the Lublin reservat, the site where Jews were concentrated prior to their shipment to extermination. "If the plan [partition] is criminal, what are we to say about Jewish consent to this plan?" Begin went on,

For years the *Nazo-British* oppressors have been marching over the bodies of our people – burned, shattered bodies, countless corpses – towards their goal ... But what can one say about Jews, about Jewish "leaders," who are willing to consent to a *programme of annihilation*? What is to be said about a leadership willing to profiteer on the blood of tens of thousands, ready to become – despite their "patriotic" prattle – a *Judenrat*? If the dismemberment of the country is a crime, then to consent to its dismemberment is a two-fold crime.[59]

The UN Partition Resolution of 29 November 1947 was for Begin "the dismemberment contract" and he stated that "the dismembering of our homeland was illegal. It will never be recognized. The signature of institutions and individuals on the dissection contract is totally invalid."[60] A day after the state was proclaimed, Begin said to his followers on the Irgun radio that even though a Jewish state had come into being,

---

[57] On the session at length, see Zertal, *From Catastrophe to Power*, pp. 232–239.
[58] Begin, *Underground*, vol. II, p. 219.   [59] Ibid. (my italics).
[60] Menachem Begin, "The Sanctity of the Indivisibility of the Land," 30 November 1947, in *Underground*, vol. IV, p. 239.

we shall always remember that the homeland has not yet been liberated ... the homeland is whole. The attempt to tear it into pieces is not only criminal; it is also abortive ... because there is an eternal law: if a separating line exists, or if someone draws such a line between the nation-state and its homeland, that artificial line is destined – to disappear.[61]

Two weeks before the Israeli army invaded Sinai in October 1956, Begin's Herut movement passed a resolution at its annual conference, stating that "the tyrant Nasser is scheming to annihilate Israel [and] constitute[s] the greatest danger to its existence since Hitler."[62] After the swift military campaign, when Israel was forced by an international coalition to retreat, and the army was withdrawing its troops, Herut accused Ben-Gurion's government of defeatism, treachery, and of reverting to the practices of the Holocaust period: "Words and expressions fail us," wrote the editorialist of the party organ *Herut*, "the heart is bursting with pain and fury, and the mind is stunned by this realization of the horrific nightmares that have been haunting us since Majdanek and Auschwitz. Capitulation, shameful, total, full, cruel capitulation, steeped in disgrace and dishonour."[63] The night after this editorial's publication, Dr. Israel Kastner was assassinated[64] outside his home as he returned from his work at a Hungarian-language newspaper. It was Menachem Begin himself who bracketed together the two events – Kastner's assassination and the withdrawal from Sinai – but from an unexpected angle. The Holocaust and what Begin saw as Mapai's only interest in clinging to power, then as now, and its willingness to do whatever necessary to safeguard it, were the double sub-text of this connection and lent it meaning:

Kastner was shot, so people say, at the precise moment when the standing of the ruling party had been undermined, inevitably, because of the insane act on the part of the government, which gave the order, in contravention of all its solemn commitments, to abandon Hebrew Gaza. What then? No my friends, this is mere speculation. Someone in Mapai can be content at the fact that Kastner has been shot at this precise moment; someone in the ruling party can try, in the wake of this assassination, to divert public opinion from the *Shoah* [the Hebrew term for the Holocaust] of the party's policy.[65]

<hr>

[61] Menachem Begin, 15 May 1948. The full text was printed in a special issue of *Herut*, which appeared on billboards. Reprinted in *Ha'mered (The Revolt)*, Tel Aviv 1978, pp. 505–511; *Underground*, vol. IV, pp. 326–333.
[62] "Resolutions of the Fourth National Conference of the Herut Movement," quoted in Naor, *Greater Israel*, p. 98.
[63] "The Third Kingdom of Israel on the Altar of Sacrifice," *Herut*, 3 March 1957.
[64] For a lengthy discussion of Dr. Israel Kastner and the affair which was to bear his name, see chapters 1 and 2 of this book.
[65] Menachem Begin, "Who is to Blame?" *Herut*, 22 March 1957.

The pre-state controversy around partition was waged not only between right and left, but within the labor movement itself. One of the "founding fathers" and leader of the Greater Israel sector in the Left, Yitzhak Tabenkin, headed the inside opposition to the central, pragmatic bloc from the late 1930s and retired, to all practical purposes, from politics on the national echelon, because of the territorial issue. Years later, after the 1967 war, Tabenkin said: "The goal of our entire project was then, and remains: A Greater Israel within its natural and ancient borders; from the Mediterranean to the desert and from Lebanon to the Dead Sea – as the reborn homeland of the entire Jewish people. This is the original Zionist ideal."[66] Whether Tabenkin's attitude to the indivisibility of the territory was based on religious foundations and the perception of the holiness of the land; whether it was born out of his revolutionary socialist viewpoint combined with his nationalist activism; or whether it reflected a purposeful rational approach stemming from his perception of the needs of Jewish settlement and society-building, he never abandoned the idea, and it became the basic tenet, article of faith, for him and his adherents. Members of his party's youth movement were taught to regard Greater Israel as a single entity, which no political treaty had the power to pull apart. "A homeland cannot be divided. One cannot rip apart a maternal bosom," was written in the movement's booklet of essays produced at the summer camp in 1937, when the 20th Zionist Congress was debating partition.[67] "Mount Gilboa stands here before us, [is] so close to our hearts, is ours, entirely ours, and no border can rob us of it. No treaty in the world could violate the covenant of blood signed among its stones."[68]

Tabenkin and his comrades perceived partition as a historical mishap, "a fleeting fact," whereas Greater Israel was defined as "inevitable," an essential factor, over which human action had no control. The indivisibility of the land "will be achieved whether by peaceful or warlike methods. If war is forced upon us, we will restore the indivisibility of the land," Tabenkin stated in 1953.[69] After the Sinai Campaign his party was actively opposed to withdrawal from Sinai and the Gaza Strip.

[66] Yitzhak Tabenkin, "Only Settlement in all the Territories Can Bring Peace," in Aharon Ben-Ami (ed.), Ha'kol – Gevulot Ha'shalom shel Eretz Israel (Everything – Eretz Israel's Borders of Peace), Tel Aviv 1967, p. 126.
[67] Yitzhak Avrahami and Ahuvia Malkin (eds.), Bi'vritkha (In Your Covenant), Tel Aviv 1938, p. 26.
[68] B. Poznansky, "The Living Spirit in the Mahanot Ha'olim," in Avrahami and Malkin (eds.), In Your Covenant, quoted in Shmuel Dotan, Pulmus Ha'haluka Bi'tekufat Ha'mandat (The Partition Polemics in the Mandate), Jerusalem 1980, p. 117.
[69] Yitzhak Tabenkin, "The Indivisibility of the Land or its Partition?," in Ha'hityashvut, Mahut Va'derekh (Settlement, Essence, and Path), Ramat Efal 1983, p. 69.

A party council declaration denounced "trends to tear away the Gaza Strip from the body of the state in order to restore it to the Egyptian dictator."[70] Tabenkin, for his part, added: "Our right to be in the Sinai desert is not new, and was gained long since. This time, however, we paid the price of the lives of 172 of our sons. This is the sacrifice. Not every death shortens a life. Some deaths extend life, extend the life of the people."[71] The spilt blood of the young sons was thus coupled with the claim of the Jewish primordial presence in and right to the land, infusing it with additional sanctity. The blood of the slain and the myth of ownership inscribed in the Bible combined into a political theology: blood and land were consecrated jointly in the name of the Ten Commandments, in the desert where the Jews became a nation; the myth of the past had been interwoven into the sacrifice of the present.[72] It was this combination, according to Tabenkin, which conferred on Israel the absolute right to Sinai. On the same occasion he added the argument which later would become the main weapon in the Israeli political arsenal – whereby every withdrawal from territory occupied by Israel during hostilities, or any Israeli territorial "renunciation," was likened to the Munich agreement on the eve of World War II.[73]

The holocaust which threatened Israel in May–June 1967 was even more devastating than that which the Nazis had inflicted on the Jews of Europe, said Tabenkin. "The pre-5 June borders have brought down *shoah* on our heads, and this *shoah* is graver than the Nazi Holocaust, because after that Holocaust some Jews remained, capable of rebuilding the nation and establishing the state, whereas if now, [Heaven] forbid, the state were to be annihilated, it is doubtful whether the Jewish people could rise again."[74] And after the 1967 victory, Tabenkin wrote that "If we had been defeated in the war, we would have been exterminated, as individuals and as a people, and thus, in this war we continued the war of the ghetto fighters." In another article, he claimed that "there was imminent danger of extermination, had we been defeated."[75]

[70] "Resolution of the Ahdut Ha'avodah-Poalei Zion Council," 20 December 1956. Quoted in Beilin, *The Price of Unity*, p. 27.
[71] Yitzhak Tabenkin, "Our Right to the Sinai Desert," *Dvarim* (*Speeches*), vol. VI, Ramat Efal 1985, p. 261.
[72] Naor, *Greater Israel*, p. 120.
[73] Yitzhak Tabenkin, "With Open Eyes – Let us Stand!," in *Speeches*, vol. VI, pp. 262–263.
[74] Yitzhak Tabenkin, "The Determinant Act," in *Lekah Sheshet Ha'yamim: Yishuva shel Eretz Bilti Mehuleket* (*The Lesson of the Six Day War: Settling an Undivided Land*), Tel Aviv 1971, p. 44.
[75] Yitzhak Tabenkin, "The Lesson of the War – Without Illusions," in *Lesson of the Six Day War*, p. 19; "We Cannot Evade the Need for Immigration and Settlement," in *Lesson of the Six Day War*, p. 36, respectively. 9th of Av is the day of the Temple's destruction.

The document "For a Greater Israel", published in September 1967 –
most of whose authors and signatories, including Nathan Alterman, Isser
Harel, Moshe Shamir, Eliezer Livneh, Hillel Dan, Avraham Yaffe,
Zerubavel Gilad, and Benny Maharshak, belonged to the various elites
of the labor movement, some of them members of Tabenkin's movement
and his associates, all of them free thinkers – was a sequel of the pre-Six
Day War Tabenkinian conception. This document extracted the war and
its fruits, namely the conquered territories, from public debate, from the
choices and decisions of Israel's citizens, and from the context of political
and international considerations: "Eretz Israel is now in the hands of the
Jewish people ... We owe fidelity to the indivisibility of our land – to the
past of the Jewish people and its future as well, and no government has
the right to renounce this indivisibility."[76] The Jewish people through
the centuries and in all its diasporas, that discursive, imagined entity[77]
in whose "hands" Eretz Israel had now been entrusted, was, in the eyes
of one of the document's authors, a refugee-nation, living forever, day
by day, in a condition of physical extermination or on the verge of extermination. "The most characteristic and horrific feature of the fate of
this refugee-nation," wrote the novelist Moshe Shamir,

is the combination of three phenomena which have always united it [the Jewish
people]. It is, at the same time, always in a condition of physical extermination or
on the verge of extermination, of attempts by individuals to escape that fate and its
framework, and of the impossibility of succeeding in these attempts ... Today,
from the Hitler of the 1930s and 1940s to whatever one chooses to call him of the
1980s and 1990s, this nation is the refugee-nation of the human race. Today it
possesses no stretch of land anywhere in the world, except for this ailing, torn,
conflict-ridden land, which is placed now on your table for scrutiny of which
justice is weighed against.[78]

Withdrawal to the crematoria

The fatal combination of the nation as a supra-political, transcendental
essence, of religion as the infrastructure of nationality, with the exclusive
reliance on military power, which too was elevated on to the religious
sphere, wedded with an ahistorical, "worldless" ghettoish conception of
Jewish/Israeli destiny, was therefore present in Israeli discourse long

---

[76] "For the Sake of Greater Israel," 22 September 1967, printed in four large newspapers,
Davar, Ha'aretz, Yedioth Aharonoth, and *Ma'ariv.* For a detailed discussion of the document see, Dan Miron, "An Israeli Document," *Politika,* **14–15,** June 1987, pp. 37–45.
[77] See Anderson, *Imagined Communities.*
[78] Moshe Shamir, "The Obligation to Know the Right," *Zot Ha'aretz,* 1 November 1968.

before Gush Emunim (Bloc of Faith) entered the arena in the wake of the 1973 war. However, this body, which sprouted from the fundamental, structural contradictions in the conception and structure of the state, and within the fuzzy spheres of its self-definition, encompassed the entire spectrum of those components, enhanced and pushed them to the edge. It did so while exploiting effectively the venerated ideologies of pioneering, settlement, and security, as well as state institutions and instruments. It usurped in the process the state's agenda and wielded these ideologies and institutions against the state itself, to become what the essayist Boaz Evron has defined as "the greatest threat to the State of Israel since its establishment."[79] Gush Emunim followers, the Jewish settlers in Sinai and the West Bank, also became the self-appointed bearers of the Holocaustic discourse in its relation to the withdrawal from the territories.

Three million Jews who happen to have been born to live in 1981 in a country named "Israel" have been called upon to determine whether to bury a 4,000-year-old dream, whether to rob ourselves of our future, and to do so, simply, by casting a slip of paper into a ballot box (just as in Sinai they once cast their jewels into the fire and out came a calf, just as the Jews of Warsaw, Berlin, and Amsterdam were not allowed to vote in the 1940s *whether* to board the trains for "resettlement in the East." In light of our experience *with ourselves* today, who knows how they would have voted

wrote the settlers' publication *Nekuda* several months before the elections scheduled for June 1981, and before the last stage of the Sinai withdrawal.[80] Sustained by the vast discursive edifice which had preceded it, *Nekuda*, the central mouthpiece of Gush Emunim and agent of the Holocaust argument, could now claim that it represented, beyond the popular consensus, a transcendental truth buried deep within the soul of the nation throughout history, and the secret code of its redemption. The State of Israel as a man-made creation, a historical and political entity established by a human group of people for purposes of conducting their joint lives, affairs, and culture, was completely worthless in the eyes of the writer, a passing cloud, as against his primordial, eternal, fixed vision of the promised land, a sacred value towering above all political decisions and anything created in the variable and relative human sphere of activity.

Nekuda, whose circulation and influence reached, from its beginning, beyond the confines of the community of settlers it represented, was considered by its contributors and readers to be a "sacred text," not

---

[79] Boaz Evron, *Ha'heshbon Ha'leumi (A National Reckoning)*, Tel Aviv (1988) 2002, pp. 374–406.
[80] Elyakim Ha'etzni, "Judea, Samaria and Gaza and the Elections to the Tenth Knesset," *Nekuda*, 25, 13 March 1981, p. 5 (italics in the original).

only of the Greater Israel ideology, but of Judaism itself which was constantly on the verge of extinction, the instrument transmitting the lament of those trapped in a death camp facing catastrophe. For several of the founders of and early contributors to *Nekuda*, the very appearance of the paper was reminiscent of the publication of a Jewish paper in Teresienstadt or Auschwitz.[81] Israel, with its mighty army, was equated, in various ways, with Jewish ghetto communities during the Holocaust, and incumbent governments were identified, as required, with the Nazis themselves or with their collaborators, both Jewish and non-Jewish.

The settlers perceived themselves, on the other hand, as the only true "Jews" of the world and of Israel, whose endless persecution and victimhood, and the Holocaustic situation in which they were living, defined them. They saw themselves as the last fighters on the wall, the handful of ghetto rebels, expecting their lonely doom in an ocean of Nazi-like hatred shared by the entire world, Gentiles, Arabs, and non-settler Israelis included. "I see an Israeli prime minister who reminds me of Marshal Pétain shaking the hand of the chief Nazi and handing over the Jews of his country," writes a woman settler after the signing of the Oslo agreement in Washington.

Around us I see the barbed wire fences and guard towers which are being erected and threaten to sequester us in a ghetto ... at the demonstration in which I took part, I saw a black-booted mounted Jewish policeman beating a Jewish child with his truncheon ... whether they wish it or not, [they] will return to our side in their fight against the SS from Gaza who will do battle with us armed with blue-and-white weapons.[82]

The world, the settler's rhetoric went, has reverted to being a world which preserves its Jews only to be able to hate and persecute them, a world where the Jews are scapegoats, atoning for the sins of the world.

No modern Western country can exist without Jews. It requires them as the objects of discrimination, feelings of superiority and contempt ... Even Germany, which killed the Jews, and Poland, valley of the same death, two countries in which there are almost no Jews, have not yet found a substitute for the Jews ... The Jews of the State of Israel are those who wear skullcaps, who carry arms, and who live beyond the Green Line, in short, Gush Emunim. Their center is Kiryat Arba, the most slandered city in Israel and in the world

wrote Elyakim Ha'etzni, chief ideologist and contributor to *Nekuda*.[83]

[81] This statement was made by Professor Hillel Weiss, resident in one of the settlements and lecturer at Bar Ilan University in the TV program "Personal Report" where the guests included Israel Harel, one of the heads of Gush Emunim and the editor in chief of *Nekuda*. TV Channel 2, 2001.
[82] Rina Ackerman, "A Nightmare Reality," *Nekuda*, 174, January 1994, pp. 7–8.
[83] Elyakin Ha'etzni, "Home-Made Anti-Semitism," *Nekuda*, 56, 28 March 1983, p. 16.

The struggle for the occupied territories within Israeli society was defined as a struggle between Jews and Gentiles, and peace – as the concern of Jews whose world had gone awry, self-hating and suicidal Jews, who were Hellenized or imitated Christian conduct. Projecting themselves on their political opponents, the settlers portrayed their opponents, peace advocates as martyrs' manufacturers and slaves of cults of the dead.

Let us caution against the priests of "peace," the bishops of retreat from Jerusalem, who with cold cynicism are exploiting the mother's cry and have already transformed it into a ritual verse, a kind of musical accompaniment to the ritual act of sacrificing Eretz Israel – and with it every ideal for which it is worth living and therefore also worth dying – on the altar of the Moloch of "now." There is something Christian about the worship of the dead by the people of "peace"

wrote *Nekuda*.[84] And in a similar act of projection, another *Nekuda* contributor pondered the emotional need of the settlers' opponents to exploit images from other times and other circumstances: "It is difficult to plumb the depths of the hatred, the malicious need to slander tens of thousands of people and to use blatantly Nazi images with regard to them."[85] He was speaking at a time when Nazi and Holocaust images – *aktziya*, yellow badge, Judenrein, Judenrat, SS, Auschwitz, and Hitler – were being enlisted by the *Nekuda* writers themselves as weapons in the ultimate battle for their Eretz Israel.

In their world, where meaning is turned inside out, which projects on to the others, the conquerers become conquered, the persecutors are turned into persecuted, wrongdoer into the victim, and this inverted order received the supreme seal of Auschwitz. Talking about conquerors who regard themselves as the conquered party, let us examine the settler Emuna Elon's complaint about the new bypass roads in the occupied territories, or the existing roads, which were marked with a yellow strip to meet the needs of the Jewish settlers, "the yellow badge roads," as she calls them. These roads, says Elon, a popular publicist in national papers and television programs, are a disgrace to Israel:

In the alleyways of El-Bireh . . . a yellow badge twists and turns on its way. Anyone who follows it will eventually find himself in Psagot: a large, flourishing settlement where wise people have spent good money to build beautiful houses overlooking a breathtaking landscape. How can these people – proud Israelis, army veterans, educated people – accustom themselves to the daily humiliation of travelling along this absurd maze? Cry, yellow country![86]

---

[84] "A Red and Black Placard," *Nekuda*, 60, 24 June 1983, p. 12.
[85] Dov Berkovitz, "We Will Not Descend to the Level of Amoz Oz and his Associates," *Nekuda*, 131, 30 June 1989, p. 18.
[86] Emuna Elon, "The Yellow Badge Roads," *Nekuda*, 153, October 1991, p. 56.

The flourishing settlement, the beautiful houses overlooking the breath-taking view, the wise people who have spent good money – all are planted in a nowhere place, in utopia. Wherever Elon's eye roams, it sees no other people, no dispossessed and persecuted men and women, no destroyed houses, no arbitrary casualties, no routine horror of occupation, no human suffering, no daily humiliation of the local population, only Elon and her like, who are forced to travel the "yellow badge roads" to their beautiful homes.

Auschwitz Angel of Death

Rhetoric of hatred does not pick and choose its images; it is not fanatic about times, places, or identities or, alternately, picks images, times, and identities, mixes them together, and does so meticulously in accordance with current needs and the issue at hand. Enemies from the past blend with today's enemies. Political opponents are branded as "others," as traitors, endangering the life of the community, deniers of its existence, and, in this fashion, are expropriated from the obligations stemming from fundamental human and political norms. The sheltering umbrella of the law and of rules of wrong and right, of the "allowed" and the "forbidden" are withheld from those defined as enemies, and this is always justified as being done for higher moral reasons, in the name of greater values. Writing in *Nekuda* about the withdrawal from Sinai, Elyakim Ha'etzni compared the Israelis to the French during World War II, most of whom, he asserted, were either active Nazis or supporters of Marshal Pétain, "the collaborator with Hitler." Likening the Israeli government at the time, which had employed force against the opponents of withdrawal, to the Judenräte, and the said opponents to the French Resistance, which redeemed France's honor, Ha'etzni wrote:

All the shouting, the condemnations and the cries of "Shame" are useless – *this scene is reminiscent of the Holocaust!* Apart from the slaughter, this total expulsion of the entire Jewish population, the destruction of an entire Jewish civilization ... can be given no other name. Those who stage an event where the victims celebrate the violence inflicted on them, those who conduct a ceremony in honor of destruction and nickname it "peace," those who pay honor and tribute to the shame of enforcement by Jews of a "Judenrein" regime on other Jews, those who adorn with festive dress and wreaths of flowers the heads of the victims of the violent sacrifice, those who arrange them in straight orderly lines to march, with a song of destruction on their lips, into evacuation and annihilation of their town and their home – those who do all this bear an appalling resemblance to the Judenrat.[87]

---

[87] Elyakim Ha'etzni, "Sinai Shall Not Fall a Fourth Time," *Nekuda*, 42, March 1982, pp. 10–11 (my Italics). For a discussion of the Judenräte and the attitude of Palestinian Zionism and Israeli society towards them in the first decade of statehood, see chapters 1, 2, 4 of this book.

A few weeks later, when Prime Minister Begin was enticed into launching the Lebanon War in order to erase through it the shame of the recent retreat from Sinai and the destruction of Yamit – and, as he himself said, to make amends for the trauma of the 1973 war, and above all to root out Arafat/Hitler from his Beirut bunker and avert a new Treblinka in Israel[88] – Begin, yesterday's Judenrat, was transformed, by the touch of a pen, into the "new Jew." In the War for Peace in Galilee, Ha'etzni now wrote, "Menachem Begin is acting like a representative of the image we dreamed would arise in this country – the image of the Jew who has no more inferiority complex and emotional need 'to prove' his noble spirit, his yearning for peace, etc." The image of the new Begin was further enhanced by contrast to the opponents of the war who, according to Ha'etzni, represented the "self-extinction attitude" in Jewish history, the "Rumkovsky–Kastner–Kreisky" approach, the "meek acceptance of the exterminator, and attempts to bring salvation through collaboration and blind obedience to the exterminator." Those who wish to inflict a Palestinian state inside Israel are introducing into the Jewish state the Jewish annihilation theory, "the Angel of Death of Auschwitz," wrote Ha'etzni.[89]

"The Holocaust, towards which we are proceeding determindedly, is one we are constructing with our own hands," wrote *Nekuda*. "Towards this oven we are being led, without being clearly aware, by our great friend, by grace of the logic of compromise on life itself,"[90] while there is no prospect that the advocates of peace,

the bleeding hearts and knights of concessions will halt even on the verge of the abyss, when they see that even the coastal strip, the "blue line," the last frontier of concessions, the Mediterranean, has already been invaded by the cancerous metastasis of retreat and the peace-of-graveyards. We learned in the Holocaust that even at the gate of the Auschwitz inferno, each and every one continued to cling to his own golden and silver idols, his wooden and stone gods.[91]

---

[88] "You know what I did and what we all did to prevent war and bereavement, but it is our fate that in Eretz Israel there is no escape from fighting with dedication. Believe me, the alternative is Treblinka, and we have decided that there will be no more Treblinka." Begin at a cabinet meeting, 5 June 1982. In response, Amos Oz wrote in "Hitler is Dead, Mr. Prime Minister", *Yedioth Aharonoth*, 21 June 1982: "There is not and cannot be balm for the open wound in our souls. Tens of thousands of Arab dead will not heal this wound. But, Mr. Begin, Adolf Hitler died 37 years ago. Sadly or not it is a fact: Hitler is not hiding in Nabatiyeh, Zidon or Beirut. He is dead and burnt."

[89] Elyakim Ha'etzni, "Three Presents for the Nations of the World and One – for the People of Israel," *Nekuda*, 45, 16 June 1982, pp. 8–9.

[90] M. Ben-Yosef (Hagar), "No More 'Nice Guy,'" *Nekuda*, 88, 24 June 1985, p. 9.

[91] Elyakim Ha'etzni, "You Too, Zubin?!, " *Nekuda*, 80, 23 November 1984, p. 25.

The process of Nazification of the Arabs which began, as noted, in the late 1940s, reached its height in the settlers' newspaper in the 1980s and the 1990s, and was accorded pseudo-scientific status, reminiscent of that which the Nazis had tried to accord to their crude and primitive anti-Semitism. In July 1991, Meir Seidler, then a Ph.D. candidate in Jewish philosophy at Bar Ilan University, stated that "the Arabs in general are today morally inferior to the Germans during the Holocaust. If they only could, they would liquidate us all, without post factum guilt feelings and without complexes and guilt feelings in the next generation, as was the case with many Germans." As a Jew born after the Holocaust and raised in West Germany, Seidler claimed that it was his "moral obligation" to examine "our enemies" through the prism of his historical knowledge.

We discovered too late the monstrous element inherent in German culture; we must reveal in good time the dangers lurking in wait for us from Arab culture. Our neighbors have only one dream – the Final Solution ... Arab culture is a culture of terror and fear, a culture based on hatred, a culture of evil, and we cannot compromise with such a culture, just as there should have been no compromise with that Austrian and his German followers two generations ago.[92]

And the writer Moshe Shamir determined that

the Arab-Muslim world in our region, as it is today, constitutes the largest and most dangerous concentration of aggressive fascism, of racist Hitlerism, of dicta-torial tyranny lacking all inner restraint ... There is no difference between the PLO's attitude towards the State of Israel and that of other Arab countries, just as there is no difference between them – and the Final Solution scheme and the liquidation of the Jewish people as perpetrated by the brutal troops of Hitler and Nazi Germany during the Holocaust. There is, indeed, one difference between Hitler and Arafat (that is, between Nazi Germany and the Arab world of today): Hitler implemented his scheme, Arafat simply cannot implement his. It is no fault of his that the State of Israel still exists and its Jews are still alive. The Israel Defense Forces have foiled him.[93]

Throughout those years only one voice was raised clearly in *Nekuda* against the industrial-scale exploitation of the Holocaust by the settlers, and the methods they adopted in order to market their Holocaust. The voice of the young journalist Uri Orbach remained a lone cry, and elicited almost no reaction from either side. And since his criticism was so excep-tional, so trenchant and daring, in particular in the context of a closed,

[92] Meir Seidler, "The Arabs of Today Are Worse than the Germans in the Nazi Era," *Nekuda*, 151, July 1991, pp. 24–25.
[93] Moshe Shamir, "What Lies Ahead," *Nekuda*, 118, 26 February 1988, p. 16.

dense, and homogeneous group like the settlers, it is worth quoting him in full:

Oh, what a beautiful *shoah*. How wonderful it is to use terms from another world in one's argument. It's frightening, it's intimidating, and they'll never dare. "Do you want Samaria to be Judenrein?" asks the expert on Holocaust and current affairs. "No," replies another *sho'ologist*, "we will not go like sheep to the slaughter." "The government is bringing down a Holocaust on our heads," another laments, and yet another adds: "The Labor Party wants us to live in a Jewish ghetto within Hebron." Oh, panic, we have returned to you, you are forever, forever in our hearts. As far as I'm concerned, and I don't care if I'm not expressing the majority view, I'm tired of this whole affair. What's this rubbish about "holocaust" and "our little town is burning?" Where does the holocaust come into the story? The first paranoids in our camp were the Yamit settlers who were stupid enough to pin yellow badges to their lapels. Then they began denouncing the reparations the government is paying the evacuees. I was ashamed then and I am ashamed today. Those who want to view the world in only two colours, black and black, should keep their colour blindness to themselves, and not inflict their world of associations on us. The bitter and horrendous memory of the holocaust should not be turned into petty, false currency. And forgive me for the heresy, the evacuation of Eretz Israel is not a holocaust. I hereby volunteer nobly and like a sheep led to the slaughter, to be accused of nowism, and of tranquillizing appeasement. Thank you. I prefer that to the thenism which begins and ends with World War II, all of whose analogies are based on speeding trains and ghettos and Holocaust and black umbrellas. Oh, *shoah* show, how good it is to have you around, the best show in town. Did I say town? *In the town of death*. Intimidate, cry out, deter, compare, and the people of Israel will be frightened, will tremble and will, of course, flock in their thousands to Samaria with certificates of residence in the Jewish street between the ghettos under the rule of Pétain and the Vichy government within the borders of Auschwitz. The mob is hereby requested not to give the Holocaust a bad name.[94]

Speech, violence, death

Politicians, journalists, and historians let themselves speak out in the name of the Holocaust dead. They/we all use Holocaust images for their/our own purposes. Some of these images are threatening, others are trivial, all are distorting. The incitement against Yitzhak Rabin and the "Oslo government" in the years between the signature of the agreement and the assassination of the Prime Minister, in which conflicting and opposed Holocaust images, from the SS officer to the Judenrat, played a central part, was no innovation, merely "more of the same

[94] Uri Orbach, "The Hour [Sha'a in Hebrew], the Shoah and the Show," *Nekuda*, 95, 21 January 1986, p. 24 (italics in the original).

thing." A Prime Minister was depicted as a traitor and collaborator with
the enemies of his people, and the incitement was not confined to written
texts but found expression in demonstrations and violent action. Central
Israeli political figures and parties, including two individuals who were
later, as a direct or indirect consequence of the assassination, to become
Prime Ministers,[95] and past and present cabinet ministers, played an
active role in these demonstrations. Finally, the provocation and violent
acts focused on the Prime Minister himself, Yitzhak Rabin.[96]

An Israeli citizen named Yigal Amir, "the salt of the earth," an
ardent Zionist, reserve soldier, a dedicated, well-educated, lover of
Eretz Israel, took it all seriously, and undertook to save the homeland
from a second holocaust even at the price of self-sacrifice.[97] Had he not
been told, this diligent student, that he who hands over even one inch
of the soil of the Promised Land is betraying his people?[98] Was he not
raised to believe that Eretz Israel can only be conquered by force and

[95] The former Prime Minister, Benjamin Netanyahu, and Ariel Sharon, who is Prime
Minister at the time of writing.
[96] The examples are countless, and a few examples will serve to bear out my argument:
"Rabin is pushing us towards the borders of Auschwitz," said Rehavam Zeevi (Gandi) in
January 1994, quoted in *Ha'ir*, 10 November 1995; "We have not yet lost our hope of
being a free people in our land. It will happen if we understand that the trains are not
travelling to summer camps, if we understand that in the smoke rising from the chimneys,
Jews are being burnt, if we send this heretic government to hell." Rehavam Zeevi, 9
March 1994, quoted in *Iton Tel Aviv*, 10 November 1995; "What happened at the Bet
Lid junction is a reminder for the anniversary of Auschwitz ... 'Quislings', that is the
correct term for them," said former Chief of Staff Rafael Eitan after the Bet Lid terrorist
attack, where numerous soldiers were killed, *Yedioth Aharonoth*, 23 January 1995; "Rabin
must not speak in the name of the Holocaust martyrs when he receives the [Nobel] prize
together with the heir of the Nazis," proclaimed a Likud press release on the eve of the
prize-awarding ceremony in Oslo, *Yedioth Aharonoth*, 11 December 1994, p. 6; "The
time has come to stop talking, the time has come to act ... now you, people of Judea,
Samaria, and Gaza, are the leaders ... You are responsible for your lives and you must
brace yourselves ... The government is handing over the settlers to armed Palestinian
gangs. They have already handed over Jews to foreigners in the past. To be a 'mosser'
[informer] and to betray others is part of the spiritual essence of the Israeli left," wrote
Ariel Sharon in June 1995, *Ha'yarden* (Likud publication), quoted in *Iton Tel Aviv*,
10 November 1995. For a detailed description of the campaign of incitement against
the Prime Minister, see Michael Karpin and Aina Friedman, *Murder in the Name of God:
The Plot to Kill Yitzhak Rabin*, New York 1998.
[97] "I am not ashamed of it, the deed I committed. I am proud, both in heart and mind, and
so I am ready to pay the price," said Amir at his trial. Quoted in *The State of Israel* v. *Yigal
ben Shlomo Amir*, Severe Criminal File (SCF) (Tel Aviv and Jaffa) 498/95, 27 March
1996, pp. 14/28. Amir also said: "It is absurd that a man who sacrificed himself for the
people, is considered a danger to the security of the state." See Yoram Yarkoni, "Yigal
Amir's Father: 'My Son Is a Fool'," *Yedioth Aharonoth*, 8 March 1996.
[98] The Committee of Rabbis of Judea, Samaria, and Gaza announced on the eve of the Oslo
agreement signature ceremony at the White House that "the nation cannot remain silent
in the face of these extremely treacherous moves with regard to Eretz Israel and thus there
will be war over Judea, Samaria, and Gaza."

suffering, and that redemption can only be gained by blood? Was he not told repeatedly throughout his adolescence, in school, at university, by the media, by the settlers' journal, in his ideological milieu, by his teachers and rabbis, by his political leaders, that withdrawal from the occupied territories would be like the annihilation of the Jews slaughtered in Europe? Was he not taught at the "nation's school,"[99] in army educational courses on the Holocaust – which were intended, among other things, to "provide a lesson for our time"[100] – that to act in a doomed situation, to take one's fate into one's own hand, was the true heroism, the kind which changes history, like the heroism of the Jewish partisan, who transformed himself "from nothing to a man in charge of his own destiny, and when he was given weapons, he underwent a spiritual transformation beyond description. The weapon not only conferred security, but also restored his personal confidence as a human being"?[101]

Identifying Yigal Amir with World War II Jewish partisans or ghetto fighters is no more blatantly untenable than likening the State of Israel to a burning ghetto or a death camp, or the outrageous comparison of withdrawal from part of the land to walking "like sheep to the slaughter" into the crematorium, or depiction of the Arabs as the reincarnation of the Nazis. Yet it was the latter assertions which made that claim applied to Amir possible. One may dispute the cliché that words can kill, but not the fact that they create a world, structure consiousness, construe a motive for action, even if not necessarily on a one-to-one basis. The personal, social, political, and religious starting point of the path that led to the assassination of 4 November 1995, and the stops along its way, are, to a large extent, dependent on one's own interpretation and perspective. The network of transitions from talk to action, from violence to the speech which represents it, from motive to perpetration and back to the speech which attributes motive to action, was by no means clarified by the narratives, all ideology-conditioned, which were related after the assassination in an attempt to explain it.[102] Rather, they helped to obscure it, as did the narcissistic mourning rituals observed by the masses all over the country after the

[99] See under "army", in Yeshayaahu Heibowitz (ed. in chief), *Hebrew Encyclopedia*, vol, XXVIII, Jerusalem and Tel Aviv 1976, p. 483.
[100] Aryeh Barnea (ed.), "The Holocaust and its Significance," in *Basic Text for Education in the IDF*, Tel Aviv (Manpower Division, Chief Educational Officer) undated, pp. 1–3.
[101] Maya Lapid (author and ed.), "Guide to the Historical Museum," *Pamphlet for IDF Education Personnel*, Jerusalem (Yad Vashem-Education Department – Army Unit), pp. 1–8.
[102] Ariela Azulai, "The Spectre of Yigal Amir," *Theory and Criticism*, 17, 2001, pp. 26–29.

assassination.[103] And as did Rabin's Labor party during the post-assassination election campaign, when it maintained total "sterility" with regard to references to the assassination and its victim, and as did the Center established in Rabin's memory,[104] and as did the state institutions charged with the task of investigating the assassination and bringing the assassin to justice.

The assassin and his world, thoughts, motives, plans, that is to say the one truly important issue, are absent from the report of the State Commission of Inquiry into the assassination, which was established hastily by the government four days after the event.[105] Instead of investigating the unknown, or the known yet purposely repressed, which had erupted in such uncanny (the Freudian *unheimlich*) manner in the act of murder, and which demanded

---

[103] Less than a week after the assassination, it was clear that Israeli society was not capable of or willing to face up to the historical and philosophical truth evident in the event, and to transform the murder into a lever for a widescale critical evaluation and reconstitution of Israeli society, and that the assassination was, instead, going to serve the discourse of national unity, conciliation, and "love of Israel." In other words, its significance would be repressed and blurred. On 10 November 1995 the present author wrote: "To the continuous killing of its sons, the obedient, authoritarian Israeli society, bred by its leaders for perpetual combat, has grown accustomed. Patricide is beyond its emotional strength. It is precisely this calamity, this yawning abyss which the Rabin legend is aimed at covering, the legend which is growing from day to day, and the mass hysterical embrace of it. It is the inner devastation, which is not new, of which the assassination is only a symptom, that this legend is intended to heal ... We must not allow this assassination to take flight into the realms of legend, we must not cover it with rituals of remembrance and reconciliation and unity, which are always enterprises of forgetting, forgetfulness, and repression. The murder of Yitzhak Rabin must be restored to history and must be left there, in all its horror, and we must delve into the depths of all its meanings. Because the violent death of Rabin is not only the consequence of three years of savage incitement by the extreme right and the so-called moderate right. It is the product of some thirty years of messianic sickness, of the fatal combination of religious fanaticism and nationalist fanaticism, which Israeli society and Israeli democracy not only did not know how to tackle, but also embraced them." See Idith Zertal, "The Rabin Legend," *Ha'aretz*, 10 November 1995. See also the remarks of the chief judge at Yigal Amir's trial, Edmond Levi, "The State of Israel versus Yigal Ben Shlomo Amir," SCF (Tel Aviv–Jaffa) 498/95, *Sentence*, 27 March 1996, p. 5. To be discussed below.

[104] The assassination of a Prime Minister naturally calls for a memorial enterprise funded, organized, and staffed by state institutions. However, from the outset, the very fact that the Rabin Center is an official institution precluded the possibility that it would foster a critical, emancipatory political critique of the event. Paradoxically enough, perhaps, the redeemers of the memory of the assassination and of its stifled significance are all affiliated to what is known as the post-Zionist left. See, for example, Idan Lando, "The Dubious Innocence of the Left," *Ha'aretz Supplement*, 29 December 1995, p. 22; Azulai, "The Spectre of Yigal Amir"; Jose Bruner, "Yigal Amir," in Adi Ophir (ed.), *50to48: Momentim Bikortiim Be'toldot Medinat Israel (Critical Moments in the History of the State of Israel)*, Jerusalem and Tel Aviv, 1999, pp. 441–449. See also Nahman Ben-Yehuda, "Saturday Night, 4 November 1995, Malkhei Israel Square, Tel Aviv: Political Assassination in Eretz Israel," *Alpayim* 12, 1996, pp. 181–210.

[105] On the appointment of the Commission, see letter from Cabinet Secretary, Shmuel Hollander, to the President of the Supreme Court, Aharon Barak, 8 November 1995.

a courageous retrospective hunt for the places and texts preaching total redemption and the one and exclusive justice, places where the murder had been conceived and formulated, the Commission focused on the self-evident, on what was blatantly obvious – the failure of security. This was no accident, since in defining the role of the Commission, the government limited its jurisdiction to ostensibly operational, professional, and technical aspects, such as the "security and intelligence arrangements" and the "safeguarding of personalities in general and at the rally where the assassination occurred in particular."[106] But if this was the purpose, an internal investigation by the security authorities responsible for the event would have sufficed, and there would have been no need for a state commission, unless the aim was hastily to restore order, or the appearance of order, and to understate the devastation. In accordance with the government decision, and almost as a matter of routine, the Supreme Court President, Aharon Barak, appointed the Commission, which included jurists and a senior army officer, but no historians, sociologists, psychologists, or experts in political culture studies.[107] Yet, however restricted the definition of the Commission's task, it could still have marked out its investigative territory and decided which questions it wished to tackle. It did little in this direction, and when it did, it expanded its investigation on marginal matters, as if it were trying to stave off evidence. The non-confidential section of the Commission's report, which obscured possible insights rather than honing them, reveals that the Commission focused mainly on the question of the limits of jurisdiction of the various bodies in charge of security at the peace rally held on 4 November 1995, and their failure. Although it examined with a fine-tooth comb what had occurred on that Saturday evening, even noting at which bus stop the assassin left the bus,[108] the Commission kept its silence with regard to ominous political events prior to the assassination, the role of certain political parties, public figures, the media, and public discourse in creating the social and cultural climate, in empowering people like the assassin and impelling them to act.

The text of the report, a fine example of a sterile, well-guarded area, defending itself against any possible infiltration of controversial political

---

[106] Shmuel Hollander to the Supreme Court President. The Commission was established in accordance with Article 1 of the Commission of Inquiry Law, 1968. See Article 1.c. of the Law.

[107] The Commission was headed by the former President of the Supreme Court, Meir Shamgar, and the other members were General (Res.) Zvi Zamir and Professor (of law) Ariel Rosen-Zvi.

[108] *Commission of Inquiry into the Assassination of the Late Prime Minister, Yitzhak Rabin: Report*, Jerusalem 1996, p. 26.

and historical information or insights, makes sparing and superficial mention of the public atmosphere prior to the assassination, and then only in the context of the deployment and preparations of the police and the security services.[109] The height of repression, however, is the report's treatment of the assassin, Yigal Amir, by no means a marginal figure in the affair, to whom the Commission devoted a mere two pages, summing up as follows:

> On the question of the motives and calculations of the assailant, nothing more need be said; particularly since the criminal trial of Yigal Amir is now taking place, and such matters are under the jurisdiction of the court. We cannot refrain, in this context, from expressing our concern and outrage at the fact that we have reached a pass where a Jewish student, an arrogant fool, could sink to depths of lowness and cruelty which found expression in the act of murder whose circumstances we are examining. He thereby was responsible for the social and psychological disaster created by the historical blot which he has left on our society.[110]

In so stating, the Commission was not only refraining from discussion of the central issue, namely "the reasons for the assassination of the prime minister" and avoiding analysis of Amir's motives and calculations, issues which "are under the jurisdiction of the court."[111] It was entangling itself in a fundamental contradiction, and inadvertently effacing the borderline between the collective – the somewhat vague "we" cited in the text – and the individual, namely the assassin, Yigal Amir. On the one hand, the Commission expressed its horror at the fact that "we have reached a pass" where a "Jewish student," a member of the said collective, could murder a Jew, and, moreover, a Prime Minister. On the other hand, the assassin was defined immediately, and unanimously, as the "other" in respect to that same collective, a total misfit, a "rotten apple" or "wild growth" according to the popular prevailing term, who acted entirely alone, and was not representative of any "we." What is more, it is unclear from the Commission's statement to which "we" they were referring; is it the Israeli collective as a whole? Is it only a part, a certain sector? How did this "we" arrive at a pass where it spawned the assassin of a Prime Minister? What had happened historically to that "we" and in what

---

[109] Ibid., p. 86. It notes, for example, police fears of clashes between right-wing demonstrators from the Zu Artzenu and Kach movements and the participants in the peace rally, and refers to the possibility that "stink bombs may be thrown."

[110] Ibid., pp. 88–89.

[111] This statement in itself is problematic, since formally speaking, it was the task of the court, rather than the Commission, to determine whether the defendant committed the crime of which he was accused and pass judgment, and not to deal with the historical and political background to the crime, although the court, too, exceeded its task whenever it found this convenient. See below.

political and social context was the assassination planned and perpetrated by the "assailant" and those who supported him? The Commission offered no answer to those critical questions, because from the outset it never asked them. Again: the vast deed, with its historic implications, committed by the "Jewish student" Yigal Amir, who had been described, because of the Commission's inability to deal with the phenomenon, as an "arrogant fool," was downplayed as a melodramatic act of "cruelty," as if it were a banal murder committed on criminal grounds, indeed very inappropriate to respectable society, rather than a calculated political and ideological move, which was both far-reaching and total, and from which there could be no return, a move that was intended to divert the course of history and succeeded perfectly in so doing.

But the cliché-ridden depictions of the assassination and the assassin do not even come close to the incongruity and dissonance of the concluding sentence of the Commission's evaluation of the assassin, who "was responsible for the social and psychological disaster *created by* the historical blot which he has left on our society." This sentence calls for analysis. State Commissions of Inquiry, more than they are charged with exposing a concealed truth, are enjoined to mend social rifts and heal collective traumas, to reestablish a shattered identity and a shaken sense of security, and to restore a damaged whole. To this end they employ soothing, appeasing, and uniting rhetoric, rather than adversarial, sharpened language. To emphasize the anomality and total otherness of the murder, the Commission felt it necessary to describe the period immediately preceding the crime as a period of normalcy, and the political and social body at the time as whole, healthy, free of all symptoms of disease, rational and sane. Consequently, the assassination was defined not as a symptom of profound social and political malaise but as a disgraceful technical mishap – doubly disgraceful because the autoimmune deficiency had occurred within the hallowed security services. Into this harmonious and healthy body, according to the Commission, an assassin suddenly burst out of nowhere, affiliated to nothing and, in effect, lacking any serious reason which was worth discussing, and assassinated randomly a Prime Minister, who too represented nothing which might have caused him to be singled out for liquidation, and thereby was responsible for a social and psychological disaster which was created *because of* "the historical blot" of the murder. (My italics.)

A meaningless assassination

The courtroom, another site where a society delineates itself and constitutes its norms, or tries to restore the semblance of order, was involved in even more profound contradictions, because it was constrained by inflexible procedures and clearly defined ritual regulations. Lest it be charged with conducting a "political trial," namely a procedure with a predetermined outcome and extra-legal objectives, the court endeavored to distance itself from even the shadow of a suspicion of political leanings. The trial was defined by the presiding judge, Justice Edmond A. Levi, as "not a political trial," but a "regular criminal trial."[112] "It was not the defendant's viewpoint regarding the sanctity of the land which stood trial, nor was it the issue of whether the Israel government's steps since the signing of the Oslo Accords were correct," declared the judge, but one sole question – whether the accused perpetrated the crime of "murder," as defined in the Penal Code.[113] Thus, like the Commission, the court devoted the bulk of its energy to self-evident and self-apparent issues – establishing that the defendant was not suffering from mental illness, that he was responsible for his actions and aware of their nature, of the circumstances, and of the possible consequences of the act. In other words, as the court phrased it, he was guilty of acting with "malice aforethought."[114] In this spirit, the court did everything possible to restrict discussion of the assassin's convictions, and cut short the defendant when he attempted to expound his ideological and political beliefs to the judges. Again and again the presiding judge – who, however subconsciously, was reflecting the general will not to hear, not to know, not to scrutinize the terrible truth of the assassination and the assassin – interrupted Amir and demanded that he stop "haranguing." In so doing, the court was also "diminishing [the assassin's] importance, and emptying his deed of rational, systematic and reasoned content," as Ariela Azulai writes.[115]

Not only the assassin was silenced by the court, as one unworthy of being granted a voice on the public, sanctified site of the court, and dammed were his views, which might then continue to disturb the peace and order already undermined by the murder. The court also obstructed any possibility of gaining knowledge and insight, which might have been embodied in the assassin's statement, as regards the ideological convictions and influences which set him in motion and propelled him to the place of the assassination on 4 November 1995, and the historical and philosophical significance of his deed. The presiding judge dismissed Amir's political and ideological pronouncements, as if they were nothing but a defensive tactic: "The decision to murder the

[112] *State of Israel* v. *Yigal Amir, Sentence*, pp. 3, 1, 2, respectively.
[113] Ibid., *Sentence*, p. 4.   [114] Ibid., *Verdict*, p. 17/28.
[115] Azulai, "The Spectre of Yigal Amir," p. 14.

Prime Minister, which was made with cold consideration and clear thinking ... was perpetrated – *at least according to the version of the accused* – against a political background," wrote Judge Levi in his verdict. And in sentencing Amir, he said: "it became clear that ... *apparently ideological motives* cut down the life of a man."[116] The assassin's utterly political declaration, reflecting the exclusively political nature of the act of assassination, namely that from the outset he had had no particular interest in Rabin's death ("My target is not Rabin himself") and had wanted, primarily, to put an end to his political functioning as Prime Minister ("My intention was to shoot him in such a way as to prevent him from continuing to function as Prime Minister"), was dismissed by the court as an attempt by the assassin to evade the weight and gravity of his deed,[117] a thesis which there had been no evidence to support, either during the police investigation of Amir or in the courtroom.[118]

On the other hand, in total conflict with the verdict, the sentence fell into the trap of a political trial. Once again, not only the assassin, his motives and guilt, were the focus of the court's attention, but also the murdered – who was no common victim of a common crime of murder, but a political leader, a head of state – and with him the murdered's community, namely, the secondary victims. For one fleeting moment, the court even constructed a political and social background for the assassin, like a theatrical backdrop:

The actions of the accused are not only a personal failing, and it is not with him alone that we are conducting a reckoning today. It is with everyone who, directly or indirectly, specifically or in general, led him to understand that it was permissible to cut down a human life on the altar of the Moloch of any ideology, whatsoever.[119]

Little more than this was said. And thus, instead of producing some truth – political, philosophical, cultural, social – however painful, which would have enabled Israeli society to commence true "work of mourning" and launch an agonizing but liberating critical process, the court broadcast messages of shock, and self-indignation. How could such a deed have

---

[116] *State of Israel* v. *Yigal Amir, Sentence*, pp. 2–3 (my italics).
[117] Ibid., *Verdict*, pp. 3/28, 17/28–18/28.
[118] Whether out of megalomania, the desire not to implicate others in his crime, or from other motives which cannot be examined here, Amir took full and total responsibility for his action. During his interrogation and in court he spoke in the first person singular. Among other things, he said: "As far as I am concerned, *Din Rodef* is written in our *Halakha* [religious law] and I don't need rabbis in order to know that. The rabbis didn't say anything to me. Someone heard a rabbi say that Yitzhak Rabin was really in the category of *Din Rodef*. I don't need a rabbi to know that." Ibid., *verdict*, p. 14/28.
[119] Ibid., *Sentence*, p. 3.

happened to *us* and "from our midst"? "We innocently believed," "it was our unsuspecting conviction," "we believed in good faith,"[120] the presiding judge said repeatedly in his sentencing decision. According to the story woven in court, as was the case with the narrative of the Commission of Inquiry, the murder was almost random, an unfortunate incident, which came from "an unexpected direction," as a surprise, "a resounding slap in the face" which shattered an illusion, "when it became clear that criminal behaviour had also reached our political life," since, in our innocence, we believed "that in this area we were not like other peoples," and that political assassination was "the inheritance of others, not our inheritance."[121]

Not only was the assassination depicted as a regrettable, anomalous incident, totally unfitting for *us*, as Jews, but it was also consequently defined as a failure, a definition that seems increasingly chilling as the years go by and the terrible historical repercussions of the assassination grow clearer. In order to veil the horror of the murder, to mend the "rift" hastily and to offer a healing message of unity and consolation, the court, in its sentence, had employed the conciliatory, blurring rhetoric of memorial days and anniversaries: "It is small consolation that not only did the assassination fail to achieve its aim, but that for a moment it brought hearts together, and there is no better evidence of this than the crowds from all walks of life who sang softly in those nights of November 1995 – 'Where can we find men like that man,'" wrote the presiding judge,[122] at a time when hearts were further apart than ever before.

Blindness

Everyone had glimpsed the face of the Gorgon, peering out of the act of assassination, dreadful, uncanny not only in the denial of the human and political, which the assassination represented, but also because it exposed something horrifying, intolerable about Israeli society, about ourselves. In order to confront that evil and overcome it, it was necessary, first and foremost, to be capable of looking it in the eye, and not to stand before it in dazzled awe, nor to fall silent in shame or to invest energies in a search for consoling myths. The fact that the fanatic right, and the settlers, could not look directly at the murder nor study it patiently, severely, and honestly, was banal. It was from their midst, from their exclusivist belief in the absolute truth and supreme justice of their cause, set above politics and human compromise, out of their zealous rhetoric and violent

[120] Ibid., pp. 2–3.   [121] Ibid., pp. 2–3.   [122] Ibid., p. 5.

practices that the murderer emerged. "Responsibility for the assassination of Rabin," wrote the philosopher Avishay Margalit, "was not confined to a direct assassin or assassins. The murder of Rabin – like that of Walter Rathenau or Jean Jaurès – was a statistical assassination: a system of denunciation and incitement marks out the victim and the question of assassination becomes a statistical question – who will actually commit the deed."[123] On the other hand, the fact that the Right succeeded in dissociating itself from the murder, policing the discourse about the murder and making it somehow improper even to discuss it, and the way in which the Right divested the 1996 elections of their single most significant issue, the political assassination of the Prime Minister, and has continued this practice vis-à-vis political discourse in general since the murder, have been much less banal. In order to silence the cry for justice for the slain Prime Minister and to render discussion of the assassination tabu in the public space, the right had need of a partner, and found one with ease within the camp of the murdered Prime Minister, within the Israeli labor movement.

Can it be that the nationalist fanaticism, the messianic belief in a borderless Greater Israel, the practices of power and violence, and the rituals of blood, victimhood, and the Holocaust, which the Israeli Left attributed to the Right in the wake of the murder, as Idan Lando wrote, contained a reflection of the Left's own shadow image, or of its distorterd outgrowth, and that it was from this that it turned away its gaze and became mute? Or was it silent because there was no way in which it could establish in-depth, stringent criticism of the assassination without facing up to the yearnings and practices of the central trend in Zionism and of the state, its institutions and elites, namely those of the labor movement itself?[124] The Left, wrote Idan Lando, "knows, in the depths of its heart, that the fanatics of the Right, with their pioneering rhetoric and brutal activism, are its own stepchildren, illegitimate offspring of the demonic coupling between labor and religious worship, between Mapai and *Adonai*, and it watches them with growing dread, its own distorted image, shamelessly taking its own darkest sides to extremes."[125]

For many years Yitzhak Rabin himself, warrior, beautiful and beloved son of the Zionist utopia, represented the dimension of its dark,

[123] Avishay Margalit, "How to Remember Yitzhak Rabin," in Yeshayahu Liebman (ed.), *Retzah Politi, Retzah Rabin U'retzihot Politiyot Ba'mizrah Ha'tichon (Political Assassination, the Rabin Assassination and Political Assassinations in the Middle East)*, Tel Aviv 1998, p. 64.
[124] On this see Bruner, "Yigal Amir."
[125] Idan Lando, "The Dubious Innocence of the Left," *Ha'aretz Supplement*, 29 December 1995, p. 22.

intoxicating power until, in the most heroic act of his life, he broke out of the framework of his foretold biography, and cast himself on to the dangerous path of peace, of partition of the land, and of delineation of the final borders of the State of Israel. At first the price he paid was loss of his eternal youth and happy princedom, then his life, a price he was apparently ready to pay, and, as maintained by his companions in the days preceding the assassination who witnessed his indifference to his personal safety, he may have been seeking, if only subconsciously, to pay.[126] And so this man of few words, who never spoke in vain in the name of the *Shoah* or the *Ge'ulah* (Redemption), became a martyr with his death, a witness to the catastrophe of political messianism and to the absence of salvation in this world.

---

[126] Yehudah (Judd) Neeman expounds a fascinating theory, though difficult to prove, regarding the heavy burden of guilt weighing on native-born Israelis with regard to the Jewish Holocaust and the Palestinian calamity, which is translated into self-chastisement and longing for punishment and breaks out in the form of ritual murder. "Because of his life story, but mainly because of the vast weight of guilt of the mythological sabra ... Rabin was doomed to be sacrificed on the altar of guilt." See Neeman, "The Wolf that Devoured Rabin," *Plastika*, **3**, Summer 1999, pp. 82–86.

Biographies

Nathan Alterman (1910–1970) – Considered as poet laureate of the Ben-Gurion era, a leading publicist, and an influential voice in Israel's political and cultural life. Born in Warsaw, Poland, he immigrated to Palestine in 1924, attended the Herzliya Gymnasiun in Tel Aviv, and later was qualified as agriculture engineer at the Higher Institute of Agriculture in Nancy, France. On his return to Palestine he started publishing essays, political articles, and poems first in *Ha'aretz*, later on in *Davar*, which became for many years his home journal. His "Poems of the Time and the Tide," as he called them, among them his weekly Seventh Column published in *Davar* in the years 1943–1965, referred to any major issue in Jewish, Zionist, and Israeli life. Close to the Palmach and its commander Yitzhak Sadeh, he later became an ardent advocate of Ben-Gurion's authoritarian étatisme (*mamlachtiut*), and joined his splinter party Rafi in 1965. In 1967 he was one of the leading members of the Movement For Greater Israel, and its most prominent voice. He got the 1968 Israel Prize for literature.

Mordechai Anielewicz (1919–1943) – Commander of the Warsaw ghetto uprising in 1943, and leader of ŻOB (Żydowska Organizacja Bojowa, Jewish Fighting Organization) during the insurrection. Born and raised in a poor Jewish quarter of Warsaw, Anielewicz joined the Zionist-socialist youth movement Ha'shomer Hatzair, and soon became one of its leaders. At the outbreak of the war, he fled from Warsaw to the border region in south-east Poland, where he was involved in smuggling Jews to Romania and out of occupied Europe. In January 1940, back in Warsaw, he started creating underground cells in ghettos all over the country. Following the first mass deportation of Warsaw Jews to Treblinka in the summer of 1942, he established himself in the ghetto, reorganized ŻOB and transformed it into a fighting force, and was appointed its commander in November 1942. On 18 January 1943, on the launching of the second mass deportation, ŻOB fighters joined the columns of deportees and attacked the Germans. Street battles followed under Anielewicz's command. Four days later the deportation was halted. On 19 April, the last deportation of Jews was launched, and the signal for the final rebellion was given. The fighting lasted for almost a month and was finally crushed by a large German military force. Anielewicz and a small surviving group of rebels took their own lives in the ŻOB bunker at 18 Miła Street on 8 May 1943. "My life's dream has come true; I have lived to see Jewish resistance in the ghetto in all its greatness and glory," Anielewicz wrote in a letter to his second in command on the Polish side.

Aharon Barak (1936–) – Incumbent President of Israel's Supreme Court. Survivor of Kovno ghetto in Lithuania, Barak reached Palestine in 1947 with his mother. Law professor at the Hebrew University of Jerusalem and Israel Prize Laureate for Social Sciences and Law for 1974, he was appointed State Attorney General in 1975. A prominent intellectual and author of influential works in jurisprudence, Barak is known to be a leading advocate of judicial activism. According to the government's decision in November 1995, Barak appointed the State Commission of Inquiry in the matter of the assassination of Prime Minister Yitzhak Rabin.

Menachem Begin (1913–1992) – Follower of Zeev Jabotinsky, Begin was born in Brest-Litovsk, studied law at the University of Warsaw, and was appointed Commissioner of Betar in March 1939. On the German invasion, he fled to Lithuania, was arrested, and condemned to eight years of hard labor, but was released in 1941 as a Polish citizen to join a Polish army company formed in the USSR to fight the Nazis. Still in army uniform he reached Palestine in May 1942, where he became the ETZEL commander. He was on board the Irgun ship *Altalena* (after Jabotinsky's pen name) in 1948, which approached Tel Aviv with immigrants and a consignment of arms, contrary to the orders of the newly formed Israel Defense Forces. The government ordered the shelling and sinking of the ship. Begin transformed ETZEL into the Herut (Freedom) party in the Knesset in 1948. In 1952 he led the party's protest against the reparations agreement with West Germany. On the eve of the Six Day War, he became a national unity cabinet member. He left the government in 1970 after its acceptance of the US plan of Israeli withdrawal from the territories. In 1973 he formed the Likud bloc under his leadership. After winning the 1977 elections he became Prime Minister. It was during this tenure that he and Egyptian President Anwar Al-Sadat received in 1978 the Nobel Peace Prize for the peace treaty they would sign the following year, after returning most of the Sinai Peninsula to Egypt. He was reelected in 1981 for a second term, and a few weeks after the violent evacuation of Jewish settlers from the town of Yamit, he ordered, in June 1982, the Israeli invasion of Lebanon. He stepped down in September 1983 and spent the rest of his life in total seclusion.

David Ben-Gurion (1886–1973) – Born in Plonsk, he joined at the age of seventeen the Jewish socialist Po'alei Zion (Zion workers') movement. Arrested twice during the failed 1905 Russian Revolution, he immigrated to Palestine in 1906, to found there the Po'alei Zion party. A prolific writer and political essayist, he soon stood out as a capable political leader and organizer. He went to study law in Turkey to prepare himself for a professional political career, but was exiled by the Turks during World War I. He went to New York where he started organizing groups of Jewish youth to immigrate to Palestine. In 1920 he was instrumental in founding the general workers federation, the Histadrut, and was elected its general secretary, his first major political role. In 1930 he formed Mapai, the Palestine Labor party, and in 1935 he became chairman of the executive committee of the Jewish Agency for Palestine. Leading the Zionist struggle for a Jewish state and what he called the Combatant Zionism, for the decade starting in 1939, he proclaimed independence for the State of Israel, on 14 May 1948, in Tel Aviv art museum.

Founder of Israel and its shaper in its first fifteen years, he led his governments and the country in an authoritarian style through a stormy period, during which Israel fought two wars (the War of Independence and the Sinai Campaign). He remained Knesset member until he retired from politics in 1970. He died in his kibbutz Sdeh Boker in the Negev desert, in October 1973.

Yosef Haim Brenner (1881–1921) – Born in the Ukraine, Brenner joined as a young man the Bund, a Jewish socialist anti-Zionist movement, but under the impact of the first Zionist congresses, he became an ardent Zionist, and advocate of Jewish immigration to and settlement in Palestine. In 1902 he was enlisted in the Russian army, but on the outbreak of the Russia–Japan war he defected, crossed the border, and reached London, where he lived until 1908. Earning his living as a typesetter, he edited the monthly *Ha'meorer* (the awakener), and published his first plays. On his arrival to Palestine in 1909, he started publishing his harsh, critical essays, novels, and plays in various publications, among them *Ha'poel Ha'tzair* and *Kuntress*. Brenner was the most prominent literary figure in Palestine and one of the most influential moral voices of his time. He was killed by Arab rioters in Jaffa in 1921.

Haim Cohen (1911–2002) – Born in Luebeck, Germany, to a Jewish orthodox family, he became a leading figure in Israel's legal system, and served the state in a variety of functions. In the 1950s he was State Attorney General, Ben-Gurion's legal strong man, and advocate of security prominence and *raison d'état*. In 1953 he initiated and was head of prosecution at the libel trial in the case of Malkiel Grunewald, which was soon transformed into a public, political trial on the Holocaust, the Jewish conduct, and the role of its leadership in both the Diaspora and Palestine during World War II, known as the Kastner–Grunewald Affair. In 1960 he was appointed Supreme Court justice gradually to become one of its most liberal and progressive members. He helped to establish the Association for Civil Rights in Israel, and was Honorary President of the International Center for Peace in the Middle East.

Moshe Dayan (1915–1981) – Born in Israel, and raised in the first Moshav (agricultural settlement) of Nahalal, he became the emblematic *Sabra*. He joined the Haganah and was company cammander in the Palmach. During a military mission to Lebanon he lost his eye in battle, and his black eye-patch was until his death his world-famous trademark. As IDF's fourth Chief of Staff, he was considered an original and militant general, advocating military solutions to political problems. On his retiring from the army in January 1958 he became active in Israel's political life as leading member of Mapai and Ben-Gurion's close associate. He held several ministry portfolios in Ben-Gurion's and Levi Eshkol's governments. Following a stormy campaign aiming at delegitimation of Premier Eshkol on the eve of the June 1967 war, Dayan was appointed Minister of Defense, and consequently won world fame with Israel's swift military victory. In the wake of the war, while being responsible for the administration of the occupied territories, he designed the "open bridges policy," and tried to bequeath to both Palestinians and Israelis the notion of "enlightened occupation."

Marek Edelman (1921–) – Co-organizer of ŽOB (Jewish Fighting Organization in Warsaw Ghetto) and one of the commanders of the Warsaw ghetto uprising. Born in Warsaw, Edelman joined the Zukunft organization, the youth movement of the Jewish Socialist Workers' party, the Bund, and later on became member of the party's central institutions. In November 1942, he was appointed as representative of his party in the fighting organization's command, and led some of the harshest battles against the Germans in April 1943. Upon defeat he refused to be part of the collective suicide of Anielewicz and his followers and crossed over to the "Aryan" side of Warsaw where he fought in the summer of 1944 as member of the Polish resistance in the Warsaw Polish Rebellion. After the war, Edelman published some books on his war years, became a renowned cardiologist, and in the early 1980s was a leading member of the Solidarity Movement.

Levi Eshkol (1895–1969) – Born in the Ukraine, Levi Shkolnik-Eshkol immigrated to Palestine in 1914 and became politically active in the ranks of Ha'poel Ha'tzair, later to be united with Achdut Ha'avodah to form Mapai (1930). Outstanding in his organizational and financial skills, he was among the prominent builders of the country's infrastructure. In 1947 he joined forces with Ben-Gurion to organize the new army and the whole security system. In 1951 he was elected Knesset member (where he served until his death in 1969). He first headed the Ministry of Agriculture, and a few months later he was appointed Minister of Finances, leaving his deep imprint on Israel's economy. On Ben-Gurion's resignation, in June 1963, Eshkol became his natural successor as Prime Minister and Minister of Defense. Known for his sense of humor, non-adversarial temperament, and for being politically milder than Ben-Gurion, he created a more flexible political climate in the country, and dismantled the Military Rule on Israel's Arab citizens. Although his was a crucial role in the build-up and modernization of the army, he was forced in June 1967 to resign from the Ministry of Defense and cede his place to Dayan.

Israel Galili (1911–1986) – Born in the Ukraine, he immigrated as a child to Palestine (1914), had to work in his youth, joined the youth labor movement Ha'noar Ha'oved. In 1930 he was among the founders of kibbutz Na'an, where he lived until his death. Between the years 1946 and 1948 he was Head of National Staff of the Haganah, and was one of the leaders of the new Achdut Ha'avoda, founded in 1944, and later on a leading member of the Labor party. Knesset member from 1955, he was appointed Minister without Portfolio in Eshkol's and Golda Meir's governments, serving as their *éminence grise* and close adviser. In the years 1970–1977 he was Chairman of Ministerial Committee for Settlements, responsible for a large Jewish settlement in the occupied territories.

Haim (Gurfinkel) Guri (1923–) – Poet, essayist, and journalist, and considered as a national moral conscience, Guri was involved in and served as witness to almost every major event in Israel in the second half of the twentieth century. A native of Palestine and born to a prominent Zionist-socialist family, he joined the Palmach, and fought in the war of 1948. His first collection of poems, *Flowers of Fire*, expressed the whole generation's war and death experience and made of him a leading voice of the new Israeli-ness. In 1961 he covered the Eichmann trial in

Jerusalem in daily reports published in the newspaper *Lamer'hav*, later to be collected in the book *Facing the Glass Booth*. In 1967 he was among the first signatories of the document For Greater Israel, and became an advocate of Jewish settlements in the occupied territories, and the settlers' moral ally. He is recipient of 1988 Israel Prize for literature.

Benyamin Halevi (1910–1996) – Born in Germany, he got his doctorate in law from Berlin University, and immigrated to Palestine after the Nazi seizure of power in 1933. He first served as Peace Justice, and in 1948 was appointed to the District Court in Jerusalem and soon became its President. In 1954–1955 he presided over the case of Grunewald, helping the defense counsel Shmuel Tamir in transforming a marginal libel case into a major political trial. Presiding over the military court established to try the perpetrators of the massacre in Kafar Kassem in October 1956, he ruled in his verdict that it was forbidden to obey overtly illegal orders, on which "a black flag is waving." He was one of three judges at the Eichmann trial in 1961, and in 1963 he was appointed Supreme Court Justice.

Gideon Hausner (1915–1990) – Born in Lemberg (Lvov), Poland, Hausner replaced Cohen as Israel's Attorney General just a few weeks before Ben-Gurion's announcement in the Knesset of the capture of Adolf Eichmann, and the plan to put him on trial according to the Nazi and Nazi Collaborators (Punishment) Law 1950. As head of the prosecution at the trial the rather greyish lawyer gained world fame. After his tenure as State Attorney General, he was elected Knesset member, representing the Independent Liberal party. In the years 1969–1990, he was Chairmen of Yad Vashem, Israel's Holocaust Remembrance Authority.

Zeev (Vladimir) Jabotinsky (1880–1940) – Born in Odessa, Russia, Jabotinsky was a brilliant intellectual, prolific author, and essayist. He studied law at the University of Rome, and served as correspondent for several Russian newspapers. The Kishinev Pogrom of 1903 spurred Jabotinsky to undertake Zionist activity. He organized self-defense units, fought for minority rights for Jews in Russia, and was elected delegate to the 6th Zionist Congress. Following the outbreak of World War I, he served as military correspondent. While in Alexandria he met Yosef Trumpeldor, and from then onward, worked for the establishment of the Jewish Legion. From 1921 onwards, Jabotinsky was a member of the Zionist Executive. After having seceded from the Zionist movement because of its cooperative and lenient attitude toward the British Mandate, he established in 1925 the Union of Zionists-Revisionists (Hatzohar) which advocated the immediate establishment of a Jewish state. He founded and was world leader of the youth movement Betar (Brit Yosef Trumpeldor), of militarist and nationalist orientation. In 1929, while he was on a world lecture tour, the British administration denied him reentry into Palestine. He resigned in 1935 from the Zionist Executive, after it had rejected his political program, and founded the New Zionist Organization (NZO) demanding free Jewish immigration and the establishment of a Jewish state. In 1937, he founded ETZEL and became its leader. In 1939–1940, Jabotinsky was active in Great Britain and the United States for the establishment of a Jewish army to fight side by side with the Allies against Nazi Germany. Jabotinsky died while visiting the Betar camp in New York in 1940.

Berl Katznelson (1887–1944) – Native of Bubroisk, Belarus, he joined the Jewish self-defense organization in his home town and later joined the socialist wing of the Zionist movement. Reaching Palestine in 1909, Katznelson became a prominent figure of the Second *Aliyah* (second wave of immigration). Settling in the commune of Kinneret, he created the Council of Galilean Farm Workers. Later on he helped establish a consumer cooperative known as Hamashbir, and the health services for workers. At the same time he created a vast program of cultural activities including lectures, libraries, Hebrew translations of classical works, publication of new books, and became a spiritual leader of the labor movement. As of 1920 he joined forces with Ben-Gurion to lead the united labor movement. Katznelson laid out the party platform which advocated "rebirth" of the Jewish people in Palestine and the creation of a socialist society based on liberty, egalitarianism, cultural and economic autonomy, and the collective ownership of land and natural resources. In 1925 he founded the movement's daily newspaper *Davar* (of which he was first editor in chief) and its publishing house, Am Oved (working people), whose aim was producing quality books at low prices.

Abba Kovner (1918–1987) – Underground leader and partisan during World War II, poet, writer, and a prominent figure in Israel's cultual and political life. Born in Sevastopol, Russia, Kovner was educated at the Hebrew high school in Vilna and at the school of arts. In 1940–1941, under Soviet occupation, Kovner was an underground activist. On German occupation in June 1941, Kovner first found refuge with a few friends in a Dominican convent then returned to the ghetto and, following the mass execution of the ghetto Jews, he published a manifesto calling for Jewish armed resistance. "Hitler plans to kill all the Jews of Europe," he wrote on 31 December 1941. "Let us not go like sheep to the slaughter." In 1942, the United Partisan Organization was founded in Vilna. After the capture of its first commander, Yitzhak Wittenberg, in July 1943, Kovner took his place. While the ghetto was being liquidated and its last Jewish dwellers deported to the death camps, Kovner organized the fighters' escape into the forests; there he commanded the Jewish Unit composed of ghetto fighters and the Nakam (revenge) group. After liberation Kovner became one of the Brichah (escape) leaders, who organized Jewish survivors' escape out of Europe. Kovner reached Palestine in 1945 to gather means and support for revenge activities and liquidation of Nazis. He was arrested, and released. In 1946 he joined kibbutz Ein Ha'choresh along with his wife the partisan Vitka Kempner. In the War of Independence he served as an indoctrination officer (*politruk*) in the Givati brigade on the southern front, and published daily calls for battle designed to invigorate the soldiers' motivation to fight. After the war Kovner returned to his kibbutz and dedicated most of his time to writing. He won the 1970 Israel Prize for literature.

Moshe Landau (1912–) – Born in Danzig, on the German–Polish border, he immigrated to Palestine in 1933, and had a brilliant career in Israel's judiciary. Appointed Justice of Peace in Haifa in 1940, he became District Court Justice in 1948 and Supreme Court Justice in 1953. In 1961, he was appointed presiding Judge at the Adolf Eichmann trial in Jerusalem, and won world acclaim for the way he handled the judicial procedure during the trial. He served as member of the Agranat Committee, which investigated the IDF's failures in the Yom Kippur War. In 1980–1982 he was the President of the Supreme Court. In 1987 he headed the Landau Committee, whose task was to inquire into the methods of investigation used by the Israeli Security Service.

Yitzhak Sadeh (1890–1952) – Military commander, poet, and essayist. Born in Lublin, Poland, Sadeh served in the Tsar's army during World War I, and commanded a troop of the Red Army following the October Revolution. In 1917 he assisted Yosef Trumpeldor with self-defense operations in Petrograd, and in the He'chalutz organization. Sadeh immigrated to Palestine in 1920, joined Gedud Ha'avoda (Labor Battalion) and the Haganah, moving up swiftly within its commanding hierarchy. He initiated the concept of "going out of the fences," an offensive orientation which had a far-reaching impact on IDF. In 1941 he founded the Palmach and served as its commander until 1945. In 1945–1947 he was Chief of Staff of the Haganah. Following the establishment of the State of Israel and his retirement from military service, he became a member of the socialist-leftist party Mapam.

Meir Shamgar (1925–) – Born in Danzig, Shamgar immigrated to Palestine in 1939, and became a member of ETZEL. Shamgar was deported in 1944 to a British detention camp in Kenya, where he studied law (in correspondence with the University of London), and was qualified as an attorney. Upon his return he fought in the 1948 Independence War, after which he joined the military's attorney staff. In 1961 he was appointed Chief Military Attorney, in which capacity he laid the legal infrastructure for the military government, which served the army following the Six Day War. In 1968 he was appointed State Attorney General, and as such he broadened the realm of activity of his office. In 1975 Shamgar was appointed Supreme Court Justice, and in 1983 he was appointed President of the Supreme Court. After retirement, he served in several state commissions of inquiry, among them as Chairman of the State Commission of Inquiry in the matter of the assassination of Prime Minister Yitzhak Rabin.

Moshe Shamir (1921–2004) – Writer, playwright, essayist, and political activist, Shamir was born in Israel, started his political activity in Ha'shomer Hatza'ir, joined the Palmach and was a kibbutz member. In 1948 (during the war), he edited IDF's newspaper *Bamachane* (in the camp). In the wake of the Six Day War, Shamir was among the initiators and founders of the movement For Greater Israel. He wrote its main manifesto and was one of its prominent speakers. In 1973 he joined the Likud. In 1977 he was one of the founders of the right-wing La'am party and elected Knesset member. Following the Camp David Accords, he founded, together with Geula Cohen, Brit Ne'emanei Eretz Israel (alliance of trustees of the land of Israel). He was Israel Prize laureate.

Yitzhak Tabenkin (1887–1971) – Tabenkin began his public activities within the ranks of Po'alei Zion and the Bund in Russia and Poland. He immigrated to Palestine in 1912, joined the defense organization Hashomer, founded Achdut Ha'avoda and the Histadrut. He later resigned from urban activity to join

Trumpeldor's Gdud Ha'avodah (Labor Battalion) and in 1921 became one of the founding members of kibbutz Ein Harod, which later formed the main core of the kibbutz movement Ha'kibbutz Ha'meuchad. Tabenkin firmly believed in the kibbutz values and way of living, and supported the idea of large kibbutzim or collective settlements open to large pluralistic membership. He became involved in labor movement politics and was one of the founders of Mapai and of Mapam. He was advocate of Greater Israel as of the 1930s, and opposed the 1937 Partition Plan. His support for the Greater Israel ideology following the Six Day War was compatible with age-old ideology. Knesset member, an untiring orator, Tabenkin, who lived in his kibbutz until his death, was a charismatic popular leader among his followers.

Shmuel (Katznelson) Tamir (1923–1987) – Born in Jerusalem, to a family of political activists, he joined the ETZEL, became its deputy commander in Jerusalem (1946), was arrested twice, and deported in 1947 to Kenya. In his detention camp he completed law studies and qualified as an attorney under the British Mandate government. In 1948 he was one of the founders of the Herut party, but resigned in 1952 in protest against Menachem Begin's leadership. He was appointed counsel for the defense in the Grunewald–Kastner trial, and succeded in transforming what was meant to be a marginal case into a major public, political event against the leading party Mapai. Tamir helped found Hamishtar Ha'chadash (the new power), a political movement which sought, among other things, to ensure human and civil rights without limitations within a constitution, to found a federate alliance with Jordan and a confederate alliance with Lebanon. Tamir was elected Knesset member in 1965, representing Gahal (Gush Herut Liberalim), an alignment of Herut and the Liberal party, to become in 1973 part of the Likud. Following public disagreements between Tamir and Begin, Tamir was suspended from membership of Herut. In 1967 he left Herut and founded Ha'merkaz Ha'hofshi (the free center), an independent party. Following the Six Day War, he coined the expression "occupied territory will not be returned." He switched parties, and was appointed Minister of Justice in Begin's government in 1977, as representative of the newly founded centrist party Dash. In 1978 he was one of the heads of the liberal movement.

Glossary

Achdut Ha'avodah (Heb.: united work) – Zionist Socialist Labor party founded in Palestine in 1919. The dominant workers' party with the aim of uniting all workers in Eretz Israel in a non-political structure. Achdut Ha'avodah's first leaders were David Ben-Gurion and Berl Katznelson. The party published a weekly newspaper by the name of *Kuntress*. In 1930 it merged with Ha'poel Ha'tzair and formed Mapai. Seceded from Mapai in 1944 and was reunited in 1968 as part of the Israeli Labor party.

Al Hamishmar (Heb.: on guard) – A daily newspaper founded in 1943 by the Ha'kibbutz Ha'artzi movement, serving mainly the ideology of left-wing, pioneering Mapam. *Al Hamishmar*'s circulation was limited to party members. It was closed in 1995.

aliyah (Heb.: going up, ascent) – A term used to denote the immigration of Jews to the Land of Israel. The term is loaded with religious and ideological connotations. *Aliyah* is also used for "going up" to the altar to read from the Torah.

Bund (abb. for "Allgemeiner Yiddischer Arbeiter Bund") – A Jewish socialist party founded in Russia in 1897, devoted to non-territorial Jewish autonomy, secular Jewish nationalism, and sharply opposed to Zionism. Following World War II, the Bund founded an international organization based in the United States.

Davar (Heb.: the word) – A daily newspaper, founded in 1925 by Berl Katznelson, serving the ideology of the Histadrut, and later Mapai. One of *Davar*'s most prominent columnists was the poet Nathan Alterman. *Davar* ceased to appear in 1996.

ETZEL (acronym for Irgun Zva'i Leumi – National Military Organization) – An underground resistance group, split from the Haganah. It was founded in 1931, for the purpose of driving away the British Mandate from Palestine and establishing a sovereign Jewish state. It was disbanded in 1948 along with other underground organizations, with the establishment of the State of Israel.

Gush Emunim (Heb.: bloc of faith) – An Israeli national-religious group, founded in 1974, following the Kippur War. Gush Emunim was the core settlers' movement in the Occupied Territories, its main tenets being that the "Greater Land of Israel" is the fulfillment of the age-old Jewish-Zionist dream and a step in the process of Redemption (Ge'ulah). It was opposed to the withdrawal from any of the territories conquered by Israel in the Six Day War (June 1967). It was formally replaced by Yesha Council, which is the political umbrella organization of the Settlements.

Ha'aretz (Heb.: the land) – A daily Israeli newspaper, founded in 1919. Privately owned, it has belonged since the 1930s to the German-Jewish Schocken family, and expresses a liberal worldview. In line with the Brit Shalom group, *Ha'aretz* favoured a binational solution to the local conflict. Secular, liberal, pluralistic, and leftist in the context of the Israeli–Palestinian conflict, *Ha'aretz* is considered to be the Israeli intelligentsia's newspaper.

Haganah (Heb.: defense) – The main paramilitary body of the Zionist labor movement, it was established in December 1920, following the miserable battle of Tel-Hai (1 March 1920), and in response to the growing security needs of the Jewish settlement in Palestine. Up to 1948 it was the main military underground organization, first linked to the labor movement and later encompassing other political groups. The source of IDF's original ethos of ethical, defensive warfare.

Ha'kibbutz Ha'meuchad (Heb.: the united kibbutz) – A kibbutz movement, whose founding father was Yitzhak Tabenkin. It was founded in 1927 and merged into the United Kibbutz movement in 1980. It was the most activist segment within the Jewish-Israeli labor movement, which was opposed historically to the partition of Palestine into two states. Among its second-generation prominent leaders were Yigal Alon and Israel Galili, who were also its political representatives.

Ha'makhanot Ha'olim (Heb.: the ascending camps) – A pioneering studying youth movement, founded in Palestine in 1926, defining itself ideologically as related to Ha'kibbutz Ha'meuchad and Ha'noar Ha'oved.

Ha'noar Ha'oved (Heb.: working youth) – An Israeli youth movement, founded in 1924 as an integral part of the Histadrut with the intention of uniting the youth for economic and socialist national and education purposes. Among its members were Israel Galili, Moshe Dayan, and Shimon Peres.

Ha'poel Ha'tzair (Heb.: the young worker) – A labor party, founded in 1905 by pioneers of the Second *Aliyah* (second wave of immigration), stressing Jewish labor as Zionist value. First indigenous workers' party, whose members helped in the founding of the first collectivist communes and settlements (kibbutzim and moshavim). In 1930 it merged with Achdut Ha'avodah and formed Mapai.

Ha'poel Ha'tzair (A monthly [later weekly] magazine) – First published in 1907, it was the first and for many years central publication of the Zionist labor movement in Palestine. Was distinguished by its literary supplement, among whose first contributors were Yoseph Haim Brenner, Shmuel Yoseph Agnon, and Moshe Smilansky. Politically related first to the Ha'poel Ha'tzair party and later to Mapai, it was closed in 1970, after the party merged with other labor groups to create the Labor party in 1968.

Ha'shomer (Heb.: the guardian) – First Jewish paramilitary organization in Palestine, founded in 1909. It was dismantled after the founding of the Haganah (labor-related main military organization, predecessor of Israel's army) in 1920.

He'chalutz (Heb.: the pioneer) – An association of Jewish youth, founded in Russia in 1905. Its aim was to train its members to settle in Eretz Israel. During the 1920s, branches were established in Britain and the United States, and during the inter-war period, also in continental Europe, Australia, South Africa, and Mediterranean countries.

Herut (Heb.: freedom) – Political movement in Israel established in 1948 by ETZEL members to continue as a parliamentary party with the ideals of Zeev Vladimir Jabotinsky. Its political agenda was the holiness (and wholeness) of the historic borders of Israel. Since 1955 Herut has been the second largest party in Israel, led by Menachem Begin. In 1977 the Herut dominated Likud under Begin's leadership, won the general elections, and for the first time replaced the political reign of Mapai.

Herut (newspaper) – A daily newspaper, which existed between the years 1948 and 1965. Served as the organ of the Herut political party.

Histadrut (Heb.: organization; abb. for General Organization of Hebrew Workers in the Land of Israel) – Jewish labor federation founded in 1920 in Palestine, subsequently renamed Histadrut Ha'ovdim Be'Eretz Israel, which is a collective body of trade unions, comprising a majority of the country's labor force. The Union originally incorporated all laborers in Israel with the aim of providing for social, cultural, and economic needs of all workers in the country.

IDF (acronym for Israel Defense Forces, Tzahal) – Israel's armed forces (army, air force, and navy), formed following the founding of Israel in 1948. The predecessors to the IDF were the Haganah (in particular, its operative detachment, the Palmach) and the British Jewish armed forces, in particular the Jewish Brigade that fought during World War II. After the creation of IDF, the three Jewish underground groups, Palmach, ETZEL, and LECHI (an extreme right splinter group), came under the control of the IDF.

Jewish Agency – Organization formed in 1929 as the formal representative of the Jewish community vis-à-vis the British mandatory government. It gradually acquired the attributes of a proto-government for the Jewish community. After the establishment of the State of Israel, the Jewish Agency shifted its focus to issues common to the state and to the Jewish world in large.

Joint (American-Jewish Joint Distribution Committee, AJJDC) – A United States Jewish philanthropic organization, founded in 1914 to assist Jewish needs during World War I. The non-Zionist organization served as the overseas charitable arm of the American Jewish community. It still operates all over the world, and has a large branch in Israel.

Knesset – The Israeli parliament first assembled in 1949. Its name and the number of its members are based on the "Knesset Hagdola" of the early Second Temple period. It is composed of 120 representatives of different political parties, elected in general elections for a four-year term.

Kuntress – A weekly newspaper published by Achdut Ha'avodah. It became the porte-parole of the labor movement in its early years.

Ma'ariv (Heb.: evening; Jewish synagogue evening prayer or service) – A daily newspaper in Israel, founded in 1948 by Azriel Carlebach, former editor of *Yedioth Aharonoth*. Nationalist in its orientation, *Ma'ariv* rapidly became a high-circulation newspaper. Populist in its journalistic approach.

Mapai (acronym for Party of Eretz Israel Workers) – A Zionist-socialist labor party in Israel founded in 1930 by the union of Achdut Ha'avodah and Ha'poel Ha'tzair. During the pre-state period, Mapai played a major role in the Yishuv (Jewish community prior to the state), laying the foundations for a sovereign Jewish state. In 1948 Mapai, led by David Ben-Gurion, declared Israel's independence. In 1968 Mapai merged along with other labor parties to create the Avodah party, and dominated the political arena until 1977, when the right-wing Likud first came to power.

Mapam (acronym for the United Workers party) – A left-wing labor Zionist party in Israel, founded in 1948 when Ha'shomer Ha'tzair merged with Achdut Ha'avodah-Po'alei Zion. Supporters of Mapam were essentially the hard-core Marxists of Ha'kibbutz Ha'artzi. In 1992 Mapam merged with Ratz and Shinui to form Meretz.

Mossad Le'aliyah Beth (Heb.: Institute for Illegal Immigration to Palestine) – A special, underground organization, founded in 1939 by the Haganah, in order to plan and implement clandestine Jewish immigration into Palestine. This was done most often by ship, and was funded primarily by the Joint. Between 1945 and 1948, the Mossad ships with their Holocaust survivors, became Zionism's main political weapon.

Nekuda (Heb.: point) – A monthly published since 1980 by Gush Emunim (later to become the Yesha Council). Ideologically oriented, it publishes writings of settlers in the West Bank and the Gaza Strip and voices the tenets of the extreme right wing and Greater Israel.

Palmach (abb. for Plugoth Machatz, striking troops) – Strike force within the Haganah, founded in 1941 in order to activate the organization's profile and participate in the war effort against Nazi Germany. Was mainly composed of native Jewish-Palestinian youth, and thus became the symbol of the Jewish-Zionist new type of man/woman. The Palmach was disbanded by Ben-Gurion in 1948, with the creation of the IDF, in the midst of a political storm within its own camp.

Rafi (abb. for Reshimat Poalei Israel, List of Israel's Workers) – A centrist laborite political party founded in 1965 by David Ben-Gurion who left his own historical party, Mapai, together with Moshe Dayan and

Shimon Peres, as part of the struggle against his successor Levi Eshkol. It was merged into the Labor party in 1968.

Unit 101 – An IDF special infantry unit formed in 1953. Its offensive line of operation set an example for other combat units of the IDF. Its commander was Ariel Sharon, and it consisted of no more than forty-five men. The unit was responsible for the bloody "reprisal operations" in the 1950s, and was criticized for its partisan-like ways and unrestrained violent conduct.

UNSCOP (acronym for United Nations Special Committee on Palestine) – Appointed in April 1947 to investigate the situation in Palestine and propose solutions. The majority of the committee recommended the partition of Palestine into two states. The Arab Higher Committee rejected the partition plan, while the Jewish Agency accepted it. UNSCOP recommendations were accepted by the UN General Assembly on 29 November 1947.

Yedioth Aharonoth (Heb.: latest news) – A daily, privately owned Israeli newspaper, founded in 1939. In 1948, a group of its leading journalists and staff members left to form another newspaper – *Ma'ariv*. Both evening papers (*Yedioth* and *Ma'ariv*) vehicle nationalist, populist attitudes, propelled also by their rivalry.

Bibliography

BOOKS

Agamben, Giorgio *Ce qui reste d'Auschwitz*, Paris 1999.
Améry, Jean *At the Mind's Limits: Contemplations by a Survivor on Auschwitz and its Realities*, Bloomington, IN, 1980.
Anderson, Benedict *Imagined Communities: Reflections on the Origins and Spread of Nationalism*, London and New York 1983.
Arendt, Hannah *Eichmann in Jerusalem: A Report on the Banality of Evil*, New York 1963.
Arendt, Hannah *Essays in Understanding, 1930–1954*, ed. Jerome Kohn, New York 1994.
Arendt, Hannah *The Human Condition* Chicago 1958.
Arendt, Hannah *Men in Dark Times*, Harmondsworth 1973.
Arendt, Hannah *The Origins of Totalitarianism*, New York (1951) 1972.
Arendt, Hannah *Rahel Varnhagen: The Life of a Jewish Woman*, New York (rev. edn.) 1974.
Ascheim, Steven A. (ed.) *Hannah Arendt in Jerusalem*, Berkeley 2001.
Bentley, Eric (ed.) *The Storm over the Deputy*, New York 1964.
Bernstein, Richard J. *Hannah Arendt and the Jewish Question*, Cambridge, MA, 1996.
Borges, Jorge Luis *Labyrinths, Selected Stories and Other Writings*, London 1970.
Brightman, Carol (ed.) *Between Friends: The Correspondence of Hannah Arendt and Mary McCarthy 1949–1975*, New York 1995.
Burleigh, Michael *The Third Reich: A New History*, New York 2000.
Byatt, A. S. and Sodre, Ignes *Imagining Characters*, New York 1995.
Canetti, Elias *Crowds and Power*, trans. Carol Stewart, London 1962.
Canovan, Margaret *Hannah Arendt: A Reinterpretation of her Political Thought*, Cambridge, MA, 1992.
Cassirer, Ernst *Essay on Man*, New Haven 1944.
Certeau, Michel de *Heterologies: Discourse on the Other*, trans. Briar Massumi, Minneapolis 1986.
Cohen, Avner *Israel and the Bomb*, New York 1998.
Feldman, Ron H. (ed.) *Hannah Arendt: The Jew as Pariah, Jewish Identity and Politics in the Modern Age*, New York 1978.
Finkielkraut, Alain *La mémoire vaine*, Paris 1989.
Friedländer, Saul *Nazi Germany and the Jews*, vol. I: *The Years of Persecution 1933–1939*, New York 1997.

Friedländer, Saul (ed.) *Probing the Limits of Representations: Nazism and the "Final Solution,"* Cambridge, MA, and London 1992.

Gary, Romain *Education Européenne*, Paris 1945.

Gutman, Israel (ed. in chief), *Encyclopedia of the Holocaust*, 4 vols., New York and London 1990.

Halbwachs, Maurice *Collective Memory*, New York 1980.

Hertz, Frederick *Nationality in History and Politics: A Psychology and Sociology of National Sentiment and Nationalism*, London 1944.

Hilberg, Raul *The Destruction of European Jews*, Chicago 1961 (2nd and expanded edition in 3 volumes, New York 1985).

Hobsbawm, Eric *Age of Extremes: The Short Twentieth Century 1914–1991*, London 1994.

Howe, Irving *A Margin of Hope: An Intellectual Autobiography*, New York 1982.

Isaac, Jeffrey C. *Arendt, Camus, and Modern Rebellion*, New Haven 1992.

Karpin, Michael and Friedman, Ina *Murder in the Name of God: The Plot to Kill Yitzhak Rabin*, New York 1998.

Kimche, David and Bawli, Dan *The Sandstorm*, London 1968.

Kohler, Lotte and Saner, Hans (eds.) *Hannah Arendt Karl Jaspers: Correspondence, 1926–1969*, New York 1992.

Krall, Hanna *Shielding the Flame: An Intimate Conversation with Dr. Marek Edelman* (trans. Joanna Stasinka and Lawrence Weschler), New York 1986.

Kristeva, Julia *Le génie féminin, Hannah Arendt*, Paris 1999.

Lahav, Pnina *Judgement in Jerusalem: Chief Justice Simon Agranat and the Zionist Century*, Berkeley 1997.

Lazare, Bernard *Job's Dungheap*, New York 1949.

Leibovici, Martine *Hannah Arendt, une Juive, expérience, politique et histoire*, Paris 1998.

Levi, Primo *Conversazioni e interviste*, Turin 1997.

Levi, Primo *The Drowned and the Saved* (from Italian: Raymond Rosenthal), New York 1988.

Levi, Primo *The Reawakening*, trans. Stuart Woolf, New York 1986.

Levin, Murray B. *Political Hysteria in America: The Democratic Capacity for Repression*, New York 1971.

Liebman, Charles and Don-Yehiya, Eliezer *Civil Religion in Israel*, Berkeley 1983.

Lyotard, Jean-François *The Differend: Phrases in Dispute*, Minneapolis 1988.

Morris, Benny *Israel's Border Wars, 1949–1956: Arab Infiltration, Israeli Retaliation and the Countdown to the Suez War*, Oxford 1993.

Mosse, George *The Fallen Soldiers: Reshaping the Memory of the World Wars*, Oxford 1990.

Netanyahu, Benjamin *A Place Among the Nations*, New York 1993.

Nora, Pierre (ed.) *Les lieux de mémoire*, vol. I: *La République*, Paris 1984.

Novick, Peter *The Holocaust in American Life*, New York 1999.

Ophir, Adi *The Order of Evils*, New York 2005.

Parker, Richard B. *The Politics of Miscalculation in the Middle East*, Bloomington, IN, 1993.

Perlov, Yitzchok *The People of Exodus*, Tel Aviv n.d.

Prinz, Joachin *Arendt Nonsense*, New York 1963.

Quandt, William *Peace Process: American Diplomacy and the Arab–Israeli Conflict since 1967*, Berkeley 1993.

Robinson, Yaakov *And the Crooked Shall Be Made Straight: The Eichmann Trial, the Jewish Catastrophe and Hannah Arendt's Narrative*, New York 1965.

Rousset, David *Les jours de notre mort*, Paris 1947.

Scholem, Gershom *Walter Benjamin: The Story of a Friendship* (from German: Harry Zohn), Philadelphia 1981.

Segev, Tom *The Seventh Million: Israelis and the Holocaust* (trans. Haim Watzman), New York 1992.

Semprun, Jorge *L'écriture ou la vie*, Paris 1995.

Shapira, Anita *Land and Labor: The Zionist Resort to Force 1881–1948* (trans. William Templer), Stanford 1992.

Silberstein, Laurence J. (ed.) *New Perspectives on Israeli History: The Early Years of the State*, New York 1991.

Strachey, James (ed.) *The Standard Edition of the Complete Psychological Works of Sigmund Freud*, 24 vols., London 1953–74.

Sturken, Marita *Tangled Memories: The Vietnam War, the Aids Epidemic, and the Politics of Remembering*, Berkeley 1997.

Trouillot, Michel-Rolph *Silencing the Past: Power and the Production of History*, Boston 1994.

Vernant, Jean Pierre *Mortals and Immortals*, Princeton 1991.

White, Hayden *Metahistory: The Historical Imagination in Nineteenth-Century Europe*, Baltimore 1973.

Wistrich, Robert and Ohana, David (eds.) *The Shaping of Israeli Identity: Myth, Memory and Trauma*, London 1995.

Yerushalmi, Yosef Hayim *Freud's Moses: Judaism Terminable and Interminable*, New Haven and London 1991.

Young, James E. *The Texture of Memory, Holocaust Memorials and Meaning*, New Haven 1993.

Young-Bruehl, Elisabeth *Hannah Arendt: For Love of the World*, New Haven and London 1982.

Zertal, Idith *From Catastrophe to Power: Holocaust Survivors and the Emergence of Israel*, Berkeley 1998.

Zerubavel, Yael *Recovered Roots, Collective Memory and the Making of Israeli National Tradition*, Chicago 1995.

BOOKS IN HEBREW

Alterman, Nathan *Ha'hut Ha'meshulash* (*The Triple Thread*), Tel Aviv 1971.

Alterman, Nathan *Ha'tur Ha'shevii,* (*The Seventh Column*), B, Tel Aviv 1975.

Alterman, Nathan *Ir Ha'yona* (*City of the Dove*), Tel Aviv 1972.

Avinoam, Reuven (ed.) *Gvilei Esh* (*Scrolls of Fire*), Tel Aviv 1952.

Avrahami, Yitzhak and Malkin, Ahuvia (eds.) *Bi'vritkha* (*In your Covenant*), Tel Aviv 1938.

Bar-On, Mordechai *Etgar Ve'tigra: Ha'derekh Le'mivtza Kadesh – 1956* (*Challenge and Dispute: The Road to the Sinai Campaign – 1956*), Be'er Sheva 1991.

Bar-On, Mordechai *Sha'arei Aza: Mediniyut Ha'bitahon Veha'hutz shel Medinat Israel 1955–1957* (*The Gates of Gaza: Israel's Security and Foreign Policy 1955–1957*), Tel Aviv 1992.

Bar-Zohar, Michael *Ben-Gurion*, B, Tel Aviv 1977.

Barnea, Aryeh (ed.) *Basic Text for Education in the IDF*, Tel Aviv undated.

Begin, Menachem *Ba'mahteret* (*Underground*), vols. II and IV, Tel Aviv 1976.

Begin, Menachem *Ha'mered* (*The Revolt*), Tel Aviv 1978.

Beilin, Yossi *Mehiro shel Ihud: Mifleget Ha'avodah ad Yom Ha'kippurim* (*The Price of Unity: The Labor Party up to the Yom Kippur War*), Tel Aviv 1988.

Ben-Ami, Aharon (ed.) *Ha'kol – Gevulot Ha'shalom shel Eretz Israel* (*Everything – Eretz Israel's Borders of Peace*), Tel Aviv 1967.

Ben-Gurion, David *Ba'ma'arakha* (*In the Battle*), Tel Aviv 1957.

Ben-Gurion, David *Yoman Ha'milhama* (*War Diary*), A, Tel Aviv 1983.

Dayan, Moshe *Avnei Derekh* (*Milestones*), Tel Aviv 1976.

Dinur, Ben-Zion *Israel Ba'gola: Mekorot U'teudot* (*Israel in the Diaspora: Sources and Documents*), Tel Aviv 1926.

Dinur, Ben-Zion (chief ed.), *Sefer Toldot Ha'haganah* (*History of the Haganah*), vol. II, part 2, Tel Aviv 1964.

Dotan, Shmuel *Pulmus Ha'haluka Bi'tekufat Ha'mandat* (*The Partition Polemics in the Mandate*), Jerusalem 1980.

Dror, Levi and Rosentzweig, Israel (eds.) *Sefer Ha'shomer Ha'tzair* (*Ha'shomer Ha'tzair Book*), B, Merhavia 1961.

Evron, Boaz *Ha'heshbon Ha'leumi* (*A National Reckoning*), Tel Aviv (1988) 2002.

Feniger, Ofer *Ha'olam Haia Betokhi* (*The World Was Inside of Me*), Tel Aviv 1972.

Firer, Ruth *Sokhnei Ha'lekakh* (*Agents of Zionist Education*), Tel Aviv 1985.

Gilad, Zerubavel (ed.) *Sefer Ha'palmach* (*The Book of the Palmach*), A, Tel Aviv 1953.

Guri, Haim *Mul Ta Ha'zekhukhit* (*Facing the Glass Booth*), Tel Aviv 1963.

Gutman, Israel (ed. in chief), *Encylopedia shel Ha'shoah* (*Encyclopedia of the Holocaust*), 5 vols., Jerusalem and Tel Aviv 1990.

Haber, Ethan *Hayom Tifrotz Milhama* (*A War Will Break Out Today: Memoirs of General Israel Lior, Military Secretary of Premiers Levi Eshkol and Golda Meir*), Tel Aviv 1987.

Hefer, Haim and Yanko Marcel, *Misdar Ha'noflim* (*The Parade of the Fallen*), Tel Aviv 1968.

Kafkafi, Yitzhak (ed.) *Shnot Mahanot Ha'olim*, B (*Mahanot Ha'olim Years*, B), Tel Aviv 1985.

Katz, Shmuel *Jabo, Biografia shel Zeev Jabotinsky*, vol. I (*Jabo, a Biography of Zeev Jabotinsky*, vol. I), Tel Aviv 1993.

Katznelson, Berl *Ketavim* (*Collected Writings*) 12, Tel Aviv 1950.

Klinger, Hayka *Yoman Ba'ghetto* (*Diary of the Ghetto*), Tel Aviv and Ha'ogen 1959.

Laor, Dan (ed.) *Nathan Alterman Al Shtei Ha'drakhim, Dapim min Ha'pinkas* (*Nathan Alterman's Two Paths: Pages from a Notebook*), Tel Aviv 1993.

Leibowitz, Yeshayahu (ed. in chief) *Hebrew Encyclopedia*, vol. XXVIII, Jerusalem and Tel Aviv 1976.

Liebman, Yeshayahu (ed.) *Retzah Politi, Retzah Rabin U'retzihot Politiyot Ba'mizrah Ha'tichon* (*Political Assassination, the Rabin Assassination and Political Assassinations in the Middle East*), Tel Aviv 1998.

Lipovsky, P. *Yosef Trumpeldor, Ishiyuto, Hayav, Peulotav* (*Yosef Trumpeldor, his Personality, Life and Deeds*), Kovno 1924, Jerusalem 1947 (revised expanded edn.).

Lubetkin, Tzivia *Yemei Kilion Va'mered* (*Days of Destruction and Rebellion*), Tel Aviv 1979.

Mardor, Munia *Rafael: Research and Development for Israel's future*, Tel Aviv 1981.

Morris, Benny *Tikun Ta'ut, Yehudim Ve'aravim Be'Eretz Israel, 1936–1956* (*Correcting an Error: Jews and Arabs in Eretz Israel, 1936–1956*), Tel Aviv 2000.

Naor, Aryeh *Eretz Israel Ha'shlema, Emuna U'mediniyut* (*Greater Israel, Belief and Policy*), Haifa and Lod 2001.

Ophir, Adi *Lashon La'ra* (*Language of Evil*), Tel Aviv 2001.

Ophir, Adi (ed.) *50to48: Momentim Bikortiim Be'toldot Medinat Israel* (*Critical Moments in the History of the State of Israel*), Jerusalem and Tel Aviv 1999.

Oz, Amos *Be'or Ha'tkhelet Ha'aza* (*In the Fierce Blue Light*), Jerusalem 1990.

Rogel, Nakdimon *Parashat Tel Hai: Teudot Le'haganat Ha'galil Ha'elyon Be'taraf* (*The Tel Hai Affair: Documents on the Defense of Upper Galilee in 1921*), Jerusalem 1994.

Rogel, Nakdimon *Tel Hai: Hazit Bli Oref* (*Tel Hai: Front without Hinterland*), Tel Aviv 1979.

Rosenfeld, Shalom *Tik Pelili 124* (*Criminal Case 124*), Tel Aviv 1955.

Rosenthal, Ruvik *Kafar Kassem, Iru'im U'mitos* (*Kafar Kassem, Events and Myth*), Tel Aviv 2000.

Scholem, Gershom *Dvarim Be'go* (*Explications and Implications*), Tel Aviv 1975.

Scholem, Gershom *Walter Benyamin, Sipura shel Yedidut*, Tel Aviv 1987; *Walter Benjamin, the Story of a Friendship*, Philadelphia 1981.

Shaham, David *Israel: 50 Ha'shanim* (*Israel: Fifty Years*), Tel Aviv 1998.

Sharett, Moshe *Personal Diary*, Tel Aviv 1978.

Tabenkin, Yitzhak *Dvarim* (*Speeches*), vol. VI, Ramat Efal 1985.

Tabenkin, Yitzhak *Ha'hityashvut, Mahut Va'derekh* (*Settlement, Essence, and Path*), Ramat Efal 1983.

Tabenkin, Yitzhak *Lekah Sheshet Ha'yamim: Yishuva shel Eretz Bilti Mehuleket* (*The Lesson of the Six Day War: Settling an Undivided Land*), Tel Aviv 1971.

Tevet, Shabtai *Kinat David, Ha'karka Ha'boer* (*David's Zeal, The Burning Ground*), Tel Aviv 1987.

Weitz, Yehiam *Ha'ish She'nirtzah Paamayim: Hayav, Mishpato U'moto shel Dr. Israel Kastner* (*The Man Who Was Murdered Twice: The Life, Trial, and Death of Dr. Israel Kastner*), Jerusalem 1995.

Yaari, Meir *Be'derekh Aruka* (*The Long Road*), Merhavia 1947.

Zertal, Idith and Zuckerman, Moshe (eds.) *Hannah Arendt: Hatzi Mea shel Pulmus* (*Hannah Arendt: A Half-Century of Polemics*), Tel Aviv 2004.

Zuckerman, Yitzhak (Antek) *Sheva Ha'shanim Ha'hen* (*Those Seven Years*), no place and date.

Zuckerman, Yitzhak and Basok, Moshe (eds.) *Sefer Milhamot Ha'getaot, Bein Ha'homot, Ba'mahanot, Ba'ya'arot* (*The Book of the Battles in the Ghettos, between Walls, in Camps, in Forests*), Tel Aviv 1954.

ARTICLES

Barshack, Lior "Death and the Political," *Free Associations*, **47**, 2001.

Brossat, Alain "La place du survivant. Une approche arendtienne," *Revue d'histoire de la Shoah*, **164**, September 1998.

Cohen, Richard I. "Breaking the Code: Hannah Arendt's *Eichmann in Jerusalem* and the Public Polemic: Myth, Memory and Historical Imagination," *Michael: On the History of the Jews in the Diaspora*, **13**, 1993.

Don-Yehiya, Eliezer "Memory and Political Culture: Israeli Society and the Holocaust," *Studies in Contemporary Jewry*, **4**, 1993.

Jaffee, Martin S. "The Victim-Community in Myth and History: Holocaust Ritual, the Question of Palestine and the Rhetoric of Christian Witness," *Journal of Ecumenical Studies*, **28**, Spring 1991.

Laqueur, Walter "The Arendt Cult – Hannah Arendt as Political Commentator," in Steven A. Ascheim (ed.), *Hannah Arendt in Jerusalem*, Berkeley 2001.

Lee Klein, Kerwin "On the Emergence of Memory in Historical Discourse," *Representations*, **69**, Winter 2000.

Lipstadt, Deborah "America and the Memory of the Holocaust, 1950–1965," *Modern Judaism*, **16** (3), October 1996.

Prost, Antoine "Les monuments aux morts," in Pierre Nora (ed.), *Les lieux de mémoire*, vol. I: *La république*, Paris 1984.

Young, James E. "When a Day Remembers: A Performative History of Yom Ha'shoah," *History and Memory*, **2** (2), Winter 1990.

Zertal, Idith "The Bearers and the Burdens: Holocaust Survivors in Zionist Discourse," *Constellations*, **5** (2), June 1998.

Zertal, Idith "From the People's Hall to the Wailing Wall: A Study in Fear, War and Memory," *Representations*, **69**, Winter 2000.

Zerubavel, Yael "The Politics of Interpretation: Tel-Hai in Israel's Collective Memory," *AJS*, **16**, 1991.

ARTICLES IN HEBREW

Azulai, Ariela "The Spectre of Yigal Amir," *Teoria U'vikoret*, **17**, 2001.

Ben-Yehuda, Nahman "Saturday Night, 4 November 1995, Malkhei Israel Square, Tel Aviv: Political Assassination in Eretz Israel," *Alpayim*, **12**, 1996.

Bilsky, Leora "The Kastner Trial," in Adi Ophir (ed.) *50to48: Momentim Bikortiim Be'toldot Medinat Israel* (*Critical Moments in the History of the State of Israel*), Jerusalem and Tel Aviv 1999.

Bisahra, Azmi "The Arabs and the Holocaust: The Problematics of the Word And," *Zmanim*, **53**, Summer 1995.

(Brenner), Y. H. B. *Revivim*, **3–4**, 1913.

Bruner, Jose "Yigal Amir," in Adi Ophir (ed.), *50to48: Momentim Bikortiim Be'toldot Medinat Israel* (*Critical Moments in the History of the State of Israel*), Jerusalem and Tel Aviv 1999.

Glickson, Moshe "The Day of Commemoration," *Ha'poel Ha'tzair*, **28**, March 1921.

Gutman, Israel "Arendt-style Self-Hatred," *Yalkut Moreshet*, **4** (6), December 1966.

Habibi, Emile "Your Holocaust, Our Catastrophe," *Politika*, **5**, 1986.

Kemp, Adriana "The Janus-faced Border: National Space and Consciousness in Israel," *Teoria U'vikoret*, **16**, 2000.

Lufban, Yitzhak "Tel Hai Day," *Ha'poel Ha'tzair*, **28**, March 1921.

Miron, Dan "An Israeli Document," *Politika*, **14–15**, June 1987.

Neemam, Yehudah (Judd) "The Wolf that Devoured Rabin," *Plastika*, **3**, Summer 1999.

Ram, Uri "Then and Now: Zionist Historiography and the Invention of the Jewish National Narrative: Ben-Zion Dinur and his Times," *Iyunim Bitekumat Israel*, 1996.

Simon, Akiva Ernst "Hannah Arendt: An Attempt at Analysis," *Molad*, **21** (179–180), July–August 1963.

Stern, Eliyahu "The Links between the Constantinople Delegation and Polish Jewry," *Yalkut Moreshet*, **39**, May 1985.

Syrkin, Nahman "The Defence of Life," *Kuntress*, **30**, 19 March 1920.

Yablonka, Hanna "The Nazis and Nazi Collaborators (Punishment) Law: An Additional Aspect of the Question of Israelis, Survivors and the Holocaust," *Katedra*, **82**, 1996.

Zertal, Idith "Hannah Arendt versus the State of Israel", in Adi Ophir (ed.), *50to48: Momentim Bikortiim Be'toldot Medinat Israel* (*Critical Moments in the History of the State of Israel*), Jerusalem and Tel Aviv 1999.

NEWSPAPERS

Der Yiddisher Kempfer
Le Figaro
Le Populaire
Menorah Journal
New York Times Book Review
New York Times Magazine
New Yorker
Sunday Times

NEWSPAPERS IN HEBREW

Ba'ma'aleh
Ba'mahaneh
Davar
Edut
Ha'aretz
Ha'ir
Ha'poel Ha'tzair
Ha'uma
Ha'yarden
Hazut
Herut
Iton Tel Aviv

Kuntress
La'merhav
Ma'ariv
Masa
Mi'bifnim
Moznayim
Nekuda
Politika
Yedioth Aharonoth
Ynet – Yedioth Aharonoth web site
Zot Ha'aretz

DOCUMENTARIES

Danny Siton and Tor Ben Mayor, *Kapo*, 2000.

ARCHIVES

Central Zionist Archives
IDF Archives
Kibbutz Artzi Archives
Kibbutz Ha'meuhad Archives
Knesset Minutes
Labor Archives
Labor Party Archives
Scholem archive in the National Library, Jerusalem

MISCELLANEOUS

Attorney General v. *Elsa Trank*, Verdicts E (District Courts), S.V. 2/52.
Attorney General v. *Malkiel Grunewald*, Criminal File 124/53, 1965.
Attorney General v. *Yehezkel Anigster*, Verdicts E (District Courts) S.V. 9/51.
Commission of Inquiry into the Assassination of the Late Prime Minister, Yitzhak Rabin: Report, Jerusalem 1996.
Hirsch Berenblatt v. *Attorney General*, Criminal Appeal No. 77/64, Legal Verdicts, Vol. 18, 1964.
Lapid, Maya (author and ed.) "Guide to the Historical Museum," *Pamphlet for IDF Education Personnel*, Jerusalem (Yad va-Shem-Education Department – Army Unit).
Nazis and Nazi Collaborators (Punishment) Law 1950. Codex 57, 9 August 1950.
The State of Israel v. *Yigal ben Shlomo Amir*, Severe Criminal File (SCF) (Tel Aviv and Jaffa) 498/95, 27 March 1996.
Yaakov Honigman v. *Attorney General*, Criminal Appeal No. 52/22, Legal Verdicts Vol. 7, 1953.

Index

Adenauer, Konrad 97
Almogi, Yosef 110
Alterman Nathan 10, 31, 36, 37, 41, 42, 43,
    51, 64, 167, 182, 190
  as Ben-Gurion's poetic alter-ego 40, 41,
    108
  and the collaboration by the Judenräte 141
  on Eichmann trial 108
  poem "Memorial Day and the Rebels"
    40–42, 43–44
  poem "Page of Michael" 47–48
  on Warsaw Ghetto uprising 10, 40
Améry, Jean 53, 55
Amir, Yigal 198, 199, 200, 202, 203
  trial 203–206
Ammar, Abdel 116
Anderson Benedict 1, 9, 95
Anielewicz, Mordechai 27, 28, 35, 36, 37
  Kibbutz Yad Mordechai 37
Anigster, Yehezkel 71, 75
  appeal to the Supreme Court 75
  trial 71, 72, 72–75
Arafat, Yasser 174, 175, 195, 196
Arendt, Hannah 6, 7, 43, 54, 55, 56, 75, 76,
    79, 87, 97, 99, 128, 167
  Arendt–Scholem correspondence 7, 129,
    131, 141, 146, 147–157
  opinion on Zionism, Israel, and the
    Jewish people 157, 164–167
  see also Eichmann in Jerusalem: A Report on
    the Banality of Evil
Aron, Raymond 147
Auschwitz 4, 52, 53, 54, 56, 57, 80, 86, 89,
    91, 110, 113, 114, 124, 125, 126, 139,
    146, 187, 192, 193, 197
  Auschwitz-Birkenau 67, 68
  Auschwitzian reality 56
  see also death, of Auschwitz
Azulai, Ariela 204

Babi Yar 86
Baeck, Leo 143

Balfour Declaration 93
Barak, Aharon 200, 201
Barzilai, Eliyahu 138, 143
Beatos, Franja 37
Becher, Kurt 81
Begin, Menachem 46, 126, 167, 168, 183,
    186, 187, 195
Belzec 86
Ben-Gurion, David 4, 17, 29, 30, 32, 42,
    59, 61, 82, 89, 90, 109, 118, 119, 120,
    122, 123, 124, 160, 167, 176, 178,
    181, 185, 187
  on the connection between Tel-Hai
    and the Warsaw ghetto 25–26
  on Eichmann capture 95
  and the Eichmann trial 6, 89, 95, 96–109,
    110, 111, 112, 114
  on Exodus refugees 46–48, 50
  on German reparations 94
  and nationalization of the Holocaust
    commemoration projects 84, 93–94
  and the nazification of the Arab enemy
    172, 173
  radio address after the Kibbya massacre
    176, 177–178
  on Tel-Hai 17, 21, 22
Ben Ovadia, Shlomo 127
Ben-Porat, Yeshayahu 123
Benjamin, Walter 146
Berenblatt, Hirsch 76
  appeal to the Supreme Court 77–79
  trial 76–77, 78
Bergen-Belsen 138
Berman, Avraham 87
Bishara, Azmi 176
Blum, Léon 44–45, 47, 48
Blumenfeld, Kurt 147
Boger, Haim 84
Borges, Jorge Luis 60
Brecht, Bertolt 127
Brenner, Yosef Haim 22, 25, 182
Brit Shalom 146, 160

Buchenwald 113
Bund 34, 35

Camus, Albert 158
Canetti, Elias 121, 156
Cassirer, Ernst 18
Chizik, Ephraim 24
Chizik, Sarah 24
Cohen, Haim 6, 65, 77, 82, 87
    attitude in Berenblatt's appeal 77
    and the Kastner affair 81–84, 88, 138
    and Nazi and Nazi Collaborators
        (Punishment) Law 1950 83–84
collaboration 6, 42, 43, 74, 80, 137, 139,
    141, 198
    and the Grunewald–Kastner trial 90
    and Nazi and Nazi Collaborators
        (Punishment) Law 1950 60, 61–62,
        63, 75–76, 83, 87, 95
Commission of Inquiry Law 201
community 2
    imagined 121, 122–127
    national 2
    victim 2
Courts (Offenses Punishable by Death)
    Law 107
    amended law ("The Eichmann Law")
        107–108
Crime of Genocide (Prevention and
    Punishment) Law 61
crimes against humanity 69, 71, 74, 75
Croce, Benedetto 12
Czerniakow, Adam 31, 37, 38, 80, 143

Dan, Hillel 190
Davar 40, 41, 129, 131
Dayan, Moshe 109, 120, 123, 124, 176
    eulogy over the grave of Ro'i Rothberg
        176, 178–182
death 1, 3, 178
    of Auschwitz 28, 195
    beautiful 26, 28, 30, 113, 168, 179
    culture of 1
    of "the drowned" 54
    memory of 1, 3
    politics of 1
    suspension of 18–19
    Zionist "theory of death" 26
Dinur, Ben-Zion 23, 54, 61, 84–87
Dobkin, Eliyahu 31
Dreyfus Affair 143

Eban, Abba 112, 122, 123, 126
Edelman, Marek 27, 28, 34, 35–38
    Shielding the Flame 38

Eichmann, Adolf 66, 100, 101, 102, 103,
    107, 109, 129, 132, 135, 139, 142,
    146, 153, 153, 175
    capture 96, 97, 103, 104, 105, 155
    execution 130, 133
    and the Mufti of Jerusalem 102, 103
Eichmann in Jerusalem: A Report on the
    Banality of Evil 6, 43, 78, 96, 97,
    128–163
    banality of evil 133, 135–136
    Ben-Gurion's role in the Eichmann trial
        145
    conduct of the Jewish leadership 136–145
    Eichmann personality 134–135
    Israel's right to try Eichmann 145
    misunderstanding of the Nazi regime and
        its policy of mass murder 145–146
    see also Arendt, Hannah
Eichmann trial 6, 43, 66, 67, 76, 77, 78, 90,
    91, 92, 114, 119, 128, 154, 156, 162
    and the Arab–Israeli conflict 97, 109,
        110–112
    legacy of the trial 114–115
    as national pedagogy 103–107, 108–109
    as turning point 6–7, 67, 92–93, 96–97,
        99, 104–107, 109–110
Einstein, Albert 127, 140
Eitan, Rafael 198
El Alamein battle 29
Elon, Emuna 193, 194
Eshkol, Levi 113, 116, 119, 120, 122, 123,
    124, 124, 124, 124
Evron, Boaz 131, 191
Exodus 5, 9, 10, 44–48
    Léon Blum on 44–45, 47, 48
    Nathan Alterman on 45

Feniger, Ofer 111–113
Freud, Sigmund 121, 157, 200
Friedländer, Saul 4

Galili, Israel 32, 185
Gary, Romain 171
Gaulle, Charles de 123, 123
Gerry, George 14
Gestapo 76
ghetto 5, 9, 87, 174, 192, 197, 199
    Warsaw ghetto uprising 10, 27–28, 44,
        84, 86, 125
    connection between Tel-Hai and the
        ghetto uprising 28; ghetto uprising as
        Zionist act 29; Zionist comments on
        the uprising 28–29
Gilad, Zerubavel 190
Glickson, Moshe 20, 23

Goebbels, Joseph 63, 103, 176
Goering, Hermann 103
Golomb, Eliyahu 26
Greenbaum, Yitzhak 32, 32
Grunewald, Malkiel 42, 80–81, 89, 90
  pamphlet 81–2
Grunewald–Kastner trial 6, 42–43, 58, 77,
  78, 88, 89–90, 138, 140
  see also Kastner affair
Guri, Haim 92, 109, 125, 126, 169, 170
Gush Emunim (bloc of faith) 191, 192
Gutman, Israel 27, 37, 130, 131

Ha'aretz 10, 14, 37, 118, 119, 120, 121,
  123
Habas, Bracha 50
Habibi, Emile 127
Ha'etzni, Elyakim 192, 194, 195
Haganah 26, 32, 171
Halbwachs, Maurice 1, 24, 24
Halevi, Benyamin 90, 138, 139
Hammarskjöld, Dag 179, 181
Harel, Isser 190
Hart, Liddell 10
Harzfeld, Abraham 14
Ha'shomer (the guardian) 171
Hausner, Gideon 102, 141, 148, 154
Hefer, Haim 167, 183
Heine, Heinrich 127
Hertz, Frederick 185
Herut 90, 187
Herut 187
Herzl, Theodor 166
Heshin, Shneour Zalman 65
Heydrich, Reinhard 103
Hilberg, Raul 137
Himmler, Heinrich 63, 102, 103, 140, 175
Histadrut (Workers' Union) 15
Hitler, Adolf 61, 63, 87, 98, 99, 101, 103,
  105, 106, 107, 118, 119, 120, 121,
  140, 172, 175, 187, 190, 193, 194,
  195, 196
Hobsbawm, Eric 4
Hollander, Shmuel 200, 201
Holocaust 2, 3, 4, 5
  and the borders of Israel 190
  and the establishment of Israel 3, 44, 86,
    93, 128, 167
  and the Israeli–Arab conflict 4, 91,
    97–103, 167, 176, 177
  in Israeli discourse 4, 6, 7, 167–208, 182
  and the Israeli nuclear bomb 99
  memory 3, 5, 6, 59, 86, 87, 94, 95, 138,
    167, 183
  political resource of 5

survivors 5, 6, 10, 48, 58, 60, 61, 66, 69,
    83, 86, 93, 113, 145, 168, 170, 171,
    177, 178; and Exodus refugees 45,
    46, 47, 48, 49–51; and the state
    and nation-building of Israeli
    statehood 58, 93, 95, 167
  victims 4, 95, 96, 104, 128, 133, 137,
    167, 168, 177, 180, 197, 198
Holocaust and Heroism Commemoration
    Day Law 39
Holocaust and Heroism Law – Yad Vashem
    54, 84–87, 88
  draft and Knesset debate 61, 85, 87
Holocaust and Heroism Memorial Day 38
Honigman, Yaakov 65
Howe, Irving 130
Husseini, Haj Amin El- (Mufti of
    Jerusalem) 100–103, 174, 175, 176
  see also Eichmann and the Mufti of
    Jerusalem

identity 5, 194
  Israeli 59; David Ben-Gurion on 59
  Jewish 7, 164
  national 9
IDF – Israel Defense Force (Tzahal) 110

Jabotinsky, Zeev 10, 11, 12–13, 19
  see also Tel-Hai
Jaffee, Martin S. 2, 3, 9
Jaspers, Karl 99, 132, 148, 156, 157, 158
Jaurès, Jean 207
Jewish Agency 47, 81
Jewish Fighting Organization (ŻOB) 34
Joint (American-Jewish Joint Distribution
    Committee) 34
Judenräte 78, 80, 88, 141, 152, 169, 186,
    193, 194, 195, 197

Kafar Kassem massacre 172–173
Kafka, Franz 146
Kafkafi, Yitzhak 30
kapo(s) 64, 71–72, 73, 74, 80, 83
Kastner, Israel (Rejo) 42, 43, 81, 89, 90,
    139, 144, 195
  assassination of Kastner 90, 187
  Kastner affair 80–84, 88, 104, 108, 138,
    139, 140, 143
  see also Grunewald–Kastner trial
Katznelson, Berl 17, 21, 22, 26, 28
Kennedy, John F. 99
Kibbya massacre 176–178
  see also Ben-Gurion, David, radio address
    after the Kibbya massacre
Klinger, Hayka 33, 34

Koretz, Zvi 138
Kovner, Abba 36, 37, 125, 141, 157, 167,
    173, 174–175
Krall, Hanna 35, 36
Kristeva, Julia 159
Kuntress 13, 14, 16, 19, 25

Labriolla, Antonio 12
Lamm, Yosef 74
    minority opinion in the Anigster case 74,
        75
    on the Nazi and Nazi Collaborators
        (Punishment) Law 1950 65, 74
Landau, Moshe 77, 79, 132
    opinion in Berenblatt's appeal 77–78
Lando, Idan 207
Lazare, Bernard 143, 146
Lebanon War 195
Le Figaro 124
Leibovici, Martine 147
Le Monde 117
Le Populaire 44
Lerer, Tzipora 28
Levi, Edmond 8, 200, 204, 205
Levi, Primo 52, 54, 55, 57, 70–71, 91, 127
Levin, Murray 121–122
Livneh, Eliezer 183, 190
[London] *Sunday Times* 97, 100, 105
Lubetkin, Tzivia 28, 28, 35
Lufban, Yitzhak 21, 21, 26
Lyotard, Jean-François 26, 27, 56, 57–58,
    113

Ma'ariv 96
McCarthy, Mary 148, 156, 162
Maharshak, Benny 190
Majdanek 187
Mapai 42, 43, 81, 83, 89, 90, 103, 110, 187,
    207
Margalit, Avishay 207
martyrology 2, 208
Massada 5, 24, 30, 32, 183, 183
Maulnier, Thierry 124, 126
Meir, Golda 150
Melnikov, Avraham 20
memory 1, 1, 126
    as agent of culture 1, 3
    collective memory 1, 23–24, 85, 92,
        114, 118
    national memory 5, 96, 104, 168
    relation to history, society, and culture
        1, 96
Michelet, Jules 3, 3, 9, 9, 104
Mishali, Yael 173
Mofaz, Shaul 180

Mossad 49, 50, 104, 123
Mosse, George 19, 19
myth 2, 3, 5, 9, 10, 105, 164, 167, 183,
    185

Nahmani, Yosef 171
Nasser, Gamal Abdel 116, 117, 120, 121,
    122, 187
nation 2
    Israeli nation-ness and nationalism 1
    national building 85
    national honour 87
National Military Organization (Irgun Zva'i
    Leumi, also ETZEL or the Irgun) 46,
    81
Nazi and Nazi Collaborators (Punishment)
    Law 1950 6, 58, 60, 61, 73, 75–76, 80,
    87, 89, 95
    courts and the law 69, 73–75, 76–79
    Knesset debate on the law 60–62
    Knesset Sub-Committee debate on the
        law 62–63
    law aimed at and wielded 64–66, 67
    trials held under the law 66–69
Neeman, Yehudah (Judd) 208
Nekuda 191, 192, 193, 194, 195, 196
Netanyahu, Benjamin 167, 174, 175–176,
    198
Neustadt, Melekh 33
New York Times 98
New Yorker 6, 99, 132, 133
Nora, Pierre 20
Novick, Peter 103, 130
Nuremberg trials 61, 81, 132, 172, 174
Nurock, Mordechai 65

Ofer, Shalom 172, 173, 174
Olshan, Yitzhak
    attitude at Berenblatt's appeal 78–79
Orbach, Uri 196
Oslo Agreement 192, 197, 198, 204
Oz, Amos 178, 195
Ozick, Cynthia 149, 151

Palmach (Haganah's fighting unit) 26, 167,
    170, 183
Pétain, (Marshal) Henri Philippe Omer
    192, 194, 197
PLO (Palestine Liberation Organization)
    116, 196
Plotnitzka, Frumka 28, 31, 33
Plotnitzka, Hancha 28
Pocherer, Mira 28
Ponar 86, 111
Printz, Joachim 129

Rabin, Yitzhak 5, 197, 198, 200
  assassination of 5, 8, 197, 199, 200,
    206–207; discourse after 207–208;
    discourse before 197–200;
    memory of 200; State
    Commission of Inquiry into
    200–203, 204, 206; trial of (see also
    Amir, Yigal 203–206)
  as Israeli Chief of Staff 115, 116, 117,
    117, 183
Rafael (Israel Council for the Development
  of Military Means) 117
Rapaport, Nathan 36, 37
Rathenau, Walter 207
Reitlinger, Gerald 137
reparations from Germany 4, 89, 94, 98–99,
  103, 104, 172, 173
Revisionist movement 81
Ribbentrop, Joachim von 175
Rogel, Nakdimon 13
Rosen, Pinhas 60, 62, 64, 66, 83
Rosen-Zvi, Ariel 201
Rothberg, Ro'i 176, 178, 179, 180, 181
  see also Dayan, Moshe, eulogy over the
    grave of Ro'i Rothberg
Rottenstreich, Nathan 59
Rousset, David 54
  Les jours de notre mort 54
Rubashov, Zalman see Shazar, Zalman
Rumkovsky, Haim 195

Sadeh, Yitzhak 26, 167, 170
  homily "My Sister on the Beach"
    170–171
Schiller, Friedrich 162
Schmidt, Anton 141, 155, 157
Scholem, Gershom 7, 146, 147, 148, 149,
  150, 151, 152, 153, 154, 155, 157, 160
  see also Arendt, Hannah,
    Arendt–Scholem correspondence
Segev, Tom 87
Seidler, Meir 196
Semprun, Jorge 54
settlers and the Holocaust discourse
  191–197
Shamgar, Meir 201
Shamir, Moshe 190, 196
Shapira, Anita 21, 23
Sharett, Moshe 176
Sharon, Ariel 123, 167, 176, 178, 198
Shazar (Rubashov), Zalman 29, 29
Sheftel, Aryeh 63
Sher, Aaron 15
Shneourson, Pinhas 14, 16
Simon, Ernst 130

Smilansky, Moshe 19, 20
Sobibor 86
Sontag, Susan 92, 96, 126
Sprinzak, Yosef 31, 32
SS 134, 136, 154, 192, 193, 197
State Education Law 84–85, 88
survivor 52–54, 55
  see also Holocaust, survivors
Syrkin, Nahman 19

Tabenkin, Yitzhak 17, 29, 30, 182,
  188–190
Tamir, Shmuel 89, 90
Tel-Hai 5, 9, 10, 15, 16, 17, 20, 44, 50
  as a symbol before the battle 17
  battle of 10, 11, 13–15
  myth of 15, 16, 18, 18–23, 24–25
  Zeev Jabotinsky on 11–12, 17
  see also Ben-Gurion, David, on Tel-Hai
Tennenbojm-Tamarof, Mordechai 37
Teresienstadt 192
Tevet, Shabtai 29, 29
totalitarianism 132, 155, 156, 157
Trank, Elsa 67, 71
  trial 67–69
Treblinka 80, 86, 143, 195
Trevor-Roper, Hugh 97, 100–101, 105–108
Trouillot, Michel-Rolph 112
Trumpeldor, Yosef 5, 10, 11, 12, 13, 14, 15,
  24, 26
  last words before his death 14–15
  see also Tel-Hai
Tuchman, Barbara 129

UNSCOP (UN Special Committee on
  Palestine) 45, 50

victimization 2
  victim as both victim and victor 2
  see also Holocaust, victims
Vilner, Yurek 28

Wahrhaftig, Zerah 62, 63, 87
war crime(s) 69, 71, 73
War of 1948 (War of Independence) 81, 98,
  109, 172, 174
War of 1956 187
War of 1967 (Six Day War) 6, 7, 91, 92,
  112, 113–114, 115, 162, 169, 185
  events before the war 115–118
  Holocaust anxiety and discourse
    before, during, and after the war
    6, 112–113, 118–121, 122–127,
    182–184, 188
War of 1973 191, 195

Weizmann, Haim 47
Wiesel, Eliezer (Elie) 57, 113, 126
Wisliceny, Dieter 102, 143

Yaari Meir 49, 172
Yad Vashem 86, 103, 170
    see also Holocaust and Heroism
        Law – Yad Vashem
Yaffe, Avraham 190

Yedioth Aharonoth 95, 119, 123, 125
Young, James E. 39, 59

Zamir, Zvi 201
Zeevi, Rehavam 198
Zerubavel, Yael 18, 25
Zuckerman, Antek 27, 28, 35, 38
    Those Seven Years 38
Zweig, Stefan 127

Books in the Series

1. Parvin Paidar, *Women and the Political Process in Twentieth-Century Iran*
2. Israel Gershoni and James Jankowski, *Redefining the Egyptian Nation, 1930–1945*
3. Annelies Moors, *Women, Property and Islam: Palestinian Experiences, 1920–1945*
4. Paul Kingston, *Britain and the Politics of Modernization in the Middle East, 1945–1958*
5. Daniel Brown, *Rethinking Tradition in Modern Islamic Thought*
6. Nathan J. Brown, *The Rule of Law in the Arab World: Courts in Egypt and the Gulf*
7. Richard Tapper, *Frontier Nomads of Iran: The Political and Social History of the Shahsevan*
8. Khaled Fahmy, *All the Pasha's Men: Mehmed Ali, His Army and the Making of Modern Egypt*
9. Sheila Carapico, *Civil Society in Yemen: The Political Economy of Activism in Arabia*
10. Meir Litvak, *Shi'i Scholars of Nineteenth-Century Iraq: The Ulama of Najaf and Karbala*
11. Jacob Metzer, *The Divided Economy of Mandatory Palestine*
12. Eugene L. Rogan, *Frontiers of the State in the Late Ottoman Empire: Transjordan, 1850–1921*
13. Eliz Sanasarian, *Religious Minorities in Iran*
14. Nadje Al-Ali, *Secularism, Gender and the State in the Middle East: The Egyptian Women's Movement*
15. Eugene L. Rogan and Avi Shlaim, *The War for Palestine: Rewriting the History of 1948*
16. Gershon Shafir and Yoar Peled, *Being Israeli: The Dynamics of Multiple Citizenship*
17. A. J. Racy, *Making Music in the Arab World: The Culture and Artistry of Tarab*
18. Benny Morris, *The Birth of the Palestinian Refugee Crisis Revisited*
19. Yasir Suleiman, *A War of Words: Language and Conflict in the Middle East*
20. Peter Moore, *Doing Business in the Middle East: Politics and Economic Crisis in Jordan and Kuwait*
21. Idith Zertal, *Israel's Holocaust and the Politics of Nationhood*
22. David Romano, *The Kurdish Nationalist Movement: Opportunity, Mobilization and Identity*
23. Laurie A. Brand, *Citizens Abroad: Emigration and the State in the Middle East and North Africa*
24. James McDougall, *History and the Culture of Nationalism in Algeria*
25. Madawi al-Rasheed, *Contesting the Saudi State: Islamic Voices from a New Generation*

26. Arang Keshavarzian, *Bazaar and State in Iran: The Politics of the Tehran Marketplace*
27. Laleh Khalili, *Heroes and Martyrs of Palestine: The Politics of National Commemoration*
28. M. Hakan Yavuz, *Secularism and Muslim Democracy in Turkey*
29. Mehran Kamrava, *Iran's Intellectual Revolution*
30. Nelida Fuccaro, *Histories of City and State in the Persian Gulf: Manama since 1800*
31. Michaelle L. Browers, *Political Ideology in the Arab World: Accommodation and Transformation*
32. Miriam R. Lowi, *Oil Wealth and the Poverty of Politics: Algeria Compared*
33. Thomas Hegghammer, *Jihad in Saudi Arabia: Violence and Pan-Islamism since 1979*
34. Sune Haugbolle, *War and Memory in Lebanon*